Eric Lee Goodfield's book is, in fact, two books in one.... Both elements are strikingly well conceived and defended. Goodfield's Hegel here is freed from over a century of a scholarship aimed more at dismissing or domesticating him than in taking his most striking claims seriously. As such, it is among the most important works on Hegel and contemporary political theory in recent memory.... Goodfield's Hegel stands as an immensely instructive reminder to engage the full scope of political theory with its attending metaphysics and not merely the parts that affirm our own prejudices.

David Lay Williams, *DePaul University, USA*

This splendid book embodies a welcome effort to do justice to the ambitious multi-dimensionality of Hegel's philosophy, particularly with respect to the inseparability of its metaphysical and political aspects. Eric Goodfield fruitfully places Hegel in the context of positivistic revolts against idealistic philosophy in general, and Hegel's philosophy in particular, in the nineteenth and the twentieth centuries. Among its excellences is its intelligent recuperation of a rich sense of political theory, by contrast with political science's more positivist inclination. It courageously and deftly takes issue with recent revisionist readings of Hegel in which the metaphysical dimensions have been expurgated. In helping restore a more genuine Hegel, Goodfield offers very thoughtful suggestions for the reassessment of contemporary political thought with an eye to a renewed engagement with the resources of the philosophical tradition. Very warmly recommended.

William Desmond, *KU Leuven, Belgium, Villanova University, USA*

This outstanding book does many things. The book begins by connecting the ... nineteenth-century critique of Hegel to the emergence of ... analytic philosophy. The rejection of Hegel's philosophy ... is then in turn connected to the contemporary emergences of both a political science based on methodological positivism and a reading of Hegel ... that separates his political philosophy from its logical and metaphysical antecedents ... [It] offers a reading of Hegel's *Encyclopaedia* Logic as an attempt to resolve the ancient problem of universals ... [and] provides an original account of Hegel's political philosophy [as a] 'resolution to the problem of universals in political terms' ... [Goodfield] concludes the book by arguing that ... our [political] 'responses to metaphysical problems are inescapably metaphysical'. Thus, it is only through a return to Hegel ... that a war of position might be waged.... Goodfield's phenomenal book deserves to be read closely and taken seriously by philosophers and political scientists, as well as anyone interested in Hegel and his influence on contemporary philosophical discussion.

Matthew Smetona, *Temple University, USA*

In his engaging new book, Eric Goodfield argues persuasively for the significance of metaphysics to Hegel's political thought, and indeed to political thinking more generally. His reconsideration of the metaphysical basis of Hegel's position and the nature of political theory as a whole represents a significant development and contribution. His conclusions are timely and important, and will be of great interest to all those concerned with Hegel's work and with how modern political science and theory have developed, and should be developed in the future.

Robert Stern, *University of Sheffield, UK*

I am delighted to see Eric Goodfield remind political theorists and metaphysicians alike that Hegel's political theory, like all political theory, involves metaphysical commitments necessarily. All the better that the implicit metaphysics of Hegel's treatment of universality turns out to be Hegel's own metaphysics of universals.

Ruth Porter Groff, *Saint Louis University, USA*

[Goodfield's] book goes beyond existing defenses ... by providing a more extensive treatment of Hegel's logic and by attempting to link the position that we should abjure appeals to metaphysics to what he calls the 'liberal-positivist school' of political science ... I want to emphasize that he deserves to be commended for laying out the controversy so starkly and pointing to a deeper issue about the role of metaphysics in political theory that is of concern to a wider audience than students of Hegel.

Mark Tunick, *Florida Atlantic University, USA*

This book happily pursues the re-emergent and salutary tradition of reading Hegel's political philosophy explicitly in the light of his larger metaphysical system. At the same time, it effectively situates Hegelian theory securely within its broader intellectual contexts. As such, it makes a notable contribution to the history of political thought.

Peter J. Steinberger, *Reed College, USA*

# Hegel and the Metaphysical Frontiers of Political Theory

For over 150 years G.W.F. Hegel's ghost has haunted theoretical understanding and practice. His opponents first, and later his defenders, have equally defined their programs against and with his. In this way Hegel's political thought has both situated and displaced modern political theorizing.

This book takes the reception of Hegel's political thought as a lens through which contemporary methodological and ideological prerogatives are exposed. It traces the nineteenth-century origins of the positivist revolt against Hegel's legacy forward to political science's turn away from philosophical tradition in the twentieth century. The book critically reviews the subsequent revisionist trend that has eliminated his metaphysics from contemporary considerations of his political thought. It then moves to re-evaluate their relation and defend their inseparability in his major work on politics: the *Philosophy of Right*. Against this background, the book concludes with an argument for the inherent metaphysical dimension of political theorizing itself. Goodfield takes Hegel's reception, representation, as well as rejection in Anglo-American scholarship as a mirror in which its metaphysical presuppositions of the political are exceptionally well reflected. It is through such reflection, he argues, that we may begin to come to terms with them.

This book will be of great interest to students, scholars, and readers of political theory and philosophy, Hegel, metaphysics and the philosophy of the social sciences.

**Eric Lee Goodfield** is Assistant Professor, American University of Beirut, Civilization Studies Program and Department of Political Studies & Public Administration.

# Hegel and the Metaphysical Frontiers of Political Theory

Eric Lee Goodfield

LONDON AND NEW YORK

First published 2014
by Routledge
2 Park Square, Milton Park, Abingdon, Oxon OX14 4RN

and by Routledge
711 Third Avenue, New York, NY 10017

*Routledge is an imprint of the Taylor & Francis Group, an informa business*

First issued in paperback 2016

© 2014 Eric Lee Goodfield

The right of Eric Lee Goodfield to be identified as author of this work has been asserted by him in accordance with sections 77 and 78 of the Copyright, Designs and Patents Act 1988.

All rights reserved. No part of this book may be reprinted or reproduced or utilized in any form or by any electronic, mechanical, or other means, now known or hereafter invented, including photocopying and recording, or in any information storage or retrieval system, without permission in writing from the publishers.

*Trademark notice*: Product or corporate names may be trademarks or registered trademarks, and are used only for identification and explanation without intent to infringe.

*British Library Cataloguing in Publication Data*
A catalogue record for this book is available from the British Library

*Library of Congress Cataloging in Publication Data*
Goodfield, Eric Lee
Hegel and the metaphysical frontiers of political theory / Eric Lee Goodfield.
  pages cm. – (Routledge innovations in political theory; 58)
  1. Hegel, Georg Wilhelm Friedrich, 1770–1831 – Political and social views. 2. Natural law. 3. State, The. 4. Political science–Philosophy–History–19th century. 5. Political science–Philosophy–History–20th century. I. Title.
  JC233.H46G66 2014
  320.01–dc23                                                2013050456

ISBN: 978-0-415-69847-4 (hbk)
ISBN: 978-1-318-64921-7 (pbk)

Typeset in Times New Roman
by Wearset Ltd, Boldon, Tyne and Wear

The image on page iv is by Albrecht Dürer, *Kleine Eule*, 1508.

# Contents

*Acknowledgments* x

**Introduction** 1

**PART I**
**Background, history and critique** 9

1 **From Feuerbach to Moore: Hegelian metaphysics and the origins of positivist revolt** 11
   *The word become flesh: Feuerbach, Marx and the German origins of the revolt against Hegelianism 11*
   *The denial of experience: William James and Hegel's "vicious intellectualism" 25*
   *G.E. Moore's "refutation of idealism": the Anglo-American origins of the break with metaphysics 30*

2 **Origins of the prescriptive problematic: the behavioral revolution and the schism of political science and philosophical tradition** 47
   *Charles Merriam 49*
   *George Catlin 53*
   *David Easton 55*
   *The legacy and persistence of positivism: scientific and theoretical 60*
   *Behavioralism, rational choice and the "post-positivist" era 65*

3 **Negating negation: twentieth-century revisionism, the rehabilitation of Hegel's political thought and the descriptive challenge** 73
   *Guilt by idealistic association: world war and Hegel's place in the Anglo-American theoretical imagination 75*

viii    *Contents*

> "For Hegel's numerous critics the implications ... are
>    monumental.": the defense and deformation of Hegel's
>    legacy  81
> Conclusion  92

### PART II
### Metaphysics and politics in Hegel's thought   101

**4  Hegel's metaphysics of thought: toward a logic of universals**   103
*Introduction  103
The problem of universals between antiquity and modernity  104
Why/how metaphysics?  110
Hegel's metaphysical corpus and the context of the* Encyclopedia
    Logic  *111
Introduction to the* Logic  *115
Being  132
Essence  138
Concept  143
Syllogism and the problem of universals  160*

**5  Political dialectic: the metaphysical vocation of political
philosophy**   170
*The metaphysical vocation of political philosophy  170
Political logic and the speculative presuppositions of the
    Philosophy of Right  174
The philosophical context of Hegel's modern political
    project  180
Foundations of the modern state  182
Coordinating categories  197
The sovereignty of the metaphysical in Hegel's political thought  200
Dialectic paralyzed: the distortions of the non-metaphysical
    reading  202*

### PART III
### Political theory, thought and metaphysics   219

**6  Political theory and the metaphysical presuppositions of
thought**   221
*Metaphysical foundations and the theorizing subject of political
    thought  222*

*Political theory and the metaphysical frontiers of the
   liberal-positivist paradigm 228*
*Political and metaphysical: analytic and continental 235*

*Select bibliography* 239
*Index* 246

# Acknowledgments

There are quite a few people to thank and recognize for their generous assistance in the writing of this book. C.J. Berry, Michael Marder, William Bluhm and Henry Richardson all offered opinion and advice at different stages. Preston Stovall, Angela Harutyunyan, David Lay Williams, Thom Brooks, Ruth Groff, James Farr, John Gunnell, Melissa Lane, David Ricci, Matteo Morganti and Octavian Esanu offered readings and in-depth commentary on various chapters. Peter Steinberger, William Desmond and Catherine Hansen were active readers, commentators and intellectual comrades whose passionate interest and sympathies contributed to the overall design, argumentation and philosophical vision which permeates this book. In addition to the tremendous benefit and enjoyment that was gained from all of these supporters, the person of Robert Stern was of particular importance in the creation of a book that would deal with Hegel's thinking and our own. His generous and reflective friendship was beyond account and saw me through the deepest and most difficult sections of the work—the chapters on Hegel's logical and political thought—where few are able or willing to tread.

# Introduction

For over 150 years Hegel's ghost has haunted theoretical understanding and practice. His opponents first, and later his defenders, have equally defined their programs against and in terms of his. In this way modern political theorizing has been both situated and displaced by his own. The dialectics of Hegel's reception, representation as well as rejection, is a mirror in which our thinking is exceptionally well reflected.

My ultimate goal in this book is to make a case for the inherency and value of metaphysical questions and thinking for contemporary political theory. In order to do so, I rethink the relation of G.W.F. Hegel's politics to his metaphysics in light of the controversy this issue has inspired over the last century. I read Hegel's devotion to fundamental metaphysical problems as both useful and necessary to the progression of contemporary political thought. Recognition of the inseparability of core metaphysical and political questions amounts to a controversial approach on at least two counts. In the first place, it responds to a widespread prejudice in Anglo-American political theory that often dismisses the possibility of the practical and ethical import of the consideration of fundamental philosophical and metaphysical questions. In the second, it calls for exchange across the theoretical gulf that often stands between post-metaphysical, analytical and empirically oriented political thought and a philosophical tradition that informs continental political thought and critique.

To these ends, the book carries out four primary tasks. First, it critically examines and excavates the nineteenth- and twentieth-century origins of the positivist revolt against idealist philosophy and Hegel's legacy. Second, it covers political science's positivist turn away from philosophical tradition in the twentieth century. Here the impact this turn had on political theory is critically examined through the lens of its revisionist reception and representations of Hegel's political thought. Third, the book presents an in-depth reading of the continuity of Hegel's metaphysical and political thought in the context of the history of ideas. Here I seek to illuminate the value and inherence of their interdependence in his thought against the majority opinion of mainstream Anglo-American Hegel scholarship and commentary. Finally, I close in taking the third task forward by making a case for the reassessment of contemporary political theory and its reengagement with philosophical tradition and its conceptual potentials.

The overall procedure of the book, then, takes the reception and broadcast of Hegel's political thought as a lens through which methodological and ideological prerogatives of contemporary political theory are exposed. On the basis of this study I conclude by moving beyond Hegel scholarship to make an argument for alternatives to these theoretical norms and conventions with an emphasis upon the inherent metaphysical dimensions and commitments of political theorizing.

After providing a historical narrative of the modern criticism and defense of Hegel's thought starting with the latter half of the nineteenth century in Chapters 1 through 3, I trace his response to the classical metaphysical problem of universals through his metaphysics and into his politics in Chapters 4 and 5.[1] I consider this metaphysical theme and its systematic inclusion in Hegel's political thought as a means of challenging contemporary trends in Hegel scholarship which have variously argued, in the main, that Hegel's political thought is separable from his metaphysical considerations and retains its integrity as such. This argumentative development is not taken up in defense of Hegel's teleological metaphysics of the spirit.[2] Rather, it is advanced in recognition of the inevitability of metaphysical questions informing the conceptual groundwork of thought and language within which political theorists work as they conceive and deploy concepts as common as the state and the citizen, freedom and obligation, and negative and positive liberty.[3] From this discursive basis I move forward to conclude that the metaphysical questions that arise with thinking carry over to ground and structure our political conceptions, representations and, ultimately, practices. It is this overlapping that centrally interests me, and it is one that transcends Hegel scholarship per se.

The first and primary reason that scholars present for dismissing the metaphysical grounding of Hegel's political thought has been and continues to be a consistent rejection of the legitimacy of his metaphysical commitments. This wholesale repugnance was originally reinforced by a second and historically prior objection: Hegel's political thought was an apologetic prelude to conservative statism and authoritarianism, and these excesses were given metaphysical justification by ultimate reference to the historical advance of spirit as consummated by Western Christianity. For these reasons, a variety of post-World War II critics such as Karl Popper and Isaiah Berlin rejected Hegel outright. Latter-day defenders such as T.M. Knox and Zbigniew Pełczyński, writing in the wake of this criticism, have invariably tried to cleanse Hegel's political thought of its metaphysical roots in order to put a thinker on offer who is compatible with the liberal norms of the Anglo-American academic world and its canon. As is manifestly clear, however, these two divided camps generally agree on one position: Hegel's political thought ought to stand away from the quagmire of metaphysics should we want to grant and preserve its theoretical respectability. This *prescriptive* attitude, I argue, has become a cornerstone of the majority approach to Hegel's political thought. Amongst the most prominent members of this group of contemporary Hegel scholars dedicated to presenting an apologetics for his political thought, Zbigniew Pełczyński, Charles Taylor and Allen Wood more recently have made strong and uncompromising cases for the superfluousness of the metaphysical elements of Hegel's theory of right. The prescriptive argument is thus made that Hegel's political thought must remain divorced from its metaphysical component in order to preserve its practical status as political theory "we" can take seriously.

As Adriaan Peperzak and a small group of others have argued, this trend of eliminating the non-metaphysical from the metaphysical in Hegel's thought amounts to an unspoken and unsubstantiated cliché that "the fight against metaphysics is over"[4] and that, as a result, the whole enterprise of metaphysics is deemed "outdated, pre-modern or pre–postmodern, somewhat infantile ... and in any case unworthy of twentieth century intellectuals."[5] Frederick Beiser asserts collaterally that this normative orientation has led to a drastic deformation of our renderings of Hegel's thought in its own right, regardless of whether we embrace metaphysics or not. As I argue and expose, this contemporary *prescriptive* attitude has led many political theorists sympathetic to Hegel into a commitment that is very much the result and residue of the intensified anti-metaphysical stress with which post-World War II Hegel scholarship was ideologically and methodologically saddled. As I bring out in Chapter 3, these circumstances have impelled authors sympathetic to Hegel to embrace a *descriptive* representation of Hegel's political thought which bears no significant reference to his metaphysics in the first place, or simply neuters the import of the latter's influence. The broad norms of Anglo-American social and political thought brought out in Chapter 2 in this way led to reification and resignation in that the representation of Hegel's political thought as non-metaphysical had become a forgone conclusion. As I argue, the anti-metaphysical *prescriptive* culture within which much contemporary Hegel scholarship has emerged has led to a *descriptive* non-metaphysical representation of his thought.

As I have previously argued,[6] the rush to the prescriptive critique and proscription of Hegel's metaphysics grounded in part one of his *Encyclopedia of the Philosophical Sciences in Outline* (hereafter referred to simply as "*Logic*") has subsequently led to an impoverished understanding and appreciation of his political thought as it is presented in the *Philosophy of Right*. On the descriptive question I hold that Hegel's political theory stands firmly on metaphysical grounds and only makes sense as such. On both the descriptive and prescriptive challenges, I argue that the largely unexamined and misunderstood metaphysical roots of Hegel's political thought demand recognition and reconsideration. As I will present, the charges of obscurantism and mysticism so often levied at them are undermined when their commitment to the resolution of philosophical problems that have direct practical utility and applicability are brought to light; i.e., the metaphysical problem of universals and its direct relevance for the resolution of the political problem of the universal by extension.[7] In order to develop and defend these positions, this book works textually between Hegel's logic as it is presented in part one of the *Encyclopedia of Philosophical Sciences in Outline* and his *Philosophy of Right* in order to assert the political treatise's conceptual dependence upon the *Logic,* and follows this up with a defense of the viability and cogency of this relationship.

Having accomplished these ends and in light of these findings, the book concludes beyond the confines of Hegel scholarship to argue on behalf of the inherent value of metaphysical problems and thinking for the practice of political theory. Theoretical responses to the metaphysical problem of universals and the correspondent epistemological questions that arise for a theory of knowledge have a direct bearing on the way we argue about the relatedness or non-relatedness of citizens and states, individuals and political communities. My demonstration and defense of Hegel's complementarism of metaphysics and politics provides the basis for making this case. If a conception of political community works from the position that the state is no more than the agglomeration of its individual parts, its concrete citizens, then a pluralistic basis for authority is given priority. Such a conclusion prevails in the thought of those like Thomas Hobbes, William James and Isaiah Berlin and naturally lends weight to the endorsement of negative and individualistic forms of liberty. However, if the state or political collective is asserted as a unity of its own, as an analytically indissoluble and categorical whole, a conceptual whole greater than the sum of its parts, its status as a universal purchases it a special and privileged seat of authority in relation to the limited capacity of its citizens. Hegel, Marx and contemporary communitarians make just such arguments, and this lends to the endorsement of positive forms of liberty. Inevitably, interrelated epistemological and metaphysical issues participate in the ways theorists knowingly or unknowingly approach, conceive and debate political questions bearing upon individual and collective belonging and the ways identity participates in or negates these types of affiliations. Far from endorsing Hegel's systematic and doctrinal position on the question, my primary interest is to defend the promise and importance of the way conceptions of the relations of ideas and things—epistemologically and metaphysically understood—participate in debates concerning seemingly unrelated practical political concerns. From this basis, I move beyond Hegel's thought to the broader assertion that the conceptual grounds upon which political theorists operate are inherently informed by and interwoven with metaphysical concerns and require attention as such.

This introduction is followed by five main chapters and a conclusion. Though the descriptive thesis,[8] as I term it, has become academically primary for much contemporary Hegel scholarship, the book first addresses the prescriptive thesis[9] in order to establish how and why it came to prominence as a standard scholarly lens. The first chapter then provides a critical overview of major nineteenth- and twentieth-century Young Hegelian, pragmatic and analytic critiques of Hegel's metaphysics, which successfully led to its wholesale discrediting amongst mainstream philosophers in the English-speaking world. This section involves in-depth coverage of the relevant writings of Ludwig Feuerbach, Karl Marx, William James and G.E. Moore. Primarily historical, it presents a critical overview of the origins of the anti-Hegelian and anti-idealist movements that would lead to the normalization of positivist epistemological orthodoxies in the twentieth century. This sets up the second chapter's examination of the twentieth-century trend within political science of severing ties with all but positivist approaches to social and political inquiry. It also anticipates the critical examination of the revisionist excesses of twentieth-century Anglo-American Hegel scholarship in the third chapter by presenting critical insight into its roots in the origins of the nineteenth-century revolt against Hegelianism and idealism.

Chapter 2 examines the impact of the twentieth-century Anglo-American positivist turn in political science by way of looking at the thought of several key figures—Charles Merriam, George Catlin, David Easton—behind its methodological regimentation within the discipline. This coverage examines the prescriptive culture of methodological positivism and the norms set up in its wake within political science (and theory by extension), which proscribed and discouraged scholarship beyond its boundaries. Chapter 3 takes this forward by examining the specific impact of positivist inclined political science in general and on Anglophone Hegel scholarship in particular. Here I outline the liberal-positivist[10] synergy, dominant for much of the twentieth century, which asserted that serious political inquiry "ought" to be distanced from metaphysics in order to preserve the former's practical and scientific value. This chapter makes the case that there has been a profound proliferation of this view and that this evolved into a project to rehabilitate and salvage Hegel's political thought by arguing for its inherent autonomy from the metaphysical component of his thought or the latter's mere non-existence. I argue that the extremely wide influence this *prescriptive* posture has enjoyed has led to a *descriptive* culture such that many commentators cursorily and axiomatically purge Hegel of his metaphysical orientations and proceed to a representation of his political theory divested of its deeper philosophical commitments.[11] While many of these authors would concede the presence of metaphysical elements in Hegel's political thought, the appropriative renderings they ultimately offer often tell another story.

Chapters 4 and 5 respond to the transformation of Hegel into a non-metaphysical theorist whose political thought is granted autonomy from metaphysical ambiguity and confusion. These two chapters reply to the descriptive challenge raised in the third by establishing a necessary and inherent bond between Hegel's logical (Chapter 4) and political (Chapter 5) thought through an exegetical examination of the deep and developmental relationship between his primary metaphysical and political texts.[12] On the question of separability, these chapters take their course from Karl Heinz Ilting's assertion that "Only an exposition of the dialectical structure of his *Philosophy of Right* makes clear whether or not this is the case."[13] They make use of close readings of Hegel's *Logic* in making the case that the *Philosophy of Right* takes its lead and sense of purpose from this work, and argues that Hegel's theorization of the state is first and foremost a philosophical project in which political problems are subjected to the remedying logic of metaphysical resolution. Working between the *Logic* and the *Philosophy of Right*, then, these chapters trace Hegel's resolution of the problem of universals originating in Aristotle's thought and illuminate the ways in which this becomes the paradigm for the resolution of the problem of the political universal and particular—state and citizen—by example. Far from providing a defense of Hegel's metaphysical system, this section excavates

Hegel's mobilization of the common conceptual language underlying philosophical and political problems and exposes their synergistic—in Hegel's case "syllogistic"—interaction.

The metaphysical problem of universals emerges directly out of the terms of the epistemological debates between nominalism and realism: do universals have an existence independent of the things that are said to instantiate them? Hegel's attempt to respond to this problem is motivated by his philosophical pursuit of the absolute and the intent to reunite the facts of mind with those of the senses in and against modern skepticism.[14] This holistic pursuit substantially mirrors political projects of positive liberty that posit strong versions of social universality and unity. Hegel's metaphysical concern with the absolute finds diverse forms of restatement beyond philosophical discourse. In theological terms we find it in the union of humanity and the divine and in the social realm in versions of positive collectivity that include Rousseau's *Volonté générale*, Hegel's *Sittlichkeit* and Marx's species-being. Frederick Schmitt's comment upon contemporary analytic debates in social metaphysics resonates beyond its intended discursive boundary:

> Virtually all of the discussion in the metaphysics of sociality has turned on how individual human beings figure in social relations and collectivities. The key question is whether a social relation amounts to something significantly over and above the nonsocial relations and properties of the individuals related and whether a collectivity amounts to something over and above its members standing in nonsocial relations.[15]

I hold that the purely conceptual problem of universals—both for Hegel and for us—is directly relatable to the formulation of a basic problem of politics and society and its attendant questions, and that this is anticipated in the conversion/translation of the metaphysical problem of universals into the political problem of the universal.[16] To talk in terms of "the problem of the state," as Peter J. Steinberger does,[17] is to recognize the ways the conceptual languages of politics and philosophy are crucially linked.

To close out this two-chapter section and having made the case for the indissolubly metaphysical nature and dimension of Hegel's political thought, I turn to consider the way the non-metaphysical reading is deformed by virtue of its omissions. In particular, and as a case study, I critically examine the field-leading work of Allen Wood to illustrate the inherent shortcomings and distortions that the non-metaphysical view issues in its representations of Hegel's political thought.[18]

The elaborate demonstration of Chapters 4 and 5 forms the basis of my closing argument in Chapter 6 for the viability and importance of linking metaphysical questions to the investigations of political theory. Having made the case for the value of metaphysical thinking for politics and their interdependence within Hegel's corpus, I conclude by applying this understanding to the practice of political theory writ large. Here the book extends its excavation and defense of Hegel's rationale for a metaphysically grounded political theory, making the case that metaphysical concerns and frameworks are redeemable and useful, if not inevitable, for contemporary political theorization in the face of post-structuralist, post-modern, liberal and positivist positions to the contrary. Through consideration of contemporary authors such as Peter J. Steinberger and Ruth Groff, both of whose work centrally focuses upon issues of political ontology and metaphysics, I argue that the conceptual "glue" that binds the metaphysical and political together reinforces a recognition of the fundamental metaphysical questions and conditions of thought which reflect, anticipate and underwrite the depth and richness of political theoretic debates.[19]

As I conclude, reflection on the problem of universals is but a step on the way towards a larger understanding of how our political forms of conception tap into the full spectrum of metaphysical problems which inform and ground our thinking. The alter ego to liberal-positivist inclined political theory, then, is a theoretical outlook that reflects upon politics in recognition of the conceptual and historical seams which bind thinkers, and not merely things, together in the world.

## Notes

1 The classical problem of universals raised the question of the mind independent status of ideas and is, in an important sense, progenitor to all attempts to reconcile or relate things and ideas, subjects and objects. The medieval philosopher Boethius traced the problem to Aristotle's *Categories* through Porphyry's writings. I discuss the problem at greater length in the introduction below as well.
2 As he presented them primarily in his volume on logic in part one of the *Encyclopedia of the Philosophical Sciences in Outline*.
3 To be clear, I am making a general case for the position that metaphysical concerns inherently inform and shape our efforts at theorizing, and not that Hegel's legacy requires that we do so.
4 Adriaan Theodoor Peperzak, *Modern Freedom: Hegel's Legal, Moral, and Political Philosophy* (Dordrecht; London: Kluwer Academic, 2001), 9.
5 Ibid.
6 Eric Goodfield, "The Sovereignty of the Metaphysical in Hegel's Philosophy of Right," *The Review of Metaphysics* 62, no. 4 (2009), 849–73.
7 The analogy between the metaphysical and political problems of universals is fairly straightforward; the question asks in one case whether ideas exist independently of their particular things or instances, and in the other whether political collectivities exist independently of their particular members.
8 The descriptive thesis represents Hegel's political thought as inherently non-metaphysical; that it "is" so.
9 The prescriptive strategy charges that all political thought "ought" to be non-metaphysical.
10 The "liberal-positivist" program, as I lay it out in Chapter 2, connotes the broad methodological and ideological program that came together within the social sciences. It became ascendant in the post-World War II period and, I will claim, the influence of this program continues in substantial ways to this day.
11 Authors of concern include Zbigniew Pełczyński, T.M. Knox, Allen Wood, Dante Germino, Mark Tunick and Michael Hardimon amongst various others.
12 Insofar as the *Logic* represents the articulation of a metaphysical system within his corpus; a position that certainly coheres with Hegel's own.

13 K.H. Ilting, "The Dialectic of Civil Society," in Z.A. Pełczyński, *The State and Civil Society: Studies in Hegel's Political Philosophy* (Cambridge, UK; New York: Cambridge University Press, 1984), 211–26: 212.
14 The core of his struggle with the skepticism emerging from empiricism.
15 Frederick F. Schmitt, *Socializing Metaphysics: The Nature of Social Reality* (Lanham, MD: Rowman & Littlefield, 2003), 1. Other contemporary authors working within the wide margins of social metaphysics include Margaret Gilbert, Seumas Miller, David-Hillel Ruben and others.
16 That is, the question of the authority of states as collectives vis-à-vis citizens as parts and vice versa.
17 Peter J. Steinberger, *The Idea of the State* (Cambridge, UK; New York: Cambridge University Press, 2004), 3.
18 Allen W. Wood, *Hegel's Ethical Thought* (Cambridge, UK; New York: Cambridge University Press, 1990).
19 Steinberger, *The Idea of the State*; Ruth Groff, *Ontology Revisited: Metaphysics in Social and Political Philosophy*, Ontological Explorations (New York, NY: Routledge, 2013).

# Part I
# Background, history and critique

# 1 From Feuerbach to Moore
## Hegelian metaphysics and the origins of positivist revolt

### The word become flesh: Feuerbach, Marx and the German origins of the revolt against Hegelianism

#### Introduction: withdrawal from the citadel of idealist dialectic

Ludwig Feuerbach's intolerance of Hegel's metaphysics of the absolute, as presented primarily in his two volumes on logic, is intensive and thoroughgoing.[1] From his critical vantage point, Hegel's idea of history and its unfolding of a master narrative takes up and subsumes all human thought, feeling and purpose. In so doing, Feuerbach held that Hegel derided the very essence of what it is to be human, taking what is most substantial out of the developmental history of the subjectivity he wishes to defend. It is in recognition of these ends that Feuerbach cites the violence done to real difference and particularity in both Hegel's logical and historical dialectics. The theoretical role of the *Aufhebung* (sublation, dialectical "synthesis") may seem neutral, indifferent and even tolerant, but in it Feuerbach witnessed the harshest tool of conflation and reduction. Dismantling differences and justifying coherences and compatibilities by reference to the higher order logic of the dialectic of the Idea dismisses the concrete differences which the categorical entities undergoing transformation themselves attest to in their essences. It is this insistence upon the immediate primacy of the real which sits at the root of Feuerbach's problem with Hegel's metaphysical systematization of history, and the way human experience is situated within it. Herein Feuerbach took forward the central plank of Schelling's assault upon Hegelianism: that in his concentration on the "ontological absolute, [he] had ignored the anthropological and practical problems that are of central importance to human beings and, therefore, to philosophy."[2]

This critical emphasis upon the alienation of the actual and the concrete—of positivity—in favor of abstract categorical and ideal comprehensiveness would remain a cornerstone of anti-Hegelian, and anti-idealistic, schools of thought from Schelling, through the young Hegelian revolt to James's radical empiricism, reaching its zenith with the origins of the analytic program initiated in Moore's highly influential "Refutation of Idealism." Insofar as a program of skeptical Hegel commentary is initiated with Feuerbach, it is important that we understand and examine his arguments as a watershed and crucible of the movement which ultimately up-ended Hegel's relevance for a century.[3] This is especially so given that Feuerbach's appeal is neither scientific nor empirical in any sharp sense, but rather emerges from an immanent and exegetical critique of his teacher's idealistic alienation which would only find completion, theoretical as well as practical, in and through Marx.

Though a progression of argumentation is suggested, this chapter does not consolidate a single historical thread of anti-idealist thinking or tradition. Rather, it renders a synoptic narrative of the influential anti-idealist critiques of disparate thinkers who, though they often markedly diverged on the actual status of the empirical, contributed to the eventual eclipse of idealism's wide-ranging influence in the nineteenth and early twentieth centuries.[4]

## *Feuerbach on Hegel's universalism and the curse of metaphysical ascription*

Feuerbach's first systematic and influential critique of Hegel's system was set out in his 1839 essay entitled "Towards a Critique of Hegel's Philosophy" and published in Arnold Ruge's *Jahrbücher*. Its complaint regarding the subordination of lived experience to intellectualism was based upon Feuerbach's assessment of Hegel's logic and extrapolated as a grievance against the claims of Hegel's system as a whole. By implication, where and when Hegel claimed to crystallize the content of the absolute idea all further thought is null and void such that philosophy "warps the mind for it sets up the indirect and formal thought in the place of the direct, original, and material thought. It kills the spirit of invention."[5] Hegel's system, which claims not only to represent truth but also to be the demonstrative representation of this truth in philosophical form, is to take all readers and listeners captive. Feuerbach's countering notion of philosophy strips Hegelian thought of its self-suspending character in formalism and replants it in the soil of discourse as a relational continuity between thinkers and thoughts. This conception of philosophy condemns Hegel's collective subject—spirit as the ultimate defeat of philosophical participation and agency. Here, none are truly permitted access to Hegel's holy of holies, his disembodied metaphysical system speaking into history as an extra-historical actor. As a result, the dialectic itself becomes a "speculative Dalai lama"[6] disclosing its esoteric truths into time from a beyond accessible only to initiates. The formalism of Hegel's method thus presents us with a scripture of philosophy whose very presentation and outline is our own conclusion and present thought in the elaboration of a reality which is conducted for all witnessing disciples. This pedantry "proceeds abstractly from the pre-existence of the intellect, and that ... does not appeal to the intellect within us."[7] Hegel's intellectual solipsism becomes the annihilation of the student and reader, and with them the defeat of the essence of philosophical intent. It is a relationship for Feuerbach where all further critical consideration is abandoned to the cultic liturgy of the dialectic in the presence of the holy spirit of truth.

## The doctrine of being and the illusion of origination

It is with the outset of Hegel's system of logic that Feuerbach identified the primary fallacy of Hegel's system. Being is placed as the preliminary step on the way to its realization in the Idea, but this being itself is made dependent upon its fulfillment in the Idea. Here Feuerbach identifies a tautology. Hegel makes the idea dependent upon being as its telos but nonetheless wants to claim the Idea as the primary, the truth of the process. Yet in order to claim this truth as the result, the process as a whole is denied. In order for us to accept the Idea as the final realization of truth we must also accept being as its presupposition which contains the conclusion in its own definition: "The starting point could just as well be the Absolute Idea because it was already a certainty, an immediate truth for Hegel before he wrote the Logic."[8] Thus the question of the difference and antithesis of being and idea is glossed over in the dialectic's apparent dual devotion to circular as well as linear progression.

Where being already presupposes the idea as its inner and necessary result, the idea is already present and so explodes the claims of being as an unmediated unity of origination. Where being is dismissed as the starting point of Hegel's logical system, the system itself is undermined as system. It rather becomes a recursive play of the Idea in its isolation, where all categories are anticipated in the conceptual antecedence of the divine Idea as absolute identity. None of the transient categories participate with the actual autonomy which Hegel ascribes to them in the dialectic and, as such, the whole affair is reduced to a tragic monism of the first order. The monistic limits and pitfalls of Parmenides' Eleaticism are not far off in Feuerbach's meaning here and he resounds with Schelling's earlier admonitions which ran that Hegel "hypostatized the concept with the intent of providing the logical movement—which, however independent one takes it to be of everything subjective, can nonetheless always exist only in *thought*."[9] The fervor and devotion to the absolute are made into Hegel's own unhappy consciousness.

## Critical approaches on the problem of universals

For Feuerbach, the primary problem with being as a starting point and its logical subordination to the Idea is evident in its incapacity to fully ground the concrete. Where Hegel abstracts from determinate being to its fulfillment in unmediated being, Feuerbach—borrowing once again from Schelling—invokes the problem of universals as a response: "Your indeterminate and pure being is just an abstraction to which nothing real corresponds, for real is only real being? Or else prove if you can the reality of general notions!"[10] For Feuerbach, Hegel's commitment to ideas requires that they exist independently of those things which they are taken to instantiate. The very notion of unmediated and pure being as a starting point is thus, as Hegel admitted, a vacuous idea, but it is problematically operative in the life of the idea in its primordial moment. While infinitely empty and devoid of content, it nonetheless plays the objective role of idealistic generation in Hegel's system. Feuerbach herein charges Hegel with positing a dialectic reconciliation of idea and thing, and of overcoming substance dualism, but only through abstractions which displace the intransigent opposition of the dualism itself:

> Do we not thus come to those general questions that touch upon the truth and reality not only of Hegel's Logic but also of philosophy altogether? Is the Logic above the dispute between the Nominalists and Realists (to use old names for what are natural contraries)? Does it not contradict in its first notions sense perception and its advocate, the intellect? Have they no right to oppose the Logic?[11]

Here experience and perception mount the first criticisms of the all-encompassing synopsis of thought and being in the Idea. From this point of view, Hegel's abstract and idealized notion of being alienates the concrete and the empirical. The notion of being as a posit of experience forms an inferior level of being which must betray itself in resignation to the primacy of the Idea and its concept. But Feuerbach protests this transference: if we exclude from a being that which makes it a being, we can conclude that it never was a being as such. A human being whose specific being is denied in the concept of the human is a contradiction in terms. Feuerbach's variation of the "third man" argument arrests Hegel's notion of being as a definition which denies its own necessary content and, in so doing, loses all meaning and referential substantiality: "It is impossible to think of being in separation from specific determinations."[12] Thus, while the particular may be more elusive than the general, and though language may be bound by its dependence upon generalization, there is no less reality in the singular than there is in the species, the many than the one. Do we necessarily lose our mothers in their uniqueness because they are generically named "Mary"? Are they any less real to us—by this or any other name—because of the lack of specificity of the name itself? Here Feuerbach restates Schelling's argument that the Hegelian science of reason is culpable of

> the illusion that [it has] not just grasped *what is real*, but [has] also grasped reality, or that [it has] grasped how what is real *arises* in this way, so that this merely logical process is also the process of real becoming. In this alone nothing else occurs save thinking.[13]

As Feuerbach's critique of dialectical idealism intended to assert, thought understood only in its autonomy is alienated from man and takes over the latter's sense of purpose and story. Hegel's narrative of historical progression within thought in association with all particular and individual action thus amounts to the surrender of real and actual being for an over-beyond of the absolute, divested of human content and access. For Feuerbach, it is through humanist materialism rather than idealism that thought may recover its potency in and against the challenges which finite contingency and relativity present to the human condition; precisely in and against the fictive dispossession and reification of particular agency into abstract ideation.

The real actors in Hegel's world on Feuerbach's account are categories of instantiated being which nonetheless take their ground in an absolute of thought which "is unable to cleave itself from itself, that it cannot step out of itself to be able to reach being."[14] It is the opposite of the absolute, in difference and differentiation, in which being must be sought and this stands as the imprint of Schelling's influence on Feuerbach's accedence to a positive philosophy. The supposed transcendentalism of Hegel's *Begriffe* (concept) is replaced by Feuerbach with thought which is grounded in being as it is immediately accessible where "Being is not a general concept that can be separated from things. It is one with that which is. It is thinkable only as mediated, that is, only through the predicates which constitute the essence of a thing."[15] The Kantian abyss of subject and object, phenomenon and noumenon, and the Hegelian project of reintegrating the subject's concept with its basis in the concreteness of substance are herein renounced in favor of a self-satisfying conception of being: one which asserts the primacy of the immediate over the mediate, and the historically embodied intellect over the metaphysically severed subject historically idealized.

## *Idealism suspended: the primacy of sensuous experience*

Feuerbach's deferral to sensuous consciousness and common sense sought to refute Hegel's appeal to the Idea as the innermost truth of sense perception. It is not in the universal that we find the particular and, even if it is so for philosophical knowing, the standpoint of sensuousness remains an unaddressed opponent to Hegel's form of logical, speculative knowing. Indeed, for "sensuous consciousness it is precisely language that is unreal, nothing."[16] The problem of universals—the status of ideas in relation to that which they are held to instantiate—here plagues Hegel's categories as self-standing moments of the dialectic. Perceptual common sense on Feuerbach's accounts demands epistemological recognition prior to subsumption within thought itself. Where the most severe antithesis to Hegel's logical system is found in the claims of empirical understanding, the former must take these claims seriously should it wish itself to be taken seriously. Hegel's pathway to the absolute abrogates its philosophical responsibility to this its primary intellectual opposition. The apparatus of demonstration in the form of the dialectic—though not in the vitriolic sense of Schopenhauer's later claims—is reduced to sophistry. While his critique of Hegel emphasizes the empirical lacking and shortcomings of the system, Feuerbach nonetheless leaves us with a very dark—and ultimately prophetic—precaution against turning completely in the other direction:

> Futile, too, is the speculative philosophy that has risen against Hegel and is in vogue now—the speculative philosophy of the positivists. For instead of going beyond Hegel, it has actually retrogressed far behind Hegel in so far as it has failed to grasp precisely the most significant directions suggested by Hegel and his predecessors.[17]

Feuerbach here asserted that worldly phenomenon can only offer a comprehensive understanding where "they are grasped not only empirically, but also metaphysically; i.e., philosophically."[18] In these words Feuerbach anticipates the revolution to come and its complete distrust of the Idea as an end in itself or as the antithesis of the sensuous world of empirical datum.[19]

## *Metaphysics and the incomplete evacuation of theology*

In a theme anticipating much of Marx's later post-Hegelian program, Feuerbach's 1843 *Principles of the Philosophy of the Future* located the origins of the modern philosophical project in Hegel's thought and set its sight on wresting reason from its internment in the theological metaphysics within it. This work followed up on and extended his earlier 1841 humanist critique of theology *The Essence of Christianity* that had such a great impact on the young Hegelians, Engels declaring that upon reading the book "we all became at once Feuerbachians."[20] Here Feuerbach would lay out a positive program for an emancipatory politics that integrated theory and practice, and heart and mind so as to reunite sensuousness and rationality in lived experience. For Feuerbach, Hegel's appropriation of reason in the abstract form of metaphysics sustained its alienation from the sensuousness of experience; Kant's critical project foundered on the shores of Hegel's commitment to a metaphysics of the spirit. Truth devoid of this foundation is severed from its own epistemological basis and becomes a sensuousness evacuated of content in sacrifice to the otherworldly Idea. That is, in theologies—monotheistic or pantheistic—the divine subsumes the human essence and is herein idealized in an alien being. With Hegel, though reason had taken hold of the divine for humanistic purposes, it had not yet gone far enough in asserting its immediate claim on truth as a possession of its own knowing and doing. Anticipating Marx, Feuerbach asserted that:

> To make out of mediation a divine necessity or an essential quality of truth is mere scholasticism.... Who would, therefore, give mediation the status of necessity or make a principle of truth out of it? Only he who is still imprisoned in that which is to be negated; only he who is still in conflict and strife with himself. Only he who has not yet fully made up his mind—in short, only he who regards truth as a matter of talent, of a particular, albeit outstanding faculty, but not of genius, not of the whole man. Genius is immediate sensuous knowledge.[21]

Hegel's initiation of the modern project and the importation of the absolute from theology thus sits at the beginning of the modern project, but the metaphysical rapprochement made with the heavenly and the hereafter in mind as an ideal stratum beyond human experience remains trapped in medieval alienation for Feuerbach. From this point of view, modern philosophy maintains roots in the old, pre-critical metaphysics. The new critical philosophy, issuing from Kant and Hegel, while overtly seeking to resolve antique metaphysical dilemmas by means of critique and speculation, are embroiled in the self-same metaphysical commitments that betray the human purposes for which they were conceived. Thus the "contradiction of the modern philosophy ... consists of the fact that it is the negation of theology from the standpoint of theology or the negation of theology which itself is again theology"[22] finds it most concentrated expression in Hegel's thought.

Drawing a line from Plato to Hegel, Feuerbach argued that it is material and factual reality as the medium of experience that is consumed and sacrificed in thought so as to derive eternal truth. Yet in this relationship, matter is imbued with the very same degenerate characteristic of the flesh which theology once attributed to it: matter once again becomes the abject which must be converted into a higher form in order to verify and secure its essence from the point of view of thought. Here, in idealism, Feuerbach found the sacrosanctity of the Idea trumping over matter and rupturing the reality of experience for its own sake at the expense of the senses, the body and its passionate needs. The degenerate humanism issuing from Hegel's metaphysics thus becomes the asceticism of the monk and the solipsism of the platonic commitment to an otherworldly order which demonizes the problematic life of the self in its abject political and material striving.[23]

Against the Hegelian apotheosis of the mind and its absolute idea in-and-for-itself, Feuerbach seeks to recover the passionate seeking after the lost other of the subject—the world of objects—in the boldest terms:

> Only those determinations are productive of real knowledge which determine the object by the object itself, that is, by its own individual determinations but not those that are general, as for example the logico-metaphysical determinations that, being applicable to all objects without distinction, determine no object.[24]

This possession of the subject and the object in the Idea here amounts to the exhaustion of human purpose and the determination of the subjective will in the subsuming force of the Hegelian concept historically understood. The recovery of particular will and purpose, in and against that which is universal and absolute, dissolves identity philosophy[25] and sets philosophy on terms which sideline Kantian, Schellingian and Hegelian commitments in exchange for those which are bound to historical action, contingency and the epistemology of an immanent, materialist humanism. It is this very critical sense of vocation which Marx would take up from Feuerbach in his conversion of the sensuous dimension into that of conscious labor. Regardless of these divisions, Marx and Feuerbach stand side by side in their embrace of the second clause of Hegel's double dictum where the rational is taken as the actual. As Löwith makes clear, as young Hegelians it was their joint emphasis upon the revolutionary import of the future for the present and the rationalization of the actual that drives their humanisms towards practical realization.[26]

As Nietzsche and Marx would later argue, with a clear indebtedness to Feuerbach's insights, the theological principle of an immutable absolute is manifest in

Hegel's Protestant preservation of the same in philosophical attire. The god of the philosophers, having come to subjective and enlightened self-consciousness in historical development here, inherits the Abrahamic throne. The pluralism and liberalism of the modern world inform Hegel's revision of Protestant theology without doing violence to its foundations in individual conscience. Feuerbach's Hegel has brought theology up to date and has insisted upon its coming to terms with a rationality whose pluralization recognizes no forms of exclusion in birth, privilege or class. Yet, and despite these commitments, the French revolution's imprint upon Hegel's thought is undone in the philosophical conversion of the eternally divine into the ideally absolute:

> The Hegelian philosophy is the last grand attempt to restore a lost and defunct Christianity through philosophy, and, of course, as is characteristic of the modern era, by identifying the negation of Christianity with Christianity itself. The much-extolled speculative identity of spirit and matter, of the infinite and the finite, of the divine and the human is nothing more than the wretched contradiction of the modern era having reached its zenith in metaphysics.[27]

The curse of metaphysics remains despite its reconfiguration to the purpose of overcoming the social and political arrangement embedded in theology's *ancien régime* of metaphysics. To this end the rationality which it would realize is already sacrificed in a commitment to a beyond of thought which leaves the human bereft of spiritual essence.[28] The "regime" of the metaphysics of the absolute Idea is the absolute subject of spirit itself—the only subject of possible enlightenment in Hegel's scheme—and, as such, is the reassertion of history theologically conceived as the arena of providential agency. This result is clearly reflected in Hegel's claim regarding the state: "It is the way of God with the world that there should be the State" (*Es ist der Gang Gottes in der Welt, dass der Staat ist*) that has garnered as much scrutiny as confusion.[29]

From Feuerbach's perspective, this exclusion of human agency from history condemns Hegel's logical system of metaphysics and its practical expressions in the *Philosophy of Right* and subjective spirit. Hegel's metaphysics thus produces for humanity an ideal narrative of philosophical participation which never touches it and in which it never truly participates:

> The reproduction of the world of ideas which circumscribes all abstract thought—from Platonism through later theological Christianity—stands in for concrete subjectivity and actual endeavor where the judgment, the conclusion ... are not our concepts, judgments, and conclusions; no, they are objective forms existing absolutely and in and for themselves.[30]

Hegel's logical categories become accretions of historical development and no more than the fiction of an Aristotelian transcendental mind immersed in its own eternal meditation. In Feuerbach and later Marx, this restatement of the divine as thought thinking itself and the medieval communion of mind with the godhead as the realization of human essence becomes the complete sacrifice of human purpose and ends. Here "Absolute Philosophy externalizes and alienates from man his own being and his own activity! Hence, the violence and torture that it inflicts on our mind."[31] The dialectic diversion imposed upon human intentions, desires and needs is filtered through a beyond which strips them of their worth and subjects them to a doctrine devoid of reciprocity with the human condition or recognition of its contingency.

In conclusion, and to put Feuerbach's contribution to the critique of the Hegelian system into context, his critique of the shortcomings of the theological basis of being was set against his own conception of nature that rejected the dialectic as a failed and one-sided imitation. Hegel's foundationalist "flowering" of reason he held to be of importance, but, as in nature, not as superior to or as substitutable for the role of the "leaves." Hegel's elevation of reason results in the sacrifice of all that is subordinate to its historical and political fulfillment, leaving the contents of human experience and its diversity an abject remainder. The sterility of the dialectic robs from the multifariousness of a plural nature only to present this as a gift in worship to the seamless unity of the divine idea. For Feuerbach, Hegel's historicism epitomized this renunciation of natural development and an equilibrium of ideal and material parts. The presence of historical time as the unfolding of spirit displaces and overshadows the actuality of the entities inhabiting dialectical categories.

Spatiality, as the complement to the development of the Idea, is thus curtailed and leveled to the status of the immaterial; only the idea is that which is present in a rarified metaphysical spacelessness. Under Feuerbach's gaze, Hegel is made a monist whose metaphysics disparaged spatial and, by extension, sensuous being. His coherence with Schelling's philosophy in which Feuerbach found "the orientalism of the philosophy of identity"[32] provided Hegel with a foundation for an intellectual preoccupation which "loses sight of differences in [its] preoccupation with unity."[33] The irony is not lost; in Feuerbach's estimations, Hegel's overt attendance to difference and the phenomenal does not allow him to escape the problems of a substance monism issuing from his primary idealist commitments. Rather, the phenomenal beings which participate in the narrative of the dialectic—transgressed and expropriated from reality—become categorical fodder where "they continue to exist as nothing more than shadows or moments, nothing more than homoeopathic drops on the level of the absolute."[34]

Feuerbach's materialist challenge to Hegel's monistic thought invokes nature as an alternative dialectic and one which evades the disparaging reductionism of difference for the sake of historical growth and metaphysical monumentalism. The teleological program which drives Hegel's idealism and justified its sublations of difference here becomes nothing more than the dissolution of real being in time; its evaporation into categorical contiguity. The divine grounds of Hegel's purpose and the theological overtones of his spiritual identity of substance and subject—achieved through the conceptual violence of the dialectic—provided a critical point of departure in Feuerbach's relation with his teacher from which he denounced his own earlier idealistic convictions. In their stead he sought out a worldly ground of embodied experience that would come to form the trunk of the nineteenth- and twentieth-century Marxian uprising as well as many of its critical branches.[35]

## *The young Hegelians and the ambiguities of Feuerbach's legacy*

Published several years prior to Feuerbach's first critique of Hegel's thought and nearly a decade to his last, Karl Friedrich Bachman's *On Hegel's System and the New Transfiguration of Philosophy* stood in essential agreement on the problematic discontinuity between thought and being, metaphysics and empirical experience in Hegel's system.[36] Despite his later defection from the Hegelian school, the young Feuerbach had once provided a thorough criticism of another of Bachman's earlier works in his *Criticism of the Anti-Hegelians* in 1835 in defense of Hegel.[37] This turn from seemingly devout Hegelianism to a thoroughgoing counterposition led the "old Hegelian" Karl Rosenkranz to comment: "who would have thought that the Hegelian philosophy, which Feuerbach defended, together with me, against Bachmann in his polemic against the Anti-Hegel, would have fallen so low in his view."[38]

Feuerbach's move from the inside to the outside of the school galvanized his criticism with an inner and acute awareness of the nuanced deficiencies and challenges facing its primary allegiance to welding pre-modern and modern, spiritual and material and the metaphysics of being with the passionate claims of subjective becoming. In this sense Feuerbach's revolt in intellectual earnest went further than Schelling's assault of spite and romantic conservatism towards damaging Hegel's legacy. As Joachim Ritter has brought out, even Rudolph Haym's spectacularly influential if sophistic assault of 1857 in *Hegel und Seine Zeit*, assailing Hegel's metaphysical defense of Prussian nationalism, was indebted to the young Hegelian program that found its origins in Feuerbach's work.[39] With this it must be made clear that, as Marx and Engels would later testify, the bones of the young Hegelian critique were effectively laid bare by Feuerbach. Yet by and large Haym's critique became the last word on German idealism, on Hegel and on his value for future scholarship. As Ritter stressed as recently as 1982:

> Haym's critique was effective. For decades Hegel's philosophy remained without influence; the repute of statism and of the reactionary absolutization of state power has persisted till today. One still cannot speak of Hegel's political philosophy without having to reckon with the image of the Prussian reactionary Hegel.[40]

The clarity of this allegiance and descent to and from Feuerbach is clear in the nuances of Haym's assault upon the logical understructure of Hegel's system. In his most passionate reactions to Hegelian science, Haym echoed the central theme fleshed out in Feuerbach's careful exegesis and critique of Hegel: the victory of mind over matter, the idea over the flesh:

An intelligent contemporary ... has compared the Hegelian Logic to the gardens of Semiramis; for in it abstract notions are artfully twisted into Arabesques: these notions are ... without life and without root. With the practical philosophy of Hegel, it is not otherwise than with his metaphysic. Where he persuades himself that he is most and deepest in reality, he penetrates only superficially into its outside. His practical notions have the withered look of plants that root only in the flat surface. In the entire depth of individual life, in the concrete inner, lie the mighty motive and matter of reality. Into this richest mine of living actuality the absolute idealism disdains to descend. It esteems subjectivity only so far as it has ceased to be subjectivity and clarified itself into the universal.[41]

The recognition of a contamination of Hegel's practical thought by the metaphysics added urgency to Feuerbach's critique, and illuminates the ways Hegel's metaphysics provided a foundation for the political world of the *Philosophy of Right*. The condemnation of this seemingly lifeless foundationalism as a precursor to politics is Haym's primary concern and one which resounds with Marx's *The German Ideology* as a thorough-going critique of the young Hegelian captivity to abstract categories. Thus, unlike Feuerbach, Haym's full-spectrum rejection of Hegel's metaphysics is a prelude to his rejection of a reactionary and conservative *Philosophy of Right*, the "scientific home of the spirit of Prussian restoration."[42]

In this movement from Hegel's system of logic towards a condemnation of the *Philosophy of Right*, Haym stands closer to Marx, albeit from a liberal base, taking Feuerbach's work as his critical point of departure. Yet long before Haym's 1857 anti-Hegelian tome stood Feuerbach, the former disciple turned teacher to a generation. By 1840 his theoretical worth recognized and established, a general turning towards the politicization of Hegel had engendered what, perhaps, Hegel himself had foreseen—and perhaps intended—in the interstices of his commitments to gradual reform and a compromise between the ideality of progress and the reality of power.

In the wake of the dangers posed by young Hegelian materialism after Hegel's death, the resurgent influence of romantic thought and the conservative European restoration repressed the taint of Hegelian philosophy, and its elimination from Prussian academies was completed in the 1840s. The radical potential of the dialectic made practical, political, had become the bane of the conservative Prussian state. While the young Hegelians saw the political state as the new religion, Feuerbach amongst them, the theology of the actually existing state was enthroned and with it the proscription of the young Hegelian ideological program. Yet, as Löwith has pointed out, where the earlier age of the reformation and its tumultuous material and intellectual wake wrested the heavens away from the church, there nonetheless arose a counter-reformation which enshrined a new "political Catholicism" to replace the old theological version.[43] A new phase in the struggle for the state had begun and Germany's metaphysical revolution become material would be taken up within the emerging cause of

Europe's new humanist secularism. Marx thus becomes Feuerbach's torchbearer in the ongoing struggle of the Hegelian left toward the political universalization of the particular and the triumph of reason over the real.

## *Contra Feuerbach: Marx and the materialist termination of Hegelian idealism*

Much as Feuerbach had done with Schelling and Hegel, Marx distinguished himself from Hegel's idealism and Feuerbach's materialism in recognizing a crucial metaphysical emphasis in both. In Hegel, Marx found process, development and history, albeit in idealized and semi-theological forms. As Löwith has brought out:

> Marx destroyed Hegel's concrete analyses on the basis of their philosophical claim, but he was able to make use of them against Feuerbach, and conversely he was able to understand Hegel's principles from Feuerbach's anthropological point of view. He defends Hegel against Feuerbach because he has grasped the decisive significance of the universal; he attacks Hegel for casting a veil of philosophical mystery over the universal relationships of history.[44]

Marx's theoretical task was to establish a human truth that was historically derivative of human experience such that it constituted a human nature which resists all abstraction. In Feuerbach, he found the potential for the historical grounding of theory and practice in the category of sensuousness and the resolution to the problem of otherworldliness which plagued Hegel's thought. Yet the formalistic residue in Feuerbach's conception of human nature bore too close a resemblance to the generic form that colored Hegel's metaphysical conception of human subjectivity for Marx. The task of theory then was to "unmask self-estrangement in its *unholy forms*"[45] and the young Hegelian practice of criticizing theology, religion and heaven was refocused to come to terms with the social and political liberation of humanity as it historically finds itself.

In his "Eleven Theses on Feuerbach," Marx carried through with this expurgation of Hegelian abstraction in taking issue with Feuerbach's prime category of sensuousness as one which takes as metaphysical what is in essence material, historical. The mechanical determinism which issued from Feuerbach's materialist doctrine resulted, Marx charged, in the metaphysical justification of class and socio-economic stratification: "alienation." Class, the result of this theoretical trend, finds its historical resolution only in a revolutionary practice which recognizes active labor as the foundation of a materialist conception of history; it is simply not sufficient to posit a material humanism without recognizing the fundamental ways in which the material world of society is politically organized to resist such a project. The "essence of man"—human nature—is social constitution, not an abstraction to be spent on the poetry of progress and liberation. As Marcuse makes clear, "Feuerbach disregarded this material function of labor altogether. Not satisfied with abstract thought, Feuerbach appeals to sense-perception [*Anschauung*]; but he does not understand our sensuous nature as practical, human-sensuous activity."[46]

Where human essence is understood as a property which remains historically unbound and general in Feuerbach, Marx took the existing critique of Hegelian metaphysics yet further. He charged that the remnant of Hegel's essentially contemplative project is preserved in Feuerbach's conception of human nature. While Feuerbach had successfully overcome the divide of human experience and thought in the notion of sensuousness, it remains just that, a notion, for Marx. The abstraction of human essence in sensuousness thus awaits its reintegration with a historically and ideologically embedded characterization; the flesh of the social world had yet to be laid upon the abstract bones of historical experience understood as an aggregate faculty.

Hegel's spirit transformed into Feuerbach's sensuousness finally unfastened the person particular from an immense historical framework—theological and teleological—and severed the subjective from the imposition of a metaphysical commitment to a higher order subjectivity. However, it remained flawed in its ahistorical commitment to the abstraction of human potentiality. Marx's own notion of species-being would take up Feuerbach's crystallization of Hegel's notion of the spirit in sensuousness, but would reinstate a teleological framework that recognized its inherent historical vocation and social purpose. The historical solipsism of Feuerbach's materialism and the atomism which potentially issues from it was for Marx none other than the presence of bourgeois ideology. While this social and political stage of development is advanced over the older order of feudalism and its "theological regime," it nonetheless sustained its primary asymmetries of class and subjectivity, albeit in a new form of material and social reproduction: "The highest point reached by contemplative [*anschauende*] materialism, that is, materialism which does not comprehend sensuousness as practical activity, is the contemplation of single individuals and of civil society [*bürgerlichen Gesellschaft*]."[47]

Having recognized the overarching trajectory of historical development towards the social equalization of the whole and the part, Marx juxtaposed the visceral subjectivity of Feuerbach's sensuousness with a revised version of Hegel's teleological narrative to the ends of incarnating the essence of the absolute idea in spirit—the divine substance—within the confines of human historical space and time. The divine time elaborated in Hegel and its atomistic suspension and punctuation in Feuerbach is up-ended, synchronized and rejoined to a historical narrative that envisions society as the new socio-historical "holy of holies." Feuerbach's negative mediation with Hegel was, in this scheme, an essential step in the revision of Hegelian teleology into its Marxian materialist and practical form.

Unlike the young Hegelians, who by and large sustained the Hegelian dialectic as part of the project of dismantling theology, Marx saw Feuerbach as being the solitary figure wholly dedicated to and capable of the task of overcoming its traces in Hegel's method. In working out of Hegel towards Hegel's own unrealized emphasis upon transformational change and the political potentials of reason, the young Hegelians had remained largely under the sway of their master in their struggle against conservative restoration and "right" Hegelianism. Marx charged that, excepting Feuerbach, they failed to see through Hegel's own impoverished metaphysical commitments. Bauer, Ruge, Stirner and Strauss are all in turn held accountable by Marx for reiterating the ahistorical dialectic and reifying historical subjectivity into abstraction. In so doing, Feuerbach dismantled what Marx considered to be the remnants of the old theological alienation in its new philosophical form. Yet, where all of the Young Hegelians remained critical of the old, including Feuerbach, they were unable to wholly pass over the Hegelian threshold to the concrete historical world beyond critique and theory. Their revolution against the old orthodoxies left them unable to overcome the fossilized abstractions inherent in the method of critique which they had inherited where—alongside the conservative camp of old Hegelians—the young were "equally far from the true historical situation—whether the consciousness they insist upon is "human" (Feuerbach), "critical" (Bauer), or "egoistic" (Stirner)."[48]

At a deeper level, however, where Marx saw in private property and religion the essential objectification and sacrifice of human potentialities and essence to alien entities, Marx and Feuerbach were in basic agreement. The spiritualization of human essence in the form of theological or economic practice are, ultimately, one and the same form of appropriation of life for the sake of abstract, the real for the sake of the ideal. Life is given over to the dialectic and a new subject arises as the philosophical consciousness of history, displacing the human consciousness which it conceptually feeds upon. This parasitism of the absolute is that which led to Feuerbach's concrete, materialist sensuousness as well as Marx's evolution of this paradigm towards a historical materialism of social organism. Marx asserted that nature absorbs the work of Hegel's logic into itself and triumphs over it, the latter exhausting itself in its eternal recycling of the idea from its universal to its singular forms:

> [W]hat is the absolute idea? It is compelled to supersede its own self again, if it does not wish to go through the whole act of abstraction once more from the beginning and to reconcile itself to being a totality of abstraction which comprehends itself as abstraction knows itself to be nothing; it must relinquish itself, the abstraction, and so arrives at something which is its exact opposite, nature. Hence the whole of the *Logic* is proof of the fact that abstract thought is nothing for itself, that the absolute idea is nothing for itself, and that only nature is something.[49]

Such a nature is not nature intuited or thought, but a nature lived and understood through the definite needs and relations of human beings as they find themselves in the historical world of society. While abstract thought is "nothing for itself," neither is the raw datum of the senses something in its independence. As Marcuse has interjected, Feuerbach's response to Hegel was to hand over all that was formerly ideational to the raw experience of the senses.[50] Yet in agreement with Hegel's intermediations of thought and practice with nature, and against Feuerbach, Marx recognized the basis of labor to be the transformation of nature as opposed to a passive adherence to the truths it discloses to the senses. Feuerbach's materialistic intuitionism (*sinnliche Anschauung*)[51] where nature inscribes truth upon the mind as a *tabula rasa* is rejected by Marx in favor of a dynamic and reciprocal relationship which submits nature to historical transformation and vice versa. Nature makes its impact upon the mind but only as transformed by human labor and the transformation of the senses into organs of historicized understanding. Contra Feuerbach, the raw data of the senses are in no way prepared to participate in the historical induction of sense experience so as to be able to apprehend the universal alienation of the individual and its labor. The realm of negative liberty in civil society and its regime of the senses in effect had to be reconciled to the project of positive freedom at the level of *Sittlichkeit*. While species-being initiates the project from the objective fact of concrete material existence, it has yet to be universalized so as to realize its immanent ethical content through the emancipation of human labor and the project of its creativity. For Marx, "A critical analysis of that process thus yields the final theme of philosophy"[52] where metaphysics is fully and finally subdued in reference to its real historical purposes and material bases of development.

The transformation of self-standing thought in the Hegelian school initiated the negation of philosophy. Marx carried out this task for the sake of its subordination to a renaissance of human historical development and the overcoming of its alienation in the abstract. The teleological vocation of the absolute Idea is terminated in Marx in order to regain direct access to the human potentials so long hidden away in a heavenly beyond. This beyond had been sublimated and made inaccessible to consciousness over the millennia under the weight of the progressive institutionalization of material domination and the immense cultural world and ideological imagination it had furnished for itself. In this epic transition, metaphysics was subdued to the repurposing of theory and the practical transformation of the material world of human need in recognition of the actual conditions of social reproduction such that "Philosophy [had] become Marxism, an immediately practical theory."[53]

## The denial of experience: William James and Hegel's "vicious intellectualism"

The transition in Hegel criticism from Feuerbach and Marx to Anglo-American empiricism and William James is not as wide as would be imagined. Feuerbach's announcement of the termination of the theological narrative sounded an explicit call to an empirical turn and Marx was merely the first to have comprehensively read history in this light. While he duly warned against its more vulgar expressions, a new materialist epistemology had thoroughly displaced all vestiges of Hegelianism in Germany. Hegel's idealist thought, though, had found sympathetic refuge in the English speaking world in England and to a lesser degree America.[54] In his 1909 *A Pluralistic Universe*, based on his Hibbert Lecture series given the year prior in Manchester, William James set out to challenge what he considered to be the thoroughgoing monism which issues from idealistic philosophy. He heralded an age in English philosophy which was slowly but surely coming to challenge the continued dominance of the German idealist tradition emanating from Kant and Hegel that persisted in British and American idealist thought. In 1908, James publically pronounced that:

> Oxford long the seed-bed, for the English world, of the idealism inspired by Kant and Hegel, has recently become the nursery of a very different way of thinking. Even non-philosophers have begun to take an interest in a controversy over what is known as pluralism or humanism. It looks a little as if the ancient English empiricism, so long put out of fashion here by noble sounding Germanic formulas, might be repluming itself and getting ready for a stronger flight than ever. It looks as if foundation were being sounded and examined afresh.[55]

Here James made his intentions eminently clear, and restated an anti-idealistic, anti-Hegel program that had its roots in his prophetic writings of the 1880s. The goal of his lecture was to sweep away the remnants of the influence of German idealism in the English-speaking world and to provide a thoroughgoing critique of what he considered to be the fallacies, excesses and wrongheadedness which were part and parcel of the idealist program. Within the scope of this program, James could not find a greater source of concern, and often contempt, than for Hegel's legacy.

In his 1908 lectures, James brought a variety of criticisms to bear upon the idealist legacy and its influences: the flawed vision of the absolute spirit in Hegel's version of reality as a finite mind which contained none of the perfection of the divine; that god is not coequal with the absolute and infinite but rather, as god is known and loved, finite; that Hegel's idea of the absolute in spirit may bring calm and peace to the world but only at the cost of subsuming all within the whole and leaving nothing to the parts; that, echoing Feuerbach and Marx, Hegel was guilty of a vicious intellectualism which theoretically coerced the world of experience to bend and cohere to the logical dialectic of categories. These sorts of admonitions led James to conclude that Hegel was in fact a "seer"—part mystic and part professor—rather than a philosopher, and one who stood in logical contravention of the dictates of the law of contradiction.[56]

Beyond these primary sins, James took issue with Hegel's writing and his dense vocabulary that he witnessed as a "refusal to let you know whether he is talking logic or physics or psychology" in a deliberate form of obscurantism such that his "present-day readers wish to tear their hair—or his—out of desperation."[57] This impenetrable aspect of Hegel's writing led him to conclude that Hegel was in fact not a logician at all, but perhaps an unwitting charlatan who presented a very interesting model of the cosmos. His rejection of Hegel could not have been more unequivocal, writing that Hegel's dialectical apparatus "counts for nothing in my eyes."[58]

On the question of Hegel's absolute, James held that the concept itself was nonetheless irrational despite the fact that the position seemed to offer a calming and pacifying function in its ability to reconcile human beings to the contingencies of existence. The dilemma, one which James denoted as "the so-called mystery of evil and of error,"[59] was rooted in the paradoxical circumstance that, while the whole was perfect and fully self-conscious, the parts reflected none of this perfection. This then begs the question as to how such a whole could emerge from such parts. While this problematic absolute conferred a certain benefit of peace and sublime unity in its taming of the apparent transience and incoherence of reality, it nonetheless was irrational and in need of replacement. Such a replacement he held could only come from a science of the sensorial finite in what he called the "immediately given."[60] It is here that we witness the beginnings of the naïve empiricism that Wilfrid Sellars later christened "the myth of the given," the simplicity of which provided both the imperative and the capacity for a wholesale renunciation of the idealist creed.[61]

The problem of Hegel's abstract gloss further spills over into James's analysis of his "vicious intellectualism." His accusation runs that Hegel had upended reality as it is presented in experience, opting instead for his dialectical system of logical categorization and definition. The force of negation in Hegel's dialectic is taken to mean that the definition of any singular entity or thing inherently presents the negation of all else, its inherent opposition to all else. The being of other entities, in relation to the primacy of the prior and preliminary thing in its being-in-itself, takes up a similar oppositional and negative role in relation, and provides for the dynamic and generative process such that "the pulse of dialectic commences to beat and the famous triads begin to grind out the cosmos."[62] For James this sort of deduction is no less than oracular irrationalism, inaccessible to interrogation or proof by rigorous logic. In agreement with Moore and Russell, things simply do not participate in this form of inner-relatedness with all else such that their being and becoming are also tied up with that of all others.

This tradition James held as a carryover from Plato who took the definition over that defined, and the concept over the reality so as to dismiss appearances altogether.[63] For James, both Plato and Hegel indulge in a conceptualism that places the reality of the concept above the reality of the thing; guilt by association with Plato was a harbinger of criticism to come. That which fails to live up to its definition is simply lacking in reality for these philosophers from James's point of view. As Gay Allen notes, "The arguments by which James finds Hegel's rationalism irrational are too complicated for brief summary, but ... his main objection is that Hegel's reasoning leads away from the 'strung-along unfinished world in time' "[64] in which men actually live; in essence Hegel, like Plato, had thrown out the causal baby with the sensory bathwater. Lamberth furthers this observation in that "For a spiritualistic thinker such as Hegel (particularly as James reads him) ... the rational is taken to be prior to (and in fact productive of) the world, and as such, nothing in fact could falsify it."[65] James's primary stance takes root in his adamant argument that empirical experience is overcome by Hegel's appeal to a fallacious apparatus of rationalist explanation, the validity of which is established solely in relation to itself. At the heart of James's screed against the vicious intellectualism at the heart of Hegel's doctrine of internal relations, rekindling Feuerbach's critique of the logic's origination in being, is a revolt against what he took as the tautology that grounds the dialectic, its conclusions arrived at in direct reflection of its presuppositions.

This wholesale rejection of the senses from James's point of view led Hegel to a rejection of finite reality and a vision of the universe that is immunized from the obstacles which sense and flux seem to present for human understanding. This is the basis of James's rejection of monism; too great a portion of experience is dismissed and made irreconcilable with the universal definitions that issue from a rationalism like Hegel's. For this reason James, in coherence with the published title of his lectures, opts for a version of pluralism that seeks to salvage what he claims monistic rationalism must necessarily abandon. Where intellectualism epistemologically condemns the variegated impressions of the senses, only the absolute can present philosophy with a reliable notion of truth. James claims that in order to overcome "the contradictions with which intellectualism has found the finite many as such to be infected,"[66] Hegel opted for a vision of a unified reality in the absolute idea which alone was able to cope with the negations generated by his vicious intellectualism. In this vicious intellectualism James witnesses a response to the problem of universals where the parts are taken as "fatal" for the reality of the whole; the whole seems to collapse into its parts and as such is severed from reality. Monism's response is to cancel the finitude of the parts in order to accomplish the whole, which for James makes the status of idealism's absolute destructive and absurd.[67]

James's earlier 1882 article published in *Mind*, "On Some Hegelisms,"[68] was even more dismissive of Hegel's corpus than were the Hibbert Lectures delivered some 26 years later. Here he argued that "Hegel's philosophy mingles mountain loads of corruption with its scanty merits."[69] The point of his writing was, in the midst of the prestige of idealist and Hegelian views in the Anglo-American academic world of the 1880s, to convert a new generation of philosophical readers to the view that there was an alternative to the bloated and corrupt monism that idealism endorsed. He made clear his hope that he would "soon be followed by somebody else's heavier musketry"[70] in this struggle. Against the idealists he sought to assert the "jolting" relevance of empirical fact that ruptures Hegel's continuity on every level; a recognition of the epistemologically banal which is apparent as soon as we take seriously the pre-conceptual primacy of the fact of materialist causality. In direct assault upon Hegel's notion of the internally related necessity of all particulars, James asserted that "atoms themselves are so many independent facts, the existence of any one of which in no wise seems to involve existence of the rest."[71] James sought to supplant Hegel's organicism with his own pluralism, seeing in the latter the appropriate recognition of the fact of individuation, rather than collectivism, that constitutes reality. In protest of the broad entrenchment of Hegelian views in the English-speaking world of his day, James lamented that idealism had garnered so much influence that "all existence must bend the knee to its requirements"[72] and the irony that "we do not call its owner monster, but philosophical prophet."[73] Ultimately the notion of interpenetration, mutual necessitation or organic unity of an ontological form are "silly Hegelian all or nothing insatiateness once more."[74] For James, simply responding to Hegel's claims results in arguments which themselves seem strange such that "the sense of a universal mirage, a ghostly unreality steals over us, which is the very moonlit atmosphere of Hegelism itself."[75]

Alongside of Moore, Russell and, perhaps, Peirce, Williams James was extremely influential for the unseating and eventual decline of Hegel's influence for Anglo-American academia at the turn of the nineteenth century. His primary and most influential attack on idealism is most clearly on display in *A Pluralistic Universe*. As Richard Bernstein has brought out, "the primary effects of a pluralistic universe was to help kill off philosophical interest in Hegel. After James's apparently devastating attack, it was difficult for any American philosopher to take Hegel seriously."[76] The influence and spread of positivism in the Anglo-American world would later entrench the conclusions regarding idealism and Hegelianism which his early critics had respectively asserted.

James was likely provoked into challenging the idealist edifice by the persons of Josiah Royce and F.H. Bradley: the former, an idealist and broadly Hegelian philosopher, was a respected junior member and colleague of James's on the Harvard faculty, the latter the preeminent British philosopher and a Cambridge professor.[77] Despite illness and age, at 65 James took up the Hibbert lecture series in earnest in 1907 where "with all his grace, wit, and philosophic charm, James ridiculed and exposed what he took to be the excesses and absurdities of the infatuation with the Absolute."[78] While absolute idealism flourished in late nineteenth-century England, it enjoyed no similar success in America. It's major defender, Josiah Royce, had little influence on subsequent philosophical progress in the wake of the likes of Dewey, James and Peirce.[79] As Tom Rockmore has brought out, James's misperception of Hegel as an enemy of empiricism was part and parcel of his own hostility to Hegel in particular and idealism in general.[80] Though a variety of the early pragmatists had a fair grasp of his legacy, James cannot be counted amongst this group. James's own criticism was not terribly different from what "budding analytic philosophers were at the time in the process of launching against British idealists. In both cases being to discredit, if not idealism, at least its Hegelian form."[81] As well James himself admits to his difficulty with reading Hegel so that the best he could muster was an "impressionistic" view. Rockmore sums up their differences and suggests a very poor showing for James:

> [H]e correctly suggests that no one accepts Hegel's view of absolute truth. [That it] is a doctrine to which Hegel was also never committed ... James construes [the absolute] in the religious terms of Royce, rather than in the secular terms of Hegel's concern with the idea of the whole.... Multiplying references to Leibniz, Lotze and McTaggart does not suffice to get at

Hegel's difficult conception of the absolute.... James's conclusion that the absolute affords religious peace but remains irrational bears no obvious relation to Hegel's view. James's own interest in a finite conception of God is utterly irrelevant to Hegel's conception of method.... His suggestion that the absolute is not forced on us by logic ... completely misses Hegel's insight that one can only think ... on the basis of an overriding whole.[82]

James's radical empiricism clearly brought him into a compulsively critical relation with Hegel, his intellectual commitments making Hegel's ideas alien and repugnant. Nonetheless he felt compelled to work towards expelling them from serious consideration in the most expedient way possible. While he dedicated much time and text to upending Hegel's influence, he nonetheless, at best, made theoretical and analytic contact with views held by Bradley and McTaggart, leaving Hegel's own system and arguments largely untouched. Unfortunately the purchase of his criticism would achieve much the same result Haym's had in Germany.

James's impact was undeservedly widespread and his misreading and misrepresentation of Hegel's thought contributed to an animus against Hegel which persists to the present in analytic and pragmatic veins of philosophy. Where James deemed Hegel a failure, he saw Hegel's conceptualism as "abandoning reality for the realm of concepts."[83] Despite its weaknesses, his influential late nineteenth- and early twentieth-century critique carried on with Feuerbach's revolt against disembodied idealism and foreran Moore and Russell's contempt for idealism's apparent reduction of experience to a cognitive phenomenalism and dialectical ontology predicated upon the doctrine of internal relations.

## G.E. Moore's "refutation of idealism": the Anglo-American origins of the break with metaphysics

### *Introduction*

As has been brought out, the young Hegelian and Marxist assault on Hegel's corpus had substantially contributed to the defeat of Hegelianism in Germany.[84] Despite this, important centers for the study of idealism in general and Hegel in particular cropped up in the English speaking world. Clearly the most important of these was Great Britain, where two generations of British idealists had come to dominate academic philosophy. Loosely described, this group counted amongst its luminaries Bernard Bosanquet, F.H. Bradley and T.H. Green, and, in its later and closing phase, H.H. Joachim, J.M.E. McTaggart, J.H. Muirhead and G.R.G. Mure. It was against this generational adherence to idealist thought influenced by Kant, often through Hegel, that the emerging school of analytic philosophy would rebel. At the heart and outset of this intellectual uprising, George Edward Moore's 1902 article "The Refutation of Idealism" is widely seen as the seed of analytic philosophy's rejection of idealism that it has associated, and continues to associate with Hegel to this day.[85] Not only did it form part of the basis for his own later work but it would also become a foundation for others, not least of whom was Bertrand Russell,[86] though he and Moore had earlier both been devout Hegelians.[87] Though Moore's article only identifies George Berkeley, A.E. Taylor and Bradley as targets of his critique, the thoroughgoing and pervasive appeal to commonsense was highly influential in making any and all forms of idealism illegitimate for a subsequent generation of philosophers.[88]

The effect was so widespread, as Bernstein has brought out in an essay on Hegel's fall from favor and subsequent revival some 50 years later, that

> The British form of Absolute Idealism passed away from its dominant position almost as quickly as it had arisen.... Within a few short years after the early attacks by Russell and Moore, young English philosophers were no longer "refuting" Absolute Idealists, they simply didn't read them.[89]

The first and most influential of these attacks issued from Moore's pen, Russell following in his wake, and these original dismissals of idealist epistemology and metaphysics have become part and parcel of subsequent scholarly culture.[90] As Rockmore has elaborated, the whole philosophical enterprise packed into the question of the reality status of a mind independent world which had emerged with Kant's Copernican revolution remained a question without significance for the next half century. Rockmore brings W.V. Quine's comment of the mid-twentieth century (1954) as testimony to the breadth and depth of this epistemological sea change: "We cannot significantly question the reality of the external world, or deny that there is evidence of external objects in the testimony of our senses."[91]

Against this background, I will critically rehearse the main elements of Moore's argument not so much to undermine his overall position as to continue to set the stage for subsequent analytic, and later political theoretic, dismissals of Hegel's conceptual system as a viable foundation for his political thought. As will also be seen, it contains some of the most basic and prevalent conceptions and misconceptions which have circulated and held purchase within analytic thought regarding Hegel's basic metaphysical arguments.[92] As such it provides an ideal lens with which to examine the inauguration of the analytic era which, while often ambivalent about the finality of positivism itself, rejected wholesale all epistemologies which opposed positivism's core tenets.[93] Regardless of its actual virtuosity for putting British idealism and Hegel's legacy to rest, Moore's text and its argumentative elements were foundational for a subsequent age of Hegel scholarship. As the next two chapters will expose, his analytic methodism was not merely a substantial forerunner of the positivist boundaries and prejudices of the fledgling discipline of American political science which was in its infancy at the time. Indeed, it also implicitly stands as the scholarly genesis of a trend in the study of Hegel's logical and political thought which would effectively seek to salvage the latter only at the cost of jettisoning, denying or ignoring the former as a deformed sibling. Hegel scholarship has had to come to terms with the onus of the biting and unfavorable reviews which Hegel's philosophical thought received in the wake of the analytic assault which Moore first made universally effective in the English speaking academic world. As Stewart has brought out:

> Both Russell and Moore were convinced idealists in their early years, and this conviction of youth, as often happens, became the target of the most impassioned criticism in maturity. This intellectual transition is marked by the publication of Moore's essay "Refutation of Idealism" in 1903. As analytic philosophy grew and came into its own, distinctions hardened between, on the one hand, the various schools of continental philosophy, which traced their origins back to Hegel, and on the other hand, the new analytic philosophy, which rejected Hegel and his followers categorically.[94]

For these reasons alone, and unlike the treatment of Feuerbach, Marx and James's works above, I closely and critically examine Moore's argumentative development in this particularly seminal essay for contemporary Anglophone Hegel scholarship.

To begin, Moore's argument in his "Refutation of Idealism" of 1902 seems to boil all variants of idealism down to two main claims. First, the universe is not what it appears to be. Here he asserted that a distinction between appearances and reality is made by idealists when it comes to knowing and things known. Objects which seem to be merely material, inanimate and insensitive to their fates are in fact, by reference to the spirituality of the universe attested to by idealism, conscious and sensitive beings, participating in the same discourse of sentience and consciousness which is usually reserved for humans. Second, the idealist spiritual universe is not merely a consciousness but a diverse and variegated entity which is involved in the same sorts of judgments, distinctions and perspectives which are also usually attributed solely to human beings: "When we say it is spiritual we mean to say that it has quite a number of excellent qualities, different from any which we commonly attribute either to stars or planets or to cups and saucers"[95] and "That it is intelligent; that it is purposeful; that it is not mechanical."[96]

In the face of the assumption of the idealist metaphysic as Moore has presented it, a vast gap between it and our ordinary and commonsensical view of the world is made apparent. This commonsensical view Moore himself held as a standard which needs no further proof or justification; it is given in experience and requires no further foundation or ground. In essence it grounds itself in perceptual immediacy as the givenness of experience universally, i.e., in the "natural" way humans experience and think about the world. In the ordinary view of the world rocks are subject to mechanical laws of motion, trees to those biological; and no autonomy or spirit is attributable. Only with idealistic thought does the question of mind, spirit or consciousness arise and it is here alone that spirit is made attributable. As a radical diversion from and inversion of the ordinary view—achieved only by reflective and critical reference to a sublime cognitive participation in the act of perception and its modes of thought—he held idealism to be wanting of a great deal in the way of justification and explanation. For Moore, its claims are made vulnerable by its reliance on a web of abstruse arguments which, on the surface, seem to run completely contrary with those of the commonsense view of the world and its categories of experience and reality. From Moore's point of view, it is not the commonsense view of mind and its world which requires further justification, defense or apology.[97]

In seeming anticipation of the broad influence his refutation would come to enjoy, Moore himself warned that the subject of the legitimacy of the idealistic project is far too complex to solve in the short exercise he is proposing. To expedite matters, he chose to focus on a key pillar of the program: it is idealism's claim for the mental spirituality (i.e., consciousness) of the universe that is its central support and an investigation of idealism's validity could therefore focus on this key pillar. Despite Kant's own division between noumenal and phenomenal forms of knowing, the question as to whether all forms of idealism must necessarily infuse the real world with a spiritual dynamic is not raised by Moore. We can certainly hold that, on Kant's account, the world is only spiritualized by the cognitive conditions of knowledge embedded in perceptual experience. The question of the spirituality of the noumenal world, of ultimate reality, in Kant's critical thought, however, is never raised by Moore, and his ascription of a spiritual metaphysics to all forms of idealism, including a version which restricts itself to an epistemological claim, is clearly a blind spot in his approach.[98] Moore partially responds to this issue in recognizing that idealists may be of different brands which may or may not hold for the ultimate spirituality of the universe in the same way. On this basis Moore proceeded to orient his refutation of idealism towards, what he termed, the universally accepted supporting argument necessary for the defense of all idealisms: "I do propose to show that one reason upon which, to the best of my judgment, all other arguments ever used by Idealists depend is false."[99] This presupposition is Berkeley's "*esse est percipi*" maxim.

Loosely translatable as "to be is to be perceived," the notion entails a view seemingly in direct contradiction to any commonsense oriented realism holding for the independent existence of the reality we perceive. The maxim itself implies that what is in the senses is a datum of the mind first, referring us back to the perception of sensuous experience as determinative of existence itself. The underlying cognitive apparatus of perception and its imposition of the conditions of knowledge becomes the primary basis of experience as opposed to a supposed array of mind independent entities empirically ascertained. Thus the actual status of things perceived becomes epiphenomenal and an irresolvable issue in the sense that they are not directly knowable. Perception presents us with an experience of objects, and it is the former, alone, which we can know. Unfortunately, Moore's thumbnail sketch failed to take into account disclamations by both Berkeley and Kant. Both insisted that the epistemological inversion of realism in idealism does not imply that the world of things does not exist, but rather that it is inaccessible to unmediated knowing. Our version of the world and reality, the only one we can attain to, is representationally and not directly disclosed to mind in perceptual experience.

### *The reduction of idealism to the* **esse est percipi**

Moore held, however, that in treating idealism we must make a slight alteration to the primary idealist presupposition in order to fully assess its validity for a spiritual ontology: the problem is that *esse est percipi* alone cannot actually aspire to the claim that reality is spiritual. Rather, as Moore clarified, idealists must go as far as holding that *esse est percipere* such that being itself must be perceptual (i.e., that being is percipient) in order to support its claim that "that Reality is mental."[100] For Moore, simply making the claim that to be is to be perceived does not, in and of itself, support the idealist metaphysic that being itself is percipient (*percipere*). This latter claim, he asserted, is what is minimally necessary for idealists to adhere to the claim for a spiritualized reality/universe though they mistakenly take it as implied by *esse est percipi*. If idealists are thus given the benefit of the logical doubt such that we can in fact logically move from the first to the second proposition (i.e., from *esse est percipi* to *percipere*), the whole enterprise stands or falls on the claim that to be is to be perceived. Moore held that this dependence is both logically and historically accurate: idealists have always proceeded from the first argument to the second; from being which is *percipi* to one which is *percipere*. In this he claimed, and as his refutation of idealism below follows, that they wrongly identify and conflate being with perception as a presupposition to the claim for a spiritualized ontology. On the strong version of idealism, then, if being turns out to be independent of perception all spiritual arguments derived from the contraposition must fall. In essence Moore's refutation proceeds on the assumption that the claim to a spiritual universe has never been coherently supported, and that the grounds upon which it must be so supported depend upon the validity of the claim to a perceptually validated reality (*esse is percipi*).

From the foregoing, it is apparent that the truth or falsehood of *esse is percipi* did nothing for the establishment of the claim to *esse est percipere* for Moore. If the first claim turns out to be true there is as yet no support for the follow up claim. If *percipi* can be proved false, however, all of idealism's arguments which have been historically built upon it also fall. Moore's previous suggestion of disconnecting the two propositions assumed that there is no logical necessity which takes us from the first to the second such that the claim to a spiritualized universe is put into doubt. While he made this assertion, it would not be the main thrust of his refutation of idealism. Rather, he here presented a second strategy of exposing idealism's spiritualist claim for its dependence upon perceptualism (i.e., *esse est percipi*): that "if esse is not percipi, they leave us as far from a proof that reality is spiritual, as if they were all false too."[101] This move Moore would take as a basis for dismissing idealism's subsequently inferred positions, or those at least which he took to be logically dependent upon them. This latter approach was his starting point for a comprehensive refutation of hitherto existing idealisms and he took this up by reducing idealism to a primary proposition: to be is to be consciously experienced or perceived. While it might not defeat the claim that reality is in fact spiritual, he took this position as one which, once

## The interrogation of the esse est percipi

With his refutative method installed, Moore set out on his interrogation of idealism's phenomonalist approach by identifying a problem in the way its use of the copula, i.e., "to be," relates being and perception. Where being and perception are held to be necessarily related, idealism is provided with its only grounds for a consistent argument.[102] The alternative would be to hold that the two terms—being and perception—are one and the same thing, and this Moore considers both fallacious and foreign to the idealist position. The first option, then, the only logically viable option to uphold idealism asserts, rather, that being and perception stand in necessary relation to each other so that we can infer perception from being. *Esse is percipi* becomes *esse* necessitates *percipi* so that where there is being there is perception. This is the principal logic which Moore took to underpin all consistent forms of idealism. In his view the only logically sensible idealist form of *esse* is *percipi* is a self-evident, synthetic proposition where perception and being are necessarily related so that to have being is to be perceived.

His definition, however, recognizes that perception is subsumed categorically in being, and not vice versa as the latter would result in the second understanding of the idealist maxim earlier elaborated (i.e., *percipere*). In essence he here charges idealist foundations with obscurantism insofar as they are incapable of grounding their primary proposition in a scrutable logic which permits distinction between the two maxims. He, however, holds that idealisms do not and have not recognized the fact that their primary presupposition is self-evident in nature and have, instead, provided fallacious arguments for it. That is, in asserting that sensuous experience contains in itself the content of experience, the idealists rely on the law of contradiction to uphold their unification of perception and experience. Where idealists reject the independence of yellow from the sensation of yellow, Moore asserted that they, on the basis of the law of contradiction, assume that they are necessarily related: since they are not independent they must therefore be dependent. For Moore this is a fallacy which has resulted in the failure to see that perception and the perceived are in fact "distinct, that they are two."[103]

Yet he witnessed that embedded in idealism's position there is also a recognition that they are two, for why else would they need to assert that perception is something distinct from the thing perceived. The very construction of the proposition that "to be is to be perceived" so that the object of experience is inconceivable without the subject explicitly asserts just this distinction. Thus, for Moore, idealism at once asserts, contradictorily, that perception and the thing perceived are at once both unified and separate. While many idealists would clearly want to assert the distinction between the object of perception and perception itself, he charges that they nonetheless run headlong into this paradox by virtue of their logical adherence to a notion of idealism that associates the reality

36  *Background, history and critique*

of the thing perceived with the perception itself. The problem thus becomes one of simultaneously holding an analytic and a synthetic proposition, amounting to an antinomy in violation of the law of contradiction. Moore held that we, problematically, tend to overlook this dilemma because consciousness of perception is a "diaphanous" and elusive aspect and, by virtue of concealing its unifying influence—of the perceived and the perception—in their proposition, idealists are satisfied in evading their own conflation.

## *The logical crisis of organicism*

Moore attributed this conspicuous violation of the law of contradiction to an interesting source. As we have seen, though he held that idealisms recognize the reality of a mind independent world, the idealist position nonetheless conceals a commitment to the identity of perception and its objects which does away with it. In this arrangement he held that the simultaneous and contradictory assertion of a synthetic and an analytic proposition arise "which cannot both be true"[104] representing a further fallacy employed to work around the glaring deficits which idealism inherited from Hegel's teachings. Where idealists hold that perception and its objects are both one and many, both independent and dependent

> A distinction is asserted; but it is also asserted that the things distinguished form an "organic unity". But, forming such a unity, it is held, each would not be what it is apart from its relation to the other. Hence to consider either by itself is to make an illegitimate abstraction.[105]

Moore charges idealism of employing the magical wand of organicism in order to evade a basic orthodoxy of logic: a part cannot be understood in its independence at the same time as the whole is held to be substitutable for the parts. Here then, for Hegelians and unsuspecting pseudo-Hegelians, the part is made equivalent to the whole and the relation evaporates in the subsumption. Where the part has no particularity and its predication is not merely part but sublimated throughout the whole, it is by definition no longer part and "this can only be because the whole is absolutely identical with the part."[106] The fallacy Moore blisteringly claims is "Hegel's main service to philosophy" and "has consisted in giving a name to and erecting into a principle, a type of fallacy to which experience had shown philosophers ... to be addicted. No wonder that he has followers and admirers."[107] Harsher criticism and condemnation could not be forthcoming.

Despite the certitude of his claims, Moore himself has evaded Hegel's rejection of the static notion of the law of contradiction in favor of a notion of dynamic ontological opposition or dialectic. Such a dynamism is emergent and developmental where "Each of the stages considered up to this point is an image of the absolute, albeit in a limited manner at first, and so it drives itself on to the whole ..."[108] Hegel's organic concept of the whole is thus not a momentary, static, overturning of the law of contradiction as Moore has represented it. Rather it invokes a notion of transformation which allows the parts to participate and merge into a new unity or be released from one. For Hegel the logical analysis that Moore participates in is itself part and parcel of an evolution of thought which is bound towards a reconciliation of subject and object, perceiver and perceived. Thus, if Moore is to sustain his scathing criticism of Hegel's "addictive" fallacy of the organic, he will have to look deeper into the notion of the absolute idea, historical spirit and dialectical transformation with which parts and wholes unite and divide.

Furthermore for Hegel, and by way of inversion, the duality of Moore's assertion for the hard division of perceiver and perceived necessary to sustain this critique results in a paradox of its own which make the forms of empirical knowledge and sensation which he wants to uphold inaccessible. As we shall see, the logical result of this critique of Hegel backed Moore into the corner of a naïve realism where mind becomes passive agent for the perception of mind independent objects. Such a version of consciousness as Moore's was already problematized in Kant's analysis of the necessary cognitive conditions of knowledge and would once again be assailed by subsequent pragmatist criticism.[109] The rejection of the unity of perceiver and perceived which is one of the pillars of Moore's refutation of idealism inevitably lapses into the skeptical problem of perception as elaborated by Hume which had originally inspired Kant's Copernican idealist turn. As Rockmore has asserted, Moore's proposed epistemological alternative to Kant's skepticism often consisted in the reassertion of what he took to be irrefutable commonsense claims, such as "Here is one hand ... and here is another."[110]

## *The idealist confusion of consciousness with its object in experience*

Moore initiated the final stage of his refutation of idealism by questioning what idealists mean by proposing that one thing is the content of another, such that blue may be said to be the content of consciousness. He presents us with the traditional view which holds that the sensation of the blue stands as content in relation to a blue object in the same way as the color blue—in consciousness—stands in relation as content to a blue sensation: the former predicates the latter and, in this sense, is contained by it. Though the sensation contains consciousness in addition to the sensational content of blue, an idea such as blue consciousness would be to confuse the content of the sensation with the sensation itself. Consciousness and blue are thus the distinguishable contents or parts of the sensation of blue which is analyzed as the whole: the part consciousness is the content and the part blue its quality. For Moore, however, the content theory of sensation is altogether wrong where "The true analysis of a sensation" attests that blue is an awareness of blue, not an awareness of a sensation as distinct from blue itself. Our knowledge of blue is not merely a relation of consciousness to content. The knowledge of blue is not the awareness of a mental object which contains blue so that our knowledge is but reflection or representation of blue content in the mirror of mental representation. Rather our knowledge is the awareness of the awareness of actually existing blue: knowledge presents blue as an awareness of the perception of blue where "To be aware of the sensation of blue is not to be aware of a mental image—of a 'thing', of which 'blue' and some other element are constituent parts."[111]

While Moore, unfortunately, gave little explanation of how "awareness" replaces consciousness or interacts with it, what seems clear from his commonsense realist position is that the mirroring aspect of the mental object as a thing-like container of perception must be set aside where perception presents us with a direct link between a mind independent and objective blue fact on the one hand, and our representational awareness or idea of blue in perception on the other. On this account, consciousness of the objects of perception is thus not a content of the perception of the sensation alongside the other perceived contents, as the idealists have confused them. Thus, a notion of "blue consciousness" on Moore's reading is fallacious and must be replaced by a notion of the consciousness of blue and the removal of the middle term in the content theory of sensuous experience: we are not conscious of our consciousness of blue but rather aware of blue itself. Consciousness must not be projected into the experience of sensation which itself merely discloses an object to consciousness in, what Moore refers to as, awareness. In fact Moore does away with the whole notion of consciousness in relation to experience where we are made "aware of an awareness of blue; awareness being used, in both cases, in exactly the same sense."[112] Whether this means to say that we are not capable of consciousness or that consciousness is somehow related to awareness is left wholly unexplored. What seems clear, is that consciousness is removed as a middling term between the perceiver and the perceived, idea and thing.

Far from proving his point, Moore merely proceeds to state that the direct and unmediated conception of perception is neglected by the content theory. While it may be neglected as an alternative, Moore had done little to show that, being more than just an alternative, it is a necessary remedy to the ills or limitations presented by idealist conceptions of consciousness and perception. As C.J. Ducasse made clear in his 1919 critique of Moore's article:

> It is only because Dr. Moore fails to consider ... the hypothesis that blue is a species and not an attribute of awareness, that he is able to dismiss the hypothesis of "blue awareness" as unimportant even if true.[113]

The best explanation offered for the confusion of consciousness and awareness was presented in terms of the elusive quality of consciousness itself where "When we try to introspect the sensation of blue, all we can see is the blue: the other element is as if it were diaphanous. Yet it can be distinguished if we look attentively enough."[114] In presenting it as a direct perceptual link to a mind independent world, Moore took awareness to be analytically ascertainable. Yet, and despite this, he presented us with little illumination of how traditional treatments of consciousness, as intermediary contents of sensation, are reducible or translatable to forms of unmediated awareness. Where Moore admitted that awareness is "itself something distinct and unique, utterly different from blue"[115] and where consciousness of blue is exchanged in favor of being "aware of an awareness" of blue, however, it seems that we are no closer to direct perception than on the idealist account. As Baldwin has brought out:

> any half-awake defender of Moore's phenomenalist principle will reject its relevance by distinguishing between colours as objective qualities and as phenomenal qualities. For with this distinction, Moore's phenomenalist principle will not entail that "a sensation of blue ... differs from a blue bead in exactly the same way in which the two latter [the blue bead and the bead] differ from one another"; what blue is in the first case (a phenomenal quality) will itself differ from what it is in the other (an objective quality)....
> Moore's influential refutation of "idealism" (i.e., phenomenalism) in RI ["The Refutation of Idealism"] is a total failure. It is only fair to add that Moore himself later expressed much the same opinion (PGEM [*The Philosophy of G.E. Moore*], p. 654), and, indeed, may have held this opinion when in 1922 he commented in the preface to PS [*Philosophical Studies*] (p. viii) that RI was "very confused" and embodied a "good many downright mistakes".[116]

Thus, the epistemological problem yet resides in the gap between awareness and its object, and the idealist strategy for intermediating knowledge and its objects in consciousness remains a viable alternative. What transpires, and how the object is transformed into an object of perception by mind, and whether this amounts to a form of perception, so that an original awareness of blue becomes a form of blue consciousness, is neglected by Moore. He seems to simply want to say that, ultimately, the mirror of perception should not be confused with the objects perceived in the mirror's reflection. The problem, however, remains that what Moore referred to as the ultimate awareness of blue, our knowledge of it, presents a mode of experience of the reflection of blue and the reflection of blue in the passive "mirror" of awareness simultaneously. From this point of view, the simultaneity of mind and sense which he intended to analyze into its discrete parts, however, still seems to participate in the constituting of experience in a way compatible with Berkeley's proto-idealist maxim *esse est percipi*. In fact Hegel himself had presented this very argument against orthodox realism in his writing on sense certainty in the *Phenomenology*:

> [S]ense-certainty appears to be the truest knowledge; for it has not as yet omitted anything from the object, but has 'the object before it in its perfect entirety.... An actual sense-certainty is not merely this pure immediacy, but an instance of it ... in sense-certainty, pure being at once splits up into what we have called the two "Thises", one "This" as "I", and the other "This" as object.[117]

Moore's reframing of sensation as consisting of a contrastable dichotomy of awareness and object is simply not a persuasive dissolution of the problem of intermediation where the mirror of awareness itself cannot be assumed to be cognitively neutral or merely "reflective." Perhaps Moore himself recognized this limitation where in his discussion of the difficulty of pinning down consciousness in the relation to the objects of perception and awareness he admits "I fear I shall have succeeded very ill"[118] in clarifying this relationship.

Moore wished to satisfy the analytic demands of his argument in the distinction of mind and sense with an appeal to introspection and analysis. Introspection enables us to appropriate from experience a form of awareness which has "to blue the simple and unique relation the existence of which alone justifies us in distinguishing knowledge of a thing from the thing known."[119] However, the simple act of deducing awareness or introducing it into the relation of "mind" and "matter" does not make it so. Rather, as one aspect of his analysis implies, it may be taken that he invoked awareness as a proposition which bestows it this relationship by definition and not demonstration: awareness relates to the object of awareness precisely because awareness is defined as something which is not itself perceived and must therefore be other than that which is perceived. Thus, his reduction of the diaphanousness of consciousness to tangible awareness resolved the idealist epistemological problem, but only by translating the idealist's sublime and inaccessible nature of underlying consciousness into something sequentially apparent and discrete, i.e., the mind's relation in awareness to the object of sensation.

The presentation of awareness in the experience of sensation in this way allows Moore to casually conclude that there is "no question of how we are to 'get outside the circle of our own ideas and sensations'. Merely to have a sensation is already to be outside that circle."[120] The epistemological skepticism arising from the problem of mediation that idealism issues is set aside and rejected in this deduction. Instead we have a form of realism which permits for direct vision and knowledge of mind independent existence, albeit through the reflecting lens of awareness in correspondence with its object. With Hegel before him, Ducasse sharply points out, however,

> the fact that the awareness can be distinguished from the blue no more proves that the blue can exist independently of the awareness of it, than the fact that in the dancing of a waltz we can distinguish dancing from the waltz proves that the waltz can exist independently of the dancing of it.[121]

Where the objects of the senses are to awareness as the senses are object to mind, Moore presented us with a two-tier system of experience. The realism which issues from this he took as a ground to claim that objects of sense are to sensuous awareness what the objects of sensuous awareness are to mind at a higher level: our sensory awareness of objects itself becomes an object of awareness for mind. Lack of awareness of what registers to sensuous awareness does not deny the reality of what is sensed or, what is more, what is not sensed: trees successfully fall in the forest with or without observers. It is on the basis of these arguments that Moore's realism dispatches with Berkeley's *esse est percipi* and

Kant's skepticism regarding the analogy of raw sensuous experience on the one hand and the subjective experience of sense impressions for mind on the other. While this is all quite lucid, Moore had not cogently or persuasively made the case that the relation of sense impressions to consciousness is analogous to consciousness's relation to its object. For the most part he merely asserted it against a caricature of metaphysical idealism and the paradoxes which such a position generates where the same "reason for doubting the existence of matter ... will prove conclusively that our experience does not exist either."[122] Yet it was only the paradoxical failure of this caricature that provided a basis for his bold, if unsteady, realist claim. As Baldwin has argued:

> From the failure, as he saw it, of the phenomenalist account of sensible qualities, Moore inferred the truth of his own strongly realist account of the intentional objects of sense-experience. According to this theory, in sense-experience we are directly aware of objects in space.... Furthermore, by treating the sensible qualities we experience as entirely "objective" (rather than merely "phenomenal"), Moore is led to interpret these objects of which we are directly aware as qualities of material objects in physical space. The resulting position is the most naive of naive realisms, whose difficulties soon became apparent to him.[123]

Kant's idealist skepticism thus withstands Moore's refutation simply because the cognitive conditions of knowledge may still be said to influence what is or can be known. The application of Moore's critique of British idealism to Hegel appears even less solid. Quite simply, "Hegel was little studied by the British Hegelians with the exception of McTaggart, whose views (so C.D. Broad famously said) made orthodox Hegelians blush all over."[124] John Lamb takes this critique further to expose the "literalism" of Moore's career of critiquing idealism in which he problematically assailed individual idealist claims out of their systematic contexts.[125]

## *The refutation of idealism and the origins of positivism*

Moore's seminal article furthered and radicalized Feuerbach's contention that the senses themselves had been shut off and obscured by Hegel's prioritization of mind and idea. His attempt to find a direct link between subject and object, asserting the primacy of the latter, represents his wholehearted project to overcome what he and other realists perceived as the rampant subjectivism, solipsism and heterodox conclusions which many idealists explicitly or implicitly held concerning, for example, issues as mundane as the existence of an external world or time. Moore's seminal article is also in lockstep with William James's earlier claim that, amongst other fallacies, Hegel's doctrine of organic relations represents a gross violation of the law of contradiction—a doctrine which he claims imposes the absolute on experience and reality in order to evade its dissolution into the myriad parts of experience that endorses a pluralistic universe. Moore's revolutionary refutation in this sense stands as a mid-point between Feuerbach's influential rejection of Hegel's metaphysics and James's empiricist project on the one hand, and the latter Moore–Russell positivist project that would put the mainstream of Anglophone philosophy beyond the gravity of idealistic claims and epistemological concerns for the better part of the twentieth century.

With this background behind us, the next task is to consider how this philosophical realism and its methodologically positivist implications anticipated, influenced and coalesced with the inauguration of the scientific study of politics in the English speaking world at the start of the twentieth century.

## Notes

1 For Feuerbach, Hegel's logic as it is presented in his *Science of Logic* and *Part 1* of the *Philosophical Science in Outline* are Hegel's metaphysical works.
2 Alan White, *Absolute Knowledge: Hegel and the Problem of Metaphysics*, Series in Continental Thought (Athens, Ohio: Ohio University Press, 1983), 10.
3 As White has brought out, Schelling foreran many of the critical movements which assailed Hegel's legacy. Despite this succession then, I start with Feuerbach as a result of his place amongst the young Hegelians and as a predecessor to Marx who had such an indelible mark on our reception of Hegel academically as well as politically.
4 James and Moore are often held to be attacking straw men rather than Hegel himself. Despite this, they are relevant for this chapter where their direct and indirect critiques of his thought, regardless of competence, came to high and prolonged influence.
5 Ludwig Feuerbach, *The Fiery Brook: Selected Writings of Ludwig Feuerbach* (Garden City, NY: Anchor Books, 1972), 67.
6 Ibid., 56.
7 Ibid., 68.
8 Ibid., 74.
9 Friedrich Wilhelm Joseph von Schelling and Bruce Matthews, *The Grounding of Positive Philosophy: The Berlin Lectures*, Suny Series in Contemporary Continental Philosophy (Albany: State University of New York Press, 2007), 151.
10 Feuerbach, *The Fiery Brook*, 70.
11 Ibid.
12 Ibid., 71.
13 Schelling and Matthews, *The Grounding of Positive Philosophy*, 133–4.
14 Feuerbach, *The Fiery Brook*, §24.
15 Feuerbach, *Principles of the Philosophy of the Future* (Hackett, 1986), §27.
16 Feuerbach, *The Fiery Brook*, 77.
17 Ibid., 94.
18 Ibid., 93.
19 John Edward Toews, *Hegelianism: The Path toward Dialectical Humanism, 1805–1841* (Cambridge, UK; New York: Cambridge University Press, 1980), 334–5. Toews identifies Feuerbach's emphasis on the empirical as his defining break with orthodox Hegelianism.
20 Friedrich Engels, "Feuerbach and the End of German Classical Philosophy," in Karl Marx and Friedrich Engels, *Karl Marx and Frederick Engels: Selected Works* (London: Lawrence and Wishart, 1968), 602–3.
21 Feuerbach, *Principles of the Philosophy of the Future*, §38.
22 Ibid., §21.
23 The parallels to the banausic prejudices of Aristocratic Greece are sustained in Feuerbach's genealogical association of Hegel with Plato.
24 Ibid., §49.

25 In the sense of a romantic project that seeks to rehabilitate unified being through the reunion of mind and world, self and other.
26 Karl Löwith, *From Hegel to Nietzsche: The Revolution in Nineteenth Century Thought* (New York: Columbia University Press, 1991).
27 Feuerbach, *Principles of the Philosophy of the Future*, §21.
28 Not unlike Arnold Ruge, Feuerbach leaves this essence somewhat indeterminate. It finds a more developed expression in Marx's species-being as the introversion of the absolute idea embodied in the personification of class consciousness and will.
29 Walter A. Kaufmann, "The Hegel Myth and Its Method," *Philosophical Review* 60, no. 4 (1951), 460–1.
30 Johann Karl Rosenkranz, cited in Löwith, *From Hegel to Nietzsche*, 73.
31 Feuerbach, *Principles of the Philosophy of the Future*, §23.
32 Feuerbach, *The Fiery Brook*, 53.
33 Ibid.
34 Ibid., 55.
35 As Marcuse points out, it is the otherworldly content of religion that requires a revision to reflect human content such that theology must become an anthropology: "The realization of religion requires its negation." Herbert Marcuse, *Reason and Revolution: Hegel and the Rise of Social Theory*, 2nd. edn (London: Routledge & Kegan Paul, 1955), 267.
36 Carl Friedrich Bachmann, *Über Hegels System und die Notwendigkeit einer nochmaligen Umgestaltung der Philosophie* (Aalen: Scientia-Verlag, 1968).
37 Ludwig Feuerbach, *Kritik der Anti-Hegels: Zur Einleitung in das Studium der Philosophie*, 2nd edn (Leipzig: Wigand, 1844).
38 Johann Karl Rosenkranz, in Löwith, *From Hegel to Nietzsche*, 73.
39 Joachim Ritter, *Hegel and the French Revolution: Essays on the Philosophy of Right* (Cambridge, MA; London, England: MIT Press, 1982), 83.
40 Ibid., 36.
41 Rudolf Haym, *Hegel und seine Zeit*, cited in James Hutchison Stirling, *The Secret of Hegel: Being the Hegelian System in Origin, Principle, Form, and Matter*, 2 vols (London: Longman, Green, Longman, Roberts, & Green, 1865), 496.
42 Rudolf Haym, *Hegel und seine Zeit: Vorlesungen über Entstehung und Entwickelung, Wesen und Werth der Hegel'schen Philosophie* (Berlin: Gaertner, 1857), 359.
43 Karl Löwith, *From Hegel to Nietzsche*, 82.
44 Ibid., 411.
45 Karl Marx, *Early Writings*, Penguin Classics (Harmondsworth; New York: Penguin in association with New Left Review, 1992), 244.
46 Marcuse, *Reason and Revolution*, 272.
47 Marx, *Early Writings*, 423.
48 Löwith, *From Hegel to Nietzsche*, 101.
49 Marx, *Early Writings*, 397; Löwith, *From Hegel to Nietzsche*.
50 Marcuse, *Reason and Revolution*, 271.
51 This is meant in the sense of an immediate disclosure of the objects of reality to the senses. Marx refers to this as a "perceptual materialism" (*anschauende Materialismus*).
52 Ibid., 273.
53 Löwith, *From Hegel to Nietzsche*, 95.
54 Bradley and Royce being the most notable members of these movements. The American tradition had historical roots in the Cincinnati and St. Louis schools.
55 William James, *A Pluralistic Universe: Hibbert Lectures to Manchester College on the Present Situation in Philosophy* (New York: Longmans, Green and Co., 1909), 3.
56 For two strong and well informed challenges of this latter position, see Robert Pippin "Hegel's Metaphysics and the Problem of Contradiction" and Robert Hanna "From an Ontological Point of View: Hegel's Critique of the Common Logic," in John Stewart,

44  *Background, history and critique*

   *The Hegel Myths and Legends*, Northwestern University Studies in Phenomenology and Existential Philosophy (Evanston: Northwestern University Press, 1996).
57 James, *A Pluralistic Universe*, 88.
58 Ibid., 74.
59 Ibid., 124.
60 Ibid., 129.
61 Wilfrid S. Sellars, "Empiricism and the Philosophy of Mind," *Minnesota Studies in the Philosophy of Science* 1 (1956), 253–329. More on the myth in my examination of G.E. Moore's writing below.
62 James, *A Pluralistic Universe*, 106–7. A similar position in opposition to Hegel's employment of negation can be found in William James, "On Some Hegelisms," *Mind* 7, no. 26 (1882), 186–208: 201–2.
63 James, *A Pluralistic Universe*, 218.
64 Gay Wilson Allen, *William James*, University of Minnesota Pamphlets on American Writers (Minneapolis: University of Minnesota Press, 1970), 34–5.
65 David C. Lamberth, *William James and the Metaphysics of Experience*, Cambridge Studies in Religion and Critical Thought (Cambridge, UK; New York: Cambridge University Press, 1999), 177.
66 James, *A Pluralistic Universe*, 188.
67 Ibid.
68 James, "On Some Hegelisms," *Mind* 7, no. 26 (1882).
69 Ibid., 186.
70 Ibid. By 1902 he would be, with the printing of Moore's "Refutation of Idealism."
71 Ibid., 188.
72 Ibid., 192.
73 Ibid., 192.
74 Ibid., 204.
75 Ibid., 205.
76 Richard J. Bernstein, "Why Hegel Now?" *The Review of Metaphysics* 31, no. 1 (1977), 29–60: 32.
77 Ibid., 31.
78 Ibid.
79 Rockmore gives only the first and the last of these authors credit for at least paying close attention to Hegel's own intentions, in Tom Rockmore, *Hegel, Idealism, and Analytic Philosophy* (New Haven: Yale University Press, 2005). Both of these authors sustained ambivalent relations with Hegel's thought itself. For more on this, see Robert Stern, *Hegelian Metaphysics* (Oxford; New York: Oxford University Press, 2009) and Paul Fairfield, *John Dewey and Continental Philosophy* (Carbondale: Southern Illinois University Press, 2010).
80 Rockmore, *Hegel, Idealism, and Analytic Philosophy*, 68.
81 Ibid., 70–1.
82 Ibid., 73.
83 Lamberth, *William James and the Metaphysics of Experience*, 190.
84 Hans Sluga, "Frege as a Rationalist," in Matthias Schirn, *Studien Zu Frege = Studies on Frege*, 3 vols, Problemata 42–4 (Stuttgart-Bad Cannstatt: Frommann-Holzboog, 1976), vol. I, 28; James, "On Some Hegelisms," 186–208; James, *A Pluralistic Universe*, 15. Neo-Kantian, Millian and Comtean trends played instrumental roles as well.
85 Thomas Baldwin, *G.E. Moore*, The Arguments of the Philosophers (London; New York: Routledge, 1999), 20, 64–7; Bernstein, "Why Hegel Now?" 11; Peter Hylton, "Hegel and Analytic Philosophy," in Frederick C. Beiser, *The Cambridge Companion to Hegel* (Cambridge, UK; New York: Cambridge University Press, 1993), 445–85: 445; Rockmore, *Hegel, Idealism, and Analytic Philosophy*"; Rockmore, "Analytic Philosophy and the Hegelian Turn," *The Review of Metaphysics* 55, no. 2 (2001): 341–69.

86 Russell admits that "It was towards the end of 1898 that Moore and I rebelled against both Kant and Hegel. Moore led the way, but I followed closely in his footsteps," in Bertrand Russell, *My Philosophical Development* (London: Allen and Unwin, 1959), 54.
87 Peter Hylton, "Hegel and Analytic Philosophy," 448.
88 Yet, as Stewart Candlish has brought out, a successful attack upon Bradley would not necessarily extend to Hegel. See Stewart Candlish, *The Russell/Bradley Dispute and Its Significance for Twentieth-Century Philosophy*, Pbk edn, History of Analytic Philosophy (Basingstoke, UK; New York: Palgrave Macmillan, 2009), 142.
89 Richard Bernstein, "Why Hegel Now?" 34.
90 For a view contesting Peter Hylton's orthodox rendering of the Cambridge origins of the analytic revolt against idealism, see David Bell, "The Revolution of Moore and Russell: A Very British Coup?" in Anthony O'Hear, *German Philosophy since Kant*, Royal Institute of Philosophy Supplement, (Cambridge, UK; New York: Cambridge University Press, 1999), 193–208.
91 W.V. Quine, *The Ways of Paradox, and Other Essays*, Rev. and enl. edn (Cambridge, MA: Harvard University Press, 1976), 229, reprinted in Rockmore, *Hegel, Idealism, and Analytic Philosophy*, 63–4.
92 Though Moore's article itself must be understood as first and foremost an assault upon British idealism in general and F.H. Bradley's thought in particular.
93 Bernstein provides us with a well rounded overview of these tenets:

> It would be irresponsible for us to ignore the challenge that positivism presents—a challenge which may be formulated as follows: Whatever disagreements there may be about the characteristics of the natural sciences, mathematics, and logic, there can be no doubt that these disciplines are the exemplars of warranted knowledge.
> Richard J. Bernstein, *The Restructuring of Social and Political Theory* (Philadelphia: University of Pennsylvania Press, 1978), 207

94 Jon Stewart, The Hegel Myths and Legends, 5–6.
95 G.E. Moore, "The Refutation of Idealism," *Mind* 12, no. 48 (1903), 433–53: 434.
96 Ibid.
97 As will be explored and asserted below, Wilfrid Sellar's "myth of the given" was a key ingredient in Moore's refutation of idealism.
98 Rockmore comes to a similar conclusion:

> Moore's critique rests on a conflation between the ontological claim that sensation is sensation of something, hence of that which is outside spirit, outside experience but given in it through sensation, and the epistemological claim that what is given in sensation is identical with, or the same as, what stands outside experience.
> Rockmore, Hegel, Idealism, and Analytic Philosophy, 67

99 Moore, "The Refutation of Idealism," 435.
100 Ibid., 436.
101 Ibid., 437.
102 Understood here simply in the sense of *esse est percipi*.
103 Moore, "The Refutation of Idealism," 442.
104 Ibid.
105 Moore, "The Refutation of Idealism," 442–3. A further and related critique of Hegel's violation of the laws of contradiction is carried out in G.E. Moore, *Some Main Problems of Philosophy*, Muirhead Library of Philosophy (London, New York: Allen & Unwin; Humanities Press, 1953), 190–1 and in *Principia Ethica* (Cambridge, UK: Cambridge University Press, 1959), 34.
106 Ibid.
107 Ibid.

## 46  *Background, history and critique*

108 Georg Wilhelm Friedrich Hegel, Klaus Brinkmann, and Daniel O. Dahlstrom, *Encyclopedia of the Philosophical Sciences in Basic Outline. Part 1: Science of Logic* (Cambridge,UK; New York: Cambridge University Press, 2010), 237.
109 A classic example being Wilfrid Sellars's treatment of the myth of the given in Wilfrid Sellars, Richard Rorty and Robert Brandom, *Empiricism and the Philosophy of Mind* (Cambridge, MA: Harvard University Press, 1997).
110 Moore, cited in Rockmore, "Analytic Philosophy and the Hegelian Turn," 346. Hylton concludes very similarly in "Hegel and Analytic Philosophy."
111 Moore, "The Refutation of Idealism," 449.
112 Ibid.
113 C.J. Ducasse, "Introspection, Mental Acts, and Sensa," *Mind* 45, no. 178 (1936), 181–92.
114 G.E. Moore, "The Refutation of Idealism," 450.
115 Ibid., 449.
116 Baldwin, *G.E. Moore*, 36–7. Hylton takes a similar position in "Hegel and Analytic Philosophy," 463.
117 Georg Wilhelm Friedrich Hegel, J.N. Findlay and Arnold V. Miller, *Phenomenology of Spirit* (Oxford: Clarendon Press, 1977), 91–2.
118 Moore, "The Refutation of Idealism," 450.
119 Ibid.
120 Ibid., 451.
121 Ducasse, "Introspection, Mental Acts, and Sensa," 181–92.
122 Moore, "The Refutation of Idealism," 453.
123 Baldwin, *G.E. Moore*, 37.
124 Nicholas Griffin, *The Cambridge Companion to Bertrand Russell* (Cambridge, UK; New York: Cambridge University Press, 2003), 89.
125 David Lamb, *Hegel: From Foundation to System*, Martinus Nijhoff Philosophy Library (The Hague; Boston Hingham, MA: M. Nijhoff, 1980), 94.

## 2 Origins of the prescriptive problematic

### The behavioral revolution and the schism of political science and philosophical tradition

> And behind all logic and its seeming sovereignty of movement, there are valuations, or to speak more plainly, physiological demands, for the maintenance of a definite mode of life.
>
> Nietzsche

> If we have taken so long and circuitous a journey towards American political science itself, it is because none of those things that predisposed it towards the "scientific method" arose from within itself.
>
> Bernard Crick

In the first half of the twentieth century, several philosophical and scientific movements led political scientists towards an acute resignation and rejection of all forms of epistemology, and ontology by extension, not strictly coherent with an empirical orientation. While the likes of Feuerbach and Marx were not vulgar materialists in any sense, their valorization of scientific methods and inquiry were part and parcel of the materialist transformation of social inquiry in general and Hegel studies in particular. Of greater salience for my consideration of the Anglo-American reception and transmission of Hegel in the twentieth century is Moore and Russell's initiation of the analytic revolution which itself was predicated upon, specifically, the rejection of all things Hegelian through the straw men of Bradley, McTaggart and other idealists.[1] James's *ad hominem* attacks on Hegel's work and character in the late nineteenth century preceded these later developments which, in combination with the lacerations of Hegel in his later works, were certainly amplified in their wake.

While the majority of the young Hegelians would certainly have sought to preserve the profound historical and philosophical insights they witnessed in Hegel's idealist corpus, these authors—closest and best situated to offer critical reflection—had unfortunately little influence on the role Hegel's work would play on the new landscape. In this context, Hegel's person and works played the role of an imaginary origin and genealogical curse in early analytic assessments and reproaches of British idealist thought.

As went Hegel, so went political studies. The founding of Anglo-American social sciences around the turn of the twentieth century took its lead from the likes of Moore and Russell and their empirical rebellion against Hegelian speculation. These leaders of the budding analytic movement had honed their ideas against the nineteenth century's engagement with philosophical reflection, the history of ideas and the relative importance of idealism in philosophy and politics that had made Hegel a figure of importance in the English-speaking academic world. Many of the doubts they originally expressed about Hegel would recirculate in later critiques of the prevailing orientation of political theory by major political scientists, such as Catlin and Easton in the twentieth century. For these empirically oriented political scientists, political theory remained mired in a subjectivism, historicism and idealism that was ultimately traceable to Hegel's discredited body of thought. As the previous chapter brought out, the analytic and empirically oriented rebellion that Moore and Russell initiated in the Anglo-American worlds were motivated and formulated against the specter of Hegel's influence. As the next chapter will examine in detail, this legacy has had a very specific and far-reaching impact on the way Hegel has been received and represented ever since.

The reasons for importing the scientific model into political studies were several, and these will be considered in greater depth below. However, in order to understand, first, the transition from the nineteenth- and early twentieth-century revolutions in the philosophy of science and, second, the high instrumental and theoretical value attributed to them by the founders of the social and political sciences, some degree of emphasis must be placed on the interaction between ideological and methodological means and ends. As Bernstein has sketched the transition to positivism:

> The understanding that social scientists have of their own disciplines was reinforced by what was happening in philosophy. Once the triad of the early logical positivists had taken hold—analytic, synthetic, or meaningless—there was no legitimate place for social and political philosophy. Such a grand edifice had to be dismantled—sorted out into its proper empirical (synthetic) components and its definitional (analytic) components.[2]

In this transition "each of the social sciences ... passed through a decline of speculative and philosophical reflection"[3] and towards an optimism in reconstituting all fields of inquiry under a scientific rubric that may be broadly classified as "methodological positivism." George Steinmetz offers us a working definition:

> Its most important features are (1) an epistemological commitment to covering laws, that is, to the identification of Humean "constant conjunctions" of empirical events; (2) an empiricist ontology (although this aspect has become somewhat less central in recent decades with the ascendance of rational choice theory, which is often anti-empiricist); and (3) a set of scientistic assumptions stemming from the belief that the methods of the human and the natural sciences should be identical.[4]

This project reached its philosophical high-water mark after World War I when the Vienna circle "pivoted on a monistic theory of scientific development and a deductivist theory of scientific structure."[5] It is this trend that was realized most fully for political science in David Easton's behavioral revolution of the 1950s which, he claimed, "in its sophisticated state as found in physics or economics ... is deductive."[6] Thus, deduction became the basis of his conceptual framework of empirical theory which would serve "as an analytical model of the concrete political system."[7]

Yet these methodological imperatives were given their more basic purpose by preexisting ideological ones. As brought out by Bernard Crick in 1964, and as will be examined after my consideration of the main methodological trends of the first two-thirds of the twentieth century in political science below, there were conspicuous ideological imperatives that underwrote the call to scientific rigor. Of Merriam, Lasswell and the Chicago school Crick writes:

> The habitual confidence of their espousal of "democracy", indeed the mere fact of their congregation in the United States, began to seem more important to me than their formal claim to be scientific ... the methodology of these books seemed of little help in understanding their own obvious and intense democratic moralism: the presuppositions outweighed the propositions.[8]

In short, scientific methodologies as well as ideological imperatives were intertwined within the new science of politics movement, marrying the materialist revolt against idealism initiated in the nineteenth century to the political interests of liberalism in an Anglo-American context. This admixture of empirical means and liberal ends unified the founders of the American Political Science Association and the subsequently highly influential Chicago School, tying together A.F. Bentley, Charles Merriam, Harold Lasswell, Herbert Tingsten, Gabriel Almond, David Truman, Abraham Kaplan, David Easton and others who pioneered the methodological regimentation of the discipline. What is critical for my narrative here is that philosophy had become political, and an understanding that the methodologically and ideologically *prescriptive* forces which were behind this movement would have a direct and indelible impact on the way Hegel's political thought would be received and appropriated in the latter half of the twentieth and the beginning of the twenty-first centuries. Prior to telling that story in the next chapter, however, we must examine the campaign for methodological rigor and its ideological presupposition that first transformed political science in the first half of the twentieth century and, by extension, subsequent political theory and philosophy.

## Charles Merriam

The methodological regimentation of contemporary political science has its thickest roots in the soil of the 1920s science of politics movement. At the forefront of this movement was Charles Merriam, who had inherited the mantle of leadership from Graham Wallas and Arthur Bentley, forerunners of the movement at the turn of the century.[9] Anticipating David Easton's pioneering program by more than 30 years, Merriam's concern was to overcome the subjectivization of the discipline, taking his starting point in the advances made toward methodological rigor which the social sciences had enjoyed in the fields of sociology and, especially, economics. While he conceded that political ideas and systems are themselves very much the outcome of historical forces, he nevertheless intended a program to overcome "economic determinism" and "social environment" in the maintenance of the scientific standing of a discipline.[10] The way forward, he argued, was the standardization of the "measuring scales of facts and forces,"[11] and his main concern was the degree to which the field had progressed in these empirical areas. Ultimately he lamented that the social sciences had been generally outstripped by the so-called natural sciences, admitting that the political scientist "often has no laboratory equipment at all"[12] and that the state of the collection of "political data for scientific purposes" remained underdeveloped.[13]

Not unlike Harold Lasswell after him, there is a clear assertion in Merriam's arguments that a scientific grounding of the study of politics would provide immunization against its ideological manipulation by authoritarian projects. Merriam's early conclusions in the 1920s were that quantitative data gathering and statistical analysis offered a sobering restraint on political discourse, as well as the hope of much sought after progress on the understanding of political systems. Yet, as Bernard Crick, James Farr, David Ricci and others have brought out,[14] Anglo-American political science's project of scientization was intimately bound up with liberal-democratic biases that sought to root out the manipulation of political analysis and so to immunize it from illiberal use. Merriam's hope was that the methodological progress he witnessed in psychology and biology could be emulated by political research where "these new inquiries seem likely to evolve methods by which many human reactions ... may be much more accurately observed, measured and compared."[15] The hard sciences, in short, could provide iron-clad and tamper-proof methodological foundations upon which political science could evolve, on the assumption that its findings and contributions would be inherently compatible with democratic and pluralist ideological principles. The ends of such a methodological revolution were clear: social controls could be modified in order to sustain and deepen democratic structures.[16]

So intense and optimistic was Merriam's commitment to ensuring a democratic landscape through methodological regimentation that he held out hopes of its resolving the fundamental problems of politics. Human nature itself seemed to "stand on the verge of definite measurement,"[17] he claimed, where psychology had mobilized the tool of scientific inquiry and observation. Political science stood to gain from these developments where it could finally begin to count on the value-free objectivity and systematic rigor which had been creeping through the social sciences in the West since the late nineteenth century. Here Merriam anticipated the behavioral revolution to come, claiming that "The statistical use of psychological material offers to the student of politics large areas hitherto unexplored, and insight into springs of political action up to this time only imperfectly observed."[18] This confluence of politics with science he witnessed as the frontier of progress for the discipline and, ultimately, as the bedrock upon which a secure democratic future could be laid. The goal of world and national peace he imagined as the potential fruit of a science of instinct where "the possibilities of training, education and reorganization" promised self-mastery to the end of "the cooperative enterprise of democracy."[19]

Merriam's apologetics for social science asked whether we have "overdone 'nature' and underdone 'man' scientifically,"[20] such that the line between the two had blurred the fundamental commonalities between spheres of inquiry. Merriam deferred to Joseph LeConte's positivist counsel of the late nineteenth century that politics must embrace science through the lens of an empiricist framework, where a "wise empiricism"[21] would direct and guide scientific inquiry towards salient political concerns. The key methodological and political goals of such a program were based on the staunch belief that "social and political control may be found to be much more susceptible to human adaptation and reorganization than they now are."[22] The belief that such control was made legitimate by reference to scientific inquiry and democratic, if not instrumental, teleology made the irony of its inherent authoritarian potential opaque to Merriam. This is made all the more controversial given his explicit support for Wallas' paternalistic and elite project aiming at "the creation of opinion by the deliberate exploitation of sub-conscious non-rational inference"[23] which Wallas' student, Walter Lippmann, would take to new heights. Merriam's 1921 article thus stands as his manifesto against what he considered to be the crisis of the discipline, bordering on "anarchy in social science, or chaos in the theory of political order."[24] The crisis he witnessed within the discipline was thus a microcosm of the ideological instability and insecurity he perceived in the American and international political landscapes writ large. In short, the scientific turn in American politics during the interwar years was implicitly a means of protecting the democratic masses from themselves through the advent of a strict regimen of scientific research and control.

Four years after his critical assessment of the discipline, Merriam set out to put political science on a surer footing. In his 1925 *New Aspects of Politics*, he outlined the obstacles which political science needed to clear in order to come to terms with the "adoption of more scientific and intelligent methods in the study and practice of government."[25] This, and not the depoliticization of society and the diminishment of the state, was the answer to the pressing problems of the time and the crises of war, revolution and the oppression of the individual. Science, it was clear for Merriam, would complete the primary tasks of the liberal enterprise: "these are the tests of scientific politics."[26]

In the face of the historical abuses and excesses of governance that threatened the just use of power in the West and beyond, Merriam asked whether political society had "not reached the time when it is necessary to adjust and adapt more intelligently, to apply the categories of science to the vastly important forces of social and political control?"[27] Clearly then the project of science and its value neutrality were part and parcel of the ideological apparatus of the science of politics as Merriam saw it. Science was here understood as a neutral tool in the beneficent hands of the ideally liberal democratic state, both as instrument of control and insurance against illiberal abuse. Where government had all too often proven to be a refuge for antiquated and irrational social impulses, imposing a scientific regimen promised not only that human technological organization would be firmly grounded but that the governance of those productive forces would itself be reined in as well. Where science never "turns its titanic forces over to a government of ignorance and prejudice, with laboratory science in the hands of jungle governors"[28] Merriam re-envisioned a Platonic kingdom of an empowered scientific elite.

Certain that the social sciences only needed time to gather to themselves the authority and mastery already possessed by the hard sciences, Merriam implored that "the methods of social science and of political science be thoroughly scrutinized and that they be adapted to ... the remarkable physical world into which we are swiftly coming."[29] Here then the study of politics and of political agents and communities is made a derivative of the material organization that physics and biology study. The political agent merely had to be understood in its physicality in order to be rendered the subject of the control and regulation of science to the ends of peace. In essence, and despite Merriam's claims to the contrary, science brings about the end of politics understood as strife and conflict and ushers in a technocracy of governance under the auspices of the conservation and canalization of human energies. So certain was this new scientific regime of control and peace in its confrontations with human nature that Merriam was willing to argue that "it has not been demonstrated that political behavior is any more complex than that of the atom."[30] The implications here are obvious; the cynicism with which humans have come to view so-called human nature is itself a function of a failed methodology of understanding and regimen of control. With these scientifically remedied and redrawn, the behavioral "atom" of human historical strife and conflict in human nature could be brought to heel through scientific intervention.

Despite his overt loyalties, Merriam's ambivalence concerning democracy is clearly on display here. On the one hand, the phenomenon of mass rule brings the question of mass irrationality to the fore. On the other, an elitist ideal of autocratic and paternal authority risks the erasure of the nature of modern society and its emphases upon individual autonomy, enterprise and non-state interference. Science would be the surer hand that could reign in the excesses of liberal democratic enterprise and ensure the ideal democratic balance between the equally undesirable politics of the few and the many. The forces of modernization had so transformed politics and society that a "technique of government"[31] founded on a new basis required inauguration. In his view progress had made this possible and the potentials of twentieth-century society meant that an evolution of mass society was at hand. Political science needed not merely to reflect and describe, but to actively contribute to these events as a partisan.

The traditional, nineteenth-century distinction between the natural and social sciences had put the latter in a place where truth had become unattainable. Yet

Merriam pointed out that progress had been initiated in this area by Auguste Comte's positivist agenda in initiating a scientific program for the field of social inquiry as a whole.[32] For Merriam it was clearly the scientific progressions of the nineteenth century in the fields of "history, sociology, economics, statistics, psychology, biology, engineering, anthropology, and ethnology"[33] that political inquiry needed to emulate. The new social and material conditions which modernity had furnished demanded new techniques of political inquiry and control and the sciences formed the essential and unassailable basis for further progress. The problems of scientific society could only be brought to heel by the force of a scientific study of politics; modern problems, Merriam argued, could only be resolved in reference to modern methods. Political inquiry had to come to terms and address itself to the new world built by technical progress: one which rendered possible leisure, education, unconventional thought, scientific data, the mastery of nature and the possibility of inclusivist government on scales never before known. Seeing in education and eugenics the two pillars of a future scientific governance of "political control"[34] he pioneered a science of politics which actively and openly petitioned for the refashioning of society, and as no mere neutral or academic observatory of human action. The normative questions implied by these interventions into human life and the implications of eugenics—an agenda in American academia that would soon be silenced by the confrontation with Nazism—Merriam intentionally left open as the inevitable inheritance of the coming technical polity. His early efforts to bring methodological rigor into political science modeled on the natural sciences would be tremendously influential. As Farr notes:

> Before the Second World War, a number of Merriam's colleagues and students—especially the imaginative and prolific Harold D. Lasswell—would join him in constructing and publicising a new science of politics that was enthusiastic about methods and realistic about democracy in the wake of the First World War. Their efforts would be continued well into the 1950s and 60s by their behavioral descendants.[35]

## George Catlin

One of Merriam's colleagues and contemporaries was George Edward Gordon Catlin. Following swiftly in Merriam's wake, Catlin's 1927 tome on political science, *The Science and Method of Politics*, argued that the field had lost its capacity to forge new knowledge. Echoing and anticipating the core of Easton's 1951 position on the decline of political theory, Catlin asserted that political science had descended into a historicism which had rendered the subject neutral, observational and passive.[36] The result, he argued had reduced the field to a "collection of essays and belles lettres."[37] The attempt to bring political studies to the status of a science remained an uphill battle where the "metaphysician dislikes its empiricism, the natural scientist suspects its human uncertainty, the historian abhors its attempt to theorise."[38] Holding that political science "had a bad start," he pushed for the transformation of the discipline to match subjects like chemistry in their use of "abstract hypotheses and of a scientific method."[39] Relativistic and anthropocentric doctrines had stultified political studies at the level of the street and the contest of opinion held sway as the measure of all things. As Easton would later argue, where no science could found a standard set of parameters for the discipline, it was itself subject to the unending contests of the politics of the field, themselves a microcosm of the larger political world and its struggles. Against this relativistic whorl of subjectivist contestation at the heart of political science as he had come to know it, Catlin made his views clear: "a scientific method is necessary in the treatment of Politics."[40] Far from being satisfied with folk wisdom, he required that politics become as practicable and rigorous as possible.

To the ends of initiating his science of politics, Catlin took aim at a cornerstone of the nineteenth-century humanities: the widely held view that natural rules of mechanical causality do not apply to the spiritualized and intentional realms of society and history. The humanities' rejection of the applicability of mechanical causation to historical phenomena, one which justified the division of natural and social scientific methodologies, was wholly unsatisfactory in Catlin's view. Rather it was their "common characteristics which have pragmatic value."[41] Conceding that a political science may not plumb the depths of human historical experience, his purposes clearly cohere with those of Merriam where control and regulation of the observable are concerned. It was through the psychological canvass that they sought to yield regularities of political behavior which would permit both prediction and policy oriented application. It is not the specificities and peculiarities of either human or natural events and entities which interest this science, but rather the broad commonalities under which the two coalesce: in essence it is the world of the empirically observable that is of primary importance and not the world of internal motivation. While denying the crude materialist mechanism of the Enlightenment, Catlin nonetheless believed that the assumption of a deterministic matrix of human behavior was itself a valuable and viable hypothesis for the progress of a practicable political science.

This intention to remove and distance political science from its subject of research, such that "Politics must view social phenomena externally,"[42] had a very important and practical goal. That is, and reproducing Merriam's position, this political science must be a politics of control which methodologically washes out human bias and prejudice in order to evince "increased control, control of men over the hitherto alarmingly uncontrollable behavior of man."[43] Thus the removal of the so-called anthropocentric dimension inevitably manifest in relativist, intuitionist and intentionalist approaches to political science must be exchanged for this higher order, "objective" approach. Catlin's political science, like Merriam's, aspired to the regulation of human behavior precisely through the disciplines' own intentional withdrawal from concern with will and intention as filtered out by scientific method. The irony, and naïveté, is all too apparent: a value free science set up to the ends of a presupposed ideological program assumes its ideological—normative—bases to be immune to its observations and vice versa. As will be examined in the next chapter, this ambiguity in the methodological constitution of twentieth-century political science would play a central role in the way a generation of Anglophone political theorists would interpret and deploy Hegel's thought.

On the basis of his hope for a "positive" politics, Catlin could afford to christen political science as a science of prediction. He sought a procedure to lay out a comprehensive organization of the governing principles and conditions within which political acts take place: in essence the boundaries of the "political system" that Easton later sought to furnish for the discipline. Formalizing the totality of the political context in this way, Catlin, we must agree, was genuine about his project to reduce political inquiry to an empirical mode of method and measurement. The question he did not answer, however, is whether the elimination of subjective willing from the data stream he configured would not also eliminate the essence of the political itself. The practical orientation and emphasis upon control here, as well, raises questions regarding the degree of validity of such a science of politics where control and not fact is the actual goal.

Speaking in the language of the Enlightenment, Catlin saw in the normative and idiographic subfield of political theory the very worst of the methodological backwardness of political studies as a whole, where "men have been permitted to cast without challenge the rubbish of uncritical speculation and the burning oil of enthusiasm to fling the bodies of opponents and to sacrifice to strange idols."[44] Catlin anticipated and pioneered the project of methodological critique and rejuvenation that Easton would centrally adopt in his prescriptions for political theory and the field as a whole. While Easton was nowhere near as enthusiastic about the purified project of a positivist approach to politics, the key elements of Catlin's and Merriam's challenges to traditional political research and scholarly practice would be largely taken on board.

## David Easton

David Easton's 1951 assault on political theory, "The Decline of Modern Political Theory," took up largely where Catlin had left off, charging political theory with a degenerate antiquarianism. Easton early on made the point that he would later drive home in his work on American political science in 1953: the historicism of then contemporary political theory had become backward looking and had ceased to pursue its sole redeeming characteristic of normative theorization. In addition, where other fields made use of theory to bring scientific rigor and conceptual coherence to field research, political theory had made little contribution in this way. Political theory could not be taken seriously in terms of its factual claims until it began to reckon with "systematizing its empirical base."[45]

Easton argued that political theory was an essentially impoverished branch of political science which had neglected a "systematic empirically-oriented theory"[46] dedicated to the study of political behavior. His position implicitly held contemporary political theory up to an empirical standard where he sighted Talcott Parsons' dismissal of the field for its lack of conformity to "purely empirical social science."[47] Political theory would have to convert itself to an empirical orientation or see itself dismissed from the discipline as both untheoretical and unscientific. In essence, theory ought to be wedded to the disciplines' empirical aspirations which Easton held were the core of political science, and align itself with the scientifically progressive movement toward the study of "political behavior and institutions."[48] His rejection was thoroughgoing in asserting that neither had political theory ever really held itself up to the standards of political science, and instead "stumbles along behind,"[49] nor had it been guided by the proper impulse to be a "truly theoretical organ for political science."[50] In short, political theory needed to shape up or ship out of the discipline. To be any better than an editorial columnist, the theorist needed to get beyond insight and participate in the systematic grounding of a theory of politics so as to lay a scientific groundwork for inquiry.

Theorists who did not embrace the task and involvement in the systematization of theoretical inquiry into political behavior—read positive political phenomena—could never raise their assessments above the status of common sense. Theorists as Easton knew them were a lot of pseudo-wise men who either span semi-causal sociological depictions of historical contexts, or exegetes who busied themselves with the true intentions of this or that canonical figure. The demands of the discipline of political science had updated themselves to include a core scientific regimentation, and political theory's intransigent antiquarianism only served to hinder the field's movement in this direction as a whole. A resentment of theory's reluctance to pursue the scientific aims is quite sharp in Easton's critique and it clearly aligned itself with Catlin's earlier arguments. In fact, in retrospect upon the first half of the twentieth century, Easton recognized only Catlin and a select few other theorists who took the project of building a solid base for the scientific inquiry into politics seriously. Yet it was in Catlin's arguments alone that he saw an explicit program for the transformation of the discipline into an integrated project of positive political research.

In this context, Easton's approach to the transformation of political theory within political science required of it a new methodological attention to empiricist rigor. While Easton conceded that to impose the same rigor as the natural sciences on the social would be to lose much of what makes them unique, he nonetheless prescribed a regimentation of the field that logically implied nothing less than a rupture with past practice. Where the conceptual systematization of political theory would become the basis for a new integration of empirical research, it would cast off its traditional philosophical enterprise once and for all, and, in so doing, adopt a wholesale empirical resolution of the great metaphysical and epistemological questions. Easton's revolt is witnessed in Bernstein's reflection on larger "Anglo-Saxon philosophy" where "the tradition of political and social philosophy had been broken."[51] Having surrendered its association to the great questions, political theory would thus be interred as conceptual handmaiden to Easton's scientific study of politics.

While Easton envisioned an engaged and critical version of political theory, what normative authority or legitimacy could it have had under the weight of the strictures of logical and empirical positivism? While Easton spoke not of a break with past research but rather of a continuity, he nonetheless envisioned a project "for political theory to assimilate itself to the main current of empirical research in political science"[52] on the basis of its failed historicist orientations over the first half of the twentieth century. His project was thus far more radical than he was overtly willing to concede. Despite his allowance that theory continue with normative inquiry as well as methodological foundation laying, it is clear that the latter project's own metaphysical assumptions—existence is synonymous with the sensorially observable—bear serious implications for the continuance of the former. Where moral and ethical research is married to the project of an assumed empirical epistemology, many of the core philosophical questions which have traditionally informed and inspired ethical and political thought will have been muted. In short, the tradition of the cross-fertilization of classical philosophy with political thought could not but be brought to an end.

Two years later, in his 1953 classic, *The Political System: An Enquiry into the State of Political Science*, Easton took this assault upon traditional political theory to new heights. Not merely assailing by way of a general juxtaposition with the supposedly superior and more dynamic approach of positive political science, Easton now laid out a plan for the thorough integration of theory into the new positivist, behavioral project. In assessing the field of political science as lacking a core theoretical method with which to systematize its fragmented insights and observations into knowledge, Easton laid out the details of a revised methodological vocation for theory. Political science he held was unable to cope with the political challenges of its age and was lagging seriously behind other empirically regimented fields. In his estimation the broad conceptual foundations of political inquiry had become overly fluid and capricious, and had led only to contradictory, repetitive and incommensurable research and conclusions. Without a systematic integration of concepts, generalization would remain impossible or at best erratic and the field would remain disintegrated and disorganized. A theoretical framework was needed to bring consistency to the meaning and use of the terms which political scientists employed. The benefits of such a reframing would be real progress and a surge in practical applicability and usefulness: to turn what is an art into a science.

To these ends, Easton took it from the natural sciences that a deductive system of theoretical generalization provided greater knowledge. A growing base of relevant and reliable universalization would provide an indicator of adequate knowledge. While this is by definition true, the assumption of predictability and consistent causal relation drawn from natural science over to political phenomena remained, then and now, far from a given. Easton's ultimate theoretical system is thus somewhat foundationalist, albeit empirically and pragmatically so. That is, one begins with the broadest assertions and generalizations and deductively moves to narrower ones to the point where specific and particular assertions are made and then empirically tested. Through this circuit of theorization Easton hoped to evoke the type of paradigm construction and testing that fields such as economics and sociology had, he believed, successfully undertaken. What Easton did not consider, however, was how political theory ought to relate to itself; how thinking is a form of political agency and not merely a handmaiden to positive political phenomena as we observe them empirically.

In his own time Easton took most major theoretical thinkers to be concerned with "the meaning, internal consistency, and historical development of past political values"[53] rather than with the pressing issues of the day. As a result the historical method seemed a stultifying force to Easton: "This preoccupation with problems of history, rather than with problems of reflection about the desirability of alternative goals, is what gives contemporary research in political theory its special significance."[54] In contrast, he held that political theory ought to take what it could from the past to better understand its present in order to better reflect and innovate to the end of a "political synthesis or image of a good political life."[55]

Easton understood American political theory's descent into historicism in terms of the discipline's own embeddedness within the West and its values, thus leading it to a normative passivity and conformity with tradition. In this way it had lost its critical capacity and had become an unwitting rubber stamp and reinforcing institution to these values. In addition, its acceptance of the nineteenth century's historicist thesis of the relativism of political programs had contributed to theory's retrogressive viewpoint where the "belief in the ultimate equal worth of all moral views is the product."[56] In Easton's post-Nazi context this value monism was clearly flawed and implied the need to reground theory on a basis which would allow it to recover its critical and normative potentials.

The failure of political theory was also a recent development for Easton. Theorists of the past had been active in consideration of political phenomena from diverse perspectives. In contrast, the theoretical inquiries of the first half of the twentieth century had severely contracted their fields of view to issues of scholarly research in the history of political thought. In doing so, in his view, theorists had done a disservice to political science in general where these concerns had concealed and obscured theory's potential to bring the discipline up to date though conceptual integration. Yet Easton here engaged in a naïve empiricism; the assumption that theory's role is more than just normative—as he claims was the case with theorists such as Locke—and ought to provide rules of generalization and conceptual order for the field is to assume that theory ought to be concerned with the scientific organization of the field to the detriment of its moral and ethical projects. That is, the conceptual "bureaucracy" of the field that he envisions where theory "ought to devote itself to analyzing and constructively formulating causal as well as moral theory"[57] implies a policing not only of moral inquiry, past and present, but a duty to provide conceptual guidance for the ordering of empirical research as well. From another standpoint, this marriage of orientations provides an awkward vocational burden for theorists where they must at once plumb the depths of the "good life" as well as instruct their field-research oriented fellows on how to proceed with empirical domains of inquiry.

Nowadays, some six decades after Easton published his work on the state of American political science, the conceptual and methodological progress he hoped for has largely emanated from the disparate field-oriented areas of political research themselves, rather than from political theorists.[58] The priority of consistency in empirical research has rarely been a concern for those who have made theory traditionally understood a primary concern. Of course, Hegel saw political theory as a project of integrating and reconciling higher order philosophical concepts with political experience as opposed to a geometric prefiguring of conceptual puzzle pieces for the purposes of positive political research and prediction. While he may have permitted theory some leeway, for Easton it must ultimately be held accountable to empirical criteria where "All that we need demand of theoretical research is that in principle we are able to test it by reference to sensory data."[59] This of course is to assume that all theory may ultimately be testable by such criteria and that the political and social phenomena and ideas that theorists apply themselves to are scrutable in this way.

Clearly, it was political theory's commitment to the history of ideas and ideological pluralism that had informed Merriam, Catlin and Easton, all of whom called for the reengagement of political research with the real world of hard political fact to democratic ends. While Easton avoided the overt discourse of democracy and instead focused upon the dual role of theory as a normative as well as systematizing engine, he nevertheless was deeply involved in the same American program that Merriam and Catlin championed. That is, he was a leading pioneer in the establishment of a science of politics which deduces methods of research from theoretical generalities precisely in order to make the data acquired part and parcel of a practical project of political prediction and, ostensibly, control. In pointing to the likes of Catlin, C.J. Friedrich and Lasswell, as well as recognizing that democratic faith is not in and of itself a sufficient insurance against its excesses,[60] Easton endorsed a conceptual reordering and purification of political study. This he argued was minimally necessary in order to achieve a science which would be democratically effective, precisely by its being insulated from the stifling prejudices of democratic pretense and political culture.

Finally, and as earlier referenced, part of what had kept political science as a whole stagnant for Easton had been its proximity and intimacy with institutional power, a proximity that curtailed its critical potentials vis-à-vis the unifying myth of democracy. The absence of its involvement in such ideological controversy lead to a softening of its critical role on the American scene. Yet his claim that there was no overarching conceptual framework within contemporary twentieth-century political thought in particular remains conspicuous, conflicting with what others have witnessed as the post-1920s American turn towards positivist political science.[61] In short, Easton failed to take sufficiently seriously that the likes of Lasswell, Catlin and Merriam, and those members of the science of politics movement beyond the Anglo-American West, had envisioned the discipline as a handmaiden to higher ideological ends. Easton's own critique of the theoretically constraining influences of democratic and Western prejudices does not spare him from scrutiny. While recognizing the fragmentation of Western values in the wake of World War II as a call to political theorists is to his credit, he nevertheless innocently extended a methodological project which had been setup as a bulwark of liberal democratic values and institutions. Gunnel reinforces the point, representing Easton as the principal spokesperson of the behavioralist movement in political science which was "less a revolution in many respects than a recommitment to the visions of both the scientific study of politics and liberal democracy that had informed the discipline for nearly a half century."[62] The very fact that he recognized the degree to which liberal democratic prejudices were part and parcel of the descent into historicism ought to have informed him of the correlative fact of their inevitable and continuing influence on the science of politics movement in the United States and beyond; especially in the wake of the grotesque illiberalism of Nazism. While Easton's vision of the interaction of political theory and field research is largely heuristic, his own critique of the failings of political theory should have led him to a deeper consideration of his predecessors' work, such as that of Catlin, and to reconsider the degree to which science could actually assist the study of politics in advancing the cause of the good life in the first place.

These shortcomings of reflection—both the adherence to positivistically driven political research and liberal democratic norms—became prejudices of the field and would have grave implications for the ongoing reception of Hegel's work and its influence. These cornerstones were simply taken for granted in Easton's extension of the science of politics movement even as he admonished the field precisely for taking American institutional values and norms for granted. While behavioralism in the 1950s and 1960s could not include most scholars as card carrying members, "a positivist undercurrent largely informed the dominant aspirations of the profession."[63] Easton's own confessional 1968 American Political Science Association Presidential address would once and for all make clear that democratic realism married to a science of politics as an elitist project had not moved forward the cause of the greater democratic good in Western countries. From this revised vantage point, political theory would no longer need to act as conceptual handmaiden to empirical method and research. On his revised account, political theory's crucial task would be to act as a watchdog to guide and command attention to the ethical application of research. Despite Easton's confession and the subsequent intellectual creativity which has marked the development of theory, political theory is still haunted by the positivist pretensions of the discipline.

## The legacy and persistence of positivism: scientific and theoretical

As Roy Bhaskar has argued:

> [T]he positivist conception of science that had dominated the first two-thirds of the twentieth century ... [was] based squarely on Humean empiricism....

*Origins of the prescriptive problematic* 61

The positivist vision of science pivoted on a monistic theory of scientific development and a deductivist theory of scientific structure.[64]

The initiation of the early twentieth-century positivist project in political science would weigh heavily on the future development and scientific regimentation of the discipline. Bernstein evades all equivocation on the matter: "as philosophers of science became clearer about the primary characteristics of the natural sciences and the precise role that theory plays in them, they extended a powerful influence on methodologically sophisticated social scientists."[65] This program coalesced with growing post-World War II skepticism regarding the certainty and stability of liberal democratic frameworks for the ongoing development of Western nations and their institutions.[66] The autonomy of the natural sciences from ideological commitment was the only way forward; not towards a doctrine of emancipation and enlightenment, but towards technical and instrumental mastery. Politics had infected science with its aspirations and irrationalities and this had to be beaten back in order to procure for politics a secure democratic bedrock it had proved unable to attain and secure for itself. With this Bernstein is able to declare of the social sciences of the mid-1970s—all the while looking back to the transformation that took place in the 1950s—that mainstream social scientists were those "who are convinced that the greatest success is to be found in emulating, modifying, and adapting techniques that have proven successful in our scientific understanding of nature."[67]

The influence of the movement has been pervasive within political science such that, as Bernstein has claimed, "thinkers in the Anglo-Saxon world cannot underestimate the extent to which their thoughts, attitudes, beliefs, and even feelings have been shaped by empiricist, scientific, and pragmatic traditions."[68] Many of these views had their origins in the Enlightenment and the belief that a cleansed vision of nature would not only be instrumentally beneficial, but normatively as well. Merriam, Catlin and Easton and many of the behavioralist "persuasion" broadly shared in these views. The shedding of *overt* liberal ideological dogmas that Easton called for to the end of a value-free study of politics is only comprehensible in the wake of the great excesses that were born of Weimar liberalism. Easton's program is very much an evolutionary step beyond Catlin's desire for democracy, seeking to thread the needle between the extremes of mass irrationality and elite paternalism, and came about only against the background of the great challenges and failures which liberal democracies had suffered in the first half of the twentieth century. Most social and political scientists vied either to progress with or move beyond theory, the latter strategy taking it as an irredeemable vestige of subjectivism and historicism that was best shuffled off to the humanities. Regardless of the path, both sides viewed "intellectual life as passing through the dark ages of theological, metaphysical, and philosophical speculation, only to emerge in the triumph of the positive sciences."[69]

The turn-of-the-century Anglo-American struggle against idealism anticipated the wider revolt that would spread throughout its social sciences; G.E. Moore's "Refutation of Idealism" had indeed been an uncanny trumpeting of a new age of intolerance of all forms of knowledge which did not adhere to the bookends of empirical and quantitative form. As Melissa Lane has brought out, the philosophical movement which issued most directly from Merriam realized its fullest expression in the behavioral revolution of the 1950s, making "the behaviorists in the social sciences [the] legitimate heirs of the positivist creed."[70] The installation of positivism in this way had a powerful and pervasive impact on the social sciences in general and political science in particular.

Where the empirical thrust was not influential, the logical thread manifested itself in the trends of rational choice, mathematical modeling, game theory, linguistic and conceptual analysis and, in general, quantitative and analytic methodological orientations. The Vienna Circle was crucial in making verifiability a touchstone of intelligibility, Carl Hempel demarcating between statements "which have empirical content" from those "of transempirical metaphysics, which admit of none."[71] Thus the very incapacity to speak outside the confines of empirical logic presented a constraint that was powerfully influential for political science and theory such that it became the benchmark of intelligibility and sobriety. Hegel's work was thus under assault from multiple directions: both by those who took issue with his supposed illiberal commitments to the Prussian state as a precursor to National Socialism, and those who found fault with his religious and metaphysical commitments which were assuredly ominous for their collectivist and illiberal orientations.

As Lane reminds us, the logical positivism of philosophers such as A.J. Ayer had a direct influence on political philosophers such as T.D. Weldon, and many others by extension, resulting in "a bracing (or chilling) effect on Anglophone political philosophy in the 1950s and 1960s."[72] Under these influences, the classical set of questions that had traditionally driven not merely political thought, but the philosophical enterprises of epistemology, ontology and ethics as well had become antiquated. Within a few years of the release of Easton's book, Peter Laslett had declared political theory dead under the positivist shadow.[73] Despite the commitment to self-critique and the thoroughgoing adherence to empiricist methodology, the behavioralist movement "uncritically oriented their studies toward the accepted foundational American values of equality and democracy."[74] As a trend, it stretches back to APSA's (American Political Science Association) first president Frank J. Goodnow and the origins of American political science, and meaningfully at least as far as Wallas' 1908 anticipation of behavioralism in his *Human Nature in Politics*. This supports the view that Easton's methodological project, despite its overt inclinations, was ultimately unable to immunize its vision for political research from the prevailing ideological prejudices of American academia and its larger institutional landscape.

The confluence of elite political prerogative in the guise of scientific establishment and democratic idealism Farr has aptly named the "enlightened elitism of democratic realism."[75] This ideological project's disingenuous populism took up for itself the goal of a "science of democracy"[76] which really signified nothing less than Lippmann's elitist end-run around popular sovereignty through the psycho-social mechanisms of the manufacturing of consent. These views

*Origins of the prescriptive problematic* 63

remained intact at the end of World War II and beyond. Where the "members of the great society cannot live up to democratic morals,"[77] for those of Merriam's students such as Lasswell it became imperative that the academic establishment push a policy platform that sustained democracy despite the capricious ideological orientations of its citizens. The irrational, ambivalent and unconscious desires of the anti-democratic masses posed an inherent threat to the great pillars of liberalism (freedom), capitalism (private property) and democracy (popular sovereignty) and could only be reconciled in this elitist and sadly ironic bargain.[78] To these public ends, empirically and analytically oriented political thought centered in Anglo-Saxon and English-speaking academic establishments were "detached from deep metaphysical questions about the meaning of human life and the place of human beings in the cosmos"[79] and frequently dismissive of attempts to overcome or challenge these prejudices.

Later, and despite the decline of the science of politics movement with the onset of social strife and protest in the late 1960s, Easton's 1969 confessional revision in favor of a "post-behavioral revolution" and the pervasive critique of positivism that had come to prominence in philosophy, the skeptical conclusions regarding the positivist paradigm "in the philosophy of science had little subsequent impact on the principal discourse of social science."[80] Gunnel commented in 1986 that few in contemporary political science overtly accepted the vulgar positivism that had infected the 1950s and 1960s but that "the basic ideas remain very much the same."[81] Thus the legacy of the behavioralist revolution has remained potent in the form of the residual methodological positivism that persisted after the former program's collapse in the late 1960s. Further illustrating this inertia Lane has suggested as recently as 2008 that the variety of American political science associations generally contain "political philosophy as one isolated corner of a field which remains broadly proud of its positivist ancestry"[82] and that "the battles between positivism and anti-positivism may not yet be played out."[83] Steinmetz's 2005 comments reinforce this viewpoint reporting that, despite ongoing efforts by social theorists to surmount it, "the disciplines continue to experience a positivistic haunting."[84]

It is precisely this lineage that has etiolated and deformed our capacity to appreciate, if not embrace, Hegel's view of the relation of political thought to philosophical problems that stood prior to the construction of the modern scientific edifice. For, regardless of whether we accept that Hegel is an uncritical and unapologetic metaphysician or a critical philosopher who seeks to rehabilitate the tradition in the wake of Kant, the very metaphysical questions that reside behind the edifice of science so crucial to Hegel's work—and upon which science itself depends for its claims and existence—have been obscured. As a result, Hegel's primary concerns with the metaphysical tradition and his response to its inner contradictions could only seem perverse and unworldly to those on this side of the epistemological divide that William James, G.E. Moore, Russell and others inaugurated for philosophy, and by extension, political science and theory. The infamous and influential misreading of Hegel's "es ist der Gang Gottes in der Welt, daß der Staat ist" as "the state is the march of God in the world"[85] remains a prime and conspicuous example of the mistreatment and intolerance directed at Hegel's political thought.

As the next chapter will explicate, the institutional and scholarly gravity of this movement, amongst philosophers as well as political theorists, was a driving force behind the emergence of revisionist readings of Hegel's political thought. This would advance under the influence of the rancor which "the alienation of political theory in political science"[86] had brought about for controversial and contentious members of political theory's canon: that is, for thinkers like Hegel who were fundamentally alien and anathema to the positivist program and its presuppositions in liberal democratic ideology.[87] In essence the positivist movement in the philosophy of science and the science of politics sustained an "underlying and profound fear and suspicion of theory as tainted by metaphysics and speculation."[88] These were seen as inherently anti-liberal and irrational and the force of this intolerance would lead a generation of scholars to reconsider Hegel's philosophical and political works in two main directions: first, to effect his rejection or dismissal from the cannon (Karl Popper, C.J. Friedrich, etc.) or, second, to salvage his contribution by way of a revisionist rehabilitation of Hegel's legacy that purged his thought of abject elements in conflict with the Anglo-American, liberal-positivist temper (Pełczyński, Taylor, Wood, etc.).

*These powerful prescriptive trends would lead many sympathetically predisposed to Hegel's political thought to take up, what I refer to as, the descriptive strategy. That is, they have represented Hegel's political thought as a secular and rational politics—usually compatible with contemporary liberalism—in absence of its supposedly odious metaphysical doctrines.* In essence, the wide influence this prescriptive posture (the "ought") against metaphysics has enjoyed has led to a descriptive culture (the "is") such that many commentators cursorily purge Hegel of his foundationalist orientations and proceed to a presentation of his political theory divested of its metaphysical commitments. The remainder, as I will expose in the following chapter, is a standard understanding which has come to take the deformation and morbidity of Hegel's metaphysical presuppositions for granted.

Where the "myth of the given"[89] had become part and parcel of the naïve positivist aspirations of philosophers of science and social scientists alike, there was little room for Hegel's metaphysical speculations. These related to the epistemological conditions for experience itself, conditions which the positivists' own empirical outlooks took for granted and which are most glaringly on display in the pioneering critique of the idealist legacy at the genesis of the analytical movement itself: Moore's "Refutation of Idealism." The challenge for contemporary readers of Hegel in a "post-behavioral" intellectual landscape, and that of political thought itself, is clear where "the persistence of the myth of the given and the instrumental interpretation of theory is now grounded in academic tradition, philosophical self-interest, and social scientific timidity."[90] Against this background, we must seek to reinvest political thought with an appreciation of the larger context of philosophical inquiry and tradition which was and continues to be eclipsed and diminished by the lingering methodological hygienics of positivism in its empiricist, quantitative and logical forms.

As Gunnel has brought out, the rationalizations for the preservation of the positivist creed in the face of the creeping critique of methodological positivism in the latter half of the twentieth century took many apologetic forms. In "social science and political theory that attempted to implement those notions or rationalize their activity in terms of them,"[91] wholesale revisionist readings of seemingly cantankerous authors like Hegel were the inevitable result. Here, under the powerful *prescriptive* pressures of "positivism and logical empiricism the philosophy of science had a normative character."[92] As a result there remains a need within political studies[93] to reconsider the way Hegel, and political thought by extension, has been received and read since at least the early twentieth century, and how this trend continues to inform scholarship today. The task would be to consider how and to what degree this legacy has deformed the representation and reception of Hegel's political thought and impoverished our ability to appreciate his theoretical contribution as both a unique thinker and an exponent of the eclipsed and discredited pre-positivist tradition of political philosophy. Sheldon Wolin's 1969 claims against methodism, that it had restricted "the "reach" of theory by dwelling on facts which are selected by what are assumed to be the functional requisites of the existing paradigm,"[94] seems as valid today as it was in 1969 when it comes to matters of retrieving the value of the non-positivist tradition of political thought for and by contemporary political theory.

## Behavioralism, rational choice and the "post-positivist" era

Alongside of the lingering influences of positivism in the social sciences, there is another powerful and perhaps more overtly influential contemporary theoretical actor to consider. The absence of some consideration of rational choice theory in this chapter would be all too conspicuous. I will deal with it briefly here for it does not evade the specific charges of ideological investment levied at the social sciences narrated above. Contemporary rational choice methods and theories are now dominant in the social sciences, the heir to behavioralism has become the preeminent trend in political science.[95] With its conceptual roots in logical positivism, rational choice approaches have set their sights on producing a new "prophetic" political science that has predictive power.[96] Yet, while rational choice grounds itself on an anti-positivist platform, Andrew Collier asserts the influential persistence of positivist roots in political science. Anti-positivist trends, Collier explains, that have attempted "to move past the positivist legacy appear to have had little effect on natural and social science research disciplines ... let alone on the policies and institutions ... that such disciplines service. One can't "'just say no' to this legacy."[97] Indeed, as James Farr has pointed out, Kenneth Shepsle considers the amalgam that has become rational choice one which promises to revolutionarily transform political theory into a "genuinely scientific enterprise" by driving a wedge between it and "political thought."[98]

While behavioralism was unable to fulfill its grand unified conception of political theory and political science, its legacy has been the proliferation and normalization of quantitative and statistical procedure.[99] Where contemporary "claims to knowledge not generated via these techniques and expressed in mathematical form" are rendered suspect by rational choice prerogatives, Timothy Kaufman-Osborn witnesses "the enduring legacy of behavioralism."[100] American political theorists have worked in ambivalent tension with these pressures well into the post-positivist era, and in ways which have had direct influence on the conceptual tools, norms and reception that their institutional context has reinforced.

Yet the defense of political theory from the normative side of the "facts and values" divide has not ensured it the protection and immunity that it has often envisioned or narrated for itself. As Gregory Kasza asserts, the quantitative and deductive thrust of mainstream political science has little tolerance for what strays from, citing Thomas Kuhn, "normal science."[101] For Kasza, the rubric of normativity is one which seeks to hem political theory in so as to "isolate the virus" which might undermine the priority which scientific thinking otherwise continues to enjoy across the discipline. The results of these sorts of academic, intellectual and institutional pressures have led to what he considers to be some theorist's "buying into normal science and taking the big questions off the table."[102] This strategy, amongst its other dimensions, involves capitulating with scientific imperatives so as to purchase a seat—and meal—at the disciplinary table. In strong agreement with Kasza, the move from a robust political philosophy to a more acceptable political theory marks "a retreat from political philosophy's core mission."[103] Yet the denuding of political philosophy doesn't merely undermine theorists, indeed, "the biggest losers ... are the rest of ... the discipline, who are rendered incapable of thinking in a sophisticated way about the most basic aspects of our research."[104]

Behind the advance of rational choice and formal theorizing, we again find liberal moorings. Rational choice theory is understood by Emily Hauptmann and Sonja Amadae as the "preeminent" school of thought within the social sciences in general and political science in particular. For these authors, it takes on its ideological character as the direct expression and justification of American economic and political liberalism.[105] Unequivocally, Amadae takes William Riker's positive political theory to be "central to the entire discipline of American political science."[106] Clearly then, where "liberalism has demonstrated an almost unprecedented capacity for absorbing its competitors,"[107] as the authors of the *Oxford Handbook of Political Theory* assure us, the contribution of rational choice to the ongoing ideological orientation of the subfield should not be underestimated or go unexamined. These insights restate and update Crick's arguments presented above, exposing the way the Americanization of political science under the rubric of liberal-democratic ideology reflects a larger institutional landscape. Kaufman-Osborn's conclusion, drawn out of his reading of the *Oxford Handbook*, is what he suggests may be "the thoroughgoing enmeshment of the contemporary American academy and hence of American political science, including political theory, within the late liberal political economy of the United States."[108] Indeed, the forms of agency which rational choice theory assumes reproduce core aspects of the possessive individual enshrined by classical liberalism. Thomas Engeman reinforces this view; the "self-interested individual of economic theory is identical with the 'rationally industrious' individual of classical liberalism."[109]

While the behavioralist's positivist agenda and its broad commitment to liberalism is well documented, the roots of rational choice in similar ideological soil has been less well explored. The cold-war ideological battle was inherited by the rational choice theorists in the post-positivist period, and they sustained the very same prerogatives which the behavioralists had been committed to before them.[110] Beyond the self-seeking individual which is specific to rational choice programs and distinguishes it from behavioralism, rational choice theory serves, with Sonja Amadae, "as a philosophic underpinning for American economic and political liberalism."[111] As with the behavioralists before them, the program of rational choice carries forward the Enlightenment project of scientific methods and democratic governance into the post-positivist era.[112]

Yet where these programs fail both democracy and liberalism is in their transformations of the ethical and social foundations which had been the basis of liberalism since the Enlightenment. In the case of behavioralism and as considered above, an unholy and paternalistic alliance of empirical research and instrumental control was theorized to the ends of the preservation of freedom. In the case of rational choice, the reification of the American sovereignty of the self-interested individual-consumer is taken as the basis for the computation of matrices of rational, legitimate choice. On this account, and echoing its cold-war struggle with its perceived collectivist, authoritarian opponent, the Soviet Union, the complementarity and compatibility of individual rationality on the one hand and social belonging on the other is jettisoned where "rational choice theory holds that rational individuals do not cooperate to achieve common goals unless coerced."[113] In the prior case, a paternalistic program of social and political control strips away the forms of socially engaged autonomy which underwrote the heroic ethics of the liberal Enlightenment. The brave new world of freedom which behavioralism promised seems less the world of liberal democracy, and more the over-determination of behavioral surveillance and modification geared to the preservation of an existing American ideological order. In the latter, the very idea of these forms of autonomy are collapsed into the motivational narcissism of a thoroughgoing methodological individualism. This ethic places utility maximization and the "ever-present incentive for individuals to cheat on each other" at the heart of rationality, and wholly dispenses with the possibility of authentic community: democratic or otherwise.[114]

In both cases, these programs are betrayed by overt ideological commitments which render their claims to a value-free, non-ideological social science spurious. Amadae's writing confronts the institutional, political and academic ramifications of these commitments and this legacy. As a bulwark against first Nazi and later Soviet forms of "authoritarianism," these cold-war programs may "have eroded the meaningfulness of the term 'American society'."[115] With proliferation of rational choices methods and decision theory beyond America through neo-liberal conventions and practices worldwide, the social meanings and contexts eroded now transcend the American framework within which these methods first germinated.

This historical and intellectual background brings to light a need to revisit questions which are equally foundational for scientific, philosophical and political theoretic work. Prior to taking up this task in the final chapter and, in the context of Hegel's legacy, I will first excavate and examine the ways in which the liberal-positivist paradigm has acted both as a passive and active boundary for the reception and representation of Hegel's political philosophy in the next chapter. In so doing, we move beyond the *prescriptive* case against metaphysics in theory and practice examined here and in the previous chapter to the deeply engrained culture of revisionist Hegel scholarship—a culture that has issued a general *descriptive* representation of Hegel's political thought that is always already metaphysically neuter and generally hospitable to liberal values.

Justifying moving beyond the cultural boundaries of over a half-century trend in scholarship specifically requires a critical consideration and response to its claims and formulations. Where a prior prescriptive set of norms has become dogma, the first step towards undoing its grip is taken in bringing critical perspective and discrimination to conflations which have come to represent scholarly standards of common sense and good judgment.

## Notes

1 Beyond the Anglo-American context that is in consideration here, Gottlob Frege must, of course, be understood as preceding Moore and Russell. Frege's project, however, did not define itself in overt confrontation with the Hegelian legacy.
2 Richard J. Bernstein, *The Restructuring of Social and Political Theory*, 1st edn (New York: Harcourt Brace Jovanovich, 1976), 4.
3 Ibid., 4
4 George Steinmetz, "The Genealogy of a Positivist Haunting: Comparing Prewar and Postwar U.S. Sociology," *boundary 2* 32, no. 2 (2005), 109–35: 111.
5 Roy Bhaskar, "General Introduction," in Margaret Archer, *Critical Realism: Essential Readings*, Critical Realism–Interventions (London; New York: Routledge, 1998), ix–xxiv: x.
6 David Easton, *The Political System: An Inquiry into the State of Political Science*, 2nd edn (New York: Knopf, 1971), 58.
7 Ibid.
8 Bernard R. Crick, *The American Science of Politics: Its Origins and Conditions* (Berkeley: University of California Press, 1959), v–vi.
9 Graham Wallas's 1920 *Human Nature in Politics* and Arthur Bentley's 1908 *The Process of Government*.
10 Charles E. Merriam, "The Present State of the Study of Politics," *American Political Science Review* 15, no. 2 (1921), 173–85: 174.
11 Ibid.
12 Ibid., 175.
13 Ibid., 176.
14 Crick, *The American Science of Politics*; James Farr, "The New Science of Politics," in Richard Bellamy and Terence Ball, *The Cambridge History of Twentieth-Century Political Thought* (Cambridge: Cambridge University Press, 2008), 431–45. David M. Ricci, *The Tragedy of Political Science: Politics, Scholarship, and Democracy* (New Haven, CT: Yale University Press, 1984).

15 Merriam, "The Present State of the Study of Politics," 180.
16 Merriam, quoted by James Farr in "The New Science of Politics," 434.
17 Merriam, "The Present State of the Study of Politics," 181.
18 Ibid.
19 Ibid., 182.
20 Ibid., 183.
21 Ibid.
22 Ibid., 184.
23 Graham Wallas, *Human Nature in Politics*, 3rd edn (New York: F.S. Crofts, 1921), 18.
24 Merriam, "The Present State of the Study of Politics," 185.
25 Charles Edward Merriam, *New Aspects of Politics*, 2nd edn (Chicago, IL: University of Chicago Press, 1931), vii.
26 Ibid., ix.
27 Ibid., xi.
28 Ibid.
29 Ibid., xii.
30 Ibid.
31 Ibid., 6.
32 For an insightful overview of the parameters and influence of the positivist program on the social sciences, see William Rose, "Positivism and its Critique," in John T. Ishiyama and Marijke Breuning, *21st Century Political Science: A Reference Handbook*, 2 vols, 21st Century Reference Series (Thousand Oaks: SAGE Publications, 2011), 459–69.
33 Ibid., 15.
34 Ibid., 23.
35 Farr, "The New Science of Politics," 432.
36 Both Easton and Catlin critiqued historicism as an emphasis upon historical inquiry, context and exegesis as opposed to a historicist teleology.
37 George Edward Gordon Catlin, *The Science and Method of Politics* (Hamden, CT: Archon Books, 1964), 94.
38 Ibid.
39 Ibid.
40 Ibid., 96.
41 Ibid., 103.
42 Ibid., 106.
43 Ibid., 107.
44 Ibid., 143.
45 David Easton, "The Decline of Modern Political Theory," *Journal of Politics* 13, no. 1 (1951), 36–58: 37.
46 Ibid., 51.
47 Ibid.
48 Ibid.
49 Ibid.
50 Ibid.
51 Bernstein, *The Restructuring of Social and Political Theory*, 6.
52 Easton, "The Decline of Modern Political Theory," 58.
53 Easton, *The Political System*, 235.
54 Ibid., 236.
55 Ibid., 237.
56 Ibid., 261.
57 Ibid., 314.
58 Comparative politics being the best example I am aware of.
59 Ibid., 315.

70  *Background, history and critique*

60 Easton, "The Decline of Modern Political Theory," 147.
61 Crick, *The American Science of Politics*; Farr "The New Science of Politics"; Gunnel, "History of Political Science," in George Thomas Kurian, *The Encyclopedia of Political Science*, 5 vols (Washington, D.C.: CQ Press, 2011), 1278–85; and others.
62 John Gunnel, "History of Political Science," 1283.
63 William Rose, "Positivism and Its Critique," 464.
64 Archer, *Critical Realism*, x.
65 Bernstein, *The Restructuring of Social and Political Theory*, 7.
66 Ibid., xi.
67 Ibid., xv.
68 Ibid., xxii.
69 Ibid., 5.
70 Melissa Lane, "Positivism: Reactions and Developments," in Richard Bellamy and Terence Ball, *The Cambridge History of Twentieth-Century Political Thought* (Cambridge: Cambridge University Press, 2008), 321–42: 336.
71 Carl G. Hempel, *Aspects of Scientific Explanation, and Other Essays in the Philosophy of Science* (New York: Free Press, 1965), 3. Lane, "Positivism: Reactions and Developments," 337.
72 Lane, "Positivism: Reactions and Developments," 337.
73 Peter Laslett, *Philosophy, Politics and Society: A Collection* (Oxford: Blackwell, 1956), vii.
74 Lane, "Positivism: Reactions and Developments," 340.
75 Farr, "The New Science of Politics," 440.
76 Ibid.
77 Harold Lasswell, in Richard Bellamy and Terence Ball, *The Cambridge History of Twentieth-Century Political Thought* (Cambridge: Cambridge University Press, 2008), 440.
78 Walter Lippman embraces Freudian pessimism on this front. See Freud's *Civilization and its Discontents*, *Totem and Taboo* and *Beyond the Pleasure Principle*.
79 David Miller and Richard Dagger, "Utilitarianism and Beyond: Contemporary Analytical Political Theory," in Richard Bellamy and Terence Ball, *The Cambridge History of Twentieth-Century Political Thought* (Cambridge: Cambridge University Press, 2008), 446–69: 446.
80 John G. Gunnell, *Between Philosophy and Politics: The Alienation of Political Theory* (Amherst: University of Massachusetts Press, 1986), 43.
81 Ibid., 45.
82 Lane, "Positivism: Reactions and Developments," 342.
83 Ibid. Reinforced in William Rose, "Positivism and its Critique," 460.
84 George Steinmetz, *The Politics of Method in the Human Sciences: Positivism and Its Epistemological Others*, Politics, History, and Culture (Durham: Duke University Press, 2005), 3.
85 Georg Wilhelm Friedrich Hegel and T.M. Knox, *Hegel's Philosophy of Right* (London, New York: Oxford University Press, 1967), 279. Kaufmann corrects this to read: "It is the way of God with the world that there should be the State" (Walter Arnold Kaufmann, *From Shakespeare to Existentialism: An Original Study. Essays on Shakespeare and Goethe, Hegel and Kierkegaard, Nietzsche, Rilke, and Freud, Jaspers, Heidegger, and Toynbee* (Princeton, NJ: Princeton University Press, 1980), 98), also recognizing that, as an addendum in the *Zusatz* additions by subsequent editors, it may not have been Hegel's own. Many of these and similar misreadings are reported in Jon Stewart, *The Hegel Myths and Legends*, Northwestern University Studies in Phenomenology and Existential Philosophy (Evanston, IL: Northwestern University Press, 1996), Kaufmann and others. The mistranslation is repeated in Thomas Knox's popular translation of the *Philosophy of Right* and remains in circulation at the start of the twenty-first century.

86  Gunnell, *Between Philosophy and Politics*, 51–2.
87  Clearly the likes of Nietzsche and Heidegger have received similar scholarly treatment in some Anglo-American circles for generations and for similar reasons.
88  Ibid., 72.
89  Wilfrid Sellars' argument that positivist epistemology took a mind independent world for granted as a given without explaining the necessary conditions for that world and for minds within it.
90  Gunnell, *Between Philosophy and Politics*, 87.
91  Ibid., 88–9.
92  Ibid., 89.
93  Both within and beyond political science proper.
94  S. Wolin Sheldon, "Political Theory as a Vocation," *American Political Science Review* 63, no. 4 (1969), 1062–82: 1082.
95  Emily Hauptmann, "Defining 'Theory' in Postwar Political Science," in George Steinmetz, *The Politics of Method in the Human Sciences: Positivism and Its Epistemological Others*, Politics, History, and Culture (Durham: Duke University Press, 2005), 207–32. S.M. Amadae, *Rationalizing Capitalist Democracy: The Cold War Origins of Rational Choice Liberalism* (Chicago: University of Chicago Press, 2003).
96  Farr, "The New Science of Politics," 445.
97  Andrew Collier, "Critical Realism," in George Steinmetz, *The Politics of Method in the Human Sciences: Positivism and Its Epistemological Others*, Politics, History, and Culture (Durham: Duke University Press, 2005), 327–45.
98  The term "political thought" here clearly suggests political philosophy traditionally understood. Kenneth A. Shepsle, "Studying Institutions: Some Lessons from the Rational Choice Approach," *Journal of Theoretical Politics* 1, no. 2 (1989), 131–47: 146.
99  Timothy V. Kaufman-Osborn, "Political Theory as Profession and as Subfield?" *Political Research Quarterly* 63, no. 3 (2010), 655–73; Robert Adcock, "Interpreting Behavioralism," in Robert Adcock, Mark Bevir and Shannon C. Stimson, *Modern Political Science: Anglo-American Exchanges since 1880* (Princeton, NJ: Princeton University Press, 2007), 180–208.
100 Kaufman-Osborn, "Political Theory as Profession and as Subfield?" 667.
101 Gregory J. Kasza, "The Marginalization of Political Philosophy and Its Effects on the Rest of the Discipline," *Political Research Quarterly* 63, no. 3 (September 1, 2010), 697–701; Kaufman-Osborn, "Political Theory as Profession and as Subfield?" 699.
102 One of several strategies he suggests theory has taken to cope with the power of its positivist and quantitative neighbors.
103 Ibid.
104 Ibid.
105 Hauptmann, "Defining 'Theory' in Postwar Political Science," 227; Amadae, *Rationalizing Capitalist Democracy*, 9, 13.
106 Amadae, *Rationalizing Capitalist Democracy*, 156.
107 John S. Dryzek, Bonnie Honig and Anne Phillips, *The Oxford Handbook of Political Theory* (Oxford: Oxford University Press, 2008), http://dx.doi.org/10.1093/oxfordhb/9780199548439.001.0001., cited in Kaufman-Osborn, "Political Theory as Profession and as Subfield?" 665.
108 Ibid., 665.
109 Thomas S. Engeman, "Behavioralism, Postbehavioralism, and the Reemergence of Political Philosophy," *Perspectives on Political Science* 24, no. 4 (1995), 214–17: 215.
110 Echoing Gunnel, Amadae tells us that "there was no real shift in the underlying attention American social sciences paid to American democracy." Amadae, *Rationalizing Capitalist Democracy*, 157.

111 Ibid., 9.
112 Ibid., 255.
113 Ibid., 3.
114 Ibid., 294.
115 Ibid., 4.

# 3 Negating negation

Twentieth-century revisionism, the rehabilitation of Hegel's political thought and the descriptive challenge

The history of political science heretofore represented introduced the general and prevailing set of attitudes within which Hegel's political thought was received for much of the twentieth century in the English speaking world. While many of those who have commented on his major and minor political texts have come from outside of political science, especially philosophy, works from both areas demonstrate a general adherence to what I refer to as the liberal-positivist paradigm. While the contexts of twentieth-century political thought as it is carried out in the academic spheres of philosophy and political science, even within the Anglo-American world, certainly differ as the result of substantially different historical presuppositions and precursors, on the matter of the status of Hegel's metaphysics and the nature of its relation to his political thought the degree of commonality substantially outweighs divergence. Here, in both contexts, Hegel has been held up to the standards of an analytic school of scrutiny that are very much the legacy of the revolt against idealism which James, Moore and Russell foreran, and which have their own roots in earlier German and Austrian movements. These certainly include the works of Feuerbach and Marx who, as we have seen, called for a thoroughgoing critique of Hegel on the basis of the "positive" categories of sensory experience and a historical materialist analysis of social development.

The Anglo-American approach to Hegel, working in the face of a small minority of protesting voices such as those of Raymond Plant, Robert Stern, Robert Ware, Mathew Smetona, Stephen Houlgate, Thom Brooks, myself and a few others, has by and large held to several key positions which deny the theoretical value of the interrelation of Hegel's political and metaphysical thought.[1] As examined above, the revolt against idealism gave birth to new paradigms of theorization in the twentieth century. The *prescriptive* move against metaphysics sounded by the likes of G.E. Moore, Charles Merriam, Rudolph Carnap[2] and others, trumpeting the theoretical prowess of positivism in its linguistic, logical and empiricist formats,[3] called for an "elimination" of the metaphysical creed in a way which had direct relevance and reference to Hegel's legacy and ideas. In continuance of the previous chapter which detailed the implications of the rise of the liberal-positivist program for political thought, this chapter will economically rehearse a broad variety of opinions on the question of the nature and relation of Hegel's metaphysical and political thought.[4] In so doing it will represent the intellectual forces and climate which demanded the division of these two aspects of thought which Hegel considered to be both essential and useful to one another.

This segregation was carried out in order to procure a version of his political thought that the ideological and methodological climate of Anglo-American scholarship in the twentieth century could afford, short of divorcing itself from Hegel altogether. Of course, this latter option was considered in the works of those like Bertrand Russell, E.F. Carritt, Karl Popper and Sidney Hook[5] who, to varying degrees, have their own nineteenth-century roots in the earlier mentioned work of Haym.[6] With special emphasis upon Popper's assault that Bertrand Russell considered a "work of first-class importance which ought to be widely read for its masterly criticism of the enemies of democracy,"[7] it was these very attacks in the wake of World War II and the triumph of liberalism that set off a series of defenses and counter-attacks on Hegel's political thought. Commentators who have come to Hegel's defense have included some of the most important theorists of the twentieth century, including Herbert Marcuse, Emil Fackenheim and Charles Taylor. This debate, which continues to make itself felt today, unleashed the combined intellectual and moral resources of post-war liberal and scientific indignation. While Hegel's image as either an unabashed proto-Nazi Prussian statist or a mystic prophet and harbinger of twentieth-century totalitarian collectivism have largely been dispatched, the stain and strain of the process of his defense have, I argue, had an indelible and deforming impact on how we nowadays conceive of Hegel's political thought and its autonomous capacity to speak to us in the present. Perhaps more importantly, and as will be examined in the concluding chapter of this book, the "high tide" of liberal and positivist indignation and its aftershocks, in their suppression of the supposed "enemies" of the "open society" and its methodological institutions, have come to have a deleterious impact on what is now theoretically viable, pronounceable or conceivable.

The prescriptive pressures against Hegel's metaphysical commitments have led to a variety of strategies that have emerged as standard defenses of his political thought as a whole. There are those who, following Klaus Hartmann, have made the argument that Hegel's logical thought is in actuality not a metaphysics in the classical sense but rather an ontological system of categories.[8] Here Hegel is understood as deploying a "theory of categories or of such determinations of the real as permit of reconstruction and are thus borne out of categories"[9] rather than a bona fide idealist metaphysics. While this view has developed a following amongst Hartmann's students, a far more common position accepts that Hegel's system was painted on the canvas of a metaphysical system. Despite this admission, it is here generally asserted that Hegel's political thought is, first, not actually dependent upon the metaphysical foundations of the logical system and, second, better read in absence of the abstruse and "incredible"[10] metaphysical claims which emerge from Hegel's larger system and its claims. Thus, in the wake of the liberal-positivist *prescriptive* assault against metaphysics which has played a central role in Anglo-American scholarship since at least the turn of the nineteenth century, an overwhelming orientation to divorce Hegel's political thought from its own roots in the logical system emerged as the dominant trend. As this chapter will document, this *prescriptive* project has directly led to a prevailing *descriptive* culture which asserts the independence and arbitrary relation of Hegel's logical and political thought to begin with: i.e., that there never was a necessary, meaningful or intended overlapping to begin with. This strategy has concerned itself with salvaging, rehabilitating and putting on offer a Hegelian version of political thought which, as Allen Wood would have it, is compelling and "speaks to us today ... [to] our ethical concerns and cultural identity crises."[11] Such a revisionist strategy clearly directs itself to the ephemeral needs and concerns of a contemporary English-speaking and -reading audience and seems to carry with it the goal of sustaining Hegel's place in *our* canon of political thought.

In this context, the prescriptive force of the liberal-positivist assault upon Hegel's legitimacy has driven scholars sympathetic to Hegel to convert and remold him for our times. This has resulted in a strategy that has sought to overcome the pressures of the prescriptive critique by putting Hegel's political thought beyond the reach of metaphysical contamination. This reaction responds to not only twentieth-century, but also nineteenth-century prescriptive impulses, earlier considered, as well. In this way the descriptive strategy that there is no necessary relation between the two segments of Hegel's corpus, the political and the logical, has become a fairly influential orthodoxy. As I will document, this has resulted in a general consensus that "Hegel's political thought can be read, understood and appreciated without having to come to terms with his metaphysics."[12] as well as a train of representations which simply exclude his metaphysical component in its wake. Prior to moving on to treat the question of the necessity and meaning of the relatedness of the two chapters, I will here run through a history of opinions that stretches back to the early twentieth century. This overview will critically detail the prevalence of this symptomatic response to the core liberal and positivist-inclined contemporary complaints against Hegel. I develop this presentation here in order to display the degree to which the descriptive approach has become widespread and unreflectively asserted, and prior to moving on to an excavation of Hegel's philosophical vision of the synergies of metaphysics and politics in the following two chapters which overturns it.

## Guilt by idealistic association: world war and Hegel's place in the Anglo-American theoretical imagination

Prior to the development of the descriptive strategy there were a limited group of scholars who, with no intent to salvage Hegel's work, initiated a line of criticism of his politics with direct reference to his logic. These authors carry forward a variety of prejudicial views of Hegel that would lay the groundwork for the apologetic revisionist school of Hegel scholarship which would emerge later.

Subsequent to the early British attacks upon the idealisms of McTaggart and Bradley, it was not until 1918 that a major, perhaps the first, English language critique of the interlocking nature of Hegel's politics and metaphysics emerged. It was in this year that Leonard Trelawney Hobhouse published his critique of the logical foundations of Hegel's politics in his *Metaphysical Theory of the State*.[13] Hobhouse, a liberal politician and social theorist in the midst of World War I, argued that Hegel, the father of idealism, held that "the world at large, and in particular the social world, is, if properly understood, an incarnation or expression of the ideal."[14] In these few words Hobhouse restates the liberal critique originating in Haym's work that takes Hegel's *Doppelsatz*—"that what is rational is actual and what is actual is rational"[15]—to imply the conservative and unjustifiable legitimization of all that currently exists, with special reference to the state. Far from recognizing the aged debate between left and right Hegelians, Hobhouse emphasized and identified only the illiberal sense of Hegel's Maxim from the *Philosophy of Right*. Moreover, he reduced the *Doppelsatz* to the explicit phraseology that "the real world is as it ought to be."[16]

Under this rubric, Hobhouse informed us that, in Hegel's conservative worldview, "the lives of individuals are altogether subordinate" to the state system and the cosmic order of things. Within this arrangement of subject and substance Hobhouse found Hegel's thought to be "a much more subtle and dangerous enemy to the ideal"[17] than Hegel's harshly critical views of liberal social atomism and empirical science. Questioning the scientific value of Hegel's metaphysics and whether it could have any relevance for a politics of nationhood, he directly asserted that the true and underlying intent of Hegel's political thought was to provide cover and apology for the interests of the nineteenth-century Prussian state. Hobhouse warned his readers against taking Hegel as a rhapsodic "metaphysical dreamer"[18] as this would be to conceal his sinister premonition and anticipation of the rise of German militarism prior to and throughout World War I. Hegel's metaphysics, Hobhouse insinuated, are nothing more than the origin of Prussian and later Germanic reaction. It is specifically in Hegel's metaphysical theory of the state that Hobhouse witnessed the anti-liberal presuppositions of World War I where "the entire modern tendency" to contain and diminish the role of the state over the lives of individuals "is reversed" where the state becomes "an end in itself."[19] Witnessing in Hegel only the most reactionary, collectivist and arcane ideological elements, he held Hegel as culpable for "the bombing of London" in which he "witnessed the visible and tangible outcome of a false and wicked doctrine."[20] To Hegel he ascribed responsibility for the German "god-state" such that the victims of German aggression met Hegel's own "Gothas in mid air."[21] In short, Hegel's metaphysics of conservative apology, a view which had earlier been energetically resisted by Rosenkranz and undermined by the sheer existence of vibrant and historically influential left and center-Hegelians, had been wholly overlooked in Hobhouse's assessments.

Hobhouse's views emerge from his deformed and selective reading of Hegel's political thought largely in reflection of his emphasis on only one half of the double maxim concerning the actual and the rational. Witnessing his anti-authoritarian interpretation as a defense of liberal "humanitarian" sensibilities, Hegel's Germanic metaphysics were reduced to a bogey which stood in for the whole of "the present condition of Europe"[22] as he then found it in the midst of war. Fallaciously, World War I for Hobhouse was not a war of Germans and Britons. Rather it was fought between democracy which Hegelianism opposed on the one hand,[23] and a collectivist nationalism sponsored by Hegelianism on the other. The latter "sets the state above moral criticism, [and] constitutes war a necessary incident in its existence,"[24] initiating the life death struggle between the "democratic and humanitarian"[25] Enlightenment tradition and Hegelian metaphysical organicism. In the context of World War I, Hobhouse characterized Hegel's political thought as a "theory admirably suited to the period of militancy and regimentation in which we find ourselves."[26]

In his 1932 "Hegel's political philosophy," Henry H. Sabine of Cornell University argued, like Hobhouse before him, that the validity of Hegel's dialectic was to be considered from the point of view of its creation "as a product of German and of European intelligence."[27] With Hobhouse he took an essentially liberal stance in critique of the *Doppelsatz* seeing in it an arch-conservative's metaphysical apologetic "that what is is necessary."[28] Three years later, Oxfords' M.B. Foster, in his *The Political Philosophies of Plato and Hegel*, considered Hegel's work in light of its Platonic connections. Seeing in Hegel the antiquated taint of the Platonic autocracy of reason, Foster argued that "Hegel never doubts that the same capacity of metaphysical deduction which makes law intelligible to the reason of the philosopher, makes it also obligatory upon the will of the moral subject."[29] Where "Hegel emphatically repudiates the notion that an historical study of the genesis of an actual system of law can take the place of this metaphysical deduction" he is "at one with Plato in maintaining that the law of the just state is determined, at least in its main outlines, by a process of logic."[30] Of course Foster admitted of the essential modernity in Hegel's vision in terms of his replacing Plato's justice with the ethic of freedom. However, in Hegel's classist vision of *Stande* and station, Foster witnessed a "relic of Platonism in Hegel's philosophy of the State," a "relic of Platonism in his metaphysics."[31] This metaphysical problem for freedom becomes a permanent impediment to the possibility of subjective freedom where, as with the subjects of the Platonic polis, political rationality "is possessed *only* by the professional philosopher"[32] such that the "whole dialectical or metaphysical deduction of the State must miss its true nature, and that the real business of the philosopher is that historical understanding which makes the ruler a statesman and the subject free."[33] With a greater degree of fidelity to Hegel's thought than either Hobhouse or Sabine were willing to allow themselves in their repugnance, Foster came to essentially the same liberal condemnations of Hegel's project: Prussianist statism, mysticism and reaction.

Oxford educated political analyst John Alfred Spender's 1940 exchanges with Malcolm Knox would resuscitate these same concerns where he held that Hegel's metaphysics gave a "philosophical (or pseudo philosophical) veneer to Machiavelli's justification of the unscrupulous use of fraud and force in the service of the State."[34] His strongest admonition against Hegel's political thought took root in his "Englishman's" resentment of Hegel's "submission of the individual to and his absorption in the state."[35] Here Hegel's collective vision of positive liberty in and through *Sittlichkeit* is reduced to no more than the "mischief" and "mystification" of an amoral, regressive and anti-liberal political vision. While Hegel's political enterprise enshrined modern freedom, Sabine, Foster and Spender were all unwilling to allow that Hegel was in any way sufficiently able to detach himself from his Greek intellectual forebears, or his contemporary political lords in attaining to a modern ethic of freedom that coheres with the contemporary demands of liberalism. Inaccessible to the democratic street, then, Hegel's metaphysics became an obstacle for these authors who saw in him an obscurantist harbinger of authoritarian collectivism.

As with Hobhouse's and James' earlier screeds against Hegel, these authors took Haym's critique of Hegel's conservative, Prussian and reactionary toadyism beyond the sphere of political critique to impugn his metaphysical thought as well. Subsequent to the successful upending of the idealist enterprise and the emergence of its analytic successor pioneered by Moore's refutation and the First World War, a marked Anglophonic perspective emerged which associated Hegel with the antiquated resurgence of mysticism, romanticism and metaphysics which "common sense finds shocking"[36] and that called for the strongest response and resistance by the forces of liberal modernity. While many of his English-speaking commentators up to this time would blame Hegel's excesses on the religious antiquations embedded in his thought, Foster took our estimate of Hegel—the failed political thinker—still lower. He asserted that Hegel's failure as a political theorist was due not to a Christian influence, but rather the failure to sufficiently assimilate Christian doctrine.[37] In short, many of Hegel's Anglophone commentators since Moore and James carried out largely one-sided and myopic readings of Hegel, finding his political thought anathema, his moral foundations wanting and his philosophical views nonsensical. This whole line of Hegel bashing would find its apotheosis, of course, in Karl Popper's anti-Hegel response to Nazi expansionism.

Without delving deeply into Popper's context, it is important to understand that his *The Open Society and Its Enemies* represented a major portion of his self-proclaimed "war effort" in 1945.[38] In this way his critique of Hegel, alongside Plato and Marx, was part and parcel of liberal democracy's ideological and material war with fascism as well as socialism. With that said, Popper would crystallize and culminate a line of criticism which took philosopher baiting to a new level, and which would play a substantial and catalytic role in triggering a counter-reaction. This counter-reaction is clearly evident in the stark quantitative shift of Anglophone books which Hegel scholarship would generate after Popper's "assault" in comparison with the paltry output witnessed in the first half of the century. As a barometer of its influence and impact, the United States Library of Congress now lists 2814 books on and related to G.W.F. Hegel.[39] Of these,

2796 were published in the twentieth and twenty-first centuries. Of these, only 121 were published prior to 1945 while 2675 were published between 1945 and 2010.[40] Thus, approximately 95 percent of books on Hegel—English and non-English—have been published since Popper's. While it is beyond question that the impact of the Frankfurt School, the resurgence of interest in Marx and his origins as well as Charles Taylor's writings led many scholars in the 1960s and 1970s back to Hegel, Popper's condemnatory and ideologically charged tome set off a vivid public debate in the English speaking world.[41]

Set against Marcuse's *Reason and Revolution* published four years earlier, Popper brought the full weight of liberal commonsense and empirical methodism to bear upon Hegel in a way which makes him the unchallenged heir to Haym's critique. For Popper, Hegel had pulled "physical rabbits out of purely metaphysical silk-hats"[42] by way of his dialectical shortcut which permitted "initiation into the deeper secrets of this world"[43] more rapidly than the methodical and skeptical progress of the natural sciences. Echoing James, Popper claimed the whole ruse was rooted in the deepest forms of intellectual deception and mendacity. Moreover, the dialectic was the metaphysical apparatus through which Hegel cast a conservative pall justifying all as it is: "By its appeal to the wisdom of providence it offers an apology for the excellence of Prussian monarchism; by its appeal to the excellence of Prussian monarchism it offers an apology for the wisdom of providence."[44] Popper goes on to ask "whether it is possible to outdo this despicable perversion of everything that is decent" where "Conscience must be replaced by blind obedience" and "the brotherhood of man by a totalitarian nationalism."[45] Having initiated the "age of dishonesty,"[46] and a history that was "pure apologetics,"[47] Hegel's fantastic and magical jargon is made the veil behind which modern totalitarianism—read Nazism—concealed its raw will to power.

On the issue of the interpretation of Hegel's double maxim or *Doppelsatz*, Popper's reading follows the trend set by Hobhouse and Sabine before him. For Popper, Hegel adopted Plato's idealist doctrine that the idea is the most real, that "*Ideal=Real*." Syllogistically combined with Kant's "*Idea=Reason*," Popper claims that Hegel was led to assert that "*Real=Reason*" in turn leading him to conclude that "everything that is reasonable must be real, and everything that is real must be reasonable."[48] On this basis Popper concludes of the *Doppelsatz* that, for Hegel, all that is now real "must be reasonable as well as good." Popper's misreading of the *Doppelsatz*, as Kaufmann and others have brought out, leads to this extreme result such that Hegel's political thought is made the apologetic justification and theodicy of status quo power and injustice, with emphasis upon the "particularly good … Prussian state."[49] Yet, as Kaufmann has explained, and as is discussed in greater depth below, Hegel nowhere equates the real with the ideal but rather actuality (*Wirklichkeit*) and ideal, where the real is never historically complete in its approximation of and ongoing historical striving towards full rationality.

With James before him, Popper sought to ensure that Hegel's legacy was further asphyxiated by asserting that Hegel essentially fell prey to his own dialectical fantasies and that this deception had been exposed and registered in the English speaking world where "the interest of philosophers in Hegel is slowly vanishing."[50] Thus, not only was Hegel a fool, but his metaphysical program of deception and spell cast over the intellect had been, once and for all, exposed and dispelled in the modern, liberal-democratic world. Bertrand Russell hailed Popper's attack, proclaiming that his "analysis of Hegel is deadly"[51] while, in retrospect, we can only say that his intent was so. Through Hobhouse and Popper then, we have come to understand that Hegel was responsible for both World Wars, Russell giving this further emphasis by asserting that Hegel's state "justifies every internal tyranny and every external aggression that can possibly be imagined."[52]

By 1954, Carl Joachim Friedrich would write that "Anyone who undertakes to deal with Hegel in pragmatic, positivistic America today is running the risk of being immediately set down as a hopeless obscurantist."[53] Further,

> Hegel remained "in the doghouse," a victim of the "revolt against idealism" and of the antagonism to all things German caused by the National Socialist dictatorship ... [it] became the fashion to talk about Hegel as if he had practically written *Mein Kampf*.[54]

Eight years later, Friedrich's 1962 essay "The Power of Negation: Hegel's Dialectic and Totalitarian Ideology" took Popper's assessment of Hegel's politics further to question whether "totalitarian ideology is the 'outcome' or the 'necessary consequence' of Hegelian dialectic."[55] His assessment of Hegel's dialectical metaphysics largely sided with and extended Popper's position, arguing that "The dissolving of all definite standards, values, and beliefs, in a constant 'dialectic' of movement and change characterizes totalitarian ideology."[56] Friedrich took Hegel's logical thought as a "relentless trouble-making,"[57] citing that the "destructive character is the perfect embodiment of the dialectic."[58]

Through these comments, Friedrich, ironically a German born and trained scholar, brought the Anglophone diatribe against the Hegelian project to its fulfillment. Not only had Hegel's politics become the vicarious victim of the defeat of idealistic philosophy, but his very name had been sullied in association with the viciousness of Nazism. The ascent of the development of the caricaturing of Hegel as an arch anti-liberal, anti-modern thinker had reached its peak, putting him beyond the pale of all respectability. To note, David Easton commended Friedrich as one of only two political theorists in the first half of the twentieth century who had taken seriously the project of constructing a general theoretical framework to the end of guiding empirical research.[59] As Friedrich and others have made clear, even mere academic consideration of Hegel's work had become associated with all manners of romantic, reactionary and authoritarian projects which spanned the range of fascism, anarchism and socialism. Intellectual and scholarly influence in Hegel's thought, at a practical nadir in Germany for over a century, was now effectively obliterated in the English speaking world as well.

## "For Hegel's numerous critics the implications ... are monumental":[60] the defense and deformation of Hegel's legacy

In 1951, 11 years prior to this high tide for a trend which threw out the political baby with the metaphysical bathwater,[61] a defensive and apologetic counter-reaction began to take shape. Hegel's influence in much of the world through Marx, the Frankfurt School and existentialism in the context of the Cold War led to a reconsideration and recasting of his thought. Richard Bernstein would write a few years later "If there is one philosopher who had been thought to be dead and buried, who embodied all the vices of the wrong way of philosophizing, who seemed to have been killed off by abuse and ridicule, it was Hegel."[62] Yet Hegel had returned during a period when ideological and ontological reconsiderations had emerged to challenge a variety of liberal and positivist biases. As Bernstein has brought out, the commonalities between Hegel's time and our own had overcome the differences, and the moment had come to reconsider his thought in light of its systematic contribution to philosophy and politics against the trend of analytic deduction and reduction. Where the culture of Anglo-American thought had "sought to conquer" through dividing and subdividing, an attitude was reinforced which presupposed that "we can isolate discrete philosophic problems and make progress in solving them."[63] Against this trend, however, and as witnessed in the case of Moore's critique of Hegel above, Bernstein asserts that "our analyses spill over to other issues and other domains. We cannot make much progress on epistemological issues unless we squarely confront metaphysical issues."[64] It is in this context, and the latter liberal crisis of communitarian critique that Hegel scholarship and appreciation has returned and proliferated in myriad forms and disciplines.

In 1951, Walter Kaufman's "The Hegel Myth and its Method" sought to stem the tide of this trend of underestimating and debasing Hegel's thought, with specific reference to Popper's work. Kaufmann assailed Popper's propagandistic abuses, arguing that "one should protest against his method" which "is unfortunately similar to that of totalitarian 'scholars'—and it appears to be spreading."[65] While primarily addressing grave failings in Popper's reading of Hegel's political thought with respect to Hegel's theories of war, history and politics, Kaufmann also took up the defense of the *Doppelsatz* maxim—historically the main target and fulcrum of attacks upon the supposedly illiberal metaphysical and logical foundations underpinning the *Philosophy of Right*'s authoritarian purposes. In bringing our attention to Hegel's actual intents in the *Doppelsatz* by reference to his comments in the *Encyclopedia*, Kaufmann swept aside Popper's cursory reading of Hegel in a single pen stroke. Hegel told us that he was well aware that "These simple sentences have seemed striking to some and have excited hostility" and that "When I have spoken of actuality ... [I] distinguished it precisely not only from the accidental, which of course has existence, too, but also, in great detail, from being there [*Dasein*], existence."[66] In short, the "right-Hegelian" appropriation, and subsequent fixation of liberal criticism, upon the latter half of Hegel's doubled equation—that the actual is the rational—wholly mistakes subsisting and empirical reality for the actual when in fact it cannot be so. This analysis is in conformity with Hegel's own idealism which distinguishes the actual, as full realization of the rational ideal, from that which simply subsists or is in the process of actualization. Popper's grave error, as of those of many of his peers, was to equate the actual with the real as we find it, when no such implication is issued by Hegel's maxim when read according to his own conceptual usage of *Wirklichkeit* (actuality). The very use of the translation that "the real is the rational" that we receive from Engel's recitation, confuses the real for Hegel's use of the term "actual" (*wirklich*) with very definite consequences for subsequent interpretation.[67]

Yet Kaufmann's defense, for our purposes, began a process of selectively defending Hegelian positions; in this case the outer political consequences of a deeper dialectical relation which went unexamined in its relation to the former. For although Kaufmann persuasively undermined the assertions of the likes of Popper and Friedrich on the matter of authoritarian undertones in Hegel's thought, he responded not at all to their claims of the essentially conservative implications of his logical dialectic. J.N. Findlay, who had argued a year earlier in his sympathetic 1958 reading of Hegel's corpus that "Our own Anglo-Saxon world ... spent much of the opening years of this century in elaborately abandoning and disowning Hegelian positions we had previously held,"[68] found it necessary, at the very same time, to assure his audience that "Hegel's philosophy is one of the most anti-metaphysical of philosophical systems, one that *remains* most within the pale of ordinary experience."[69] What both Kaufmann's and Findlay's sympathetic readings of Hegel have in common, insofar as they both relate Hegel's "ideas and language to our own time,"[70] is to truncate his corpus and system of thought, at times frenetically, in order to prune an understanding that could contend and withstand the twin pressures of liberalism and positivism that had already weighed down so heavily upon Hegel's legacy. This would hold for a whole trend of sympathetic commentators as well who would assert a functional division between Hegel's political and logical thought.

Sidney Hook, who had come out strongly against Popper's reductionist reading,[71] conceded that, despite the "compatibility" of Hegel's politics and his logic, this did not mean that the latter were "therefore deducible from his metaphysics."[72] Perhaps even more telling was his need to assail the "fundamental ambiguity in that metaphysics"[73] as the basis of the retrogressive and statist elements of the *Philosophy of Right*. Here, and alongside the growth of the project to salvage Hegel's political thought, emerged a concomitant orientation to either dismiss or understate the value of Hegel's intent to wed politics to a logico-metaphysical conception. Hook even went as far as to suggest that Hegel's metaphysics of the *Doppelsatz* neutered his politics altogether; where the world is as it necessarily and rationally ought to be, there was little basis for normative claims for one political vision or another.[74] Where Hegel's metaphysical goal is "understanding and justifying history *after* it has happened,"[75] in a form of rationalist theodicy christening political reality as it is found, there is little basis for more than quietistic observation and resignation. On this reading, where metaphysics is, little in the way of politics can or should follow.

This trend of dismissive side-glances to the issue of the relation of metaphysics and politics by authors sympathetic to Hegel's politics—to varying degrees—would take a significant turn with the publication of Malcolm Knox and Zbigniew Pełczyński's *Hegel's Political Writings* in 1964. In Pełczyński's introduction he made the case that here, for the first time, was an explicit Anglophone attempt to rehabilitate and initiate Hegel's political thought into the so-called modern canon where Hegel's view on "the scope of free activity which an individual, a locality, or a sectional interest should enjoy ... can stand comparison with that assigned to them by many liberal thinkers of the age."[76] These authors set out not only to dispel the arguments of Haym and Popper, but to persuade those who have seen Hegel as outside of the "stream of Western European political theory" which favors "constitutionalism, democracy, and progress ... how little substance there is in any such interpretation."[77] With concerns over Hegel's democratic credentials addressed, Pełczyński intended to assist his readers with an understanding of just why Hegel has been held "to stand apart from other 'classical' political theorists."[78] This matter, he explained, is down to Hegel's metaphysics which had overshadowed the other elements of thought and left them largely unexplored. Pełczyński's assessment of the problem intended to clear a path for the restoration of our interest in Hegel's political thought: "once the metaphysical element becomes dominant ..., the character of political theory changes. The teaching, or the insight, it provides ceases to have any practical significance."[79]

As with Hook and others, the basis of this analysis is Hegel's metaphysical politics of the spirit which leave us, in alignment with Hook, Popper, Friedrich and others, but to ponder and "venerate" the rational beauty of the world as it is, to stand atop of a metaphysical tower in observation of the chaos below with the sole intent of discovering "new kinds of order and symmetry."[80] In identifying the conservative curse cast upon his politics as originating in his metaphysics, Pełczyński is lead to conclude that "Hegel could have kept his political theory quite distinct from his general philosophy."[81] It is this bisection which he set out to accomplish for Hegel's corpus, distinguishing between the excesses of the *Philosophy of Right* and the earlier, non-metaphysical, works of political theory which witness Hegel's sobriety, pragmatism and attention to empirical detail. Unlike Hook, who saw the metaphysical element as terminal for a politics which can do no more than acquiesce to power, Pełczyński preferred to optimistically call for a clean disconnection of the political animus from the philosophical apparatus: "Hegel's political thought can be read, understood, and appreciated without having to come to terms with his metaphysics."[82]

With the Pełczyński and Knox volume then, we have the first articulation of a project intent on purging Hegel's politics of its metaphysical presuppositions and the denial of either their necessity for its grounding or their usefulness for its comprehension. The question of Hegel's political loyalty, as set between the liberal enthusiasm of his youth on the one hand or to the Prussian monarchy

84  *Background, history and critique*

which employed and seated his professorship in Berlin on the other, here, as before, replays itself as perhaps the oldest schism amongst Hegel's interested disciples and commentators. Unfortunately, the mistranslation and misunderstanding of Hegel's second dictum that "the actual is the rational" has repeatedly circulated as a surrogate caricature and synecdoche for the larger influence of Hegel's idealism, and this case is no exception. Yet, as we know from Kaufmann and from Hegel himself, the actual is never the real as we find it. Rather, as Hegel took care to inform us a year prior to his death, God "alone is truly actual,"[83] the real—all states included—are but mere "appearance" in the process of closing the gap between themselves and their conceptual ideals. Hegel's idealism here, his naïveté if any, is found in an optimism derived from his teleological historicism. Hegel's end of history is the realization of the ongoing and underlying plan of rationality as an expression of the spirit—a vision of the living and progressive growth of human historical thought and idea towards ideal fulfillment—and not the end-state of the internal development and growth of human historical consciousness in and of itself. The Prussian state from this point of view is as much a rational apotheosis in its time as was the Greek democratic state in its own, and both appearances, both emergences of spirit, are bound to be swept away for the ephemeral instantiations of the rational ideal they are. As M.W. Jackson has brought out, "No political theorist has suffered more distortion because of a single sentence than Hegel."[84]

As is clear, the metaphysics of Hegel's historicism has confused as well as liberated his readers to a variety of complicated ends. The uses and abuses of those foundations, over time, have saddled Hegel's legacy with a grave connotation. Seen as an arch determinist and reactionary apologist for the authoritarian state writ large, Hegel's anti-positivist vision of individual and collective political life has been plagued by a *perceived* association with multiple wars, genocide, anti-scientific and mystical obscurantism, reactionary romanticism and all manner of violence justified in the name of the collective good. Pełczyński's soft denial of Hegel's metaphysics glosses over this legacy and, perhaps worse, reinforces it in the most effective manner by bringing to completion a host of under- and unexamined prejudices regarding Hegel's thought which, directly and indirectly, impugn his metaphysics. It is precisely not that his politics "ceases to have any practical significance"[85] where metaphysics is involved, but rather that the practical significances seem dark, dangerous and distant in light of our liberal-democratic and empirical commitments. Overturning Popper's profligate prosecution of Hegel will not be—fully—accomplished by burying the evidence. While much work has been done to rehabilitate elements of Hegel's thought since 1945, much of it is still caught up in this legacy of evading, denying or condemning the metaphysical dimension of his political thought. Jackson informs us of the extent of the damage done to our appreciation of Hegel's political thought as a result of the legacy of misapprehending the supposedly conservative apology contained in the *Philosophy of Right*'s Preface: "For Hegel's numerous critics the implications … are monumental."[86] This resultant "diremption"[87] witnesses one era peeling away unattractive and alien elements in a philosopher which it must, nonetheless, rehabilitate and, ultimately, assimilate. The rehabilitated vision of Hegel's political thought which Knox and Pełczyński developed, Dickey and Nisbet have made clear, responded to this crisis by attempting to "make him appear a more liberal, rational, and mainstream political thinker than he has been taken to be in the past."[88]

Why then has the English-speaking West, and beyond, needed Hegel even if it meant, at times, rewriting his thought and dismissing his own claims as to intent and meaning? Could it be that the Hegel we have sought to rehabilitate for our own time and needs is not the philosopher who then lived in Prussia, but the epic historical thinker who has lived in the specter of history and ideological imagination? As Kaufmann reminds us, "Hegel's enormous importance becomes clear as soon as we reflect on his historic role."[89] Too wide to begin to assess here, perhaps in any one book, Hegel's influence spans all major schools of political thought leading into the twentieth century, including liberalism.[90] It founded ideological programs which took material and institutional form in a variety of states—some Western—not to mention his guiding role—if inverted—in Marx's thought which provided central theoretical and ideological impetus to the sole counterweight to "Western" dominance for some seven decades during the cold war. While Hegel eventually did become something of a misplaced insider in today's canon of political thought, he does not seem fully at home there.[91] It is this ambiguity which has led to a culture of appropriating his thought; strongly identifying ourselves with certain intellectually and historically compelling aspects while, simultaneously, repelling and denying others. The legacy of the opaque theoretical logic underlying his political thought has "made Hegel a *bête noir* of English writers,"[92] and the sophistic project to overcome this crisis has often seen fit to sacrifice the tissue of Hegel's metaphysics in order to salvage the bone of his "practical" political thought. The repeal of our misapprehensions of Hegel's assessment of the relationship of the politically actual and the metaphysically rational opens up the possibility of reconsidering the latter aspect of Hegel's thought, and it must be done precisely in absence of the variety of liberal and positivist compulsions which have and continue to lead scholarship astray.

Five years subsequent to the Pełczyński and Knox translated collection, Dante Germino released his "Hegel as a Political Theorist" in the *Journal of Politics* in 1969. Here Germino would wrangle with the relevance of the Knox and Pełczyński collection of Hegel's early political writings and assert their secondary value to that of the *Philosophy of Right* for any assessment of Hegel's essential political views.[93] With this differing aside, Germino recognized that the core problem is that the *Philosophy of Right* "in the English-speaking world at least … is rarely taken seriously enough—a fate attributable in part to the author's predilection for system-construction and fondness for needlessly ponderous jargon."[94] On the basis of the seeming distraction which Hegel's logical system implied for our gaining better access to his concrete political theory, Germino, overtly "in basic agreement"[95] with Pełczyński, reasserted and extended Pełczyński's proviso for our considerations of the *Philosophy of Right*: "Hegel's political thought ... can be understood without constant reference to his total metaphysical system."[96]

As a justification for his passing over the "metaphysical system," Germino informs us that Hegel was a "man of insight" whose vision should be examined independent of the assumption that he was a "prisoner of method."[97] With no further elaboration as to how or why this need be our approach, Germino progresses with the Knox–Pełczyński line of advancing Hegel as a respected member of the "great conversation"[98] of political theory who "deserves to be listed among the leading proponents of liberalism."[99] The question of Hegel's liberal credentials aside, Germino goes as far as to say that the "excessive preoccupation with Hegel's system and with the not inconsiderable obscurity of the dialectic hinders rather than advances our appreciation of his contribution to political theory."[100] Here then we have a rejection of the influence of metaphysics upon Hegel's politics without so much as a consideration of the supposedly illiberal aspects of Hegel's supposed conservatism in the *Philosophy of Right*; a consideration which has generally had its basis in Hegel's metaphysics and which was the basis of Pełczyński's objections.

Germino has taken the Pełczyński strategy to an extreme so as to argue that the metaphysics obscure, but do not negatively obstruct, Hegel's liberal intentions. But how can he come to this conclusion in the face of Hegel's comments in the preface which has been a bone of contention from the time of its writing for essentially all of his commentators? Unsurprisingly, the inevitable result is that, by putting Hegel's metaphysics completely out of view, we eliminate the question of the interpretation of Hegel's double dictum as well as the debate over the wider historicist context of the *Philosophy of Right* altogether. This is precisely what Germino's reading achieves. The slippery slope of detaching logical from political developments in Hegel's political thought has come to the point where the former's occlusion has transformed the understanding of the latter, thus permitting Germino's unequivocal call for an end to "the all-too-common practice of making [Hegel] a favorite whipping-boy through a fundamental distortion of his teaching as illiberal and 'authoritarian' in the extreme."[101] While we may perhaps be entitled to agree with Germino, we have somehow dispensed with Hegel in the rush to redeeming and rehabilitating him for the "Great Conversation of political theory."[102]

With the appearance of Shlomo Avineri's ground breaking and influential *Hegel's Theory of the Modern State* in 1972, the question of the influence of Hegel's system for his politics no longer required so much as a comment. In the 241 pages of this work there is only one significant reference to Hegel's logical thought.[103] Avineri nonetheless provides us with a justification for this silence; if he were to consider it, he "may find himself immersed in an explication of the systematic edifice of Hegel's philosophy without ever reaching his political theory."[104] The gulf between the two portions of Hegel's corpus seems to have been made unsurpassable, and the implication has and continues to be clear; you cannot get there (politics) from here (logic and metaphysics.) Rather than assail Hegel's conception of metaphysics which cuts a clear path and argument for political relevance, this trend sees fit to sidestep the former without really explaining why.

What exactly is it about Hegel's metaphysics which provides such an obstacle to approaching his political theory? Avineri gives us a hint; where the philosophy is so "dense" as to "be more obscure than illuminating,"[105] a clear approach to Hegel's political thought is impeded. In other words, Hegel's logical thought throws more shadow than light on the politics, is unworthy of consideration and is of no substantial use or value in our considerations of Hegel's intentions and accomplishments in the *Philosophy of Right*. Yet, and as emerged from my analysis of Germino's declaration of Hegel's liberal credentials above, this is clearly difficult to sustain. Our reading of Hegel's vision of political life and action should be, and has historically been, heavily informed precisely by how we read the overt influences of his logical system within it even when it is dismissed. Sidestepping these influences and traces, as if they weren't there, is simply to reify Pełczyński's approach. It also discloses a conspicuous trend amongst Anglo-American scholars which repeatedly emancipates a liberal Hegel from a discursive and historical legacy which has witnessed deep ideological ambiguity at the heart of Hegel's political thought.

Following on the political trend of interpretation initiated by Pełczyński and Knox, a cultural trend would arise which would take much the same approach regarding the place and value of Hegel's metaphysics for the understanding of his politics. In 1979 Charles Taylor's much hailed study argued that if "Hegel's crucial proof in the *Logic* will not carry conviction today, and if this constitutes a refutation of his ontology, what interest can there be in studying his system?"[106] To answer this question of whether this lack of *our* contemporary conviction in Hegel's "proof" merits equivalency to refutation,[107] the easy answer is that it may be, or, as I shall argue in the coming chapters, that it is transformational for our understanding of the meaning of his political thought as well as its active participation in the history of ideas. Taylor spoke in complete earnest in the Preface to his 1975 *Hegel* when he informed his readers seeking understanding of Hegel's thoughts on politics, history and modernity that the section on Hegel's logic was "the most unrewarding" and that "they might skip this part."[108] Taylor's reading of Hegel's dedication to romantic expressivism and moral freedom, as historically and culturally grounded responses to Enlightenment mechanism, dismisses the primary concern or interest of Hegel's metaphysics for his "philosophical synthesis" with obvious ramifications for an understanding of his political thought.

As with Taylor, Steven B. Smith did not seek to recast Hegel as a liberal in his 1989 *Hegel's Critique of Liberalism*. Yet Smith too sought to resuscitate Hegel for contemporary thought and denies the primacy or even centrality of Hegel's logic for our appreciation of his politics where "viewing Hegel as 'first and foremost' a logician and speculative metaphysician ... tends to isolate Hegel's philosophy proper from the rudimentary human and political concerns that were never far from its center."[109] Despite distinguishing himself from the metaphysical and political interpretative camps,[110] Smith's intent is at bottom and self-admittedly an anti-foundationalist approach tempered by Hegel's "cultural hermeneutics."[111] Yet while liberal commitments may not be behind Smith's intentions for dismissing a metaphysical appreciation of Hegel's politics, his sensitivity to secular methodology most certainly is:

> Hegel seems to belong unalterably to the mystic regions of German speculative thought which, we have been assured by more empirically minded philosophers, has been superseded by the development of increasingly sophisticated logical and factual disciplines. Hegel's formidable "system" seems the very antithesis of the more skeptical spirit driving much of modern philosophy.[112]

Allen Wood's 1990 *Hegel's Ethical Thought* followed in Avineri's, Taylor's and Smith's footsteps. Seeing in Hegel's political thought the project of overcoming modern alienation, he mirrored elements of Taylor's "expressivist" and Smith's cultural hermeneutic interpretations. He too sought to sideline Hegel's metaphysics, and made strong admonition against their inclusion warning that, if one did, "you are in for a difficult and generally unrewarding time of it, at least from the standpoint of social and political theory. If you are sensible, you will try to avoid that."[113] These are very strong words. Despite recognizing the assumptions regarding Hegel harbored by "English-speaking philosophers," Wood is nonetheless remorseless in his dismissal of the speculative logic and its metaphysical implications, citing Rosen's unequivocal rejection of Hegel's metaphysics: "'What is living in the logic of Hegel?' is: 'Nothing'."[114] Like Taylor, Wood's primary concern is to resuscitate Hegel to contemporary ends, not an idealist logician and metaphysical theorist but rather "a philosophical historian, a political and social theorist, a philosopher of our ethical concerns and cultural identity crises."[115] In fact, he informs us that Hegel himself misestimated "himself as primarily a metaphysician."[116] Finally, he warned us wholly away from any consideration of the grounds of Hegel's political thought in his logic such that "we are likely to miss the connection between the two [metaphysics and politics] if ... we suppose that Hegelian social thought is *grounded* in Hegelian metaphysics."[117]

What Taylor, Smith and Wood all share in common is a recognition of Hegel's ambivalent relation with liberal politics. They all come after the so-called line of "political interpretation" started by Pełczyński and in some sense they all are primarily concerned not merely with the way Hegel recapitulates fundamental liberal convictions, but with how he founds its modern criticism. As Brooks has brought out, Wood's position against a systematic approach to Hegel's political thought takes its stand on three principles: (1) such an approach would garner little interest, (2) we would inevitably get caught up in defending such a system and (3) the task of defending Hegel's political thought would be complicated by the fact of its entwinement with his discredited idealist system. Brooks rightly questions the persuasive nature of Wood's approach to Hegel's corpus, retorting that the primary concern should be, to begin with, an understanding of the relevance of Hegel's system for his political thought, regardless of whether we choose to defend his relevance or not or the "size of our audience" in doing so.[118] This critique applies to Taylor and Smith as well, and again restates the way contemporary positivist and modern conceptions of politically theoretic norms of analysis are unreflectively advanced and have ring-fenced Anglophone assessments of Hegel's relevance to contemporary political theory, regardless of their reception of Hegel's critique of liberalism.

In this context, Mark Tunick's 1992 *Hegel's Political Philosophy* represents an updated collage of these dismissals of the relevance of Hegel's philosophical project for the purpose of considering his political thought. Tunick comes clean in admitting his "modern sensibility that rejects" Hegel's absolute idealism and metaphysical claims as "unacceptable."[119] Moreover, he restates the age-old wisdom that holds that Hegel's idealist metaphysics "forecloses debate and discussion about competing interpretations."[120] On this basis he asserts that it is best to "leave aside the metaphysics and appropriate Hegel as a theorist who can help us think clearly about our practices ... that we ... must resolve in some way."[121] Hegel here becomes captive to our political presuppositions, our needs and biases, Tunick admitting that "the Hegel [he] appropriate[s] is a non-foundationalist, non-metaphysical, that is, a rehabilitated Hegel"[122] who is not Hegel at all. On the basis that Hegel coerces political choice onto the grounds of a metaphysics which prescribes action to a rationalist and preclusive script, he holds that there appears to be little room for real political life or action. Coming out against Hegel's rationalist idealism, Tunick took up Benjamin Barber's stance that modern politics proceeds "in the absence of independent grounds for judgment."[123] On this basis Tunick concluded that "Hegel's foundationalism, his commitment to his metaphysics, makes him seem ... unpolitical and impractical. My suggestion is that we take Hegel as offering interpretation of the concepts of practices and leave aside his metaphysical claim."[124] Yet, again, this completely mistakes Hegel's *Doppelsatz* of the real and the rational as a conflation—one which Hegel clearly admonished against.

The idea that rationality for choice and agency is at any time fully accessible is foolhardy. The idea, rather, is that action participates in its own dialectical chain driving it towards greater rationality. Far from interfering with political action, Hegel's metaphysics impute an ethical intentionality into rational agency which anticipates its own fulfillment in the act to which it aspires. Having set aside Hegel's dialectical metaphysics for a more tangible world of actors and agents, Tunick has missed out on how the dialectic is not merely an impersonal scheme of action for Hegel, but reflects will, agency and subjectivity through the very act of our engaging in reason as a practice of dialectic. Of course Tunick restricts his consideration of Hegel's metaphysics to his deism and, by extension, his rationalist providence.

Yet, there is another approach to this question. From this alternative point of view, Hegel's logic of political action does not coerce agency to the metascript of a supra-personal metaphysical rationality, but rather witnesses that very rationality in subjectivity. Far from a deterministic matrix of impersonal forces,

90  *Background, history and critique*

on this reading there is a real basis of subjective contingency in Hegel's developmental appreciation of historical experience and action. The greater structures of dialectic are there as the lattice of possibility and, as we see in the *Logic*, bind together the creative oppositions of the categories of thought. Hegel's philosophy of history may crystallize the past into a representative web of necessary outcomes, but there is no tautology, no such certainty for the future which has yet to crystallize itself through us: "Philosophy, as the thought of the world does not appear until reality has completed its formative process, and made itself ready."[125] The idea of history in lived thought thus precedes the Idea of history as its resolute consummation.

Following on this trend of instrumentalist and piecemeal appropriation, from Taylor to Tunick, would come Michael Hardimon's *Hegel's Social Philosophy: The Project of Reconciliation* two years later in 1994. It would restate much the same repugnance with Hegel's theoretical context, seeking "to avoid using Hegel's technical vocabulary, to minimize reliance on his metaphysics, and to present his view in terms that we can understand."[126] While Hegel himself made it clear in the preface to the *Philosophy of Right* that the politics presupposed his *Logic*, Hardimon's interpretation teases out aspects of Hegel that seem attractive to us against the grain of Hegel's actual intentions and possibilities. In particular, his insistence that Hegel's true intentions would have been best realized in a democratic political form seems wholly ascriptive.[127]

In 1999, Alan Patten's *Hegel's Idea of Freedom* would further Hardimon's surgical appropriations in and against Hegel's self-understanding. Here he explained that, to fully understand Hegel's politics, we need to move beyond the merely metaphysical interpretation, turning "to the historicist and/or self-actualization readings for assistance."[128] In short, the self-same cultural interpretations pioneered in contemporary Anglophone readings by Taylor and Wood are necessary to augment Hegel's own systematic, largely unpalatable political project in order to salvage its usefulness and redeeming value for our age. Peter Steinberger took critical note of this equivocation, holding that Patten's "interpretation, even as it seeks to approach Hegel on his own terms, seems to back away from the full force of the larger Hegelian system ... to ignore some the boldest yet most characteristic claims of Hegel's philosophy."[129] In particular, those assertions which unite free political agency with the capacity for rational thought and a willing coherence with it.

Paul Franco's 1999 *Hegel's Philosophy of Freedom* witnesses a break with the Taylor–Wood reading, seeing in Hegel's political thought a critical liberalism that seeks to marry and balance social goods with those individual. In this he proclaimed that Hegel is "successful in defending the modern, liberal social order on a basis that goes beyond liberalism"[130] based on an assessment of his political thought that takes freedom to be the central and only necessary consideration where it is "the first, last, and in many respects *only* theme of Hegel's political philosophy."[131] Unsurprisingly, and very much in the spirit of the liberal trend of interpretation initiated by Pełczyński, Franco dispatches with the systematic concerns Hegel had woven into the *Philosophy of Right*, declaring that

"Much of the argument of the *Philosophy of Right* is intelligible on its own and can be evaluated without reference to the logic."[132] At best he sees Hegel's logic as merely a "model" for Hegel's "procedure" in his political thought, one through which a "formal understanding" of the latter is produced. In the end, and wholly in line with most other theorists working in the liberal trend, as well as Neuhouser's publication of the following year, this strategy repeatedly settled on a revised basis for the elaboration of right, "Its practical relevance to the understanding of liberal democracy at the end of the twentieth century."[133] In short, the content which freedom carries will be determined by the demands and needs of present readership, as opposed to Hegel's philosophical intentions or intended audience asserting that Hegel's "grandiose" politics do not "fit well with the skeptical temper of our times."[134]

This utilitarian and selective appropriation would continue apace with the publication of Fredrick Neuhouser's *Foundations of Hegel's Social Theory* in 2000. At the outset, renewing Pełczyński's view vis-à-vis Hegel's system, Neuhouser suggests that it is possible "to understand his account of what makes the rational social order rational and to appreciate its force even while abstracting from those more fundamental doctrines."[135] All other authors since Taylor, and perhaps before, have simply made a clear disavowal of the value and significance of such considerations. Neuhouser here, seemingly more apologetic to Hegel's intentions and project, avoids this approach in favor of a middle position. Yet he seems equivocal where he had previously stated that, in the extant literature, "it is surprisingly difficult to find one [treatment of Hegel's social theory] that goes beyond a description of the institutions Hegel favors to provide a systematic, philosophically sensitive account of the arguments that underlie his claims."[136] What seems first and foremost to concern him, however, is the very same concern with plausibility and the need for Hegel to be compelling that first asserted itself in Taylor's and Woods' works. Thus, the paring down of our reading of Hegel's political thought is warranted to produce such a result, even though we "lack access" to the more basic rational foundations which permit freedom to emerge in the first place.[137] His larger goals, as well, reproduce Pełczyński's early liberal apologetics. In seeking to salvage Hegel's legitimacy as a liberal thinker, Neuhouser witnesses only one substantial departure from the classical liberal tradition that he associates with theorists such as Locke and Rousseau. Where it is the case that Hegel makes one's class or station in civil society a conditioning, and by extension, limiting principle for one's involvement in the politics of the state, Neuhouser argues that this "is the *only* aspect of Hegel's position that is unequivocally and irreconcilably at odds with the fundamental tenets of liberalism" and that "this unattractive and archaic doctrine is a relatively expendable part of Hegel's social theory."[138] In short by withdrawing from the metaphysical and political tenets of Hegel's political thought, which are "jolting to our modern (liberal) ears,"[139] we are able to appropriate a "plausible," "compelling" and practical theory of politics from Hegel amenable to contemporary standards. The central problem for Neuhouser's strategy, as was the case for Patten before him, is that the withdrawal of the rational content from experience in emphasizing and fixating on the practical procedure of modern politics is to remove Hegel's creative assessments of what gives content to freedom in the first place, and to replace these considerations with a democratic surrogate: "a variety of forms of that ideal [freedom] that are generally recognizable as good by modern subjects."[140]

## Conclusion

While a short list of relevant works have come into print since Neuhouser's publication, this overview sums up the latent yet ongoing complaint that is deeply woven into the liberal as well as cultural trends of English speaking interpretation. These views seem to state:

> *We can't consent to Hegel's rational vision as a legitimate basis for positive politics as it would all but eliminate consent in the first place, but are willing to accept a neutered version predicated on the commonsense version of freedom that we today can live with.*

To begin with, the strategy is one which replaces normative theorization with descriptive ascription (i.e., that what is *ought* to be), unreflectively and uncritically reifying contemporary theoretical norms. The problem for scholarship arises where such readings attribute these very views and intentions to Hegel,[141] or leave Hegel altogether behind in highly selective and unreflective appropriations that universally fail to consider what value there may be behind his systematic intent in the first place. While the former represents a crisis for commentative scholarship, the latter seems to suggest a far more serious problem that goes beyond Hegel scholarship and speaks to proprietary assumptions in Anglophone political thought and philosophy. For example, most informed commentators would find laughable any intention to import Hegel's presuppositional metaphysics of the spirit into contemporary constitutional or legal frameworks. However, the same cannot be said for a consideration of our own presuppositions without which political assumptions, judgments and statements lose intelligibility, and normative force by extension, and become the outward restatement of positive convention and mere descriptions of precedent. Here, as Peter Steinberger has brought out, "the state is essentially a structure of intelligibility that embodies and renders authoritative a society's collective judgment about how things in the world really are."[142] Practical politics becomes the outlet for such "collective" metaphysical commitments where "ordinary political activity focuses largely on establishing and explicating one or another version of that [collective] understanding."[143] In short, Hegel's work should not first and foremost be taken as an invitation to dismiss his foundations in favor of our own, but rather as an opportunity to explore and extend the intelligible depths of the latter with reference to political thinking.

Too quickly do the two trends described above simply dispense wholesale with the issue of justifiable and intelligible foundations, making consistent reference to the presumptions of present methodological and political norms. As a result, they miss out on the deeper project within which Hegel is centrally involved. This largely occurs in the shadow of self-serving appropriations of useful and insightful theoretical elements in Hegel's thought, empowering these authors to advance and justify their own theoretical ends with little or no presuppositional self-inspection or interrogation. On this charge, the liberal and cultural interpretations fail Hegel's thought in their appropriations and seem wholly willing to make these instrumental appropriations with little or no will to consider the elaboration of justificatory arguments for such a project; a demand which Hegel's political thought makes a central concern. Appeals to anti-foundationalist strategies for the reading of Hegel's thought are made almost exclusively in the name of the contemporary pillars of methodological positivism and post-positivism on the one hand, and pluralistic forms of liberalism on the other, and lead one to question why these authors would choose Hegel, of all authors, as grist for their mills.[144]

As was brought out in the previous chapter, the liberal-positivist paradigm defined and reinforced a broad set of convictions and commitments that became part and parcel of Anglophone political science by the middle of the twentieth century. Philosophy had moved on to inaugurate post-positivist critical considerations in the works of the likes of Quine, Strawson and Putnam in the circles of analytic philosophy, and through reference to Husserl, Heidegger and Gadamer in those continental. Political thought, by contrast and specifically in the context of its disciplinary embedment within political science, was found to remain restricted within methodological boundaries fixed in the wake of antiquated positivist enterprises.[145] Why has this been the case? As Merriam and Lasswell had once openly aspired, and as Crick, Farr and Gunnel have exposed, the positivist undertones of political science have their historical roots in the discipline's liberal-democratic presuppositions, convictions and aspirations. No better and unimpeachable witness to this wide-ranging and banal factor than David Easton could attest to the embeddedness and beholdingness of the American discipline to its larger ideological world:

> [T]he institutional matrix within which this [political] research must be conducted has shaped and directed the growth of political science as a field more than it has the other social sciences. By the very nature of its research interests, political science is in a particularly exposed position ... its proximity to sensitive areas of political power has helped to keep it close to the level of achievement attained at the beginning of the twentieth century, when it began to feel its first strength as an independent field for empirical research.[146]

While Easton's primary concern was with the pace of methodological progress within the discipline, the underlying implications for political science and theory with it are grave. In short, his comments expose the intimacy of disciplinary commitment and institutional power and ideology.[147] Herein it becomes all the more difficult to accept the often repeated critique of the arch-conservative, obscurantist or quietistic implications of Hegel's metaphysics for his political thought which require us to take leave of his system. All the more so where they are espoused by those very authors who advance this ideological undercurrent. These have assailed Hegel's supposed apologetic metaphysics in favor of quietly, unreflectively or overtly installing and reifying their own, and, to some extent, doing so in his name. For those commentators beyond the disciplinary culture of political science, some of them tendering the cultural interpretation, the results have been largely the same. These authors have insisted upon imposing contemporary pragmatic appropriations of Hegel's politics, dismissing Hegel's explicit attempts at systematic unity and have instead insisted upon the separability of the political content from the "incredible"[148] and "discredited"[149] logical shell.

For all intents and purposes, for political and methodological reasons, the claim of separability is at the core of these authors' strategies for dealing with the place of the politics in Hegel's larger system. As Brooks has brought out, virtually all camps, systematic and non-systematic, metaphysical and non-metaphysical, concede to the presence of metaphysical elements in Hegel's political thought.[150] Yet, as has been brought out above, the resistance against the inclusion of these elements in our considerations consistently led to a revisionist strategy of selective appropriation and pruning that, in the end, finds its point of departure in the severance of the political from the larger system. The reasons repeatedly asserted against the inclusion of the metaphysical dimension of his political thought are various: the rejection of their having any practical value, the need to make Hegel's political thought relevant and compelling for a contemporary world, the odious presence of their reactionary and authoritarian character, their methodological discrediting, their opaque mysticism, etc., etc.

My concern here is to bring attention to the essentially overdetermining result that this century-old and forceful trend has had. In particular, while most commentators recognize the presence of the metaphysical elements, they nevertheless represent Hegel's political thought in ways which bear little semblance to his program of logical embedment with conspicuous consistency. The argument underlying this pragmatic, ideological and methodological dismemberment is singular; there is no necessary theoretical dependence of Hegel's political thought as it is presented in the *Philosophy of Right* on his logical system, in part or whole. This analytic procedure has taken as a starting point for its presentations and assessments of Hegel's thought a dismissal of his insistence on unity, and have realized in their interpretative appropriations a revised body of Hegelian political thought. *In short the anti-foundationalist prescriptive program set up in the early twentieth century to eliminate metaphysics in the name of positivist, logical and empirical rigor as well as liberal conviction has effected exactly that in this case. The result over 60 years is a scholarly culture which has come to take the deformation and morbidity of Hegel's metaphysical presuppositions for granted, ultimately converting the prescriptive project against metaphysics into a descriptive one.*[151] That is, the prevailing proscription of Hegel's opaque system has led to its effective elimination from our representations and understandings of his political thought. Where the revolt against idealism had once railed against the political and methodological excesses of the metaphysical creed in the likes of Bradley, McTaggart and the idealist king Hegel, it had now, ironically, rehabilitated a version of Hegelian politics on its own terms which no longer possessed the taint of metaphysics. As such, claims as to the expendability of Hegel's metaphysics clearly reflect the interested discursive conditions within which Hegel's work has been received, rather than the sober and secular apex of its illumination as has generally and confidently been asserted.[152]

Ironically, and with the full benefit of more than 150 years of its criticism behind us then, the negation of Hegel's idealism in favor of a thoroughgoing vision of a positive order of knowledge and understanding is a procedure anticipated by and forewarned against by one of its forerunners. Feuerbach's admonition of 1839 restates itself today and calls for a reconsideration of the philosophical potentials embedded in Hegel's political thought:

> Futile, too, is the speculative philosophy that has risen against Hegel and is in vogue now—the speculative philosophy of the positivists. For instead of going beyond Hegel, it has actually retrogressed far behind Hegel in so far as it has failed to grasp precisely the most significant directions suggested by Hegel and his predecessors.[153]

In this context, and over the course of the next two chapters, I will challenge this very assertion of the lack of any necessary or useful binding between the supposedly disposable metaphysics of the system and the practical political insights of the *Philosophy of Right*. After overturning the *descriptive* strategy in showing their necessity for Hegel's system, I will then return to challenge the historically prior and more basic *prescriptive* paradigm in the concluding chapter. The prescriptive paradigm has had an overdetermining influence on our estimations of Hegel's politics as well as the legitimate theoretical frontiers of political thought since the early twentieth century. This latter task will be carried out by mounting a defense of the theoretical usefulness and appreciation of metaphysical thinking and paradigmatic problems for contemporary political thinking and conception. Far from seeking to rehabilitate the supernatural and suprasensible entities of medieval imagination, metaphysical thought and interrogation discloses rather the arrays of interrogative and conceptual complexity which inform and problematize political thinking and our understanding of its place in the world.

## Notes

1 Thom Brooks, Hegel's Political Philosophy: A Systematic Reading of the Philosophy of Right (Edinburgh: Edinburgh University Press, 2007); Eric Goodfield, "The Sovereignty of the Metaphysical in Hegel's Philosophy of Right," The Review of Metaphysics 62, no. 4 (2009), 849–873; Raymond Plant, Hegel (Bloomington: Indiana University Press, 1973); Matthew J. Smetona, Hegel's Logical Comprehension of the Modern State (Lanham: Lexington Books, 2013); Peter J. Steinberger, Logic and

Politics: Hegel's Philosophy of Right (New Haven: Yale University Press, 1988); Robert Stern, Hegel, Kant and the Structure of the Object (London; New York: Routledge, 1990); Robert Stern, Routledge Philosophy Guidebook to Hegel and the Phenomenology of Spirit, Routledge Philosophy Guidebooks (London; New York: Routledge, 2002); Robert Stern, Hegelian Metaphysics (Oxford; New York: Oxford University Press, 2009); Robert Bruce Ware, Hegel: The Logic of Self-Consciousness and the Legacy of Subjective Freedom (Edinburgh: Edinburgh University Press, 1999); Stephen Houlgate, An Introduction to Hegel: Freedom, Truth, and History, 2nd edn (Malden, MA: Blackwell, 2005); Stephen Houlgate, "Hegel's Ethical Thought," in Bulletin of the Hegel Society of Great Britain, 25 (1992), 1–17.
2 Rudolf Carnap, "The Elimination of Metaphysics through Logical Analysis of Language," Erkenntnis (1932).
3 More recently in the form of rational choice theory which is discussed below.
4 As John Burbidge and others have brought out regarding both Hegel's primary metaphysical works which he entitled The Science of Logic, Hegel "would have been wiser to adopt the title used for his lectures: Logic and Metaphysics." In John W. Burbidge, The Logic of Hegel's Logic: An Introduction (Peterborough, Ont.: Broadview Press, 2006), 14.
5 E.F. Carritt, "Hegel and Prussianism," Philosophy 15, no. 58 (1940); Sidney Hook, From Hegel to Marx (New York: Reynal & Hitchcock, 1936); Karl R. Popper, The Open Society and Its Enemies, 2 vols (London: Routledge, 1945); Bertrand Russell, A History of Western Philosophy, and Its Connection with Political and Social Circumstances from the Earliest Times to the Present Day (New York: Simon and Schuster, 1945).
6 Rudolf Haym, Hegel und seine Zeit: Vorlesungen über Entstehung und Entwickelung, Wesen und Werth der Hegel'schen Philosophie (Berlin: Gaertner, 1857).
7 I. Grattan-Guinness, "Russell and Karl Popper: Their Personal Contacts," (DigitalCommons@McMaster, 1992), 10.
8 Hegel's works on logic are his Science of Logic and Part 1 of the Philosophical Science in Outline. The latter is a more concise and introductory version than the former.
9 Klaus Hartmann, "Hegel: A Non-Metaphysical View," in Alasdair C. MacIntyre, Hegel: A Collection of Critical Essays, 1st edn, Modern Studies in Philosophy (Garden City, NY: Anchor Books, 1972), 101–24: 103, 104, 107.
10 Charles Taylor, *Hegel and Modern Society*, Modern European Philosophy (Cambridge, UK; New York: Cambridge University Press, 1979), 69.
11 Allen W. Wood, *Hegel's Ethical Thought* (Cambridge, UK; New York: Cambridge University Press, 1990), 5–6.
12 Georg Wilhelm Friedrich Hegel and Z.A. Pełczyński, *Hegel's Political Writings* (Oxford: Clarendon Press, 1964), 136.
13 L.T. Hobhouse, *The Metaphysical Theory of the State* (London: G. Allen & Unwin, 1918), 17.
14 Ibid.
15 Georg Wilhelm Friedrich Hegel and T.M. Knox, *Hegel's Philosophy of Right* (London: Oxford University Press, 1952), 10; Haym, *Hegel Und Seine Zeit*, 357.
16 Hobhouse, *The Metaphysical Theory of the State*, 17.
17 Ibid., 18.
18 Ibid., 23.
19 Ibid., 73.
20 Ibid., 6. A message he prefaces his book with in a dedication addressed to his son.
21 Ibid.
22 Ibid., 137.
23 Ibid., 23.
24 Ibid., 25.

25 Ibid., 23.
26 Ibid., 25.
27 George H. Sabine, "Hegel's Political Philosophy," *Philosophical Review* 41, no. 3 (1932): 261–82: 261.
28 Ibid., 269.
29 Michael Beresford Foster, *The Political Philosophies of Plato and Hegel* (Oxford: Clarendon Press, 1935), 117.
30 Ibid., 118, 121.
31 Ibid., 164.
32 Ibid., 174.
33 Ibid.
34 J.A. Spender and T.M. Knox, "Hegel and Prussianism," *Philosophy* 15, no. 58 (1940), 219–220: 219.
35 Ibid.
36 Foster, *The Political Philosophies of Plato and Hegel*, 140.
37 Ibid.
38 Karl R. Popper, *Unended Quest*, Rev. edn, Routledge Classics (London; New York: Routledge, 2002), 131.
39 This number will be largely accurate but is approximate. Due to the use of the single search term "G.W.F. Hegel" as the most efficient means of indexing all Hegel related content in the Library of Congress' catalog, there are a minority of unrelated contents.
40 These numbers can be examined through a search of the Library of Congress's website or catalog.
41 Book publication on Hegel doubled by the end of the decade.
42 Popper, *The Open Society and Its Enemies*, 25.
43 Ibid.
44 Ibid., 45.
45 Ibid., 47.
46 Ibid., 26. Popper is here referencing Schopenhauer's views on Hegel's legacy.
47 Ibid., 45.
48 Ibid., 39.
49 Ibid.
50 Ibid., 27.
51 Grattan-Guinness, "Russell and Karl Popper," 11.
52 Bertrand Russell, *A History of Western Philosophy* (New York: Simon and Schuster, 1945), 742.
53 Georg Wilhelm Friedrich Hegel and Carl J. Friedrich, *The Philosophy of Hegel* (New York: Modern Library, 1954), xiii.
54 Ibid.
55 Don Carlos Travis and Texas University, Dept. of Germanic Languages, *A Hegel Symposium; Essays by Carl J. Friedrich [and Others]*(Austin: Dept. of Germanic Languages, University of Texas, 1962), 13.
56 Ibid., 31.
57 Ibid.
58 Ibid., 34–5.
59 David Easton, "The Decline of Modern Political Theory," *Journal of Politics* 13, no. 1 (1951), 36–58: 54.
60 M.W. Jackson, "Hegel: The Real and the Rational," in Jon Stewart, *The Hegel Myths and Legends*, Northwestern University Studies in Phenomenology and Existential Philosophy (Evanston, IL: Northwestern University Press, 1996), 19–25: 20.
61 As seen from its point of view. As the following chapters will expose, Hegel's metaphysics do not in any fundamental way condemn the politics to a thoroughgoing antidemocratic or conservative agenda.

## Background, history and critique

62 Richard J. Bernstein, "Why Hegel Now?" *The Review of Metaphysics* 31, no. 1 (1977), 29–60: 29.
63 Ibid., 38.
64 Ibid., 44.
65 Walter A. Kaufmann, "The Hegel Myth and Its Method," *Philosophical Review* 60, no. 4 (1951), 459–86: 460.
66 Hegel, in ibid., 469.
67 As M.W. Jackson points out (in "Hegel: The Real and the Rational," 20), errors such as these would subsequently reverberate in the English speaking world.
68 John Niemeyer Findlay, *Hegel, A Re-Examination*, Muirhead Library of Philosophy (London; New York: Allen & Unwin; Macmillan, 1958), 18.
69 Ibid., 348.
70 Ibid., 18. Findlay, like Kaufmann after him, was explicitly wrestling with "deep-rooted, prevailing misconceptions ... underived from anything Hegel says" (ibid., 19.).
71 Sidney Hook, "From Plato to Hegel to Marx," *New York Times*, July 22, 1951.
72 Sidney Hook, *From Hegel to Marx: Studies in the Intellectual Development of Karl Marx*, Ann Arbor Paperbacks for the Study of Communism and Marxism (Ann Arbor: University of Michigan Press, 1962), 19.
73 Ibid.
74 Ibid., 50.
75 Ibid., 50.
76 Hegel and Pełczyński, *Hegel's Political Writings*, 68.
77 Ibid., 134.
78 Ibid., 135.
79 Ibid.
80 Ibid., 136.
81 Ibid.
82 Ibid.
83 Georg Wilhelm Friedrich Hegel and William Wallace, *Hegel's Logic: Being Part One of the Encyclopaedia of the Philosophical Sciences (1830)* (Oxford: Clarendon Press, 1975), Part 1, §6.
84 Jackson, "Hegel: The Real and the Rational," 19.
85 Hegel and Pełczyński, *Hegel's Political Writings*, 135.
86 Jackson, "Hegel: The Real and the Rational," 20. For Jackson the roots of this interpretation are to be found in Haym's work on Hegel.
87 I specifically use Hegel's term to describe the process going on here.
88 Georg Wilhelm Friedrich Hegel, Laurence Winant Dickey and Hugh Barr Nisbet, *G.W.F. Hegel: Political Writings*, Cambridge Texts in the History of Political Thought (New York: Cambridge University Press, 1999), viii–ix. Though not our task here, a consideration of Hegel's function in the context of the production of cold-war ideology would seem to provide a context for this strategy.
89 Walter Arnold Kaufmann, *The Owl and the Nightingale: From Shakespeare to Existentialism* (London: Faber and Faber, 1959), 88.
90 Stewart makes this case in the clearest possible terms: "His philosophy, which marks the crossroads in the modern intellectual tradition, has given birth to virtually all of the major schools of contemporary thought: phenomenology, existentialism, Marxism, critical theory, structuralism, pragmatism, hermeneutics, and so on." Stewart, *The Hegel Myths and Legends*, 4.
91 His political thought is often given its emphasis as a precursor to Marx's, as opposed to a worthy subject of its own.
92 Jackson, "Hegel: The Real and the Rational," 21. He points out that this dominant orientation has not been the case in other European contexts.

93 Dante Germino, "Hegel as a Political Theorist," *Journal of Politics* 31, no. 4 (1969), 885–912: 885.
94 Ibid.
95 Ibid.
96 Ibid.
97 Ibid.
98 Ibid., 886.
99 Ibid., 905.
100 Ibid., 885–6.
101 Ibid., 911.
102 Ibid., 912. The capitalization is Germino's.
103 Shlomo Avineri, *Hegel's Theory of the Modern State*, Cambridge Studies in the History and Theory of Politics (London: Cambridge University Press, 1972), 221.
104 Ibid., ix.
105 Ibid.
106 Taylor, *Hegel and Modern Society*, 68.
107 In the year 1979 or beyond it.
108 Charles Taylor, *Hegel* (Cambridge, UK; New York: Cambridge University Press, 1975), vii.
109 Steven B. Smith, *Hegel's Critique of Liberalism: Rights in Context* (Chicago: University of Chicago Press, 1989), 11.
110 Ibid., 10. The former running along the lines of Royce and Rosen, the latter Pełczyński and Germino.
111 Ibid., 11. Richard Bernstein attests to the "non-metaphysical" basis of Smith's approach in his back-cover review of the 1989 edition.
112 Ibid., 1.
113 Wood, *Hegel's Ethical Thought*, xiii.
114 Michael Rosen, in ibid., 5.
115 Ibid., 5–6.
116 Ibid., 7.
117 Ibid., 6.
118 Brooks, *Hegel's Political Philosophy*, 7–8.
119 Mark Tunick, *Hegel's Political Philosophy: Interpreting the Practice of Legal Punishment* (Princeton, NJ: Princeton University Press, 1992), 3.
120 Ibid., 4.
121 Ibid.
122 Ibid.
123 Benjamin Barber, cited in Mark Tunick, *Hegel's Political Philosophy: Interpreting the Practice of Legal Punishment* (Princeton, NJ: Princeton University Press, 1992), 17.
124 Ibid.
125 G.W.F. Hegel, *The Philosophy of Right*, trans. T.M. Knox (London: Oxford University Press, 1952), preface.
126 Michael O. Hardimon, *Hegel's Social Philosophy: The Project of Reconciliation*, Modern European Philosophy (Cambridge, UK; New York: Cambridge University Press, 1994), 8.
127 Ibid., 215.
128 Alan Patten, *Hegel's Idea of Freedom*, Oxford Philosophical Monographs (Oxford; New York: Oxford University Press, 1999), 27.
129 Peter J. Steinberger, "Hegel's Philosophy of Freedom. By Paul Franco," *American Political Science Review* 95, no. 01 (2001), 205.
130 Paul Franco, *Hegel's Philosophy of Freedom* (New Haven, CT: Yale University Press, 1999).
131 Ibid., x.

132 Ibid., 140.
133 Ibid., xii.
134 Ibid., xii.
135 Frederick Neuhouser, *Foundations of Hegel's Social Theory: Actualizing Freedom* (Cambridge, MA: Harvard University Press, 2000), 4.
136 Ibid., 3.
137 Ibid., 4–5.
138 Ibid., 205.
139 Ibid., 215.
140 Ibid., 270.
141 Tunick had the good sense to voluntarily resign from any such claim.
142 Peter J. Steinberger, *The Idea of the State*, Contemporary Political Theory (Cambridge, UK; New York: Cambridge University Press, 2004), 192.
143 Ibid.
144 Of course Hegel's intellectual and historical significances, as earlier discussed, trump any such confusion. The pragmatic dismissal of the system and Hegel's logic as of no use to politics, Hegel's or ours, essentially boils down to the positivist rejection of their indeterminable authenticity and departure from commonsense.
145 Which themselves prevailed largely beyond any form of introspection well into the late 1960s.
146 David Easton, *The Political System: An Inquiry into the State of Political Science*, 1st edn (New York: Knopf, 1953), 51.
147 A set of commitments which Kaufman–Osbourn's writing has brought out has been discussed in Chapter 2.
148 Taylor, *Hegel and Modern Society*, 69.
149 Wood, Allen W., 'Reply', Bulletin of the Hegel Society of Great Britain, 25 (1992), 41. Wood qualifies this discrediting but the overall argument functions on the assumption where Hegel's logic "provides no good basis for his [Hegel's] ethics" (ibid.).
150 Brooks, *Hegel's Political Philosophy*, 3.
151 Such that our representations of Hegel's politics are non-metaphysical to begin with.
152 A mode of representation which has been especially troubling to Adriaan Peperzak. Adriaan Theodoor Peperzak, *Modern Freedom: Hegel's Legal, Moral, and Political Philosophy* (Dordrecht; London: Kluwer Academic, 2001).
153 Ludwig Feuerbach, *The Fiery Brook; Selected Writings of Ludwig Feuerbach* (Garden City, NY: Anchor Books, 1972), 94.

# Part II
# Metaphysics and politics in Hegel's thought

# 4 Hegel's metaphysics of thought
## Toward a logic of universals

**Introduction**

In combination with the following chapter on the *Philosophy of Right*, this chapter works to disclose the antique problem of universals within Hegel's logical project as a core metaphysical and animating concern. To begin with, this is taken up in consideration of Hegel's *Nuremberg Propadeutic*, and subsequently through the work of Hegel's 1830 *Encyclopedia* Logic[1] (hereafter also "*Logic*") which itself develops from a conception of Eleatic being as its philosophical, and historical, starting point. As I will argue, the culmination of the *Logic* in the syllogism represents Hegel's offering of a resolution to the problem of universals as a specifically metaphysical question, and in turn grounds his conceptual framework for a resolution of the political problem of universals in his *Philosophy of Right*.[2]

As a combined unit, these two chapters direct themselves against the descriptive strategy, assumed by authors examined in the preceding chapter, that intends to cull all dimension and import of the metaphysical elements in exchange for a "cleansed" version of Hegel's politics that "we" can live with. First, through this examination of Hegel's *Logic* and the *Philosophy of Right* in Chapters 4 and 5, I assert against the descriptive strategy and culture of Hegel scholarship that the metaphysical element of Hegel's thought is very much present, irreducible and irremovable from his thinking. From these grounds I argue that the carryover from the metaphysical work of the *Logic* to his politics is both intentional and useful, if not inevitable, in Hegel's program. In this way Chapters 4 and 5 initiate the undoing of the basic descriptive assumptions about the divisible and contingent relation of Hegel's metaphysical and political thought. Moreover, the explication of the metaphysical basis of Hegel's logical project in this chapter implicitly challenges authors such as Robert Pippin and Klaus Hartmann who have sought to recast Hegel as a non-metaphysical thinker primarily engaged either in neo-Kantian epistemology or category theorization.[3]

Having cleared these scholarly and institutional obstacles away, the final chapter issues an assault upon the more basic prescriptive claims of the inherent impracticality, absent utility and general proscription of metaphysics for political theorizing writ large. Not merely negative, it presents an argument for the theoretical virtue and perhaps inevitability of metaphysical problems and thinking for political thought in general. Prior to initiating this concluding challenge and taking the first step through Hegel's *Logic* in this chapter, however, I provide a brief introduction to the historical problem of universals and its significance to Hegel's thought as a specifically metaphysical concern.

An exegetical approach to Hegel's *Logic* is an arduous but not an unrewarding one. Through it we arrive at a fuller understanding of its fundamental strengths as well as weaknesses. It is also the standard lens through which he viewed modern and pre-modern thought, and this is exactly the record he impressed upon the *Logic*. The *Logic* is Hegel's palimpsest of the historical forms and schools of thought and the inner logics which he felt wove them together as an ongoing and purposive evolution. I rehearse much of Hegel's *Logic* on its own terms, while trying to make sense of its arguments on two levels: first, as a system of thought which responds to Hegel's own goals; and, second, as a concerted response to the traditional metaphysical problem of universals. Working through its arguments and examining the *Logic* in this way, with all its ambiguities, represents an attempt to take Hegel's own thinking seriously and to begin to reconsider the scope of its philosophical commitments in the context of his other works. While the *Logic* is extraordinarily dense, it remains reachable through its inner dialogue with the history of thought which it takes as its foundation.

While Hegel's system of logic contains enclosed and frequently self-recursive elements, I take it up to demonstrate that it is passable, that it may be understood to be diligently working on problems which traverse metaphysics and politics in substantial ways. The attempt to correct Hegel's *Logic* and make sense of it in terms which appeal to analytic and empirical common sense simply invites a reductionism of his thought to our methodological concerns. Such an approach all but ensures that we miss out on Hegel's wider ideas and program.[4] The admonitions against taking the *Logic* into account on the way to Hegel's politics are restated by authors considered in Chapter 3. To a great extent they are summed up by Shlomo Avineri in his position that "he" who considers it "may find himself immersed in an explication of the systematic edifice of Hegel's philosophy without ever reaching his political theory."[5] My task against this background is to reveal common foundations between the two texts which illuminate Hegel's political program in ways which remain opaque and beyond intelligibility in their absence: foundations which can only be understood in their fullness in consideration of the complimentarity of the two major works and within the context of Hegel's larger system itself.

## The problem of universals between antiquity and modernity

At its root, the classical philosophical problem of universals aspires to take both the individual aspect of particular things in their conceptual as well as their empirical aspects into account; that is, both the thing as thought or idea and the thing sensed. In the first case the emphasis is upon essential and definitive characteristics common to individuals; for example, the circularity shared by two or more balls, or the commonalities shared by a species of animals etc. In the second, the stress is put upon the brute fact of separateness; both balls may be circular, but circularity remains distinct in each ball despite a common visual or even geometrical shape. In other words, in this second sense, circularity remains a specific property in each case, a fact of perception that defies universalization. If one takes the first approach, one is a taking a realist strategy on the question and accepts the existence of universals, in one or a variety of ways, in appealing to a fundamental and irreducible commonality. If the second, one is adopting a nominalist approach that rejects the existence of universals. The problem is so theoretically basic and banal in its approach to the relation of ideas and things that Andrew Schoedinger has commented that "people other than philosophers are generally unaware that the problem even exists."[6] Despite this commonsensical obliviousness, the problem is real nonetheless: things can only be named according to properties and attributes, and this tears at the boundaries between the thing itself and our thoughts of it. Where "Concepts with no physical referents are necessary in order to account for that which is physical,"[7] an epistemological cleaving point and divide emerges and the metaphysical question of the independence of the universal presents itself as an inexorable, and perhaps ineliminable, problem. The debate continues to this day and responses range from nominalism to realism to its wholesale dismissal as a pseudo-problem.

While realists have always had an uphill battle metaphysically, struggling to substantiate the existence of universals, nominalists have difficulty with coming into conflict with common sense. In dispensing with universals, nominalism falls afoul of generalization. Where no general entities are said to exist, and all things are held as individual instances, acquisition of truth or even partial knowledge becomes impossible: how may we begin to describe the world we experience without categories and classes? Hannah Arendt poses the problem: "it is indeed true that once the suprasensory realm is discarded, its opposite, the world of appearances as understood for so many centuries, is also annihilated."[8]

A map, perhaps of all individual entities as an index of atomic facts, may assist us in comprehending such a world. Even such a map, however, under the strictures of nominalism would deny fundamental commonalities of individual entities and would lead to the paradoxical conclusion that, despite all outer similarities, no two entities are inherently or internally related. As such all covering laws would at best amount to a pragmatic patterning, attesting to no underlying strata of categorical commonality. The world of phenomenal correspondence and conflict would in this way be reduced to an absurd state of happenstance, contingency and coincidence. As Paul Spade has brought out, "[the nominalist's] problem is in explaining how we can know the world is the way they say it is."[9] The world of atomic facts simply does not get at the important complexity and collectivity of the world of experience. Where, as well, we ought to be inclined to ask, may we say discrete entities ultimately reside and persist? To respond with the claim of their absolute individuality and separateness only seems to beg the question of their seeming belonging and relating to one another. As well, where most of what we identify in the world as discrete is further reducible to subordinate parts, we seem to fall into infinite regression. All of these paradoxical issues and concerns have been raised by realists and nominalists in classical, pre-modern and modern contexts.

The problem of universals as a historically important philosophical concern was established by the posthumous influence of Porphyry's *Isagoge* on medieval philosophy. Written in the middle of the third century AD, Porphyry's text set out to provide an introduction to the logical work of Aristotle's *Categories* with special attention to the issues of universals raised in Aristotle's work. While Aristotle's work defined universals in *De Interpretatione* as an entity predicated of many instances, such that "man, for instance, is a universal, Callias a particular,"[10] Riin Sirkel argues that the traditional problem of universals as we know it was not explicitly formulated there or in Aristotle's text that Porphyry is ostensibly commenting upon, *The Categories*.[11] While Aristotle contributed to its development, the medieval formulation of the problem was Porphyry's own.

In his meditative interrogation of the implications of Aristotle's subdivisions of logical classification, Porphyry raised three questions which became philosophical touchstones for the vast enterprise of medieval philosophical inquiry:

> (a) whether genera and species are real or are situated in bare thoughts alone, (b) whether as real they are bodies or incorporeals, and (c) whether they are separated or in sensibles and have their reality in connection with them.[12]

While Porphyry drew attention to these issues in a stark and dramatic way at the very start of his text, he immediately resigned from the issue declaring that "such business is profound, and requires another, greater investigation."[13] This cursory third-century digression would make the question of the status of universals "famous and [was] bequeathed to the Middle Ages by Boethius through his translation of Isagoge."[14] Despite its parsing into three questions, the problem really reduces to the issue of the status of universals in relation to the particular things that are said to instantiate or "predicate" them. Porphyry's own significance on the issue is limited to this intermediation of Aristotle and later medieval commentators. He himself had little of further substance to contribute to the question and his formulation of the problem of universals would be of little note for two centuries afterwards. It was not until the fifth century, and the translation of the *Isagoge* into Latin by Anicius Manlius Severinus Boethius, that Porphyry's Aristotelian provocation would take deep root in medieval philosophical soil.

Aristotle's questions did not merely ask whether universal terms exist independently of the instances they are said to collect. His question also raised another concern, part and parcel of the third question raised by Porphyry, as to whether universals cohere as both linguistic terms and "extralinguistic entities"[15] as Spade puts it. That is: (1) do the categorical terms or concepts of universality exist as an essential bond of the plural entities which predicate them and (2) is there a more basic metaphysical relation amongst classes of things (as opposed to terms or concepts) which bond them in some essential way. The problem of universals thus presents a problem for a substantive notion of both universal categories—logical, as well as classes of things—metaphysical. In a Platonic sense it may be necessary that the latter must hold in order for the former to be true: that some inherent relation amongst classes of things must exist to give the logical rubric universal "substance" in the first place. Regardless of the logical and metaphysical aspects of the issue, its debate breaks, and continues to break, upon the nominalist and realist divide, though authors like Peter Abelard and others have taken differing positions on the logical and metaphysical sides of the question. John Duns Scotus, William of Ockham and many others would follow up on Boethius and Abelard in the thirteenth and fourteenth centuries, where the problem of universals had become a central concern of scholastic philosophy. These authors received Porphyry and Boethius, and Aristotle by extension, through Peter Lombard's *Sentences* written in the twelfth century.[16]

Yet, while the medieval problem of universals is generally traced back to Aristotle, it was a central issue for Plato as well. The problem of universals as a discrete philosophical problem was explicitly elaborated in Plato's *Philebus* as a question as to

> ... how each individual unity, being always the same and incapable either of generation or of destruction, but retaining a permanent individuality can be conceived either as dispersed and multiplied in the infinity of the world of generation, or as still entire and yet divided from itself, which latter would seem to be the greatest impossibility of all, for how can one and the same thing be at the same time in one and in many things?[17]

Thus the problem of universals, and of the one and the many by extension, raises the question as to how being can enter and involve itself with the flow of change and generation while it yet remains what it is in itself: "how can one and the same thing be at the same time in one and in many things?"[18] The problem of universals in the *Philebus* was generated in reaction to the Heracleitean and materialist supposition where being is understood as distributed over all phenomena such that it is at once both instanced and self-sufficient in any material or ideal particular.[19] The language and dialectical rendering of the one and the many here recalls the logical procedure undertaken in the primordial supposition of the *Parmenides*: one is either one and not many but singular, or one is not one and is many or plural. The fundamental question of being in the *Philebus* was taken up on the grounds of the contest between the Eleatic unmoving, *causa sui* (self-creating and standing) unity of being which embraces all, and the fluidity of the Heracleitean flux in which each moment and part of the generative flow of "the river" instances a self-contained or "monadic" entity. For Plato, the problem of the one and the many was not merely about distribution of singular qualities or properties across particulars; it also immediately implied the ontological issue of their independence and existence as well. Without the self-subsisting universality of his conceptual "forms" Plato feared that knowledge would be washed away in the flow of material change; where else could we find an unchanging foundation independent of sensorial corruption? As Moreland makes clear, "Issues and options regarding the One and Many have formed the core of the problem of universals since the time of Plato."[20]

For Hegel himself, the medieval problem was specifically concerned with the controversy over "the metaphysical opposition between the universal and the individual."[21] In line with his own dialectical commitments, he held that the debate reflected "great credit" to the scholastic age. Hegel understood the debate as centered upon the question as to

> whether ... universals are something real in and for themselves, apart from the thinking subject, and independent of the individual existing thing, so that they exist in the individual things independently of the individuality of the thing and of each other; or whether the universal is only nominal, only in the subjective representation, a thing of thought.[22]

He recognized a modern debt to these debates and saw in them an anticipation of the origins of modern philosophical concerns where the problem of universals "was in itself highly important and significant for the culture of more modern times."[23] While this is certainly true in a deep and substantial sense and directly relates to Hegel's overt systematic goal of reuniting substance and subject, few Hegel commentators have sought to come to terms with the implications of this metaphysical legacy in his thought.[24]

As an exception, the American idealist Josiah Royce took this connection seriously, pointing out in 1892 that "the Hegelian theory of Universals is intended ... to offer a solution of the ancient question as to the reality of universals."[25] For Royce, this statement is a prelude to a more basic argument: the paradoxes of thought arising from the observation of the external world "which baffle human understanding" are the gateway to the development of theoretical understanding. As in the case of the problem of universals which originated in Aristotle's thought and later manifested as a central question of medieval times:

> Philosophy is a nest of such problems. They vex men endlessly; they gave Kant his troublesome pairs of contradictory assertions about space and time; they gave Fichte the puzzle about self and not-self; they gave Hume the problem about facts and laws, about experience that could never find necessity, and necessity that continually pretended to inflict itself upon experience. A logical system of such problems and of their solutions would be a complete theoretical philosophy.[26]

The way to proceed from theory to practice for Hegel was thus a logical system which addressed these issues in a comprehensive way. The fundamental problems of philosophy were a touchstone in his work for the alleviation of the issues which had first proven an obstacle to making progress on those practical. This recalls Plato's own phenomenological genealogy which asserted that the awareness of the disturbing ambiguity of sensory impressions—the object which is both small and large, hard and soft[27]—giving rise to the awareness of a divergence of appearance and reality. In sum, politics too has roots in the dilemmas of thought, and theoretical housecleaning was as important here as it was in the areas of science and epistemology. As will be made clear in my coverage of the *Logic* below and in the following chapter on the *Philosophy of Right*, Hegel's thought is distanced from twentieth-century empirically inclined theory in that these problems simply aren't reducible to the monism of materialist explanation or conceptual analysis. Neither was Hegel satisfied with reductionist idealism. Rather, his intention was to bring the two together in a way which reunited thing and idea, substance and subject, in an overarching system which sought to reconcile the seemingly incommensurable categories of nature and spirit.

In this spirit, Royce teaches us that Hegel set out "to expound ... the nature and the solution of every philosophical problem concerning the absolute as the history of philosophy has presented such problems to us."[28] While a wildly ambitious and immodest task of philosophical zealotry, Hegel's interest in the practical implications of the resolution of the problems of philosophy was taken up as a prelude to his intent to return to the world of common sense in the wake of this deeper awareness of the shifting ontological sands upon which all seeming and appearance depends. As I will argue, far from turning away from the world of the senses in a once and for all time metaphysical hermitage, Hegel's intent is an active return to the public "cave" of appearances and opinion. Far from overturning its empirical regime of the senses, Hegel's plan sees fit to incorporate and reconcile the reflective understanding of the ideal universal with its inevitable home in the world of everyday experience and transience. Metaphysics as Hegel's method of philosophical resolution in the *Logic*, then, herein puts a skeptical turn on our deployment of linguistic categories—as stand-ins for experience—so as not to fall prey to the myth of the given. Primary impressions, the staple of empirical research and common sense, do not do justice either to the phenomenal aspect of the impression on the one side, nor to the intent for comprehension on the other. What we see is not always what we get, and the Kantian critical exposé of perception—his declaration of the inaccessibility of the noumenal and our restriction to the world of appearances—is recapitulated in Hegel's reflective attendance to the categories of experience. What concerns us as essential here is the weight of Hegel's recognition that engaging the practical categories of experience, and politics by extension, demands their interrogation in metaphysical terms, and not merely as unmediated outputs of cognition.

As I will develop below, Hegel's attendance to the fundamental problems for both theoretical and practical thought takes its roots in Aristotle's problem of universals. Royce recounts the legacy of this philosophical problem:

> When we think, we always think of classes, of categories, in brief, of universals. But, on the other hand, the facts of the world always appear to our senses to be individual. Man, as a mere abstraction, doesn't exist; individual men do.[29]

In other words, both the general and particular, fluid and discrete natures of things and ideas challenge our capacity to identify and define the entities of experience. The reality of the mind seems to come into conflict and oppose the reality presented in the senses. The question of the status and priority of general universals in and against their instantiations, "one of the most famous of the controversies of the philosophy of the Middle Ages," thus arises and is "precisely the kind of paradox that Hegel's method was peculiarly apt to ... deal with."[30]

## Why/how metaphysics?

Hegel's response to the problem of universals exposes the way he attempted to reconstitute metaphysics after Kant's critique vis-à-vis the fallacies which such a venture entailed. Kant defined metaphysics as an attempt at representation and knowledge of the absolute through reason. This rejection of the viability of metaphysics in the *Critique of Pure Reason* was based on his argument that reason outstrips itself and falls into fallacy in attempts to rationally appropriate the unconditioned absolute. Yet, as many working in his wake recognized, the Kantian dualism of understanding and sensibility was so severe that there was no choice but to return to metaphysics in order to resolve it. Thus, long before Hegel had become the locus of scrutiny for German idealism, "It had become clear to many thinkers in the late 1790s that it was impossible to resolve the problem of the transcendental deduction ... from Kant's original starting point."[31] The dualism was seen as fundamentally problematic in that it made it impossible to imagine how the timeless content of the faculty of understanding could bear any relation to that of sensibility as embedded in the time and space of experience. In some retrogressive sense, Kantian skepticism had fallen into and reproduced the substance dualistic dilemma that Spinoza had witnessed in Descartes. Invoking Spinoza, the early Hegel–Schelling project thus took up its metaphysics of the absolute in an attempt to revise the relation of nature and mind, world and idea. This they argued could be accomplished by overturning what they took as the mechanical conceptualization of nature inherent in Kant's thought, one that severed the relation of substance and subject and the natural and the spiritual realms.[32]

In this discursive context, and as will be fleshed out below in my coverage of the *Logic*, the problem of universals played a central and integral role within Hegel's ambition to reunify the spiritual and natural realms for thought. What Kant's critique had denied to metaphysics Hegel sought to regain precisely through the dialectic of the universal. As an attempt to restore the equilibrium of the empirical particular and the cognitive universal lost to Kantian skepticism, his rehabilitation of metaphysics is inherently betrothed to the problem of universals. With reference to Plato's logic of the one and the many discussed above, the problem of universals is patently metaphysical because it is directly derivable from rational attempts at representing the absolute and whole. In fact, in a fundamental way Kant's basic critique of general metaphysics may be restated, in Hegelian terms, as a rejection of the problem of universals itself where a key entry point to metaphysics is denied. It is precisely the royal road to synthetic *a priori* knowledge that Hegel intended to reopen.

As explored below, the problem is at play under the surface of Hegel's dialectic, and its two poles play the role of representing the tandem opposition of universal ideas and the particular things within which they are immanent. This classical wheel of traditional philosophical explanation thus represents a core component of Hegel's response to the problem of the understanding and the limits of empirical knowing which he found in the skeptical remainder of Kant's transcendental logic. Where influential authors such as Klaus Hartmann and Robert Pippin have sought to recast Hegel as a category theorist or as working in the epistemological vein of the Kantian tradition, then, they have largely missed out on the way Hegel's critique and reaction to Kant is every bit as definitive of his efforts as the continuity.[33] Moreover, they have not merely overlooked and underestimated Hegel's radical departure from Kant as both Frederick Beiser and James Kreines have brought out.[34] They have as well overlooked a larger historical narrative which conveys Hegel's modern recapitulation of antique and perennial philosophical concerns as a core metaphysical creed, one which further serves to substantially distinguish his thought from Kant's.[35] Indeed, the view of Hegel as post-metaphysical heir to the Kantian project dismisses these crucial dimensions where "Hegel's continuity with the prior tradition is so massively evident, and not least in his respect for the Greeks, ... that this interpretation has much to do with the commentators own embarrassments with metaphysics."[36]

## Hegel's metaphysical corpus and the context of the *Encyclopedia* Logic

Hegel's shorter logic, his *Encyclopedia* Logic, is best understood in terms of its continuity with his earlier work in *The Phenomenology* where his system of universals is concerned. As in the logic, the development of self-consciousness explicated in *The Phenomenology* originates as embedded and immediate within experience, where it must yet pass beyond itself to its "other." This subjectivization of the dialectic ultimately, in its completion, brings together both object and subject in the universal's surpassing its merely sensuous origins where, in Hegel's terms, "the relation between these two ... gains concrete form and its own proper shape and appearance, finds a place in the life of the universal individual."[37] This final shape of the developing self is the substance of the absolute which serves to form the basis of the unity of subject and object as the goal of Hegel's logic. This is the extension of the synthetic task as it was first carried out in the *Phenomenology*, and represents the true introduction of his system as a whole. The goal in both cases remains, however, a consistent articulation of the absolute in its phenomenal forms. Where the *Phenomenology* moves from the first inklings of experience through to the absolute, the *Logic* moves in the same direction through a conceptual evolution.

Against the background of his earlier *Science of Logic,* I take the older Hegel's 1830 *Logic* to represent the latest and most mature expression of his logical-thought and its direct integration into his triadic system of thought as the first of its three volumes. Hegel himself tells us of the later *Logic* that he had "gone through it several times" and that beyond the first five sections intended as a critique and communiqué with his contemporaries that "The rest I have sought to make more definite, and so far as may be clearer."[38] Both William Wallace and J.N. Findlay[39] extend this assessment, the former holding that the "Encyclopaedia is the only complete, matured, and authentic statement of Hegel's philosophical system"[40] and the latter that "the Science of Logic can be said ... to have been superseded by the Logic of the Encyclopaedia."[41] It will here be examined as the consummate expression of his metaphysics insofar as one of its central and explicit tasks is the resolution of the problem of universals and the status of its relational instantiations: i.e., the nature of the particulars that the universal organizes.

Running parallel to the logic's tracing the life of the Idea,[42] the *Phenomenology* describes the ascent of consciousness towards its own idea as self-realization, recapitulating itself as the grounding of all subsequent subjectivity: "The individual, whose substance is mind at the higher level, passes through these past forms, much in the way that one who takes up a higher science goes through those preparatory forms of knowledge."[43] The graduation of the mind from the captivity of sensuous experience towards self-othering, the root of the ultimate emancipation of the self in the recognition of the other as its own, forms the basis of reality. The absolute as thinking substance in the *Phenomenology*, as mentioned, takes up where experience leaves off and closes out the circle of the absolute which the *Logic* initiates. Hegel's own comments in the *Phenomenology* as to its introductory function/capacity to the science of philosophy he later recanted in the 1830 *Logic* "because so much that properly belongs to the concrete branches is prematurely dragged into the introduction."[44] In short, Hegel's coverage of the phases and moments of the historical and cultural progression of consciousness inevitably demanded the treatment of its plethora of expressions as the "special branches of philosophy" of knowledge "such as individual and social morality, art and religion."[45]

In order to delineate and render transparent this development, he was compelled to carry out an exposition of these historical expressions, the "existence of their concrete formations" in their various disciplinary forms. The *Logic* is thus, as Hegel termed it, his later attempt to clearly introduce and connect the historical development of thought with a sphere of seemingly abstract, and at first blush epistemologically problematic, universals as a central priority for his science of philosophy. This project takes as its self-proclaimed task the reunification of "substance and subject," articulating the life of the absolute in its ideal and temporal forms, so as to span the Humean gap between the empirical reality of particulars and a supposed universal ideality of thought.[46] Regardless of how this latter distancing from the phenomenology may be seen, the two texts embrace each other as a singular project which reflects the dialectical circle of othering and negation bonded together by the elements of Hegel's project of the absolute. The primacy of the *Logic* as Hegel's chosen introductory statement to his system, then, seems well established in his own latter references to the *Phenomenology*. In this context, the *Logic* of 1830 stands as his mature conceptualization of logical system introduction and metaphysical treatise.[47] As John Burbidge has brought out, it is directly against the background laid out in the *Phenomenology* that

> Hegel can claim that what pure thought discovers ... are not only the logical principles underlying all our thinking ... but also the metaphysical principles which make up whatever is. His objective logic takes the place of what previously had been called metaphysics.[48]

In coming out of Kant's transcendental logic elaborated in the *Critique of Pure Reason*, Hegel fashioned the task of reconciling an epistemic logic[49] of non-empirical categories with empirical reality and its transformations for himself. Such a logic for both Kant and Hegel is no system of abstractions which remains a mere intellectual reflection of reality as the epistemological "other" of being. Here Hegel worked to undo the division of concept and nature, understanding and sense, and ultimately the rupture of universality, in the prioritization of the empirical flux of particulars. The transcendental procedure works from within phenomena in recognition of the necessity of a dialectic of form which generates and permits change. In Kant, Hegel witnessed the beginnings of the procedure, though he held it as yet incomplete in its inability to find a systematic mediation of subject and object, universal concept and the particular of empirical nature, which could ground a foundation for knowledge and a conception of the absolute. In its middling capacity, then, Hegel's doctrine of logic mediates between his philosophy of historical spirit, and philosophy of nature in the syllogistic form of the particular which reconciles the universal to the individual at the organizational level of the *Encyclopedia of the Philosophical Sciences* as a whole.[50]

## First philosophy and a foundational system of universals

The 1830 *Encyclopedia* represents Hegel's integration of the earlier *Science of Logic* and the earliest Jena logic with his work on *Sittlichkeit* (customary or ethical life) and nature. With the earlier edition of the *Science of Logic* of 1812, Hegel released a preparatory text on logic for his young pupils at the Nuremberg gymnasium which acted as a synopsis of the overall dialectical trajectory of the work.[51] In this work Hegel has left out much of the treatment and development of his system of universals in order to make clear the rudimentary groundwork of his logical system of dialectic and its inner development. In this propaedutic, however, Hegel clarified the purpose of his logic and, though he left out much concerning the development of the absolute Idea, he made reference to one of its central purposes for the better understanding of his system of philosophy: "The thinking activity is, in general, the apprehension and bringing together of the Manifold into unity. The Manifold as such belongs to externality in general—to feeling and sensuous intuition."[52] In bringing the manifold of experience into unity, Hegel foreshadows the Idea as the coordination of universal concepts and the multifarious particularities of phenomena in their final entwining as individuality.[53] In his reference to thinking here, Hegel means the content of the dialectic, and by the content of the dialectic he intends the work of logic itself. In this sense Hegel is asserting the essential cognizant or active life of the Idea in the development of its instantiations, a life which is immediate and active in thinking as well as the work of philosophy. For Hegel these instantiations span the range of the natural, abstract and subjective spheres and the *Logic* itself plays the role of elucidating the inner life of the Idea for itself. In our thought, as individuals, we are merely recapitulating what is universally true of all change as the unfolding and self-development of the ideal substance of the absolute Idea; an absolute, as well shall see, which is necessarily dynamic and in tension with itself. This self-opposition and negation for Hegel is equated with the truth itself, and is precisely in line with the young Hegel's dissertational assertion that truth is found in contradiction rather than non-contradiction.

Furthermore, in this early preparatory work, Hegel addressed the question of antinomies first raised by Kant, and expanded on them by means of his dialectical method. Kant's transcendental procedure initiated the interrogation of the formal foundations of facts themselves so as to allow for the possibility of induction from the underlying ontological assumptions of empiricism. This approach acted as a model for Hegel's logical project. His participation in it is a response to the epistemological crisis set up in Kant's work by Hume's skeptical empiricism as the exclusion of god, substance and the absolute. We thus find in the early propadeutic, and under the rubric of the Kantian antinomies, Hegel directly restating the centrality of the Eleatic thesis for modern thought in asking whether "absolutely necessary Being belongs to the world" or whether "There exists no absolutely necessary Being."[54] Veiled in the language of the question of the ontological existence of god, and the question of the intermingling of metaphysical substances, lies Hegel's direct appeal to an Eleatic origination for the dialectic. That is, he asked whether being is the necessary condition of reality, and therefore truth, or whether non-being, i.e., becoming and change, is the true. Hegel argued for the truth in both positions holding that "Every change stands under its condition" and must be understood in view of the necessity of a universal. All change presupposes, it is here held, that there is an ultimate and original cause which was unconditioned. The thread of necessity which runs through the objective world is annulled. However, the expression of this primordial being, understood not as transcendence but rather as a necessary immanence, permits change; without this ultimate permanence and being there could not be that which itself changes. From this standpoint of the dialectic the universal is the very fabric of intelligible reality. Considered from the inverse and negative perspective, becoming must be the true because the idea of an immutable being "contradicts the dynamical law of the determination of all phenomena."[55] In the doctrine of becoming, all phenomena cohere, not with a universal law, but rather with the principle of ad infinitum change where no permanent being can be evinced. Change is what is real here, and thought lacks reference to a standpoint beyond experience upon which it is able to ground the permanence of being and the universality it might be able to establish; knowledge is herein excluded.

Out of these two standpoints Hegel witnesses the opposition of the principles of the necessity of the being of an absolute, on the one hand, and the contingency of becoming, on the other. In the case of the former, the thread of being and becoming originates in a primary and unchanging being. In the latter the thread of becoming lacks any such foundation; it rather asserts that the unity of the former's position falters in the absurdity of infinite regression where being, though "contingent and conditioned, yet on the whole absolutely necessary and unconditioned ... is self-contradictory... for the reason that the existence of an aggregate cannot be a necessary one if no single part of it possesses necessary existence."[56] For Hegel these two positions demand synthetic coordination and being and becoming must be understood not merely in their opposition but in there reciprocity as well, where "neither of the two moments of causality is for itself and absolute, but that it is only the *entire circle*, THE TOTALITY, that is in and for itself."[57] The Eleatic origins of the problem of universals, the opposition between realist and nominalist conceptions of being, are in this way a driving and originating impulse in the working out of the Hegelian project of coordination, and are recovered from empiricism's reduction and dismissal of logic to the formalistic abstraction of atomic facts. As foreshadowed in the *Nuremberg Propadeutic*, and as laid out later in the *Logic*, the Parmenidean conception of unpunctuated being provided the point of departure for Hegel's dialectic of the universal. This starting point provided him with a basis to confront Heracleitean becoming and move onwards through the history of metaphysical thought as the working out and evolution of the absolute Idea itself.

## Introduction to the *Logic*

*Transition to the* Encyclopedia *Logic: between Eleaticism and empiricism*

Against this background of Hegel's earlier writings, it is the project of the reconciliation and mediation of universal and particular within the *Logic* which I will here explicate in order to outline, in turn, its critical value for an appreciation of his politics of reconciliation. I here examine the 1830 *Logic* in detail in order to outline what I hold to be Hegel's fullest representation of his metaphysical groundwork of a system of universals. Though the text is at times extraordinarily elaborate and voluminous in its attention to the minute details of the progression of thought both historically and logically understood, its unique attention to its own participation in this construction makes it extremely rich. Hegel's explicit and systematic intention is to find a dynamic model reconciling the universal and particular in a way which brings together both being and becoming in the classical sense. In carrying this examination out, I *exegetically* rehearse the *Logic*'s articulation and resolution of the problem of universals. Throughout this process I draw consistent contrast with Plato's scheme of universals as a means of tying together the historical threads of the problem of universals, as well as bringing Hegel's positions into greater relief. From this starting point and having considered the three phases of the dialectic of the universal, I will move on in the next chapter to relate these metaphysical concerns to the political arguments and concrete institutions of the *Philosophy of Right*. I approach the political framework of the relations of state and citizen in the *Philosophy of Right* by way of first deriving Hegel's consummate statement on the status of the universal vis-à-vis its particulars and their mediation in individuality from the *Logic*. This program represents Hegel's pursuit of a version of truth which rests upon his system of the universal, one modeled after the development of the absolute Idea in its movements through universal being, particular essence and the individuality of the concept.[58]

In the first third of the *Logic*, or what Hegel termed "Preliminary Conception," which I will attend to first, Hegel thoroughly distinguished his framework of terms and analysis from that of his contemporaries and his forebears. Prior to mounting the three primary moments of his system of ideas—being, essence and concept—he presented this rigorous examination and restatement of the categories of thought traditionally understood. In this way the 1830 *Logic* is different from the *Science of Logic* published during his Nuremberg period. Here his intent was as much elaboration as it was apology, and in this vein the chronologically latter restatement is far shorter and more succinct. Where Hegel compressed his coverage of the actual phases of his logical system in the latter text, he extended it to clarify and contextualize its arguments for his philosophical peers and students by way of its six-part introduction. In essence the *Logic* of 1830 provided a corridor to his thought by means of its direct accessibility to the ontologies then prevalent as "attitudes" of thought in order "to meet an interest of the day."[59] The most philosophically important of these were Kant's and, as earlier conveyed, Kant's logic and categories were points of departure for Hegel.

Prior to proceeding it may be asked why it is essential, in a chapter focused primarily on Hegel's attention to the problem of universals, to spend several dozen pages running through a variety of historically discursive arguments which Hegel felt were required to contextualize, introduce and defend his thought. To this question there are several very strong arguments which make the time and effort required for such an undertaking—for both author and reader—worthwhile. First, these sections provide a much needed elaboration of many of his concepts and the way they are differentiated from the terms which conventional logic and metaphysics have deployed in the past. Second, his articulation of the problem of universals and its particulars here, and the confrontation of philosophy and science which it evokes, initiates his program of their reconciliation in a way which specifically distinguishes his logic and metaphysics from that of his intellectual opponents. Finally, and perhaps most importantly, in these sections he renders his critique of the inherent limitations of both positivism and empiricism. Given that the present book spends two of its first three chapters dealing with precisely the legacy and meaning which these two schools of thought have taken up in relation to Hegel's thought, it is profoundly important to consider Hegel's own views and concerns on the matter.

The most serious misgivings expressed in the "Preliminary Conception" were with the epistemological principles of empiricism and its metaphysical implications. Perhaps the clearest trend and intent of this section is Hegel's methodical reformulation of the basic concepts of the positivist epistemology of empiricism so as to undermine its hold on his peers. The first third of the *Logic* is thus primarily critical and apologetic, and he left the positive, constructive work of his positive philosophy—speculation[60]—for the remaining chapters. Despite this segregation of the work, Hegel's attention to the problem of universals remains central to his progress on both fronts. Where the preliminary work laid down the main contemporary attitudes of thought to objectivity, Hegel spared no efforts in ameliorating the limitations of what he saw as the one-sided commitment of the modern sciences to the isolated particular and its catastrophic epistemological implications.

The problem of universals is introduced very early in the *Logic*'s introduction. Here the absolute is traced through its various instantiations and elaborates a constant connection of phenomena with a grand design. In this recognition Hegel took up Plato's project of concretely bonding ideas with phenomena, and extended it in seeking to give immense scope to the particulars of sense without sacrificing the universal as a prior and regulating content. In following this line of his thought, we see that Hegel's approach to the problem is similar to Plato's as it worked itself out in the post-*Republic* dialogs, though it is far more systematic and less insistent upon the unchallenged primacy of the universal. Hegel made clear, where his contemporary opponents and critics held "that ideas and ideals are nothing more than chimeras and philosophy a system of such phantasms,"[61] that the origin of the division of ideality and reality is had in the analytic strand of empirical thinking itself. The Idea, far from being the mere object of intuition or judgment is thus, in fact, the central object of philosophy:

> the idea which is not so impotent as to demand that it merely ought to be actual without being so and, hence, it deals with an actuality of which those objects, arrangements, situations, etc., are only the superficial exterior.[62]

Phenomena themselves are regulated by this supersensory sphere of regulative universals borne in the form of dialectic transformation.

Hegel's method for dealing with the divide of the real and the ideal proceeded from his assessment that philosophy in the modern world had come to cohere with a post-metaphysical bias towards phenomena and empirical reality. This for Hegel stood in sharp contrast to the Greeks where reason stands aloof and above the spectacle of worldly change in order to discern and establish its pantheon of immutable ideas; philosophy is thus turned towards the ends of empirical theory in its ascertaining "fixed measures and what is *universal* [*das Allgemeine*] in the sea of empirical particulars, and with what is *necessary*, such as the *laws* governing the seemingly chaotic and infinite mass of contingent things."[63] This subordination of the Idea and universal to the condition of material existence and experience, within the bounds of empiricism's reality principle, was very much the subject and sentiment of concern of Hegel's phenomenology as well:

> Time was when man had a heaven, decked and fitted out with endless wealth of thoughts and pictures. The significance of all that is, lay in the thread of light by which it was attached to heaven; instead of dwelling in the present as it is here and now, the eye glanced away over the present to the Divine, away, so to say, to a present that lies beyond. The mind's gaze had to be directed under compulsion to what is earthly, and kept fixed there; and it has needed a long time to introduce that clearness, which only celestial realities had, into the crassness and confusion shrouding the sense of things earthly, and to make attention to the immediate present as such, which was called Experience, of interest and of value. Now we have apparently the need for the opposite of all this; man's mind and interest are so deeply rooted in the earthly that we require a like power to have them raised above that level. His spirit shows such poverty of nature that it seems to long for the mere pitiful feeling of the divine in the abstract, and to get refreshment from that, like a wanderer in the desert craving for the merest mouthful of water. By the little which can thus satisfy the needs of the human spirit we can measure the extent of its loss.[64]

It is just this turning away from the life of the Idea and forcible adherence to the movement and fluctuation of empirical experience which motivated Hegel to reinstate a balance between the ideal universal and the phenomenal particular. He held this to be necessary if philosophy was to surmount its relegation to a mere tool for the organization of sense data taken up in the "seemingly chaotic and infinite mass of contingent things." Hegel's system of universals is thus not merely an antiquarian repetition and amelioration of ancient thought problems, but also very much a restorative and remedial task taken up in the light of the scientific and analytical revolution which severed metaphysics from its rational claim on the articulation of universal ideas in-themselves. The Humean and Kantian backdrops play just this generative role in Hegel's program, revealing the degree to which his metaphysical project calls forth a conceptual turn on the political in its rendering from Grotius to Hobbes to Locke and beyond. His direct response to the empirical credo is its inversion: "*nihil est in sensu, quod non fuerit in intellectu.*" His credo that that which is experienced was first in the intellect asserts the primacy of mind—*Nous*—as a strata of universals and the motor of all particular change. This very much coheres with Plato and Parmenides' belief that the world of sense is an objectification of ideas. Hegel in fact sites the Greek idea of *Nous* or spirit as the cause of the world and a kind of ceaseless "moving mover."

In response to the possible counterclaims of science against speculative thought Hegel surmised that, in comparison to the other sciences, philosophy must bring into its considerations a wider variety of categories of determinacy for its modeling of the universal in accord with the demands of necessity. That is, logic must not be seen as a separate discipline, but rather as the root which embraces all the laws of its subordinate branches, including science, in its aspiration for wider categories as they cohere with necessity and ultimately reason. A true philosophical science must be inclusive of, as well as go beyond, the empirical model to apprehend the universal and absolute: be it freedom in the political realm, spirit in the cultural or the divine in the religious. These universals, as the content of the concept or final universal, define the task of philosophy only in addition to the task of presenting the facts of experience and sense to which science limits itself.

As Hegel had brought out in the *Phenomenology* and restated in the *Logic*, philosophy reasserts itself in the modern condition in its hunger for the universal against the constraints of empiricism. The hatred of reason or "misology" which Hegel claims Plato confronted in his time, existed in his period as well. Though a philosophical science of reason's point of departure may be found in empirical experience, its completion cannot be. The universal, in both the ancient and modern cases, is only had in the wake of thought moving beyond its immediacy in sense experience, through induction towards the Idea which represents its universal identity. This is the archetypal genesis of philosophy in raising, inducting thought beyond immediacy towards universalizing reflection as is seen in the sweeping abstractionism of Parmenides. It is merely a first negation of the problem of becoming in the thought of being. It remains incomplete at this stage and faces a further opposition out of itself:

> it at first takes up a self-distancing, *negative relationship* towards that point of departure. It thus finds satisfaction, for the time being, within itself, i.e., in the idea of the *universal* essence of these appearances, an idea that may be more or less abstract (such as the absolute, God).[65]

Yet modern science responds to the demands of the metaphysical legacy in denying its overall form of truth and its juxtapositions of essence. Natural science for Hegel asserts a vision of reality which is composed of "a multiplicity of items placed *side by side* one another and thus generally *contingent*, and to elevate this content to necessity."[66] In denying the formal unity which binds the universal essence of classical thought, modern philosophy has left itself incapable of understanding the meaningful inner-relatedness of particulars despite the profound formal conditions, the grounds of necessity which bind them one to the other in a meaningful unity. Under these conditions science "tears thinking away from that universality and the implicitly [*an sich*] assured satisfaction and impels it to *the development [of the form and content] from out of itself.*"[67] Reason is emptied of its universalist aspirations and is reduced to the handmaiden of empirical and instrumental reason, altogether denied access to any categorical criteria which would allow the assertion, or appropriation, of underlying unity.

The tension between the abstract philosophical formalism of, say, Plato and Parmenides, on the one hand, with that of the concrete materialism of empiricism, on the other, is useful for situating Hegel's task here. The former represents a formalistic and vulgar realism where the intellect merely takes the diversity of experience, reflects upon it and ascertains its truth in the abstract. The intermediation of thought is not recognized and the contents of thought are taken as immediate with the facts of perception. The latter, on the other hand, impels the former to return to experience in order to justify its absolute and universal categories, rendering them vital to thought in practical terms beyond the abstract. Here the abstractions of pure philosophy are rendered such that experience itself may experience growth and advance. Hegel witnessed the circularity of the movement from experience to the absolute and vice versa as a reciprocating progression of scientific development grounded upon historical self-consciousness. He further articulated his middle ground between the metaphysical posture of the ancients and the moderns, arguing that "When thinking remains at a standstill with the universality of ideas, as is unavoidable in the case of the first philosophies (think of *being* in the Eleatic school, *becoming* in Heraclitus, etc.), then it is rightfully accused *of formalism.*"[68]

With Hegel as with the latter Plato, to assert only the ideal and essential of things in their reflection of the universal does not do justice to the universal, but rather renders its form without giving expression to the content to which it is bound and purposed. Modern science in this way ameliorates the inherent limitations of ancient abstractionism. However, in setting up a condition which denies the universal altogether, science is already ripe with the condition of its own negation—its own contradiction with itself—where it would strive to represent a reality beyond contingency, Brownian flux and the accidental causality of atomism. Hegel's philosophical calling emerges in this very confrontation of universal and particular, being and nothingness as the task of reconciling a sphere of formalizing and regulative universals on the one hand with an actual world of transient sense experience and phenomena on the other. The absence of either extreme, either condition for Hegel, would inherently undermine progress towards an adequate conception of the individual or singular absolute, one which is essential to the condition of truth and central to his project of philosophy. The dissolution or disavowal of the problem of universals is herein made inherently inadequate responses to the problem, and both Eleatic and scientific reductions are dismissed by Hegel.

*Overcoming positivism: philosophy and the dialectical reunion of universalism and particularism*

The evolution of thought and philosophy which Hegel rendered in the opening of the *Logic* recognizes an inherent development in the ongoing discourse of ideas with the universal. Here the architect is the "one living spirit"[69] which pervades all being. Unity is the mediated moment of spirit realizing itself both as object and subject, and the beginnings of its movement to a further stage of self-reflection. Thus, the dialectical clashes of the historical movement of the Idea, despite their outward appearances, remain coherent with the inner unity of the Idea as an organic project of self-knowing. This temporalization of the universal implies the bifurcation and pluralization of unpunctuated being into both subject and object. In this way, the overturning of the scholastic and neo-Platonic worldviews in the early modern and modern periods is witnessed by the emergence of an empirical orientation which particularizes thought and action. It is this view of phenomena which demands further amelioration in recognition of its inherently fragmenting implications for Hegel:

> The origin and development of philosophy as a *history of this science* is portrayed in the peculiar shape of an *external history*. This shape bestows upon the developmental stages of the idea the form *of contingent* succession and mere *diversity* of the principles and their elaborations in philosophies of them.[70]

In fact it is the unity of his thinking substance which binds all temporal thought and ideas to an ultimate stratum of universals, one which coheres throughout the evolution of thought and the history of ideas. Despite this legacy, and its apparent self-undermining claims for a break with the past, these systematic divergences are not incompatible with the unity of the universal. As is the case with the sphere of phenomena, thought in all its expressions also expresses an inner adherence with its universal as the framework which bonds all particulars with an ongoing pattern of development.

For Hegel, then, empirically oriented studies such as biology and geography are inherently grounded in reason and ultimately rest upon the Idea, but rescind this overt relation in the face of the authority and "singularity" of the empirical facts of experience themselves. The underlying universal basis of particulars is obscured in empirical research by its overriding commitment to outward and positive expression: "what is in itself a rational starting-point passes over into something contingent due to the fact that they have to trace the universal back down to *empirical singularity* and *actuality*."[71] As sciences they reflect mechanical, contingent and chance relations which obscure what, for Hegel, is the underlying spiritualized Idea and self-uniting relation of subject and object. The inner necessity in the regulation of the universal is obscured in these fields. This is the result of the dissipating of the universals which underlie nature into the various fields—geography, physics, anthropology etc. These forms of inquiry focus upon differentiated aspects of the universal and, as a result, are simultaneously made incapable of witnessing its unity. Despite their alienation, science may nonetheless get beyond itself and actually be made accessible to the universal which brings phenomena into the development of the Idea where "due to the opposition and manifoldness of the juxtaposed phenomena, the extraneous and contingent circumstances of their conditions sublate themselves, so that the universal then comes before the mind."[72] But this epistemological union of universal and particular itself is not the priority of the empirical sciences and only reflects its inevitable alienation from the underlying and meaningful unity holding together the facts which they individually assemble. The sciences all participate within the larger frame of the absolute universal or Idea, yet they are seriously constrained and largely unable to witness the fullest significance of their work by virtue of their methodological and metaphysical presuppositions. For Hegel, positivist presuppositions remain largely beyond the purview or question of the sciences themselves "insofar as they do not acknowledge that their determinations are *finite*. Nor do they point up where these determinations, together with their entire sphere, make the transition into a higher sphere."[73] The obscurity of the universal for these fields, grounded on the comprehensiveness of the particular field which they research in its specificity and richness, reinforces their alienation from the deeper implications of the knowledge they unearth; the forest is lost for the trees. The passage into the dominance of a reality principle grounded on the nominalism and particularity of all phenomena leads the science into a form of metaphysical obscurantism, one equal in its degree to that of the formalism of the ancients. On this account, then, the abstract and empty universal of classical metaphysics is as philosophically problematic as the sweeping metaphysical denialism of positivist thought and its canonization of the empirically discrete particular.

In Hegel's thought and system, the originating and philosophical "one living spirit"[74] is the original unity of the particular principles out of which arose the diverse schools of thought and science we are now considering. Each of these schools represents a singular moment and adequate system of philosophy for-itself, and are embraced by the unity of the Idea as shards of a single project of truth. The process and sequencing of the development of thought in this way witnesses the taking up and absorption of past phases of thought in the new. The historical dialectic of thought expressed in the *Logic* makes a record of this very process whereby the inadequate ideas of the past are subjected to the dialectical forces of negation and renewal. Yet the contradiction which undoes the thesis is already implied in its own shape making its negation—and the affirmative position that emerges with it—its own theoretical offspring. It is this internal development and dynamism of thought which does away with the formalistic extremes to be found in both ancient and overtly empiricist theory, where either the particular or universal are taken as a self-subsistent principle and reified. It is only the overcoming of the contradiction of the two which permits for a complete elaboration of the evolution of truth for Hegel, avoiding a view of it as fragmented from its own earlier forms as just so many particular and unrelated frames of thought in a historical stream of understanding. It is precisely this situation which led Hegel to declare that "When dealing with what seem to be so many *diverse* philosophies one must distinguish the *universal* and the *particular* according to their proper determinations."[75] Thus he held that the universal and particular, at the level of thought, must not be confused or conflated. The derision directed at philosophy as a collection of dislocated principles by the epistemological ascendance of the positivist sciences Hegel witnessed as resultant of this very condition. The fundamental metaphysical problem of universals is a basis for progress rather than an impediment

In its intent to better understand the unstable relation of universal and particular, the Hegelian program took concrete ideas as participatory in a higher or encompassing universality. The science of thought thus must view its subject matter, itself, as both a system of concrete instances and formal universal modes in order to arrive at a comprehensive system of truth. Truth is only possible by "collecting and holding itself together in a unity," "as such it is an *idea,* and in its full universality *the* idea, or *the absolute.*"[76] The science of logic is thus the systematic rendering of the life of the universal Idea in its diverse forms, modes and alterations in the concrete: its shapes. This ground of thought in his system of universals is therefore a precondition to political understanding and theory as well, and necessarily interrelates metaphysics in the Hegelian scheme.

As earlier discussed, the ideas presented by any particular system are themselves a completion, a philosophical and adequate whole on their own. Nonetheless, each of these philosophical entities participate in the final universal, Hegel's "absolute Idea," as their ground and antecedence. Each one as a circle of completion "bursts" its own limitations and births an all-encompassing "circle of circles" which embraces the whole project of philosophy. This expresses their essential idea in conformity with the absolute philosophical Idea which is their starting point and end. On this account, any system of thought which takes a particular principle out of the context of all the principles to which it has access is no longer philosophy. Philosophy as this unpunctuated system of universals thus sees the particular in terms of its originating universal as Idea, each idea a holographic reflection of the whole philosophical Idea as a "circle of circles" in constant contraction, opposition and expansion. This ideal circuit of philosophy lends the various branches of philosophy their truth value or content in view of their organic relation to reflection of the greater unity. Philosophy as a whole itself then is just this system of integrated universals in a single science and its primary condition. Parts are only true in terms of their being integrated and non-isolated wholes themselves, that is they too must possess their own universality.

In this outline of Hegel's plan of philosophy, we see a system of universals ordered at the level of theory prior to its application to the categories of logic, nature and experience. In fact, it is in its essence, as the doctrine of the concept will comprehensively explicate and consummate, an attempt at a self-ordering and self-generating system. This process of laying out terms and concepts prior to the actual work of the *Logic* is Hegel's way of elaborating the very terms of a system of universals and their particular predicates, and vice versa. In this Hegel sought to set up the formal conditions of a system of philosophy, one which would articulate a developmental understanding of the universal and particular as primary concepts. In setting out his terms of universal and particular and the general conditions of their dynamics of relation in this way, Hegel wove the problem of universals deeply into the very structure of his thought.

## Sense, concept and thought: from epistemology to metaphysics through reflection

Hegel specifies that the universal is the basic form of all thought. Insofar as it is also considered as the agent of thinking acts, it is an active universal realizing itself as its own end. Thought is thus the generation of the universal in-itself and, in this sense, the latter is intimate with its very identity: "thought, is *the universal, the* abstract in general. *Thinking* as an *activity* is thus the *active* universal."[77] For this reason the universal is self-actualizing thought as subject, and the "I" which takes the universal as its foundation and its purpose in the concept, the ground of the Idea. For Hegel the metaphysical problem of universals is herein identical with the question of self and identity, and it is through this lens that he pursues its reconciliation with its particular other in sense and experience.

Like Plato, Hegel distinguished between the universality of conceptual thinking and the particularism of the senses in hard terms. Through the organs of sense humans perceive the individuality and specificity of that which is acting upon the senses. In simple terms, the agitation of the senses brings about the awareness of an objects' existence in conformity with the conditioning structures of the senses themselves. At this level, the multiplicity of sensible objects external to the self represents atomic units which bear no inherent or internal relations with each other; they stand in isolation at the level of phenomenal individuality and flux. Thus far his view accords with the central tenets of empiricism. Yet, at the higher level of the process of conception in picture thinking (*Vorstellung*), thought draws closer to the universal than does the raw datum of sense experience. Here mind presses together a representation of the various elements of experience, both of sources external and internal to consciousness, into a collation of relations and similarities. This is to be understood in the sense of an association of like properties taking the shape of generalizations which fall short of understanding their basis in the universal.

At yet a higher level, thought itself stands in direct and aware reflection of the dual nature of the self, the "I" which at once expresses itself to the negation of all others and at the same time excludes itself and all others from the self. This self collects the isolated fragments and associations of conception and impresses upon them a more complete universality which is the beginning of philosophical understanding. This transpires in the identity of thought and self such that the essence of self is universality and vice versa: the "I is the universal in and for itself, and the commonality is also a universal, albeit only an outer form of universality."[78] This raises sense and conception to the level of identity and the reciprocal relation of subject and object united in thought[79] is raised to the level of the subject. In this way the universal is necessarily bound up with the life of the self, standing in autonomy to the contents which it itself thinks. Thought and the universal are herein made indistinguishable from thinking, feeling and sensory experience for Hegel. In this sense the universal is ever present regardless of whether the subject overtly recognizes in its immediate form of self-consciousness and awareness:

This is why the I is thinking as a subject, and because I am at the same time present in all my sensations, representations, and states, etc., thought is present everywhere and permeates all these determinations as a category.[80]

This self creation of the self in and through the universal, in thought as well as language, is the ultimate basis of freedom in its ability to take hold of that which is foundational to its own formation. Thought captures and discloses the essence of the thing thought as well as the thinking agent. This is the outflanking or overreaching[81] of both the other and the self in thought by the universal, in anticipation of each other so "that thought and the universal are just this, namely to be itself as well as its other, that its reach extends over the other, and that nothing escapes from it."[82]

This dialectic continuity of universals with particulars entails that intermediate universals are derived as subordinate strata of greater universals. These latter are herein both a universal and a particular, as in the case of the German people and the genus which is a member of its own species. Where the "I" is taken up into a universality which is the basis of abstract freedom here, it retains itself as its individual self and yet simultaneously stands in partnership with the universal as its outward expression. Thus particulars and individuals are, in their very essences, composed and conditioned by the form giving power of the universal such that it is impossible to speak of the particular or individual without at the same time meaning the universal; "when I say 'I' I *mean* to refer to myself *as this one* individual, excluding everyone else. But what I say (namely, 'I') is precisely each and every one."[83] The universal is thus a pervasive force in the generation of thought and language and, in this Hegelian framework, requires rigorous consideration in order to stabilize any discrete conception of the particular and individual, if at all. This framework reveals the outflanking Hegelian universal as the ultimate form of both itself and its other, posing the challenge of the particular's ontological subsumption in Hegel's resolution of the problem of universals. As will later be examined, this apparent primacy of the universal stands as potentially controversial where it is understood to challenge Hegel's overt project of its reconciliation with the particular.

From this picture of Hegel's coordination of the senses and their relation to abstraction, Plato and Hegel again seem to stand on similar ground. Where on Plato's account the problem of universals arises in consciousness through the experience of the contradiction of the senses, on Hegel's it emerges with reflection upon experience in terms of the question of essence. In the latter case, a division arises between the transient experience of phenomena and the desire to understand what the phenomenon is in-itself, in its essence. This divests the outer show of the empirical of its finality and vests thought with accountability such that the "phenomenon is ... made double" and an inside and outside, reality and appearance, diverge. On Hegel's account, the outer and transient is the thing governed by the senses, and the inner and permanent—the immutable in Plato's terms—is deemed the true and universal. Reflection (*Reflexion*)[84] is thus that form of thought which pursues what is universal and permanent in contrast with what the sensible appearance provides to experience in terms of its individuality and evanescence. Reflective thought is just this original attempt to find one in the many and the universal amongst its particulars.

In this context of the emergent problem of universals for thought, Hegel tells us that the mind asserts the need for unity and aspires to find the universal in every case when it is confronted with the seemingly endless diversity that the senses present to the mind. As the individual elements of experience are transient we cannot grasp their being, their identity in the singular instance and so look higher to the species. At this level of thought and mind, reflection seeks to ascertain the governing principles which would lend stability to the apparent chaos of phenomenal world. Out of this inductive process, the universal, the essence of these phenomenal instantiations, is posited as alone true and remains unknowable to the senses without this engagement of reflection. Hence, the division of the experience of the senses and the universal understanding of reflective thought is established hard and fast. The immediacy of the senses comes to stand in a complete contrast to the "mediated, inner and universal" which alone is attained through thinking. Hegel here takes God as archetype of this form of universality and as "an absolute through which everything else has been generated."[85] The universal, the territory of the mind alone, is substance to the outer appearances of things despite their silence and seeming dissociation from one another and the self in experience. This stage of philosophy remains formalistic and, after the nomothetic power of the universal of thought, represents a metaphysics dissociated from the particulars of experience.

Yet phenomena as presented in experience do not provide the grounds for the acquisition of universals in themselves. Rather, the mind or reason must apply themselves to the facts of the senses so as to introduce the concepts which order them in reflective thinking. Hegel asserts that this application of the mind seems to contradict the philosophical intent to see things as they are beyond our purposes. Such purpose is the act of reflection and the inner being or essence of a thing may be seen in this way alone where "it has been the conviction of all times that only by reworking the immediate, a reworking produced by thinking things over, is something substantive attained."[86] Reflection then is the application of mediated, human thinking to the intelligible essence of the perceived in experience: the mind as universal encountering its world as particular other, and becoming aware of the gulf that separates the two. It is a seeking after the universal, always already inherent within the self, in the other so as to reunite what was the prior alienated content with a broader universal: Hegel's permanent substratum of the concept as the self-aware universal.

It was only with the onset of rigorous empiricism and skepticism in the modern era that this epistemological bond between the mind's idea and the object of perception had been truly challenged. As discussed earlier, Hegel largely attributed this rupture, theoretically, to orthodox empiricism. In this context, he disagreed with the common and widely held skeptical view of philosophy as a diseased science, and he took it upon himself to return thinking to a confidence in the ideal-realist unity and coherence of the thing and the thought on the ground of the universal. In coherence with the universal and its particular facts, thoughts take on an objective character in addition to their subjective side in reflection. With this Hegel asserted that "*Logic* thus coincides with *Metaphysics*" because both deal especially with the nature of thought and "expressing *the essentialities of things*."[87] The problem of universals is thus not merely an abstract metaphysical problem which Hegel took up to reunite substance and subject, world and mind; it is also at the very heart of the intellectual engine which generates his dynamic of self and other relating through ideas. In other words, the problem is not merely metaphysical, but social, psychological and linguistic as well, and, by extension, inevitably political.

In its articulation of the universal to this point, the *Logic* has developed a language of metaphysics which circumscribes and "outflanks" the divide of appearance and reality, particular and universal, and unifies them in the self-organizing and developing thought which is a person: thought is herein understood as an active agent. The *Logic* itself was intended as the historical and evolutionary compendium of this thinking personality and its attempt is to bring it to a completed self-understanding; a metaphysics of metaphysics which extends and fulfills the demands of the Kantian transcendental logic. The dialectical resolution of the universal to the particular is thus the amelioration of thought as well, and the completion of the one implies the resolution of the other. This goal of final resolution of universal thought in the Hegelian system, its final resting place in self-aware identity, is the concept, and this level holds within itself all prior moments of the universal as sense, conception, thought and reflective activity.

*Limits of the "understanding": speculative philosophy and the particular elements of a universalist logic*

Having found that the subjective and objective are entwined in the universal, we have arrived at the first stage of consideration of what Hegel refers to in the *Logic* as "understanding" and with it his science of particulars. Here the identity of things is admitted insofar as mind is able to apprehend the existence and subsistence of a thing qua identity. The ability to know the particular secures the universal for the mind, and vice versa. Understanding as *Verstand*[88] is this basis of knowledge and is the faculty or moment of thought which recognizes and frames the universal:

> the logical sphere in general is to be construed not merely as a subjective activity, but instead as absolutely universal and therefore at the same time as objective, this is to be applied to the understanding as the first form of the logical as well.[89]

Far from being a mere interpreter or passive observer of the universal, understanding itself is in its essence the developing universal, and only recognizes itself and its nature in that which it circumscribes and thinks in thought. Hegel compares this arrangement to the religious notion of the goodness or grace of

God which begets to all things the capacity both to be and to persist as individuals. It is this very capacity to exist within the universal and to simultaneously persist in particularity that grounds understanding. This faculty's ability to grasp differentiation is what provides for the basis of knowledge in a mediate form:

> understanding shows itself in every domain of the objective [*gegenständlich*] world, and it belongs essentially to the perfection of an object that the principle of the understanding receive its due in it. Thus, for instance, the state is imperfect if a specific differentiation of estates and professions has not yet emerged in it, and if the political and governmental functions that differ in accordance with the concept have not yet been formed into specific organs in the same way as is the case in the developed animal organism with its different functions of sensation, movement, digestion, etc.[90]

The universal disclosed in thoughtful understanding is the first moment of the acquisition of the discrete expressions or instances of the universal in objective form. The practice of the understanding, whether in the workings of botany, biology or statecraft, represents the human ability to arrest the universal in the flux of experience, to stabilize it in thought and to merge it with the demands of reason. With this first moment of the dialectic in understanding reason has not yet made its full appearance and, rather, remains merely foreshadowed and obscured within the as yet unrevealed dynamism of the dialectic. Understanding recognizes the overt universal and distinguishes between sense experience and its acquisition of essence.[91] Yet here it remains fixed and is unable to overcome the hard dichotomy of the appearances of sense datum on the one hand with the mutual exclusivity of the abstract universal to which it adheres as its own thought identity on the other.

Though impeded in its own right, the understanding's distinction between wholes and parts is a necessary element in the strivings of Hegel's philosophy to secure its fulfillment in the truth of the absolute Idea as *Wahrheit*.[92] The truth obtained by the understanding, however, is finite and does not fully cohere with its concept. As with Plato's conception of the polis, truth as the fulfillment of the whole is attained in the proper working out and fruition of the individual parts in coordination with the universal.[93] Dialectic is the subsequent movement of logic and proceeds from its point of departure in the understanding. It finds relation in the analytically discrete results of the understanding and brings context to its parts so that "In its distinctive determinateness, the dialectic is far more the proper, true nature of the determinations of the understanding, of things, and of the finite in general."[94] Dialectic moves beyond the understanding in bringing limit to the identities which the understanding has disclosed, and in doing so fixes the limits of the categories of the understanding for thought where "the one-sided and limited character of the determinations of the understanding presents itself as what it is, namely as their negation."[95] The power of the middling moment of the logic, of negation, thus leads to the supersession of the findings of the understanding which, at first blush, seem to stand as totalities unto themselves. This is precisely the blind spot which Hegel declares to be the limiting principle of empiricism.

The discrete identities of the understanding are not merely limited by virtue of the limited nature of the faculty. Rather they are limited from within by the very nature of their own particularity for Hegel. They are thus not merely creations of its analytic practice and thereby a subjective or psychologistic reflection of its limitations. The finite contains, of its own nature, its own limitation such that "life as such carries within itself the germ of death and that, generally speaking, the finite contradicts itself in itself and for that reason sublates itself."[96] The categories of the understanding are herein not merely the epistemologically alienated impressions of this faculty upon the contingency of the entities to which it applies itself. Rather, dialectic discloses the unreflective character of the finite understanding in its particularity where the former's purpose is "contemplating things as they are in and for themselves" and to demonstrate "the finitude of the one-sided determinations of the understanding."[97] Dialectic is herein understood by Hegel to be no mere theoretical method but rather the very working of life and of all change. Human beings, he claims, feel this level of existence and understand it naturally. The awareness of the fluidity of reality, Hegel's dialectic of the finite, and the inevitability of change is just such an awareness and through it we are inevitably confronted with its opposite. Here Hegel references Plato and Parmenides, recognizing through dialectic the inconsistencies of an atomism which bases itself on the finite abstractions of the understanding. It is just such a dialectic inquiry which evinces its opposite by virtue of its own nature in common experience:

> We know that all finite things, instead of being something fixed and ultimate, are really changeable and perishable, and this is nothing but the dialectic of the finite. By virtue of this dialectic, the same thing (as in itself the other of itself) is driven beyond what it immediately is and turns over into its opposite.[98]

Dialectic is a Heracleitean force for Hegel, where all finite things are subjected to transformation though being, in contradistinction to Heraclitus, remains.

Having passed beyond understanding, Hegel outlines the philosophical limits of dialectic as well. The inability to move beyond the negative, beyond dialectic becomes a spurious theoretical position which is the failing, for example, of modern skepticism. Here the fixation on finitude and the particulars of experience in and through understanding are overcome and, as with Hume who represents this phase of thought for Hegel, all knowledge seems to slip away. Yet this finitude is merely the outward appearance of the forms of understanding and requires a further stage of inquiry to recover its certitude for objective knowing: the positive philosophy of speculative reason.

*Spekulation* is the synthetic and sublating turn on the understanding's opposition with dialectic. It is speculative in Kant's sense of pointing beyond immediate sense certainty to a cognitive view of the objects of experience.[99] However, and unlike Kant, in passing beyond the particulars of the understanding and the dialectics of their contradiction to the reciprocity of speculation, Hegel sought to insulate his system against the nihilism which he saw as resultant of modern skepticism and its roots in empiricism. Though Hegel's dialectical logic of negative transformation also implies the formation of a new unity, the sundered presuppositions of this negation, the deposed universal[100] per se, are preserved in and through it. The formation of this new whole from the destruction of the former unity into parts invokes the third moment in speculation which "contains within itself that from which it results, containing the latter as something it has sublated, and is not without what it has sublated."[101] The negation thus contains its own overcoming, and so gives way to a positive result in its moment of completion. Speculation as the completion of the dialectic here moves beyond both understanding and dialectical negation, and is the truth of both for Hegel. It affirms in the positive the result of the logical opposition and reciprocity of these two former terms and so reinstates the universal which had first been reduced to a finite particular—at the level of understanding—and then altogether renounced—through dialectical negation. The reinstated universal, though, now resides at a higher level having taken into itself and absorbed its surpassed moments. In this way the dialectic is the process which elaborates the progressive movement and development of the universal through its various objective formalizations. Though these objective forms represent the transformation of the thinking or ideal substratum of the universal, the universal is itself ultimately unchanged, having found a merely more adequate outward form in surpassing its prior constraints.

As the foregoing brings out, the results of speculative reason are concrete thoughts which move beyond the "mere abstractions" of the understanding and its negation in dialectic. They are the outcome of the synthetic unity which bind the conceptual oppositions and fragmentation of the former two stages of thought. All individuals, for example, are made rational in their awareness of a like completed universality in the laws of one's nation. Subjection to the universal is the attainment of rational freedom at the level of the particular and Hegel describes this logical posture in political terms: citizens willing the laws of their state. Thus reasoning is the mediation of the universal at the level of the individual will. This capacity for the integration of part and whole is the merit which Hegel references in asserting the inherent rationality of all human beings regardless of how they reason. The individual will recognizes the universal power expressed in the dicta of parent, state or god and herein its own will is fulfilled in the broader scope of speculative rationality. Speculation clearly commands more than the transformations of natural phenomena and the historical forms of thought. It is also directly related to the political dialectic which ideally orders the ethical world and its institutions.

In response to critics who would reject an all-encompassing speculative system as incapable of resolving the pervasive oppositions of thought, Hegel boldly claimed that speculation is explicitly what contains those oppositions at which the understanding stops short (thus including the opposition of the subjective and the objective) and contains them as something sublated within itself and precisely by this means proves itself to be concrete and a totality.[102]

Speculation is herein Hegel's comprehensive system of logical resolution and integration. It is expressly intended as the system which brings together the finite and infinite, whole and part, so as to bring logical meaning and purpose to the seemingly insurmountable opposition which the universal and particular, objective and subjective seem to impose at the levels of the understanding. The logical meaning of Hegel's interpenetration of opposites as the conclusive moment of the dialectic in response to the problem of universals appears as a mysticism to the obstructed condition of the understanding. In Hegelian terms, and as we will explore further below, it is the syllogistic coordination of all phenomena and thought which presupposes a former synthetic basis in the universal of the speculative moment. That is, without the antecedence of the speculative or positive universal as the closure of the dialectic of understanding and negation (i.e., universal and particular), no such opposition would have been possible to begin with. The opposition itself is the progressive objectivation of the Idea or absolute universal[103] which at all times coheres with itself as essence. The grand universal merely alienates itself through these prior phases, returning totality and unity to its parts through their the cycle of dialectical transformation and generation.

As Hegel has made clear, the methodological and ontological individualism of atomism inherent to empiricism is inherently a limiting and constricting epistemology. The question of the universal at this level is only accessible at all because thought is unable to get beyond the pluralism of sensory experience so as to relate itself to its experience. In this way thought acts as a bonding substrate between the "seemingly chaotic and infinite mass of contingent things"[104] and the unified and substantial whole of universality inherent to thought itself. Although the negation of the understanding stands directly before it in the form of the unity binding and relating all particulars together, the farthest empiricism may go towards its own revision is its own negativity in radical epistemological skepticism. The simplicity of the speculative method overcomes this in its assertion of the universalist rationality which underlies diversity and the mere appearance of incontrovertible opposition in the logical status of phenomena. What takes on a necessarily rational character in speculative thinking remains a mystical impasse to the analytic understanding.

As discussed above, the first third of the *Logic* was explanatory and apologetic. His task to this point has been to dismantle the prevailing intellectual attitudes of his day and to offer general correctives outside of a comprehensive system. With the task of theoretical and essayistic reconciliation complete, the segue to the systematic work of the *Logic* has brought us to its point of departure in being.

## Being

### The Parmenidean origins of the dialectic

The history of philosophy for Hegel is a series of successive understandings of the absolute, and this narrative represents the development of the Idea towards its consummation. As each emerges and surmounts the last it does not deny its core, but rather transforms it and absorbs its content in the process of negation and speculative affirmation. "The One" of the Eleatics is the first thought phase of this evolution in the understanding of absolute being. This is the absolute of immediacy and indeterminacy and therefore remains wholly abstract; the universal understood only in terms of its universality. This represents not only the beginning of thought but the beginning itself. The serial development of philosophy therefore witnesses not the fossilized remains of the corpses of the ideas of the past for Hegel, but rather vital and necessary stages on the way to the present, and as such, the intellectual past is always present:

> the history of philosophy deals not with the past, but with what is eternal and absolutely present, and its result must be compared not to a gallery of errors of the human spirit, but rather to a pantheon of divine figures [*Gottergestalten*]. These divine figures are the various stages of the idea as they emerged successively in the dialectical development.[105]

This "pantheon" of the Idea, one which the structure of the *Logic* mirrors in its recapitulation of the dialectical phases of the historical and active Idea, begins with this development and especially with Parmenides' first thesis in his *On Nature*: Being alone is, and Nothing is not. Where the dialectic moves from the wholeness of the universal to the particular and completes its cycle in the individual, the initial phase of being presents the universal in its isolation as the starting point of the logic.[106] The search for the meaning and ultimate status of universals is thus a point of departure for Hegel. The Eleatic conception of "the One" as absolute being is herein taken as the first philosophically coherent utterance, within the putative Western tradition, as it directs itself to the problem which phenomena present for the stability of universal ideas themselves. Thus for Hegel as for the Eleatics, the problem of universals runs to the heart of the philosophical project, and, for Hegel at least, unites the partisans of philosophy in a timeless dialog—his Pantheon of the mind—seeking to ameliorate the controversy of the whole and the part, the mind and the senses, for thought.

Despite the fact that the Eleatics remained in a static and abstract conception of pure being in metaphysical understanding, Hegel recognized that to admit of an "other" to being, that there is being and its other, is absurd. What remains for being, he claimed, is precisely to confront nothing and to sink into it as opposite so as to gain the fixity of determinacy and become concrete. That is, in Hegel's elaboration, being must become something other than itself, and that is precisely the diversity of the concrete and real. This is none other than his temporalization and pluralization of being and its accessibility to the dialectic; a process regulative of both thought and materiality in their expression of the universal Idea itself as their basis. As Hegel says, no matter what primordial starting point you begin with as originating substratum, with being "whatever else may be made the beginning ... it is at first only something represented and not something thought ... [which] is only being after all."[107] In the history of the development of the Idea, "being" is the first moment and invites its own negation and moment of dialectic. Naturally, the negation of being comes in the form of "nothing" and with this Hegel confronts the impasse which both Parmenides and Plato recognized as a sophistical, and profoundly treacherous, pitfall for thought.

The dialectic of being thus set up, Hegel recognized the almost inseparable unity of being and nothing, the very same aporetic relation which Plato and Parmenides worked out of. Here the pure abstraction of being, its inability to possess any parts or characteristics, any predications, which would in any way bring about a discretion of its unpunctuated continuity makes it wholly abstract and indeterminate: being is "absolutely devoid of all determination, and nothing is the very same lack of determination."[108] In this way thought is left with no reference with which to mark off being from nothing so that the division between the two itself resides only in name. As categories these two terms have no further logical superstrata to refer to: there are no higher species which might unite them. The uniqueness of this dyad, being and nothing, makes their very distinction difficult to justify beyond the empty abstractions which the two terms represents as a polarity. The resolution of the indeterminate opposition between them is manifest in the subcategory of "becoming" as *das Werden*. Heracleitean change alone brings these two terms out of their abstract opposition into the concrete.

At the level of the pure abstraction of being and nothing, Hegel took it as a difficult truth that they may be equally held identical and opposite. The opposition exists for the mind alone though it can find no ground in either upon which to assert the distinction. This is Hegel's purest conception of immediacy, one which veils within itself both the in-itself and the for-itself so that both understanding and dialectic (universal and particular) are present, but undifferentiated. Though being and nothing present apparent stillness and identity, it is their internally mediated tension which brings about the possibility of becoming. Hegel explicates the dynamic: "the unity [of being and nothing] that as relation to itself is not merely immobile, but is within itself against itself on account of the difference of being and nothing contained in it."[109] No empirical reference to corporeal entities or things tangible can offer any resolution to the identity of these two terms for that would be to evade the thoroughgoing level of logical abstraction and formality at which they are meaningful. It is this inaccessibility to experience which Hegel realizes will perplex most who approach these categories with an empirically grounded commonsense in hand. The problem of universals at the stage of being is really *only* the problem of the universal, for particularity is not yet admitted and remains wholly latent. Things which instantiate the universal may not yet be said to exist such that the universal, itself, betokens nothing but itself. For these reasons, the Eleatic plane of thought is pure abstraction and remains a mere hypothetical starting point in the development of the idea.

At the same time, it is through this movement of ideas that the contention between Eleatic being and Heracleitean becoming is seemingly resolved. Being and nothing remain impassable in themselves as abstract opposites. The abstract conundrum is overcome only *in time* and gives birth to becoming as that which unites both, forming the first realization of the Idea in the concrete. Taken out of its abstract form and made empirically accessible, the Idea at this level discloses the presence of the universal in phenomena and that which remained merely formal is made substantial, particular and determinate. For Hegel this is a clear testament to the completion, rather than ineluctable contradiction, between the Eleatic and Heracleitean positions. The pure being of Parmenides melts into the nothingness which is at its very heart, and expresses an absolute unable to move beyond the abstract in the form of determinate being. The ineluctable tension within this intangible and nebulous unity is finally exploded in the appearance of change and differentiation. Being and nothing only become "true" in the form which emerges through their union in change. For this reason, Heraclitus completes and overcomes the impasse which Parmenides, and Plato, saw in the impassable conflict between the absolute universality of being and the degenerate particulars of transformation. It is in this light that Hegel subverts traditional logic to the metaphysics of a dialectic where truth is borne of contradiction, not of non-contradiction. That is, in looking at terms which either do not possess opposition or evade it, we look only at a singular idea in its abstraction and not its actuality in development. In fact, all terms and categories are mediated, and so stand in a relation of contradiction to each other as expressions of the universal syllogistic basis of the dialectic. Common scientific sense, understanding, and its demand for non-contradiction misses this crucial point and, for this reason, is unable to come to terms with the simultaneity of the coexistence and yet distinction of being and becoming. It is only through this recognition that Hegelian logic is able to surmount the crisis of the one of mind and the many of the senses, an expression of the problem of universals, which confronted the ancients.[110] He witnesses the failing of the Eleatics in Zeno and Parmenides' inability to move beyond an all-encompassing definition of being, desperately running the dialectical gambit in the hope of divesting becoming of all ontological merit. In this manner they arrived at systems which were distanced from the movement of these foundational categories of the dialectic and the real results which spring from their interactions.[111]

Despite this overcoming, the problem of universals persists and is implied in the very realization which becoming has brought to the abstraction of being in its incapacity to find form. That is, in becoming, being has not been undone as an immutable ground of universality and its capacity to found permanence and ideal stability is retained. Hence, the question arises as to what becoming has itself become:

contained in our representation that when there is becoming, something comes out of it and that therefore becoming has a result. But there then arises the question how becoming manages not to remain mere becoming but to have a result.[112]

Thus the particularization of being through its mediation with nothingness and its concretion in becoming, does nothing to undo the truth of the universal, of the Idea.

The question here raised, as to what becoming has become, goes to the heart of the ancient debate. The flux of negation which has exhausted being and nothingness has realized a new form as determinate being. That is, for Hegel becoming is a "fire" which "extinguishes" itself in the process of surpassing the former opposition; becoming itself as unceasing creation and negation. In doing so it recreates the old opposition of being and nothingness, but this time in a fixed form. In catalyzing the sublation of the dyad, becoming itself is overcome and returns to rest in its new found form: that which has become as determinate being. With the dialectical cycle complete, we have arrived once again to being, though it has been transformed by the interactions of its real and ideal, concrete and abstract potentialities. This form of being then stands as the first moment of a new cycle and the previous dyad of being, nothing and becoming, gives way to a new one. The genesis of actuality here begun is the transformation of real particulars through the dialectical development of the universal Idea. Absolute and unpunctuated being is undone and yet preserved in the world; the word made flesh.

In light of the self-generating dialectic of being, and in direct reference to Plato's *Philebus*, Hegel addressed the issue of limit and limitlessness (*Peras* and *Apeiron*). Here the particular instantiations of being mirrors the universal Idea so that, despite its changes and alterations through becoming, it adheres to its own nature at all time and in all places insofar as it is has been made concrete. Hegel agrees with Plato that the admixture of opposites brings about reality and reflects the truth that both ideas and material process express the same ideal dialectic; it is not a question of the universal or its particulars, but of the one *and* the other. The finite, which as determinate being is in its essence reality for Hegel, is that which has its limits but remains potentiated to change. It is alterable and thus mutable. However, this mutability is the very reflection of its being, and the notion of existence as its inherent concept is the expression of its essence. Thus the ideal universal shines through phenomena, and despite modal transformations, remains true to the unchanging being which identifies it, as if a shadow, in the limit to which it necessarily adheres.

This is what it means to be a self, an identity in essence, and such a limit immediately entails an other. Being in reality is always construed in this mediate form and embodies finitude as the content of the limit. The infinite thus set up in and against finitude fails as a true infinity, and cannot be understood under the category of determinate being. That is, insofar as there are two categories—finitude and infinity—this infinity stands as the mediate other of finitude and therefore only as a particular. This infinity is not the infinity for which philosophy searches, the "true infinite" with which Hegel portends the absolute. The ad infinitum of finite empirically observable parts is just such an example of a false infinity, and Hegel admonishes against such thinking. This is the very same dialectical admonition which Plato issued in his *Philebus* against premature approaches on the absolute, being and the One. Hegel then remains true to Plato and rejects conflations of either unitary or manifold finitude with the infinite. With this Hegel makes his own overt borrowing on the advanced logical developments of Plato's corpus.

## *Quality, quantity, measure*

Hegel's declaration on "the One" is clear: it cannot issue at the point of the indeterminate and abstract being which satisfied the Eleatics. Rather it approaches the completed form of determinate being as a particular of the understanding which is a quality. Identity emerges so as to make fully discrete an entity as a whole being for-itself in Quality (*Qualität*). Though this remains ideal, as it retains negative demarcation excluding others from its self-definition in mind, it is an infinite and self-completing "One," and moving beyond Eleatic logic, the one natively proceeds to the many. The negativity inherent in the being-for-self of the One potentiates its own overcoming in reality. Therefore the unitary nature of the One is overturned and gives way to a plurality of ones, each of them a self-completing and negating unity repelling its others in conformity with its being for self such that the "One" is the "Many."

In addressing the limitations of Eleatic logic in this way, Hegel put the question of the one and the many and of the problem of universals into stark relief: "When we talk about the One, the first thing that tends to occur to us is the Many. The question then arises where the Many come from."[113] Here, the universality of the one as being is the very precondition and starting point of the many as its particulars; they are co-dependent though the One is prior: "the One constitutes the presupposition for the Many, and it is inherent in the thought of the One to posit itself as the Many."[114] The internal negation of "the One," by its own mediating negativity, Hegel termed repulsion which he borrowed from physics. The connotation is that in the corpuscular existence of each thing, its self-identical and atomic identity as an exclusive and self-completing being, lies the necessary exclusion of all others. But Hegel goes further than this. The repulsion is not merely directed outwards, it was first an inward force of differentiation and individuation which then overcomes and rends the original unity of "the One" into the many, the universal into its particulars. With the cycle of both negation and concrete inception so presented, we have the introduction of sublation (*Aufheben*) as that force or momentum which brings together both. The whole then has become parts which are wholes in themselves and being moves from a logical state of quality to quantity.

To stop at this waypoint of the dialectic in declaring the unlimited physical alterability and transformation of being in quantity would be no more than a

*Hegel's metaphysics of thought* 137

vulgar materialism, and this for Hegel is a defect of the Enlightenment to be surpassed. The atomism of modern physics takes being in its plural and material forms as its absolute and sets up the many Ones as its final truth. More importantly, this has become the abiding atomistic metaphysics underpinning liberal thought and society:

> According to this view, the will of the *individual* as such is the principle of the state. The attractive force is the particularity of the needs and inclinations, and the universal, the state itself, is [based on] the external relationship of the contract.[115]

The development of modern science and politics stops with this repulsive particularism of concrete being and goes no further. For Hegel, amelioration of the limits of atomism comes in the form of measure, resolving the interior tensions which riddled the first two moments of being: quality and quantity. These two adhere in this one, and being retakes a fully concrete form.

Measure stands as that which unites the limited and unlimited, finite and infinite. This balance of measure between quality and quantity creates the condition for the particularizations of being in its many concrete forms. Thus not only a change in quality, but threshold changes of quantity too—extensive or intensive—transform being. Descartes' wax at the quantum of one temperature or another may be said to be vested with a different being: solid or liquid. Differences made to quality beyond a certain degree transforms a being from its current state to another as well. Quantity and quality are here understood to be held within measure as their abiding harmonization, one which signals the complete rendering of being and a passage to the question of the regulatory logic of the instantiations of this determinate being as "essence." Measure reconciles the universal finite with phenomena, being with becoming, such that the fluctuant changes of static being are in fact no more than alterations on its quantitative and qualitative arrangement. In this way he follows directly on Socrates' declaration in the *Philebus* that "when I speak of the third class, understand me to mean any offspring of these, being a birth into true being, effected by the measure which the limit introduces."[116] The limitless, in opposition, brings being to all things, and it is the limit which contains them within themselves. Quality and quantity are the expression of the admixture of finitude and infinitude for both Hegel and Plato.

With being thus fixed, mediate and capable of differentiation, pluralized being becomes implicit essence. "The One" of abstract being has become the many of concrete and determinate being, and the universality of diversity of phenomena themselves are for the first time recognized despite their outward display of transformation and diversity. With the universality of unpunctuated being restored through its resolution with the particular in measure, Hegel has delivered the *Logic* to the sphere of the particularized and mediated universal in essence.

## Essence

### Existence

At the level of essence, philosophy takes as its goal the task of linking up the outward immediacy of things with the recessed essence which grounds their particularity in existence. The being of the universal Idea sits immanently behind all transitory phenomena and the latter are understood as a "curtain" behind which essence is "hidden." Essence is a mediate reflection of being within the transitory thing, the penetration of the universal into the particular and we here witness Hegel's continuing attendance to the problem of universals and his redress of the shortcoming of dualism in the triadic structure of the dialectic. That is, he strives to provide wide range and play for both phenomena and the universal—the development of the universal Idea—without ever detaching one from the other. In so doing, he calls attention to their mutual permanence in the ongoing play of the universal within the plurality of phenomena:

> It then is also not enough merely to traipse from one quality to another and merely proceed from the qualitative to the quantitative and vice versa; instead, there is something enduring in things and this primarily is the essence.[117]

This permanence is the outer and actual or objective reflection of the universal in a mediated form; each thing identified under its universal, and all universals subsumed within the self-differentiating absolute Idea.[118] The movement and diversity of essence in phenomena must not be seen as their autonomy from being itself but rather its appearance in concrete existence.

Once the ground, the antecedence, of an existent is brought forward so as to bring together identity and difference within itself—the "indeterminate set of concretely existing entities [*Existierenden*] as reflected-in-themselves"[119]—reflection is confronted with a panoply of causes and effects. Reflection is just the mediation of thought in its moment of negating a former immediacy in the movement of the particularization of the universal thought: it is the light of the universal thrown upon into itself so as to provide mediation and distinction between a one and an other, between particulars as moments of universality. Within this river of the flux of essences, reflection and understanding themselves find no ground upon which to establish any higher principle or "firm foothold," nor unity in this "colourful play" of phenomena. From this point of view, all is in constant motion and relation, and nothing coheres with itself or any other in a way which discloses unity:

> The reflecting understanding makes it its business to investigate and pursue these ubiquitous relations; but the question concerning the final purpose remains unanswered in the process and, hence, with the further development of the logical idea, reason's need to grasp matters conceptually passes beyond this standpoint of mere relativity.[120]

At the level of the concrete interplay of existent causes and effects, the universal Idea is in its least apparent form, and the outward appearance of things at its most complete in the flux of causality. It is only speculative reason which preserves the Idea for this state of apparent affairs, making a further progression both possible and necessary; thought's pursuit of its final purpose remains yet latent due to the Idea's identification with sense experience at this stage.

## *Appearance*

Hegel's equivalent to the Platonic concept of becoming lies in his idea of appearance (*Schein*): though becoming is moving away from being for Plato whereas essence is an authentic appearance of the truth and moving towards its consummation as a universal in the Idea for Hegel. Here, being is mediated through the expression of essence into actuality so that what appears "is." This projection of being in appearance represents its movement as it "shines" through essence into existence. The universal's self-differentiation, its emanation per se, is its particularized and outward expression—"show"—of its universal basis. Thus, existence in the form of appearance finds a kindred detachment from being in these two stages in the development of the Idea: essence and existence. These remain mutually excluding for Plato, but Hegel, to avoid either a hard dichotomy or their conflation, stressed that appearance is not to be taken as a mere and false show of phenomenal flux or a mere "congeries" of events in a causal chain. Rather, existence is the outward form of the universal expressing essence in its immediacy where "appearance posited in this way does not stand on its own feet."[121] Instead, it stands precisely on its universal grounds, its antecedence in the movement of the active universal or Idea.

It is here, in the realm of the problematics of appearance and phenomena, that Hegel directly addressed the notion of Heracleitean becoming and sought to overcome its hard opposition with Eleatic being:

> When we speak of an appearance, we associate with it the representation of an indeterminate multiplicity of concretely existing things whose being is simply mediation alone and which accordingly do not zest on themselves, but instead have validity only as moments.[122]

The relativist notion remains unable to pass beyond the outward façade of the phenomenal so as to penetrate to the essential dialectic. Like Plato's shining absolute good-in-itself, Hegel witnessed an "the infinite goodness" which overflows being so as to allow "it the joy of existing." The immanent show of being in existence is always expressive of being. Hegel's immanent essence of things distinguishes between the discrete expression of the essence taken in its isolation as against the essence which is self-supporting. By this he argued that essence, and later existence, may be taken in terms of the particular only. Yet this logic does not undermine the self-standing autonomy of essence which is both the contradictory and identical moment of being. The latter configuration as opposed to the former preserves the continuity between the ground which shines and the light of appearance itself. It is the very difficulty and importance of theoretically preserving this continuity which drove Hegel to so rigorously critique the logical and epistemological failures of empiricism and Kantianism at the outset of the 1830 *EL*. The importance he here held is in understanding, that it is not the opposition of a substantive immediate being with a merely phenomenal becoming which brings the truth of actuality into relief. Rather, the recognition that the latter is what manifests the very actuality of the former and contains both moments within itself so that "appearance is something higher than a mere being." This configuration is missing in both ancient Eleatic and modern empirical understandings where the former plays out the valorization of being over becoming, and the latter dismisses the former altogether to vest the positive and empirical particularizations of becoming with a final epistemological validity and, therein, an inherently necessary causal continuity.

In relation to the question of being and becoming, then, Hegel had no difficulty in taking a wholly anti-Eleatic, anti-monist stance on their relation. Where absolute being remains static and as yet undifferentiated and developed, it has not yet passed through the phases of differentiation which bring to being a synthetic unity of self and other, whole and part. This has yet to be accomplished and, given this, he is able to hold that appearances offer us a richer category than immediate being.[123] Parmenidean being is as yet wholly unmoving and incapable of relation and correlation.[124] This stated, the necessity of finding fluid theoretical relation between being and becoming takes Hegel directly from the explication of essence to that of correlation in terms of the universal whole and its parts. The ascendance of being moves from a condition of pure immediacy through phenomena towards differentiation, all the while preserved as the ground presented in existence and experience. Yet what Hegel and Plato both witnessed and shared was the need to move beyond the Eleatic monism of absolute being, and to begin to come to grips with the metaphysical substantiality and significance of phenomena as they present themselves to the senses. Nevertheless, though they work this out at the level of the problem of universals quite differently, they both have this restorative project firmly in mind. Actually, Hegel credited Kant as the first modern thinker involved in "rehabilitating the ... difference between ordinary and philosophical consciousness."[125]

## *One and the many as content and form*

In the context of appearances and as background to his doctrine of essence, Hegel took up the logical question of the universal formally restated in terms of the physical paradox of the whole and its parts. As has been articulated, essence sits between being and its final actualization in the Idea and it is here that the work of intermediation of being and becoming, universal and particular, carries on. Prior to approaching the question of the whole and the parts, Hegel worked through the question of the nature of form and content and found their fulfillment in accession to the categories of whole and part in terms of relation and correlation. That is, form and content are at once a unity in terms of their grounding the "subsistence" or independence of an object in its transformation. At the very same time they exist as binary in their "revulsion" to each other such that the unity is fractured:

> one and the same, [namely] the content, is as the developed form, as the externality and opposition of self-standing concrete existences and their identical relation, the relation in which alone the differentiated elements are what they are.[126]

The relation of form and content, as the logical grounds upon which phenomena are transformed, is thus the logical germ seed of the problem of the whole and its parts. Form and content at once represent logical wholeness and integral object substantiality, namely, their unified opposition to external existence, and at the very same time express an inner opposition of identities which rescinds the whole.

Plato found the phenomenological origins of the problem of the one and the many in the mind's desire to overcome the conundrum which the singular body composed of parts presented for logic. Hegel deepened this insight, presenting us with a progression which articulates a body or thing in terms of the dialectic of the integrity and revulsion of form and content where the whole is essential content and the parts are form. Though the parts possess independence, their identity is necessarily grounded in relation vis-à-vis the whole. Where the part is necessarily part it is at the same time necessarily the whole and not part; the latter being the negation of the former. This relationship of whole and part is understood at the level of appearances and as the outward show of essence. In this way the metaphor of the whole and its parts is widely accessible to thought, though equally prone to misinterpretation in its appearance as a merely mechanical relation of materiality reducible to physical laws. Restricted to the level of understanding, the latter conceptualization is precisely the epistemological rock upon which positivist and empiricist accounts founder for Hegel.

The problem of universals expressed as the opposition of whole and part for Hegel was the result of "low-level and untrue concrete existences."[127] That is, the lack of harmony which appears from the conflict of form and content, part and whole, is merely a failure to recognize the larger correlative context to which the whole and part refer in their movement from self to other-relatedness. The notion of the whole is to contain parts, but if the whole is taken and made what its inner concept implies, i.e., if it is divided, it at once ceases to be a whole. Recalling Plato's *Sophist*, Hegel issued a direct reply to the sophistic claim that what is called "untrue" attributes being to that which is non-existent: that that which is false is something which itself must be true, or that the nothing which we postulate must therefore be a something. Hegel here asserted that the untrue is not a verification of non-being, but rather a recognition of the alienation of the universal Idea and the forms of existence which it temporally takes. This alienation he held to be reflective of analytically oriented philosophy and its inability to witness the dialectic of correlation which regulates the relation of the whole and the parts.

Beyond the correlation of form and content, *force* unites the movement of particulars and so bonds the whole to the parts and the parts to the whole, reinstating the momentum of the dialectic. It is the condition of identical self-relation and negative self-relation. At first the whole is made content where self-relation gives way to a process of reflection into self. The latter is self-revulsion and makes an other of itself:

> What is one and the same in this relationship (the relation to itself that is on hand in it) is thus an immediately negative relation to itself and, to be sure, as the mediation to the effect that one and the same is indifferent to the difference, and that it is the negative relation to itself that repels itself, as reflection-in-itself, towards the difference, and posits itself, concretely existing as reflection-into-another and, in reverse direction, conducts this reflection-into-another back to the relation to itself and to the indifference—the farce and its expression.[128]

The whole and the parts are equally both, but they originate in the relation of the whole to itself as a whole; its universality in inward-reflection. The consciousness of the Idea pervading the whole immediately posits the self as other and cleaves the whole as whole so that self becomes other. This intermediating consciousness is the force which regulates the mechanical relations of the whole and the parts in their objective and natural forms. As the unifying factor in the mechanical causality which serially unifies and divides wholes to parts and parts to wholes, force is immanent in their relation which for Hegel stands as "the process of the identity-with-itself turning over into diversity."[129] The relation of wholes and parts is, as was implied, a condition of causal relation. The fallacy of the problem of the whole and part is thus best expressed in the ad infinitum absurdity of the reduction of the whole to its parts, which in turn becomes wholes, etc. Force is the concept returning relatedness and integrity to the impossibility of materiality which the problem of universals, of the whole and its parts, implies for material existence. In this way it is clear that Hegel did not merely wish to undo the appearance of the dilemma of the universal. Rather, he wished to show its positive necessity for the progression of the dialectic in its dependence on the internally self-rending orientation of the universal and its capacity for self-diremption out of its own immediacy.

The whole then is finally the content which unites in itself the relation of the parts as its identity and essence. Force acts as the mediating power which brings about the transition of the whole into its parts and simultaneously preserves the whole in the relation of the parts such that "The empty abstractions, by means of which the one identical content is still supposed to obtain in the relationship, sublate themselves in the immediate transition, the one in the other."[130] Force itself gives way to its own externality in its unceasing dependence on external antecedence such that it too is subject to the problem of the whole and the parts:

force as a unity falls apart in the analytic consideration of its conditionally discrete causes and effects. The creative instability of the universal is here recapitulated throughout.

The seeming instability of the grounds of the dialectics of causality appear to require a further description and elaboration. That is, the condition of essence as appearances has reached its limit of self-consistency and requires a further logical discourse of resolution. Where appearances formerly arose out of the ground of essence and have come into opposition with it, the seemingly outer with the inner, a further progression is necessary to bring back together the condition of existence with its concomitant manifestations. This is done in a way which seeks to overcome the empirical dilemma which the physical problematic of the whole and the parts implies. The collapse of essence as the doctrine of the particularization and negation of being has brought about the moment of their reconciliation. With this overturning of the understanding's and dialectic's principles of being and essence respectively, the moment of speculative reconciliation and modernity has arrived to posit the singular individual.

# Concept

### *The subjectivization of substance*

In choosing a path to the absolute, Hegel rejected Spinoza's substance as a one-sided abstraction. The concept of substance falls one step short of the doctrine of the concept which accommodates universality, particularity and individuality. In short Spinoza's "oriental" shortcoming was, for Hegel, to be found in its monological relation of transitory and subordinate parts to a singular whole of substantial being. This being, be it god or nature or both, Hegel decried as a finality that falls short of the properly "Western" principle of individuation which demands intercession and mediation between the whole and its parts. Though Hegel's theological reduction of Spinoza's concept itself appears unconvincing given the prolific textual reflectivity of Spinoza's Judaism, he is nonetheless making a hard distinction between his own philosophy and what he considered to be the last vestiges of scholastic metaphysics. To the scholastics a proposition was held to be either true or false culminating in the argument that a thing was either finite or infinite. This bi-polar logic is rejected by the speculative premise. This said, in his critique of Spinoza, Hegel imposed the philosophical demands of modernity on the metaphysical tradition, a revolution in thought he identified with Leibniz's principle of individuation and the dawn of a modern era of thought.

Hegel was herein drawn into the final chapter of his logico-metaphysical project to surmount the challenge of the universal in a way which valorizes neither extreme in the rendering of absolute totality. This moment introduces the concept (*Begriff*) as the immediate and preliminary form of the whole sublating and overcoming Spinozian substance where "The concept is the *free* [actuality] [*das Frei*] as the *substantial power that* is *for-itself* and it is the *totality,* since *each* of the moments is *the whole* that *it* is, and each is posited as an undivided unity with it."[131] Thus the reasoning will and freedom of the parts is equalized with that of the rational and universal whole, and made co-immanent with it so that substance is made subject. The phenomenal expressions of the parts present the outward existence of the spiritual whole as their immanent content; the concept as the absolute whole or universal particularized. This inherent othering is Hegel's grounds for the principle of freedom through which he witnessed the fulfillment of self in the other that is "the liberation of having itself not as other but of having its own being and positing in something else actual with which what is actual is bound together by the power of necessity."[132] In this way Hegel presented a heterodox vision of the absolute as self-moving and creative, in direct contravention of the Eleatic metaphysics of being or the Aristotelian unmoved mover in stasis and unvarying equilibrium. The reflective realization of necessity at the level of the whole here requires the volition of the individual subject, and presents the foundational form of rationality for the appearance of moral autonomy in the individual. This identity of particular and universal Hegel called "I" and subject, and represents the concluding phase in the historical and logical emergence and self-creation of the absolute—Hegel's self-proclaimed contribution to the history of thought as well as the thought of history.

Immediate being is here in the final stages of self-reflective development in its transformation to self-aware substance, having passed beyond the phase of reflective being in the form of essence which could not move past the problem of universals. The final form of the concept as self-identical—the coherence of all parts with their universal concept—in the dialectical dynamics of the absolute Idea closes the circle which unites immediate being with its spiritual self-rendering as a self-knowing and individual thought. This cycle is the basis for Hegel's absolute idealism which takes the form of the concept as the preliminary and developmental mode of the Idea in all its stages.

Hegel sought to insulate this process of the speculative overcoming of the universal and particular divide from the charge of formalism, holding that the case had been successfully made for the inseparability of form and content, appearance and existence and universal and particular. Against his empiricist critics, the concreteness of the speculative concept is intended to fuse and overcome the distinction between real and ideal. While the ideal is no logical prison for the parts, it is nonetheless absolutely necessary for the coordination of their common identity in difference. Thus, and as was earlier brought out, the material metaphor of the whole and the parts is shown for its conceptual weakness in addressing the philosophical problem of universals:

> the concept may also be called "abstract", if by "concrete" one understands what presents itself to the senses as concrete—what can be perceived in any immediate way at all. We cannot grasp the concept as such with our hands and, when it comes to the concept, we generally have to take leave of seeing and hearing. Nonetheless, the concept is at the same time, as already noted, the absolutely concrete, and indeed is so insofar as it contains in itself being

and essence, and accordingly contains the entire richness of these two spheres in an ideal [*ideeller*] unity.[133]

Being and the sphere of becoming in the doctrine of essence are herein related and given continuity in the life of the concept. The universal whole is nowhere found as given in empirical experience, but must rather be sought in and through the life of the mind which apprehends the Idea behind it. Hegel's assault upon the myth of the empirically given,[134] one he began in his *Phenomenology*, insists upon the epistemological reciprocity of thought and its objects in experience. The Idea which they both express and reflect takes up a divergent evolutionary course, the first a spiritual one in the historical world of thought and philosophy and the latter a material one within nature.

## *The individual and syllogistic resolution*

For Hegel, the universal occupies a special significance in the elaboration of the concept vis-à-vis the individual; the individual as the third and closing moment of the dialectical circuit. The universality of the concept must be understood as distinct from the mere form of abstraction in which commonalities are collected and separated from differences so as to stand as a pattern of general relation. His choice to move beyond the language of the general universal, to speak of universals as inherently mediated by particulars, is derived from the logical threshold beyond which the concept has moved and which distinguishes it from the universal as an abstract generality:

> the universal factor of the concept is not merely something common, opposite which the particular has its standing for itself. Instead the universal factor is the process of particularizing (specifying) itself and remaining in unclouded clarity with itself in its other. It is of the most enormous importance as much for knowing as for our practical comportment that the merely common is not confused with the truly universal factor [*Allgemeinen*], the universal [*Universellen*].[135]

The universal is thus the immediate ground of the self-generating concept. It is the source of all other and subsequent dialectical activity—the ground of Hegel's absolute idealism—and is further refined in his notion of the absolute Idea both here and elsewhere in his corpus.[136]

In his doctrine of the concept Hegel appealed to the harmonizing and synthetic logic of universality which holds within itself the subordinate moments of mere universality and particularity: the universal at the level of the concept has converted being in the abstract into a concrete and actual form. Though the concept itself coheres with individuality—the absolute as individuality totalized—and this individuality is the sole concrete form of the concept, it is nonetheless the universal which defines the basal and creative form of the concept itself.[137] To what extent this valorization skews Hegel's proclaimed equalization of the universal and particular is called into question. Further, whereas the universal is self-particularizing, the individual remains effective on its own and is, as such, the subsistence of the particular alongside the former's creative priority in terms of both form and content. This problematic runs against Hegel's claim for individuality as the "reflection-in-itself of the determinacies of universality and particularity ... [which is] *determinate in and for itself* and at the same time identical with itself or universal."[138]

This issue and the problem of universals for Hegel's theory, as he openly recognized, springs from the challenge which the independent universal presents for the unified concept as a precursor to the absolute Idea.[139] Where Hegel addressed this by positing the prior creativity of the universal from which the particular springs, he seems to have evaded the problem of the opposition of the universal and its parts and achieved resolution through dialectical temporality. That is, in starting with the universal of the concept which self-mediates, the particular of the concept is made dependent on the former's dialectical antecedence. Hegel however denies, in the case of the concept, that any such antecedence is supposed where the moments of the concept are understood as indissoluble. Yet, and in response to Hegel's claim of the concept as the "truly first" and "is not to be considered something that has a genesis at all," the particular must reside in its autonomy alongside and in independence of the universal. This must be the case if, in fact, the universal at the level of the concept is subject to mediation which retains its autonomy and contains mediation within itself. The universal he claims always resides in mediate juxtaposition with the particular and does not reside in a state of prior immediacy such that it is "free sameness with itself."[140] This universal of the concept, in its constant tension with its other, is also particular and the resolution of the opposition is attained only at the higher level of the concept which takes up within itself the synthetic character of the universality deposed at the lower level. This configuration, however, challenges the finality of the concept and asks whether it does not merely present one amongst many moments in the ongoing life of the dialectic of the universal. As well, it challenges the concept as the absolute in asking whether it is not merely an elevated instantiation of the universal which is always already present.

The status of the universal, looked at under this aspect, thus seems not merely problematic for the particular, but for the concept itself. Hegel may reply that the status of the universal as inherently mediated has been established, but it has only been so for the dialectic in general and not for the unconditioned absolute. Where he wishes to establish the concept on the basis of the interpenetrating moments or functions of the universal—the particular and individual—we witness a problem of logical generation or transition: either the self-creating concept as the whole is formed at the expense of the substantial identity of its subordinate parts, or the parts persist in their meaningful identity so as to deny the possibility of their subsumption and sublation in the concept as a complete whole. Faced with the presence of the seemingly irresolvable dilemma of the universal in Hegel's discourse of the concept, the problematics of holding both to a position of dynamic permanence and differentiated unity emerges. The problem seems to arise from the bowels of the Hegelian apparatus itself and calls our attention to this aspect of the dialectic of the universal in his further elaboration of its development.

Anticipating these issues, Hegel offers us an epistemological justification of the syllogism as an ontological foundation. Here, as with Plato's good-in-itself, the concept is made the ideal foundation of all actuality and "the fullness of divine thoughts." It is through the creative power of this basis that all truth is disclosed and put beyond origination:

> It is wrong to assume, first that there are objects which form the content of our representations and then our subjective activity comes along behind them, forming the concepts of objects by means of the earlier mentioned operation of abstracting and gathering together what is common to the objects. On the contrary, the concept is what is truly first and the things are what they are, thanks to the activity of the concept dwelling in them and revealing itself in them.[141]

It is the primordial stuff of reality, its completion realized in its subjective spiritualization as the absolute Idea with no reference beyond itself: *Causa Sui*. Here Hegel holds that the three moments of the concept—universal, particular and individual—are composed as an "inseparability of the moments in their difference ... in which no difference interrupts or obscures the concept, but in which each difference is instead equally transparent."[142] However, as has been presented, he also posits the universal in a way which conditions the particular and the individual. This is presented quite openly where he states that the particular of the concept is "universal in itself," and that the individual itself is a substratum of universality. For these and the prior discussed reasons, the formal primacy of the universal takes on a privileged position in the development of the individual where the former is held as the express ground or outward objective appearance of the latter. Hegel's concept as the basis of the actuality of reality as well as the union of the natural and spiritual worlds thus seems to give the universal primacy in relation to its parts and their unification in the individual. The autonomy of the parts and the individual then seem yet to stand in questionable autonomy.

## *Judgment*

The judgment of the concept, both in the abstract and in the action, is the witnessing of the immediate presence of the universal in the individual. As was previously elaborated these two are inextricably linked in strict Hegelian terms at the level of the concept, and for this reason judgments are not mere subjective propositions of objective reality but rather the Idea realizing itself in its other. The orientation of modern empirical and formal logics to dissociate the predicate and subject are here put in check. In actuality, the inherent intimacy of the universal subject and the individual predicate come to form the particular only through their syllogistic interplay.

On Hegel's account, the equilibrium of the tripartite syllogistic structure is held in the circular, rather than hierarchical, structure of its relations; each express the other two in mediation and negation. Thus the concept passes over into the cognitive act of judgment which is its further particularization, its movement towards final self-specification and its differing with itself in the moment in which a predicate is ascribed to a universal. This specifying of the universal makes particular its otherwise abstract content and whole, while at the same time preserving the prior universality within it. Here then a form of mutual interpenetration restates the equalization of the universal and particular in the individual, and upholds the Hegelian circle against the charge of the overdetermining influence of the universal. The judgment takes the Idea a further step towards actuality, and the movement between its original formalizing potential and realization is the difference between, as Hegel described it, the universal "root" and the fully grown and particular "plant."

At this point Hegel sought to further establish the reconciliation of the universal and individual of the concept through the dialectic of the judgment, rendering a clear relational and reciprocal unity between the two extremes. The judgment bonds together the two in the copula "is" at the level of the particular, holding between the two extremes of any statement so that "The individual is the Universal."[143] In this statement, the copula discloses the prior interpenetration of the universal and individual, predicate and subject, such that neither stands as an isolated entity vis-à-vis the other. This "negative self-relation" persists at the level of particularity and holds the two extremes together without overcoming the one or the other. The universal remains empty and abstract until the specifying moment of the individual is arrived at in conceptual judgment so as to bring predicate into subject and hold them together.

From the subjective ground of the concept which brings about the judgment in order to specify and articulate the universal, the object itself as sheer individuality becomes possible. The concept moves from the ideal ground of subjectivity at the level of concept to articulate the internal negativity it possesses as its "negative self-relation" "in which the universal is this *singular* totality that has returned into itself and whose differences are equally this totality, which has determined itself to be an *immediate* unity by sublating mediation."[144] The initiation of the transition of the subjective concept to the objective descends to the individual from the level of the universal such that:

> the *object* in general is also the *one* whole, in itself as yet indeterminate, the objective world in general, God, the absolute object. But the object equally has difference within it, breaking down in itself into an indeterminate manifold (as objective *world*) and each of these *individuated entities* is also an object, an existence [*Dasein*], in itself concrete, complete, self-sufficient.[145]

Thus the fragmentation of the concept from the level of the subjective to the object witnesses the differentiation of the universal from an abstract to a positive and actual content.

To sum up and clarify this phase of thought, Hegel here wished to outline the modern analytical mood as one which equates the object particular—the simple individual itself—with none other than the universal. He held that it thereby restrains the universal to an intermediated participation in things through their predications, circumstances and accidents and dismisses and denies the unity of the concept. Hegel framed the discourse of the judgment in the context of his understanding of modern empirical and positivist thought where "In this connection the subject counts as something obtaining externally for itself and the predicate as something occurring in our head."[146] Here he directly alluded to his earlier criticism of the reductionist tendency in Hume and Kant and beyond, asserting in contradistinction the reciprocity of both universal and particular in the ongoing generative capacity of the logical dialectic of the Idea. From this point of view, the concept that particulars are comprehensible outside of their universal, and so do not bear relation to the concept, is made spurious.

This moment in the *Logic* denotes Hegel's own point of epistemological as well as historical departure from the intellectual development of his Enlightenment predecessors. It is the last moment of temporal reflection on this period, permitting for Hegel's own embarkation on the amelioration of these formerly undisclosed contradictions inherent in thought in central recognition of their own self-inclined tendency towards negation and further development.

## Syllogism and the object

### Mechanism

With the concept of the object fulfilled in judgment, being is once again found in its immediate, though variegated, form. The object represents a specialized moment of the universal for Hegel, one which at the very same moment qualifies as a particular of being in its object status per se:

> It breaks down into differentiated [moments], each of which is itself the totality. The object is thus the absolute *contradiction* of the complete self-sufficiency of the manifold and the equally complete lack of self-sufficiency of the differentiated [moments].[147]

In the object the universal is found intact where the former preserves the whole in the dependence of the parts alongside the very moment of their individuality as independent moments of multiplicity. The condition of the object here, then, is the very definition of the problem of universals, the specter of the universal raised by the implicit unity and relation of particulars. As with the subject of the concept, previously considered, the universal finds equalization and equilibrium with the particular so as to permit further instantiation in the form of the individual. The progression from one stage to another, from the dilemma of the fragmented whole to its resolution in individuality, represents the elaboration of the concept as it transits to greater forms of complexity. As will be examined below, this is achieved in ongoing reflection of an initial teleological potentiality actualized over time. In the case of the *EL*'s doctrine, itself, this is the human historical progression of philosophy as it relates to itself in its completed form: Hegel's pen as the owl of Minerva's flight at dusk. In its political instantiation, as will be examined in the following chapter, Hegel witnessed the emergence of this reconciliation in the form of the modern social and political arrangement of *Sittlichkeit*. Clearly, in the case of the logic, as opposed to his phenomenology, the life development of the Idea is understood in terms of a philosophical evolution originating with Parmenides. The philosophical consummation of the object for Hegel took form in the philosophy of Leibniz's monads as discrete totalities which sustain difference within themselves, and first represented the object in its harmonization of universality and particularity.

The mechanical relation forms the first thought of the object of the concept and is equivalent to the condition of ethical heteronomy for Hegel, one founded upon arbitrary authority. That is, mechanistic thinking contains in itself a passive recognition of discrete forces enacted upon things which seem to wholly determine their content through an otherwise formal and external series of relations. This connects itself to the level of essence which dealt with correlation and causality but at a higher level. Here Hegel made implicit reference to the materialist and physiocratic thinking of the early and high Enlightenment. This mode of the concept, of thinking, at the level of the object is itself unreflective in that it participates in a cognition of the object from its externality only, dismissing its concept as content. This form of thought is limited for Hegel and remains incapable of integrating the conceptual realms of subject, object and nature, and is thus able to pass no further. Mechanism is thus a dogmatic mode of inquiry with a "pretension of occupying the position of conceptual knowing in general and making mechanism the absolute category."[148] The attempt to read all knowledge spheres and phenomenal relations in terms of this mode of thought becomes a reductive practice which divests these of their meaningful and inward basis of relational necessity in their concept. The relation of the object as part with the object as independent whole is the dynamic basis of "absolute mechanism" and is best described by the inquiries of modern physics for Hegel.

Beyond physics, the syllogism of the object expresses the deeper correlation of the dialectic such that each moment—particular, individual and universal— each play a role as extreme and intermediary: the "relative centre" of the syllogism is in flux, and the shift from particular to individual to universal as mediating moment brings the latter two into the central position as abstract and absolute forms. That is, transient objects are the subject of the mechanical concept and expose "[t]he flawed *individuality* of the objects *lacking self-sufficiency* ... [which] is, in keeping with its lack of self-sufficiency, just as much the external *universality*."[149] Thus, the merely external or positive assessment of the object is the limit of the mechanical concept, one which dismisses the three varying and unstable moments of dialectical transition. This science of the object here takes its form in the abstract opposition of universal and individual, and so is unable to realize the reflective subjectivity which would allow it to genuinely understand their relations. This rigorous yet one-dimensional conceptual framework at once brings about the grounds for the immensely useful and precise findings of the empirical sciences, and at the same time presents its most obvious limitations for thought. Here then absolute mechanism, which rules the relations of the solar system in its configuration of a center, its satellites and their own gravitational sub-systems, becomes the analogue for a social system centered upon the universal "gravity" of the state. The metaphor only carries over in a form which approaches the objective externality of the social order, and not its inner subjective spirituality. The latter, as we clearly witness in the *Philosophy of Right*, awaits reconciliation with the objective sphere in order to form the spiritual universality of the historical state in direct reflection of the absolute Idea.

Though it is only a formal reflection of the political order, the syllogism of the object does capture the objective relations of the sphere of spirit. For example, the individual citizen at first is related to the state as universal through its particular needs as a member of a family. Second, and at the same moment the same individual intermediates between the system of particular needs procurement and the maintenance of the whole in civil society. Third and last, the universal as state forms the permanent and underlying "substantial middle [term] in which the individuals and their satisfaction have and acquire their fulfilled reality, mediation, and subsistence."[150] That is to say, the state provides the ground of mediation between private individuals and the social and institutional network through which they reciprocate and exchange. These three syllogisms,[151] are all necessary moments in the final elaboration of the organization of both the natural and historical, objective and subjective worlds. This reveals the ultramundane presence of the syllogistic form itself as the structured and persistent system of the Hegelian universal. In this way each part contains the whole, while the whole holds the parts, and, as pointed out before, the universal plays the exceptional role of the 'grounding ground'.

*Chemism*

The concept surpasses mechanism in the framework of chemism: "a reflexive relationship [*Reflexionsverhältnis*] of objectivity."[152] The neutrality and indifference of the causal sequence of mechanism is overcome and the parts overtly reveal their inherent drive towards relation: "the absolute drive to integrate themselves through and with one another."[153] Chemical interaction involves the triad of syllogisms and the difference with the mechanical concept in general is marked specifically by the overt inherence of relationality in a causal chain of differentiation. Chemism thus opposes the indifferent interactions of mechanism and so realizes the possibility of order and purpose as the rudiment state of organization. This negation through chemism brings an end to the merely formal moment of the object. This initiates the liberation of the universal of the concept in teleological thought, bringing to a close the opposition of the abstract universal in and against its dynamic parts.

## Teleology

Teleological thought is the beginning of the concept's final transition to the Idea. Through it the immediate object is held in opposition with its other as the "contradiction of its identity with itself opposite the negation and the opposition posited in."[154] In this sense the universal recognizes the necessity of its own negation as a purposive act of self-preservation. This implies the demand of closure which seeks to overcome the contradiction in a way that it "has joined *itself* together *only with itself and* has *preserved* itself."[155] As with all former states of synthetic transition from completed sublation, the isolated as well as correlated objects are given over to a higher form of causality which declares a "purpose" and final cause. No longer does thought recognize in the relations of the object a mere superficial relation in force. Rather, the purpose or telos is disclosed in the realization of the object's identity with its concept such that it overcomes this mere positive objectivity.

Borrowing on Aristotle's conceptualization of rationality, the telos-driven nature of the object expresses an inner process of rationality revealing itself in its self-transformation. Here, the effect, as the cause of the cause, becomes the basis of the rationality which reflects the teleological context of the dialectic such that "the cause ... [is in] the effect first a cause, and does it come back *into itself*."[156] Thus the object truly becomes itself in its fulfillment of its inherent concept in accord with reason as the inner map or plan of its conceptual development. The rational purpose of the effect inheres within the cause as a presupposition, and inverts the otherwise monological causal relation mechanically, or chemically, understood.

The teleological moment of purpose realized in the final cause unifies subject and object. This transpires in the course of what Hegel termed the "the dominance of the purpose," and here a purposive design realizes the inherent unity of the former opposition of subject and object. This, in fact, is the very objective of the purpose, and it too rends the division between form and content, the parts and the whole, asunder. This process is the self-realizing or disclosing of the concept as it moves through its layers of development at the level of the object. The object of the concept is here in a constant and negative relational development with the former subjective level of the concept. This is a creative development for Hegel and each step is an ongoing upwards progression not merely in relation to the former opposition, but to the triads which these former oppositions themselves contain as their own substantial and syllogistic grounds as well: "This form of syllogistic inference is a universal form of all things. Everything is something particular that joins itself as something universal with the individual."[157] The teleological realization of the purpose or final cause in the concept appears to subjectivity as finite and impermanent. Despite this appearance, Hegel assures us, however, that an "absolute Good" abides as the more permanent and "eternal" basis of objective reality. This Good stands in direct contrast to the subjective and instrumentalist good of human volition and interest which annihilates the object and its truth, and seeks to imposes its own wish.

Despite its overt intent, the latter form achieves no certitude or foundation for thought while the former, the genuine universal, always outflanks human intentions as the epistemic ground of truth itself where "it alone is the activating principle upon which the interest of the world rests."[158]

The appearance of the purpose of the concept for thought seems to suggest that the purpose itself is in the process of becoming. Yet the actual purpose is always self-subsistent and is no less than the recycling of the concept in the form of the Idea:

> The idea in its process fabricates that illusion for itself, positing an other opposite itself, and its action consists in sublating this illusion. Truth emerges only from this error....[159]

Thus the purpose sits at the very cusp of Hegel's concept of total and complete self-subsistence in the form of the absolute which is the Idea, and forms the basis of the absolute good which is also true. In this way the authenticity of human ethical purposes are bonded to the development of the concept in its fulfillment of the absolute good in coherence with the foundational universality of concept and Idea.

*Teleology and syllogistic revolution*

The dialectic of the object has moved through the three stages of mechanism, chemism and teleology. In teleology the special form of the syllogism was revealed as the underlying method or model of change for all forms of dialectic transformation. It is at this level that the syllogism made its appearance as the unifying dynamic organizing the dialectical moments of universal, individual and particular. Hegel described these as the absolute center, relative center and non-independent object in respective order. Thus three syllogisms emerge which coordinate the relations of the universal, particular and individual, where each are mediated by the other two. In setting up this comparison between his dialectical teleology and the paradigmatic phases of the methodological mechanism of the natural sciences, Hegel sought to show how his syllogistic categories permeate even the most basic presuppositions of the latter. He held that his notion of teleology stands as the one syllogistic configuration of the three terms which were "overlooked and left aside" by the scholastic tradition of logic and metaphysics whose legacy is mathematics and modern science. Here scholastic dogma isolated contradictory statements and so dismissed their syllogistic relations and potential, whereas in dialectic thought they exist in relation and within a unity which is "sublated in the whole." This integration of whole and parts is the very fabric of Hegel's speculative method and principle of totality.

As Hegel set out, each of the three primary syllogistic configurations relate directly to different formulations of the prime social or political actor or category; be it the identification of the particular with civil society, the individual with the citizen or the universal with the state. In natural scientific terms, this is the equivalent of recognizing either the individual, the species or the genus as the unit of analysis in theorizing evolution, or in material terms; the atom, molecule and element. The syllogistic form here directly addresses itself to the problem of universals, as to how an integration of the understanding of wholes and parts ought to influence our descriptions of their relations and identities. Hegel's idealistic ontology in the *Logic* made this central case, and directs itself to the most basic foundations upon which the objectivity of the sciences are claimed. In so doing he makes a claim for the value of teleological thought and applies the syllogistic complex to the forms of mechanical causality as well.

At the level of teleology, each syllogistic form in its isolation is inadequate, and the natural and empirical sciences' inability to overcome the analytical segregation of the categories of mechanical causality leads to its paralysis. It remains unable to pass beyond a chemistic conception of material, as well as social and political, reality. This for Hegel is the status of the objective understanding of the sciences of his day, and the inherent nature and limit of the empirical sciences. Where mechanism passes to its alternate form in chemism, it has simply replaced the absolute isolation of its individual parts atomically understood with a mere outward tendency towards interaction. What remains undeveloped and unresolved is the basis of the affinity of the parts, or its dissolution, so as to account for the presence of the underlying universal in an otherwise finite process. This need for further elaboration is what calls forth teleology as a consideration of purposes or final causes. The wholesale absence of the universal in the mechanical mode of analysis immediately demands a recognition of the inadequacy of its empirical outlook, and the concomitant need for an explanation of the universal's causal participation where:

> To be sure, justice must be done to finite things as such inasmuch as they are to be considered to be other than ultimate and to point beyond themselves. This negativity of finite things, however, is their own dialectic and, in order to know this, one first has to get involved with their positive content.[160]

It is this "beyond" which teleology has instantiated in design and which the Idea subsequently realizes in the form of its coherent recovery of the fragmented universal of the object in logical reconciliation. This recovery of the three moments of the syllogism has moved the concept from the status of subjectivity in judgment, to that of objectivity in mechanism to their present unification with the onset of the Idea. This progress reflects the transformation of the abstract universal at the base of mechanical thought to its completion in the concrete universal of the teleological purpose. As was the case with the syllogistic development of the concept, the teleology of the purpose proceeds from the primacy of the universal[161] to that of the particular.[162] Here the final purpose of the purposive Idea is realized in the centrality of the universal reconstituted as individual.[163] The result and completion of the concept through these syllogisms reveals that the synthetic outcome is the "universal, that as simple is reflected in itself ... *the content* that remains *the same* through all three *termini* [terms] of the syllogism and their movement."[164] Thus the individual allows the fulfillment of the purpose and inherent purpose of the object, and reflects the preservation of the true and undifferentiated universality of the unified concept through all of its syllogistic reformulations in dialectic.

In Hegel's terms, the path from purpose to idea, from object to idea through teleology, proceeds from "universality identical with itself," to the "particularization of this universal" to its recollection where "by the activity of the universal, the latter [the universal] then returns to itself by means of that content and *joins itself together with itself.*"[165] Here then the complete Hegelian circuit of the syllogism of the concept is brought forth and rendered in reflection of the universal in its self-cycling, self-differentiating nature. The syllogism is thus the basic and concise representation of Hegel's system of universals. At its core, the syllogism overcomes the disparity of the universal whole and its parts in the necessity of their interpenetrations and mutual grounding. Furthermore this contradiction of classical origin is seen as only one of the three basic forms of essential opposition and intermediation which precedes all becoming, all change.

The constant reformulation of the universal may, however, be held to trump the participations of the particular and individual in this context. The Hegelian language of the constant ebb and tide of the universal evinces just this conclusion. Yet this would seem premature and insufficient in its dismissal of the inevitable mediation of the universal itself such that it too is punctuated by the grounding presence and purposes of its others: particular and individual. The conclusion on the status of the universal is best not sought in the ascendant framework of the dialectic and syllogism, though profoundly important for the analysis of the system. Rather, it is at the level of the Idea in the very terms of the absolute, the precise point to which Hegel has directed his metaphysical project, that the status of the universal may be conclusively sought vis-à-vis its relation to its others and its participation in the Hegelian response to the problem of universals. Where the Idea subsequently sets up the ideal arrangement of the subject, object and individual in the ethical life, we may look there to see how and to what extent the triad of syllogisms play out so as to ensure a balanced integration of the political interests of each.

*Concept fulfilled: absolute Idea*

The Idea has been clearly set out as residing above and in autonomy over the individual: the self-subsistent universal over and against the individual. By individual of course Hegel is referring to conceptual individuality and not merely individual subjects themselves. Truth comes in the identity of object as form with the concept as its content:

> the truth is this, that objectivity corresponds to the concept,—not that external things correspond to my representations; these are only *correct* representations that *I, this person* [*Ich Dieser*], have.[166]

Here the problem of universals is seemingly sidestepped through an epistemological move which holds that objects of thought must cohere, not with transient human universal ideas, but rather with an absolute subject which is the truth in its eternal and ideal coherence with its objective self. This conceptualization of truth as a fully formed unity of subjective idea with its own objective existence is both the standard by which actuality may be known as well as the means by which it comes into form. At the very same moment, all individual truths as subordinate to "the one idea" are vested with actuality and ideal substantiality only through their reflection of the latter's primacy. Individuals emerge from the inner negativity—the mediation—which inheres within universals as the energetic subjectivity of the concept itself: its consciousness per se. Clearly, for Hegel the Idea is the ultimate stratum, seen either as a sub- or superstratum, which founds and terminates all subsequent strata while remaining primordial and without prior cause outside of itself and the Idea has traversed the full circle of the dialectic. On this point Hegel assures us that it is the very cause of itself. It is this self-dirempting and dynamic quality which initiates the dialectic of the concept seen in the overall structure and transition of the *Logic* from being-in-itself to essence-for-itself to concept in-itself and for-itself as fulfilled Idea.

In contrast to the self-completing and complete Idea, the lack of coherence between the particular and its inner concept defines the condition of its finitude. The particular's imperfection and subsistence upon more fully developed forms of objectivity is expressed in its transience and impermanence: in the dialectic of the concept its negation and in the life of persons, death. The weakness of the part for Hegel is disclosed in its inherent alienation from its concept whereas the universal holds to its concept and returns to itself. On the other hand "The Absolute is the universal and one idea" and we see in the fulfillment of the dialectic circle of the concept the primacy of the universal and the thematic orientation of the *Logic* itself. Though the Idea is mediated, and so holds within itself particularity, it is self-mediating and is "its own result and, as such, just as much immediate as mediated."[167] The Idea as the universal of the concept at its highest level particularizes itself in the syllogism which unites it to its individual moments. These moments are the outward truth and objectivity of the inner and abstract universality through which the highest idea shines.

Nevertheless, the particular and its individuations return to "into the one idea, their truth."[168] Here, through the outward objectification of the abstract universal, the Idea reproduces itself. The telos of both the universal concept and its moments becomes the recreation of the whole as "the one idea" where truth alone resides. This inner and outer, as well as upper and lower life of the concept is the absolute for Hegel and it is lived out in the dialectic as a subject through which teleological and purposive agency is realized. This is the coming into being of substance as subject in accord with the phenomenology, overriding what Hegel witnessed as the merely formal notions of substance in Spinoza and subject in Leibniz. These Hegel declared inadequate in view of the necessity that the absolute be no mere "thing" or object, but a person as well. The personage which is the Idea's "*negative return of it into itself* and as *subjectivity*"[169] is the conceptual frame within which the problem of universals is overcome. The part and whole are in full coordination inside the individual thought which bonds the outward objectivity of the thing with the subject's cognition of it. Here, as earlier discussed, in its thinking itself from universality through differentiation, and its return into itself as a universal subject, the absolute Idea is an agency that always already corresponds with itself. This holds in the inverse—from the parts to the whole—and this reflective symmetry restates the fundamental syllogistic movement of the entire idealist dialectic. In a similar way the object reflects the subject, and the individual always reflects the universal through its own essence. Though, as I have pointed out, the universal in important ways reigns over the particularized origination and development of the particular in the grander scheme of dialectical activity, the two are harmonized at the bonding level of negation. Where the autonomy of the universal and the particular are thus inherently unified, and superseded, in the continuity of the absolute Idea, the formal dilemma or problem of universals is seemingly overcome. However, and from a critical point of view, this is only so where the extent of the prioritization of the universal, and its privileged ontological and epistemic roles are overlooked. Where the primacy of the universal seems to threaten the genuine authenticity of the particular, Hegel's idealist correspondence theory of truth seems less the coherence of the universal and part with each other, and more the logical subsumption of the latter within the priority of the omnipresent absolute Idea; the universal as it is found in its various categorical forms.[170] This seems mandated by the upward teleological march of Hegel's idealist dialectic towards greater, and ultimately, final unity and self-correspondence.

These issues aside and with the absolute Idea arrived at, so too has the justification of philosophy been clarified. The Idea is no transcendental and otherworldly notion, and is as present in immediate being as it is in the concept; its ideal content. Here consciousness is lifted out of the analogical immediacy of the material problem of the one and the many and introduced to the philosophical problem of universals:

> we regard the world as governed by divine providence and herein lies the fact that the asundered character [*Auseinander*] of the world is eternally led back to the unity out of which it went forth and, in keeping with that unity, is preserved.—From time immemorial in philosophy, it has been about nothing other than thoughtfully knowing the idea, and underlying everything that deserves the name "philosophy" has been the consciousness of an absolute unity of what holds for the understanding only in its separation.[171]

Here Hegel's logical project responds directly to Plato's question of the universal: "What is absolute unity?"[172] It is this alleviation of philosophy from the formalism of mere understanding which for Hegel is made present again in the seriousness granted the *a priori* and the noumenal in Kant's transcendental logic; a moment which permits the surpassing of empirical formalism and mechanism in the modern philosophical discourse. Plato and Aristotle do not stand amongst those in the problematic metaphysical and dogmatic camps for Hegel, and he largely sees these as the legacy of scholasticism. Here then consciousness, is both finite and infinite, and neither predicate reveals to us the whole that is both. This unification is left for the Idea which resolves within itself their propositional tension while preserving their autonomy as antinomious, contradictory categories. Where dogmatism rejects this further stage, speculative reason proceeds. The project of conceptual liberation is no less than the legacy of Plato, and one which witnesses the re-spiritualization of the human and natural worlds.

In having surpassed being, essence, concept and the modern opposition of object and subject—as well as the plethora of subordinate syllogistic triads belonging to these concepts—Hegel held that the works of all philosophical forebears had been consummated in a principle of final resolution—a resolution inaccessible to them in the varying degrees to which each failed to see the progressive and purposive totality of thought:

> The stages considered so far, those of being and essence and equally of the concept and objectivity, are not something fixed and resting on themselves with regard to this difference among them. Instead they have been demonstrated to be dialectical and their truth is only that of being moments of the idea.[173]

In the self-identity of the concept with itself, the eternal Idea, Hegel identified the bonding force uniting the categories of opposition which have historically confounded the understanding: subject and object, finite and infinite, whole and part are herein seen to explicate each other's possibility in dialectical and reciprocal necessity. This understanding attained, the unity inherent in opposition is best expressed in the concept of reason. Here judgment transforms understanding through the recognition which the interpenetration of opposites allows. In turn, thought is no longer apt to make the mistake of taking concepts in their ideal or formal isolation as abstract and self-contained moments:

> Understanding may demonstrate that the Idea is self-contradictory: because the subjective is subjective only and is always confronted by the objective; because the finite is finite only, the exact antithesis of the infinite, and therefore not identical with it; and so on.... The reverse of all this however is the doctrine of Logic. Logic shows that the subjective which is to be subjective only, the finite which would be finite only, the infinite which would be infinite only, and so on, have no truth, but contradict themselves, and pass over into their opposites.[174]

Reason in the form of the Idea is thus the vitality which unifies apparent opposition and multiplicity as a thinking process at the level of speculation. In his idealism, the force of reason is made the bond of the objectively real and the subjectively ideal, and the ground which gives both actuality. In this way Hegel restored diversity back to unity in reflection of the primacy of the Idea as "the process of eternally intuiting [*Anschauen*] itself in the other."[175] This reflective and ongoing resonance of the absolute, in Hegel's vision of "first philosophy," resounds through the syllogistic oppositions of the individual and universal as the constant, underlying and singular thinking substance. The oppositions and dichotomies of developmental thought are thus only the limited and outward forms of the Idea. In being, the limits of sensory experience presented the opposition of the object to the mind. This opposition was only overcome in its abstract denial by the Eleatic rejection of the reality of the parts in their becoming. In essence, and on the other hand, the limits of the understanding set up the inverse condition where the thinking subject itself became the epistemological other of the object in empiricism. Here the universal was denied and the particular was made a self-completing and self-standing whole. It is the extremes of these first two phases of thought which have brought on the need of a third to undo the hard dichotomy and restore the real relationality of actuality to thought. This is Hegel's work in the *Logic* thus far.

As this brings out, the mere understanding stood for Hegel as the impediment and obstacle to this realization which is, in fact, the ground of the problem of universals. The understanding is here restrained to see in its categories of thought only opposition, formal and abstract autonomy and difference from their other. This form of thought "overlooks ... the nature of the *copula* in a judgment, which asserts of the individual, the subject, that the individual is just as much something not individual but instead something universal."[176] This is a terminal flaw for Hegel, restricting its form of thinking and permanently obscuring the dialectical foundation of the Idea. The latter alone establishes the logical identity of individual concepts through its power of relation as a direct reflection of its own dynamic unity and its perseverance in the universal. Furthermore, understanding commits the grave error of interpreting, and thereby discarding, this self-consistent unity of the Idea as a distortion or impression of mere subjectivity. That is, the interpenetrating character of the categories of thought are taken by the understanding as external to thought itself, dismissing the circumscribing power of the Idea and shattering the absolute. It is thus relegated to work out their position and apposition as formal and isolated entities. For this reason, this faculty of thought is unable to witness the relations of ground and mediation which connect the categories and force them beyond contradiction in negation. This inter-reflective character of the categories is

> the dialectic that eternally separates and distinguishes what is identical with itself from the differentiated [*Differenten*], the subjective from the objective, the finite from the infinite, the soul from the body and, only insofar as it does, is it eternal creation, eternally alive, and eternal spirit.[177]

The problem of universals, then, at both the physical and logical level, is surmountable only in reference to a conceptual framework which, though confounding to the subordinate form of reason that is the understanding, unites movement and stasis, and whole and part. This clearly recalls the divine substance of

Aristotle's special metaphysics and the work of Plato's *Sophist*. The dialectic force of syllogism generated by the Idea's development is thus the bond which adheres behind the veil of phenomenal diversity. Here, the relative autonomy of the parts always reflects the universal whole in a reciprocating dynamic.

Where the universal traverses the levels of sense, understanding and finally the concept in constant reflection of the Idea, it stands in as the representative of the overall resolution of the dialectic that is the Idea:

> Only the concept itself is free and the truly *universal*; in the idea its *determinacy* is thus equally only itself—an objectivity into which it, as the universal, continuously sets itself and in which it has only its own determinacy, the total determinacy.[178]

All subordinate categorical antinomies are extinguished in the absolute Idea which coheres with itself as the final universal. The absolute Idea is thus both the fruition and origin of the universal in its completed circumscription of all its moments. Insofar as the absolute Idea has only itself as its object, nothing standing beyond its cognitive and volitional groundings in Hegelian terms: it is thought thinking itself. Here, then, Hegel concludes with Aristotle's definition of substance and deity, in deferring to the concept of the concept as the ameliorated conceptual form of substance. Where the absolute Idea thinks itself through the objects which are its own instantiations, all truth is fully rendered and the dialectic puts the human condition into perspective in accord with a similar, albeit contingent, relation. That is, in individual knowing the subject overcomes the object as its negative other and recognizes the other as its own concept at that level of the development and recycling of the Idea. Thus the universal, through which the seemingly extraneous particular is first known, is everywhere found immanent in the latter and to hold with it a shared identity constitutive of the real. This is the grounds of the abiding identity-in-differentiation of the universal and particular for Hegel.

## Syllogism and the problem of universals

The system of the *Logic* has culminated in the total unification of subject and object, whole and part. Such a unity does not escape the problematic logic of totalization which so influenced the Eleatic and Platonic conceptions of the absolute, or the post-scholastic attempts of Descartes, Spinoza, Leibniz, or others for that matter as well. As Parmenides recognized, a conception of the absolute must necessarily embrace self-identity in a thoroughly consistent way. It cannot refer outside of itself to any other being or cause as the inference or antecedent of its own existence; there can be no need of an explanation of itself outside of itself. This extends to the premise of the ontological argument such that the reality of the absolute being is necessitated by its essential concept. On these grounds, any conceptualization of totality must embrace a comprehensive theoretical symmetry in coherence with the demands of formal as well substantial consideration. It must conform to the logical rigors of both the laws of mind and body, of philosophy and physics. For Parmenides this was analogized as a geometric form which expressed perfect symmetry, immutability and the limitlessness of unpunctuated contiguity. For Hegel these considerations of self-consistency play a role in his formal depiction of the absolute Idea as well:

> The *absolute idea* is for itself, since in it there is no transition or presupposing and no determinacy at all that is not fluid and transparent; it is the *pure form* of the concept that intuits *its content* as itself. It is content for itself insofar as it is the ideal differentiating of itself from itself, and one side of what has been differentiated is the identity with itself, in which, however, the totality of the form is contained as the system of the determinations of the content.[179]

For Hegel, however, and unlike the ancients influenced by Parmenides, unity does not mandate stasis and it is not the language of geometry which best describes the autogenous or self-constituting nature of the absolute. In large part, it is this fixture of ancient thought, in its dependence upon mathematical or geometric forms of consistency, which often confounds its more profound inner potentialities. Hegel recognized this pitfall of formalism, and sought to find a coherent conceptual language of idealism in the dynamic of mind and thought as absolute Idea. He intended that his conceptual framework, while independent of material predication, be reconciled to physical reality by virtue of the relational and generative procession of the dialectic towards an end which implies itself recursively: the Idea "that intuits *its content* as itself." The final model of the absolute then is one of mind uniting the universal with its instantiations on this highest level such that all parts are inherently the thought moments or life of the absolute Idea in mediation of itself in particular form. Inversely, the universal is contained within the part's negative self-relation as the living opposition of universality with particularity. These two syllogisms together with a third, unite the universal and its moments and are instanced in the prevailing self-continuity of the absolute Idea. Though the absolute Idea as the final universal fully coheres with itself as the final ground of concept and reality, all partial moments, as has been discussed, remain flawed and finite reflections. It is for this reason that, while the total whole prevails as a formal unity, its constituent moments forever move upon the wheel of change; the absolute Idea as the eternal axis of their phenomenal becoming. Thus, the relationship of the absolute with the universal is a specialized and privileged one, and Hegel insists that this total universality not be considered as an aggregate in any sense which would diffuse its unity:

> It can ... be said that the absolute idea is the universal, but the universal not merely as an abstract form opposite which the particular content stands as something other than it. Instead it is the absolute form, into which all determinations, the entire fullness of the content posited by it, have gone back. In this respect, the absolute idea is comparable to the old man who says the

same religious sentences as the child does, but for the old man they have the meaning of his entire life.[180]

We thus see in the mating of subject and substance, the idea and the thing, Hegel's universal persona taking up within itself the particular "experience" of its conceptual moments in their independent existences as its form. The strivings of this subject are self-constituting where its purpose and interests are its own foundations. This is the energetic basis of endeavor with which the dialectic of the absolute pushes itself forward, over-reaching or outflanking its opposing elements in a universality unceasingly striving toward further teleological resolution. This for Hegel is the life course of both "the man" and the Idea in the evolutionary coming to consciousness of their most basic identity and truth. The life development of the particular in this sublime context is delivered as the surprise to the self, once cleansed of false aspiration and denial through the perspective of speculative thought: the life lived is in actuality what we always wished for ourselves and equally knew ourselves to be.

On this point, and in concord with Plato, the philosopher is made the crucial witness of the life course of the absolute where "everything that appears limited, taken for itself, acquires its worth through inhering in the whole and being a moment of the idea."[181] It is in this organic unity of universal and particular, one which will serve as a model for Hegel's project of political reconciliation, that all particularity is potentiated to independent actuality and the former terms are reconciled in its purposive mediation. The primary recognition of the inability of formal logic traditionally understood to recognize the purposive movement of mediation, and the concomitant inversion that truth is found not in non-contradiction but in contradiction, permitted Hegel to resolve dichotomy in mediation as the ground of emergent actuality. In these tenets, established in the *Logic* through a reconsideration of traditional logical doctrine, Hegel provided direct remedy to the difficulties facing Parmenides, Plato as well as Kant in the metaphysical aporias of being formally understood.

The organic whole which for Hegel successfully accommodates the inner movements of its parts, in fact, realizes the very image of the Parmenidean "one"; "being" as the stage of the Idea which Hegel termed "beginning." As Hegel informed us, "Each of the stages considered up to this point is an image of the absolute, albeit in a limited manner at first, and so it drives itself on to the whole."[182] Parmenides' own logical and definitional strictures from *On Nature* aside, the holographic unity of whole and part achieved in the absolute Idea realizes the one as the "whole" for which he strived. That is, Parmenides' conception of being is given the self-consistent symmetry for which he expressly searched, and for Hegel it is precisely through the dialectic of actualized being that such a definition may alone be coherently rendered.

In this context, the *Logic* was fashioned as a transcendental pursuit after being, starting with the ancient metaphysics of immediate being in the Eleatics, and moves by leap and bound up to and beyond Kant. It explicitly worked to overcome the problem of universals as they confronted Parmenides' original thesis first elaborated in Plato's dialog of the same name and as later restated by Aristotle. Here, the *Logic* as a system strives to answer the question as to how a thing can both be susceptible to transformation and still be known to be the thing which it is, and truth grasped against a background of unceasing phenomenal transformation. Thus it is the absolute in the form of being which Parmenides founded, Plato problematized and Hegel sought to redeem on a wholly reconsidered platform of logic in order to restore a foundation for knowledge in the wake of the skeptical aftershocks of empiricism. The pursuit of the absolute is primary to all three thinkers' work as first philosophers, and this inner dialogue intimately connects them in their common commitment to its rational exposition.

As with Plato, immediate being moves from the stage of phenomenal perception to that of the concept as universal. For both thinkers, the development of the Idea, of philosophical conception itself, moves from the transience of the senses toward the stability of the Idea in its absolute form so that "When it means immediate being, the beginning is taken from sensation and perception."[183] However, and in contrast with Plato, where the starting point of thought "in the sense of the universality, it is the beginning of the synthetic method"[184] with Hegel. That is, where speculative thought begins with being in its universal form as concept, and moves towards it particular elements through the synthetic activity of syllogism, there is no fundamental dilemma of abstract opposition. This was the doubling of philosophical science for Hegel such that the two movements of thought permit equal access to the absolute Idea at one end and immediate being at the other, and which are tied together as the beginning of the self-same circle of truth in dialectical continuity.

This circle of the self-conception of the absolute is the revolutionary dimension of Hegel's response to the logical problem of universals. The process of dialectic thus reveals itself in moving forward in both forms such that universal immediacy is actively negated into particularity, and particularity surrenders itself to the implicit universality of the concept which it holds within itself. This is the complete arc of Hegel's resolution of the problem of universals. *The severance or bifurcation of the universal and its particulars is suspended through a process of mediation. This mediation is grounded upon the inherent conceptual relation of the two terms as part of a larger syllogism of categorical reconciliation which speculative thought makes transparent in the concept. This reconciliation is brought about in reflection of their trajectory on the circle of the absolute, one which unites the beginning and the end; universal being and the telos of spiritual individuality towards which it inherently strives in its particularized forms.*

The mediation of the purpose of the absolute Idea by the beginning of being, and vice versa, brings the *Logic* into a circle which finds its continuity outside and beyond its own boundaries. That is, the absolute Idea is completed by the objective being of nature,[185] and this latter confronts the subjectivity of spirit in mediation throughout. This circle is a comprehensive representation of the dialectical ordering of the *Encyclopedia of the Philosophical Sciences* as a whole, one which founds Hegel's system of knowledge, and his political, aesthetic and historical theorizations by extension. The *Logic* here forms the middle ground between the *Encyclopedia*'s other two terms—nature and spirit—which carry out the elaboration of the objective and subjective spheres. Nature posits the universality of being, and individualized spirit confronts it in the preliminary instance of the concept as well as in its continual dialectic extension so that, throughout the logic, "nature is posited by the spirit and the spirit itself makes nature its presupposition."[186] From the subjective realm of being (universal in-itself) to the objective realm of essence (particular for-itself) and their consummation in the conceptual, self-knowing and spiritual completion of the absolute Idea (individual in-and-for-itself), the structural development of the *Logic* is recapitulated at the higher level of the *Encyclopedia*'s overall organization. In Hegelian terms, this architecture of syllogistic reconciliation in the *Logic* and the *Encyclopedia* as a whole is the thoroughgoing coherence of philosophy with its inner concept. This reflects the extent to which the metaphysical problem of universals participates in his logical project in a fundamental way.

At the level of spirit in the human historical world, the evolution of thought has but one goal: the realization of freedom where the fullness of the conceptual diversity exemplified in the various moments of the dialectic are retained. For Burbidge, the political implications of Hegel's logic of resolution are clear where thinking or reason is

> a process of determining indeterminate universals ... that brings all the various determinations together into a single perspective ... a process of integration that understands the parts within a singular, all-inclusive unity.... The subjective end that is to be realized in history is to achieve such a freedom—to embody reason.... What does the achieved end look like? Hegel calls it the state.[187]

Where the *Logic* ends with the resolution of the metaphysical problem, the political project begins.

## Notes

1 Hegel's Encyclopedia Logic is the common name for part one of Hegel's Encyclopedia of the Philosophical Sciences in Outline.
2 The Philosophy of Right was last revised in 1827 and so was written prior to the Encyclopedia Logic of 1830. Hegel's most advanced statement of logic at the time was thus his 1816 Science of Logic. Despite this, his later work on logic remains a useful and more accessible, if somewhat condensed, entry to his logical system, and it largely retained a fidelity to the earlier edition.
3 Robert B. Pippin, Hegel's Idealism: The Satisfactions of Self-Consciousness (Cambridge, UK; New York: Cambridge University Press, 1989); Klaus Hartmann, "Hegel: A Non-metaphysical View," in Alasdair C. MacIntyre, Hegel: A Collection of Critical Essays, 1st edn, Modern Studies in Philosophy (Garden City, NY: Anchor Books, 1972), 101–4.

4 Something that I positively demonstrate in my consideration of Allen Wood's Hegel's Ethical Thought at the end of Chapter 5.
5 Shlomo Avineri, Hegel's Theory of the Modern State, Cambridge Studies in the History and Theory of Politics (London: Cambridge University Press, 1972), 221.
6 Andrew B. Schoedinger, The Problem of Universals (Atlantic Highlands, NJ: Humanities Press, 1992), ix.
7 Andrew B. Schoedinger, Introduction to Metaphysics: The Fundamental Questions (Buffalo, NY: Prometheus Books, 1991), 9.
8 Hannah Arendt, The Life of the Mind, One-volume edition (San Diego: Harcourt Brace Jovanovich, 1981), 10.
9 Porphyry and Paul Vincent Spade, Five Texts on the Mediaeval Problem of Universals: Porphyry, Boethius, Abelard, Duns Scotus, Ockham (Indianapolis: Hackett, 1994), viii.
10 Aristotle, De Interpretatione 7, 17$^a$38-$^b$1, in Porphyry and Spade, Five Texts on the Mediaeval Problem of Universals, x.
11 Riin Sirkel, The Problem of Katholou (Universals) in Aristotle (London, Ont.: School of Graduate and Postdoctoral Studies, University of Western Ontario, 2010), http://ir.lib.uwo.ca/etd/62, 1.
12 Porphyry and Spade, Five Texts on the Mediaeval Problem of Universals, 1.
13 Ibid.
14 Sirkel, The Problem of Katholou (Universals) in Aristotle, 1.
15 Porphyry and Spade, Five Texts on the Mediaeval Problem of Universals, x.
16 Ibid., xi.
17 Plato and Benjamin Jowett, The Dialogues of Plato, 3d edn, 5 vols (New York and London: Macmillan, 1892), Steph. 15.
18 Ibid., Steph. 15. J.P. Moreland agrees: "historically, the problem of universals has been mainly about the 'One and Many' (a.k.a. 'One over Many', 'One in Many'), which involves giving an account of the unity of natural classes." James Porter Moreland, Universals, Central Problems of Philosophy (Montreal; Ithaca: McGill-Queen's University Press, 2001), 1.
19 This concern extends back to work carried out in Plato's Sophist as well.
20 Moreland, Universals, 2.
21 Georg Wilhelm Friedrich Hegel, Lectures on the History of Philosophy: Vol. III (London: Kegan Paul, Trench Trübner, 1896), 77. Individual may also be understood as particular here, but does not refer to the individual—or singular—third moment of the dialectic.
22 Ibid., 78.
23 Ibid., 85.
24 While not addressing the overt historical legacy of the medieval tradition, Robert Stern's Hegel, Kant and the Structure of the Object (London; New York: Routledge, 1990) remains a wonderful and rare exception. More on the topic can also be followed up in Stern's Hegelian Metaphysics (Oxford; New York: Oxford University Press, 2009).
25 Josiah Royce, The Spirit of Modern Philosophy: An Essay in the Form of Lectures (Boston and New York: Houghton, 1892), 492.
26 Ibid., 217.
27 Plato and Robin Waterfield, Republic, Oxford World's Classics (Oxford; New York: Oxford University Press, 1998), Steph. 523e.
28 Royce, The Spirit of Modern Philosophy, 218.
29 Ibid.
30 Ibid.
31 Frederick Beiser "Dark Days: Anglophone Scholarship since the 1960s," in Espen Hammer, German Idealism: Contemporary Perspectives (London: Routledge, 2007), 79–90: 82.
32 Ibid.

166  *Metaphysics and politics in Hegel's thought*

33 Pippin, *Hegel's Idealism*; Klaus Hartmann, "Hegel: A Non-metaphysical View."
34 James Kreines, "Hegel's Metaphysics: Changing the Debate," *Philosophy Compass* 1, no. 5 (2006), 466–80; Frederick Beiser "Dark Days."
35 A subject upon which Josiah Royce is uncommonly aware amongst modern and contemporary Hegel commentators.
36 William Desmond, "Being, Determination, and Dialectic: On the Sources of Metaphysical Thinking," *The Review of Metaphysics* 48, no. 4 (1995), 731–69: 732.
37 Georg Wilhelm Friedrich Hegel, John Niemeyer Findlay and Arnold V. Miller, *Phenomenology of Spirit* (Oxford: Clarendon Press, 1977), §28.
38 Hegel, *Hegel's Briefe*, Hamburg: Felix Meiner Verlag, 1952, Vol. ii, 204.
39 Translator and author of the foreword to the standard Oxford University Press edition of Hegel's *Logic*, Georg Wilhelm Friedrich Hegel and William Wallace, *Hegel's Logic: Being Part One of the Encyclopaedia of the Philosophical Sciences (1830)* (Oxford: Clarendon Press, 1975).
40 Ibid., 31.
41 Ibid., 7.
42 I use "Idea" capitalized to refer to Hegel's "absolute Idea": one which witnesses the completion of all subordinate ideas.
43 Hegel *et al.*, *Phenomenology of Spirit*, §28.
44 Ibid., §25.
45 Ibid.
46 Certainly present in Hobbes's earlier *De Corporea* and *Leviathan* as well.
47 Though some would contend against the assessment of Hegel's work as metaphysical, he himself sees his work as coextensive with such a pursuit.
48 John W. Burbidge, *The Logic of Hegel's Logic: An Introduction* (Peterborough, Ont.: Broadview Press, 2006), 35.
49 As opposed to a formal one.
50 In Hegel's corpus, the *Logic* begins the triad in the first position but in terms of the circular system of thought, nature and subject, it mediates between nature and subject where the concept once again begins to move towards nature. For Hegel, there is no actual originary beginning.
51 Georg Wilhelm Friedrich Hegel, Michael George and Andrew Vincent, *The Philosophical Propaedeutic* (Oxford; New York: Blackwell, 1986).
52 Ibid. §2.
53 Individuality (or singularity) as the synthetic or concluding moment of the dialectical triad. I capitalize usages of the term Idea in reference to Hegel's absolute Idea as opposed to ideas in general or particular.
54 Ibid., §84.
55 Ibid., §86.
56 Ibid.
57 Here Hegel relates the resolution of the opposition of being and becoming to the resolution of the prior antinomy of cause and effect which, in his thought, is a reflection of the logical problem of universals in the sphere of nature.
58 *Begriff*, sometimes translated as "notion." William Wallace and A.V. Miller employed this alternative in their translations of the *Phenomenology* and the *Logic* respectively as well.
59 Heel, *Hegel's Briefe*, 204.
60 Understandable in general terms as the synthetic thinking which witnesses the unity in opposites, dialectically pushing thinking beyond thought which witnesses only particulars in contradistinction to one another.
61 Georg Wilhelm Friedrich Hegel, Klaus Brinkmann and Daniel O. Dahlstrom, *Encyclopedia of the Philosophical Sciences in Basic Outline. Part 1, Science of Logic* (Cambridge, UK; New York: Cambridge University Press, 2010), §6.
62 Ibid., §6.

63 Ibid., §7.
64 Georg Wilhelm Friedrich Hegel and J.B. Baillie, *The Phenomenology of Mind*, 2nd edn, Library of Philosophy, edited by J.H. Muirhead (London; New York: G. Allen & Unwin; Macmillan, 1931), §8. The James Black Baillie translation best captures Hegel's share of melancholic lament.
65 Hegel et al., *Encyclopedia of the Philosophical Sciences in Basic Outline. Part 1, Science of Logic*, §12.
66 Ibid.
67 Ibid.
68 Ibid., § 12.
69 Living thought of the unchanging absolute Idea which develops greater self-awareness through temporal experience.
70 Ibid., §13.
71 Ibid., §16.
72 Ibid.
73 Ibid.
74 Again, the historical development of conscious thought pursuing the Idea through time.
75 Ibid., §13.
76 Ibid., §14.
77 Ibid., §20.
78 Ibid., §20.
79 Both linguistically as well as conceptually.
80 Ibid., §20.
81 Despite Brinkmann and Dahlstrom's translation of Hegel's *übergreift* as "over-reach," I employ Wallace's "outflank."
82 Ibid., §20.
83 Ibid., §20.
84 *Reflexion*: Hegel's sense of basic abstraction which thinks in mediation and distinguishes between subject and object, appearances and reality.
85 Ibid., §21.
86 Ibid., §22.
87 Ibid., §24.
88 Also translatable as "reason."
89 Ibid., §80.
90 Ibid., §80.
91 The presence of the universal in the particular entities of experience.
92 Truth.
93 Though they have radically different notions how parts and individuals achieve this.
94 Ibid., §81.
95 Ibid.
96 Ibid.
97 Ibid.
98 Ibid.
99 Immanuel Kant, Paul Guyer and Allen W. Wood, *Critique of Pure Reason* (Cambridge, UK; New York: Cambridge University Press, 1998), a634f.
100 Or thesis as it is sometimes rendered in contemporary Hegelian shorthand. That said, Hegel himself never used the thesis, antithesis, synthesis formulation.
101 Hegel et al., *Encyclopedia of the Philosophical Sciences in Basic Outline. Part 1, Science of Logic*, §81.
102 Ibid., §82.
103 Hegel's "concept" presents the universal at myriad levels on its way to full logical resolution through the final stage of speculation. The concept is thus not fully realized at the previous two levels of understanding and dialectic.

168  *Metaphysics and politics in Hegel's thought*

104 Ibid., §7.
105 Ibid., §86.
106 Being is the content of the universal at the initial phase of the *Logic*, just as essence and notion play the roles of particular and individual later on.
107 Ibid. §86.
108 Ibid. §87A.
109 Ibid., §88A4.
110 The problem of the one and the many, unsurprisingly, is itself an expression of the problem of universals put in rustic terms.
111 These problematic entailments of classical Eleatic thought, and the attempt to reconcile the Eleatic One with the coordinate relation of ideas were taken up by Plato in his *Sophist* and *Theatatus*.
112 Ibid., §89A.
113 Ibid., §97A.
114 Ibid.
115 Ibid., §98.
116 Plato and Benjamin Jowett, *The Dialogues of Plato*, 3d edn (New York: Oxford University Press, 1892), Steph. 25.
117 Hegel *et al.*, *Encyclopedia of the Philosophical Sciences in Basic Outline. Part 1, Science of Logic*, §112A.
118 This will later be developed in the form of Hegel's "Concept" or "Notion" (*Begriff*): the universal of universals.
119 Ibid., §123.
120 Ibid.
121 Ibid., §131A.
122 Ibid., §131.
123 Due to their holding both being-for-itself and being-for-other within.
124 Ibid., §86.
125 Ibid., §131.
126 Ibid., §134.
127 Ibid., §135A.
128 Ibid., §136.
129 Ibid.
130 Ibid., §141.
131 Ibid., §160.
132 Ibid., §159.
133 Ibid., §160.
134 The reference to Wilfrid Sellars' critique being overt and mine, not Hegel's.
135 Ibid., §163A1.
136 In *The Phenomenology* for example.
137 This ontological prioritization of the universal for knowledge is witnessed in Plato's *Theatatus* as well.
138 Ibid., §163.
139 A similar debate has haunted Christian theology in its commitment to both the trinity and monotheistic doctrine.
140 Ibid.
141 Ibid.
142 Ibid., §164.
143 As in "the tree is brown" or "the man is good."
144 Ibid., §193.
145 Ibid.
146 Ibid., §166.
147 Ibid., §194.
148 Ibid., §195.

149 Ibid., §198.
150 Ibid.
151 U-P-I, P-I-U, I-U-P.
152 Ibid., §202.
153 Ibid., §200.
154 Ibid., §204.
155 Ibid. The William Wallace rendering seems clearer here: "the cause is in the effect made for the first time a cause, and that it there returns into itself." Hegel and Wallace, *Hegel's Logic*.
156 Hegel et al., *Encyclopedia of the Philosophical Sciences in Basic Outline. Part 1, Science of Logic*.
157 Ibid., §24.
158 Ibid., §212.
159 Ibid.
160 Ibid., §205.
161 Universal and individual mediated by particular.
162 Universal and particular mediated by the individual.
163 Individual and particular mediated by the universal individual.
164 Ibid., §210.
165 Ibid., §206.
166 Ibid., §213.
167 Ibid.
168 Ibid.
169 Ibid.
170 These forms of the universal which preserve the Idea are represented in each of the three phases of the dialectic, and in all their subordinate triads.
171 Ibid.
172 Plato and Jowett, *The Dialogues of Plato*, Steph. 524.
173 Hegel et al., *Encyclopedia of the Philosophical Sciences in Basic Outline. Part 1, Science of Logic*, §213.
174 Ibid., §214.
175 Ibid.
176 Ibid.
177 Ibid.
178 Ibid.
179 Ibid., §237.
180 Ibid.
181 Ibid.
182 Ibid.
183 Ibid.
184 Ibid., §238.
185 Schelling's petrified intelligence.
186 Ibid., §239.
187 John W. Burbidge, *Hegel's Systematic Contingency* (Basingstoke, UK; New York: Palgrave Macmillan, 2007), 150.

# 5 Political dialectic

## The metaphysical vocation of political philosophy[1]

**The metaphysical vocation of political philosophy**

As examined above, conceptions of metaphysics as valuable for theoretical considerations of practical politics have been overshadowed by contemporary positivist and liberal proscriptions for some time. This has not always been the case. For example, in the early years of the twentieth century, the Hegel scholar Henry S. Macran deemed it permissible to suggest in his introductory comments to Hegel's *Science of Logic* that

> The fundamental opposition that runs through the whole content and through the whole history of philosophic thought is ... the opposition between the thesis and antithesis or position and negation of the Hegelian triad.... Nor is it merely a philosophical opposition; as every other kind of thinking is applied logic, there is no sphere of human life that escapes the contrast. It is at the bottom of the distinction between the socialist and the individualist, the imperialist and the Little Englander, the philosopher in general and the man of affairs, the devotee and the worker, the artist and the man of science, idealistic art and realistic, experimental research and mere observation.[2]

From this point of view, dialectical logic provides both a necessary framework for the understanding of the Hegelian corpus as well as the dynamic underpinning the workings of the historical world of society and politics.[3] With Mathew J. Smetona, while there is no ultimate "foundationalist" starting point in Hegel's circle of the intermediated and interdependent unity of logic, nature and spirit, "the interpreter of Hegel's political philosophy cannot comprehend what the *Philosophy of Right* is the actualization *of* if the *Science of Logic* is dispensed with."[4] Certainly, this position coheres with Hegel's own, which took the metaphysical work of the *Logic* as a necessary component for the appreciation of his overall system. Yet, under the climate of Anglo-American Hegel scholarship prevalent since at least the 1950s, there has been an ongoing divergence from the traditional approach in terms of the relation and interdependence of Hegel's respective philosophical and political bodies of thought. Much of this program was motivated by an intent to salvage Hegel's political thought from critics who would associate him with the illiberalisms of Prussian statism, twentieth-century German nationalism or the antiquations of pre-Kantian metaphysical excess.[5]

As discussed above in Chapter 3, authors such as Zbigniew Pełczyński, Allen Wood, Dante Germino, Mark Tunick and numerous others argue that Hegel's political thought is wholly intelligible without reference to the supposedly abstruse foundations of the dialectical logic.[6] As Pełczyński has noted, "Hegel's political thought can be read, understood and appreciated without having to come to terms with his metaphysics."[7] Germino took this depreciation of Hegel's logical thought still further, asserting that the source of the problem is specifically "the not inconsiderable obscurity of the dialectic [which] hinders rather than advances our appreciation of his contribution to political theory."[8] Indeed, in his study of powerful trend towards revisionist approaches to Hegel's metaphysical thought, Frederick Beiser asserted that "The final refuge, the last redoubt, of the non-metaphysical interpretation has been Hegel's social and political philosophy ... [such that] we can clearly extricate Hegel's [political] teachings from his metaphysics."[9] In contrast, select authors such as Raymond Plant, Robert Stern, Robert Ware, Mathew Smetona, Stephen Houlgate, Thom Brooks and myself have witnessed a development of theoretical necessity in the transition from the logical component of Hegel's work to his political treatise.[10] On these accounts, his political thought must be understood as a dependent component of his philosophical system insofar as Hegel embraces the Greek "logos" with the primary intent of articulating the whole as absolute.

This contention over the value of the metaphysical underpinnings of his politics persists as a result of a lack of attention given to the influence of the fundamental philosophical problems out of which, as the previous chapter elaborately set out, Hegel himself was working. While the dialectics of the *Encyclopaedia Logic*[11] have been explored in their philosophical isolation, the role of the universalist logic driving the politics as a response to core philosophical dilemmas germane to it has not. While there have been a select few studies of the interrelationship of Hegelian metaphysics and politics, the philosophical problem of universals and their becoming, one which Hegel witnesses in the *Logic* as originating with Eleatic "Being," has not been integrated into the mapping of his political thought.[12] Hegel's primary quest to fully articulate the transformation of being out of itself—a project initiated from "being" as the preliminary phase of both the major and minor works on logic—and the need to subsequently restore this universality through dialectical change so as to sustain a self-contained and self-generating conception of being[13] should not be set aside in our estimations of Hegel's politics. Contemporary scholarship has skirted this influential presence of the dialectic in his politics and is led by those who primarily restrict themselves to Hegel the political thinker with only a side-glance to his foundational conceptual framework.[14] For the most part, the coverage of the actual intertwining of the political and metaphysical in Hegel has played at the theoretical surface of the concomitant project within Hegel's political program which seeks to respond to the philosophical paradox of transformation, "becoming," in order to preserve the value of universal ideas for his system.

Even where the traditional, pre-twentieth-century view[15] of the interdependence of metaphysics and politics in the Hegelian corpus is discounted as an antiquated or immodest expression of doctrinal adherence,[16] we are no closer to a convenient split between a metaphysical and political component in the *Philosophy of Right*. Rather, as the foregoing discussion and chapter illuminate, there has been a lack of recognition of a basic philosophical dilemma which resides at the heart of Hegel's political thought, a dilemma which emerges into the politics from the starting point of the logical system in "being" in response to the problem of universals. This shortcoming is in part due to an underestimation of his classicist and metaphysical intention to reinstate the primacy of logic and to its misapprehension as a formal apparatus within which the contents of history take independent shape.

In response to this state of affairs, I argue that such readings run wholly against the grain of Hegel's thought and purpose. Contending against the separability of philosophical form and political content, I argue that the metaphysical component, the "coincidence" of logic and metaphysics as he puts it, substantially informs his conception of state.[17] In defense of this position, I piece together what Hegel presented as a continuity between a philosophical system which responds to the dilemma of the universal, and both the practical governing and institutional formations and relationships which he formulated as political entailments. My approach is grounded in the problem of universals—how being accommodates change and unity, diversity—outlined in the previous chapter, read out of the *Philosophy of Right* as a concern which Hegel centrally responds to throughout his political dialectic in direct reference to his system of logic.

The metaphysical problem of universals becomes political in consideration of the modern tensions and ambiguities of political belonging. These arise between the specific affiliations which situate subject-individuals in the family, civil society or state institutions on one side, and that which binds them to the overall state and ethical life as an indissoluble spiritual union on the other. Plato's philosophical question as to how "one and the same thing be at the same time in one and in many things?"[18] finds its political analog in the question as to whether the state is merely equated with the fact of the multitude it contains, or as "the One" which unifies it or even presupposes it. Peter J. Steinberger restates the paradox in his treatment of the dilemma of freedom which arises with Hegel's conception of autonomous citizens circumscribed by an otherwise organic and seemingly diametrically opposed state:

> How can the individual be bound, so to speak, by the functional exigencies of the state while yet remaining free? Is not organicism fundamentally a denial of autonomy? If the hand and the other parts of the body were truly to operate freely, in utter independence from one another, surely the organism would be destroyed and the parts along with it.[19]

On this basis Steinberger is able to assert that "Hegel's political thought is importantly shaped by the apparent tension between social rules and patterns ... [and] the individual ..." such that we may "hypothesize that this characteristic problem of modern political philosophy is at the very center of Hegel's project."[20]

Theoretical responses to the metaphysical problem of universals and the antecedent epistemological questions which arise for a theory of knowledge here have a direct bearing on the way we argue about the relatedness or non-relatedness of citizens and states, individuals and their political communities. My demonstration and defense of Hegel's continuum of metaphysics and politics below provides the basis for making this case. If a conception of political community works from the position that the state is no more than the agglomeration of its individual parts, its concrete citizens, then a pluralistic basis for authority is given priority. However, if the state is asserted as a unity of its own, as an analytically indissoluble and categorical whole, a conceptual whole greater than the sum of its parts, its status as a universal purchases it a special and privileged seat of authority in relation to the limited capacity of its citizens.

Hegel argued that modern political systems require both strategies. His resultant social and political arrangement asserted a hybridity that responded both to the demands for civil liberty, as well as the reinstatement of the ethical and political unity in and through the state which the civil sphere had overturned in its emergence from pre-modern forms of collectivity. In short, Hegel intended a logico-political solution which stringently addressed itself to the primary concern of modern political thought: "To find a form of association ... by which each partner, uniting himself with all the rest, nevertheless obeys only himself, and remains as free as before."[21] The dilemma of inherent unity and individuation sits at the root of Rousseau's formulation of the central project of modern political thought, and restates the ancient problem of universals in modern political terms. As I will argue in the final chapter, the parallelism of metaphysics and politics is not limited to Hegel's species of political thinking, but rather represents an inherent dimension of political theorizing itself.

Hegel intended the theory of politics presented in the *Philosophy of Right* of 1820 as his comprehensive contribution to a science of the state, and he tells us this against the backdrop of his work presented in the section on subjective spirit in his 1817 *Encyclopedia of the Philosophical Sciences in Outline*. Though he dealt with politics in both his *Philosophy of History* and the *Phenomenology of Spirit* as well, the *Philosophy of Right* is his singular and uncompromising contribution to a theory of the state in his larger oeuvre. In order to assert the validity and utility of Hegel's metaphysics for the construction of his political edifice, I develop the ways in which the *Philosophy of Right* was explicitly conceptualized along the lines of the speculative method and coheres with "the closed circle of a science." Hegel made clear from the outset that his political treatise proceeds from the method developed in his work on logic.[22] Though he took for granted that his readers would be familiar with this work, he does not restate many of its most basic arguments in order to avoid detracting from his presentation of a comprehensive theory of state.

In this chapter, then, I first outline and excavate the deep and interlocking links between the *Philosophy of Right*'s preliminary reflection on the problem of universals in the Preface and Introduction and the design and rigor of the logical doctrine. I then treat his ethical life (*Sittlichkeit*)—the fully developed theory of modern social and political relations—in detail and examine its political structures and state–citizen relations, asserting the centrality of their reflection of his metaphysical response to the problem of universals and its implications for legitimacy. My main purpose is to expose the ways Hegel's metaphysical program of universals undergirds and guides his response to its political analogue. In doing so and in combination with Chapter 4 above, it completes a refutation of the descriptive strategy—outlined in Chapter 1 and traced through its contemporary exponents in Chapter 3—which culls all dimension and import of the metaphysical in exchange for a "cleansed" version of Hegel's politics that "we" can live with. *Where Chapter 4 asserted and highlighted the concrete presence of a metaphysical program in Hegel's system of logic, this chapter takes that work forward to show the way that program is carried over to provide a basis for a subsequent political arrangement.*[23] Not only is the presence of the metaphysical marked and substantial in both works, but they abide in a creative continuity, a branching in Hegel's terms, that takes the metaphysical as both necessary and useful for political theory and practice. Thus, I will argue that the metaphysical elements of Hegel's thought are herein very much present, irreducible and irremovable from his political thinking. That, in fact, the carryover from the metaphysical work of the *Logic* to his politics is intentional, warranted and structurally integral to Hegel's larger program in a way that makes its consideration quintessential.

Subsequent to carrying out the primary task of exploring the continuity of metaphysics and politics below, I take up the work of Allen Wood's *Hegel's Ethical Thought* as a means of demonstrating the inherent shortcomings of non-metaphysical reading. While I first make the positive case for the prolific influence of the metaphysical in Hegel's politics, I thereafter address the claims of the non-metaphysical reading. These claim, regardless of Hegel's overt metaphysical intentions, that the *Philosophy of Right* is best read in absence of these influences and that it may be seen to theoretically function perfectly well on its own.

These two tasks—the positive case that the metaphysical reading is correct and the negative that the non-metaphysical reading is wrong—complete my argument against the descriptive challenge which holds that there is no metaphysical project or that such a project may be dispensed with in our assessments of Hegel's politics. This then clears the path for critical reconsideration of the chronologically and theoretically prior prescriptive challenge in the next, concluding chapter as an injunction which has weighed heavily not merely on Hegel scholarship but on political thought as well.[24]

## Political logic and the speculative presuppositions of the *Philosophy of Right*

Hegel made clear early on in the Preface to his political treatise that it stands squarely on the work carried out in his logic. This background is the "logical spirit" and he clarified that it is "from this point of view above all that I should like my book to be taken and judged."[25] We are therefore to understand the political relations here articulated in their direct relation to the metaphysical method of syllogistic resolution he had earlier laid out in the *Logic*. The content of political theory is regulated, and preceded by the form which is philosophical science. Here and in the Introduction which follows it, Hegel sought to establish and distinguish his political logic from that of positivist liberalism. For this reason Hegel strongly differed with those who emphasized nature as the sole source for an understanding of the state and dismissed the realm of thought and idea. He here took a position contrary to the Enlightenment and empiricist legacies which witnessed a fundamental split between politics and philosophy, the practical and the theoretical. With so many opinions arising out of the relativist vacuum resultant of the alienation of philosophy from the political and normative theorization of the state—who shall rule and how—it is philosophy alone which may elevate these incessant debates to the realm of thought and the standard of a perennial truth. Philosophy alone offers a means of separating the wheat from the chaff in order to discriminate the rationality inherent in the universal idea of the state amongst its historical manifestations.

The actual philosophical thought of the Hegelian state lies in the inner identification of the actual and the rational. Here the empirical and ideal content of reason cohere with one another so as to express a deeper unity which is lost in witnessing the idea of the state as merely one amongst a plethora of ideas founded, essentially, in the subjective consciousness of mere theory. As the *Logic* asserted and the *Philosophy of Right* reinforced, ultimate actuality resides in the rational and founding substance that is the Idea: "nothing is actual except the Idea. Once that is granted, the important thing, then, is to recognize in the semblance of the temporal and transient the substance which is immanent and the eternal which is present."[26] Beneath the outer appearance of the becoming of history is revealed an inner being, a universal strata which coheres with an absolute Idea in constant self-realization. This becoming displays an "infinite wealth of forms, shapes, and appearances" but at its core is none other than what is present to consciousness itself in its nascent realization of its rational content and correspondence with the Idea.

This limitless fluidity between phenomena and the universality of the Idea is the realization of Hegel's speculative practice, dialectically overcoming the apparent alienation of the two moments of sense perception and thought; object and subject. With this Hegel assures us that the province of a theory of politics and the state belong squarely within the auspices of the logical method. The application of the speculative method to a consideration and formulation of the state requires an unearthing of the rationality inherent to the potentialities of an age. In this way it is seen not as a utopian ideal to be pursued beyond the horizons of historical possibility, but rather as the inherent potentiality presented to the age itself in terms of the disclosure of its universal idea: its "concept." In this sense his vision of the state is intended as *no* timeless formulation and eschatology of the state, but rather one's "*own time apprehended in thoughts.*"

176   *Metaphysics and politics in Hegel's thought*

The conception of reason laid out in the Preface explicitly serves to conjoin his logic with his politics in the possibility of a reconciliation between an as yet unresolved abstract ideal and the actuality real persons sensorially find themselves within. This capacity for more than a mere consolation in existence, but rather the joy of recognizing the immediacy of the ideal present in the midst of a seemingly alien and inhospitable actuality resolves humanity to its plight. Much as Plato understood philosophical insight as the light of liberation from the darkness of the cave and the initiation of a form of moral purpose, Hegel witnessed the redemptive capacity of the penetration of reason into the recurring cycle of the seemingly banal becoming of human existence and suffering. Philosophy thus directly empowers those who would engage in the thought of politics to recover its central concept, the state, as the wealth that is the rational birthright of an age.

The logical pursuit and realization of political ideals in a temporally and spatially bound form surmounts fatalism in its intermediation of either an unrealizable utopian afterlife or an overdetermining historical past. The "rose in the cross of the present" is Hegel's recognition of the rational basis underlying both subjective will and its objective, natural circumstances. Christ's legacy is thus the spiritual reconciliation of humanity to its existence and philosophy's subsequent task is its salvaging of the human present as a site for celebration beyond messianic anticipation or worldly resignation.

The trinitarian reconciliation of father, son and holy ghost here informed Hegel's dialectical transformation of the universal community into particularity and singularity. The equivalent modern political project, then, is to bring about this reconciliation in overcoming the alienation of family, individual and state in realizing their rational unity in the singular conception of the state. Yet, despite the theological dimensions of the state, his intent in the *Philosophy of Right* vis-à-vis religion is the comprehensive consideration of the *Logic* of the state considered in its own relative autonomy. Though faith both presents and preserves the dynamics of the absolute in the feeling and intuition of naïve consciousness, it is only reason which permits for its fullest realization in a modern state. Hegel's Lutheran Christian principle applied to politics is essentially a doctrine of non-deterministic intermediation where divine will is manifested through of the inherency of reason in the world without an accompanying diminishment of the subjective agency of modern individuals. Regardless, his theory of the state organizes itself within these logical parameters largely divested of an underlying religious program, and in a way which serves to sharply discriminate between theocracy and modern statehood.

Hegel's Introduction takes these insights further. The theory of right and ethics, the main grounds for a theory of state, are derived through the logic of the universal and its modes of determinations in thought, i.e., its coming into being through the reason of becoming. The *Philosophy of Right* presents the explication of the state as the realization of the concept of right inherent in thought: "This self-consciousness which apprehends itself through thinking as an essence, and thereby frees itself from the contingent and the untrue, is the principle of right, morality, and all ethical life."[27] The *Philosophy of Right* is herein intended as the explication of the inherent rationality of the idea of right, and no mere theorization out of a subjective concept. Hegel clarifies this to show that he is not dealing with a merely formal construction of state in abstract and ahistorical terms, but rather one which mirrors the essential teleological purposing of the state toward its inner concept. The science of right is thus first and foremost a philosophical task and its job is the articulation of the concept which permits politics to realize the "immanent development of the thing itself," i.e., the state.

The history which presupposes the concept, that which has made it accessible to present thought, Hegel claims, is a given. Much as the *Philosophy of Right* assumed his *Encyclopedia* Logic as the clear articulation of the speculative project for thought, it also took its historical precursors as presuppositional for what it intended to elaborate in terms of the actuality or rational potential of an age. In Hegel's case this implied no less than the formulation of a wholly modern conception of state out of an understanding of its inherent yet historically bounded concept. Reason peels back the layers of "ephemeral existence, external contingency, opinion, unsubstantial appearance, untruth, illusion, and so forth"[28] in order to see things as they actually are and to most fully realize the possibilities of the actual in accord with the rational ideal. In the case of the *Philosophy of Right,* the goal is the realization of the political concept of state in view of the demands of modern individuality and freedom. What has gone before to make Hegel's task possible, i.e., the elaborations of the dialectic in his two treatises on logic,[29] was not the task of the *Philosophy of Right* itself. Hegel's early intent in the Introduction was rather to introduce us to his fundamental categories of modern politics—right, will and freedom—in a way which intermediates between the thoroughgoing metaphysics of the *Logic* and conceptually derivative social and political arrangements.

The logically derived concept is the very basis of right, and thought its origin. Right is the expression of freedom as it manifests itself at the various levels of ethical life. Freedom forms the inner concept of right in the state where "the system of right is the realm of freedom made actual, the world of spirit [*Geist*] brought forth out of itself like a second nature."[30] Hegel asserts that freedom is the product of the thought through which the will and volition realizes the concepts of political life provided in thought itself. This link is so strong that Hegel references his work on logic as the source of the science of thought and the ultimate basis of freedom achieved there: "*That* the will is free and *what* the will and freedom are, can be deduced ... only in the context of the whole [of philosophy]."[31] *It is thus the creativity of the speculative power of thought which makes freedom possible in political life.*

The formation of the will and its connection to the dynamics of the development of thought as it is presented in the *Logic* is reinforced in his politics. Insofar as the will is "particularity reflected into itself and so brought back to universality," the individual particular is elevated to individual as universal through speculation.[32] As this makes clear, the realization of the self in individual freedom of the will is not the atomic selfhood of the individual particular, but rather "individuality in accordance with its concept" which is the universal.[33] Citing sections 163–5 of the *Encyclopedia* Logic, Hegel here draws our attention to the play of the "concept" as a structuring paradigm for the activity of the will. In thinking and dialectic, the concept gathers together the particularized universality that is instantiated in the unified individual in its universal—rather than unitary—form. As explored above in consideration of Hegel's *Logic*, both particular and universal aspects of individual willing are tied together into actuality through syllogistic reconciliation in the concept. This actualization of the will is the ultimate goal of Hegel's politics; reason's utmost purpose is to ensure that ideal actuality is brought about in accord with its concept in political form. Where the speculative activity of thought's self-relation is abandoned, our understanding of politics can get no further than understanding and the "stubborn" adherence to the reality of the particular will alone: the "third moment, which is true and speculative ... is the one into which the understanding declines to advance, for it is precisely the concept which it persists in calling the inconceivable."[34] In the modern context, the speculative coordination of universal and particular is synonymous with freedom on the Hegelian account, and it is "the task of logic as purely speculative philosophy to prove and explain ... this ultimate spring of all activity, life, and consciousness."[35]

In its bringing together the universal and individual in itself beyond understanding and dialectic, the will to freedom grasps its concept and strives to realize its inner concept of itself. This recognition of the logic's organization in the "substance of self-consciousness, its immanent generic essence"[36] tethers the political will to freedom to the logic of thought. This consciousness emerges historically as a form of "the universal which embraces its object, thoroughly permeates its determination and therein remains identical with itself."[37] In realizing itself in its striving for its inner conceptual basis, the will realizes its own potential and impresses this upon the form of the political community. Here the will of the particular individual is understood in its universality at the very foundations of the state, and it takes license in this larger will. Grounded in Rousseau's theory of legitimacy, this is the direct political implication of speculative thought for Hegel applied to the sphere of modern ethical life or *Sittlichkeit*, one which orders the community in accord with the rational dictates of the free will in reflection of right as its political concept.

Where the will's innermost purpose is had in the realization of its inner concept of freedom, it is made an engine of historical change. In this way it bonds the real to the ideal, the particular to the universal idea. Its historical realization of freedom is the creation of the condition for the will's own self-realization in reflection of its concept so that it is "*the free will which wills the free will.*" Political thought thus takes up this goal of setting agents of thought, citizens and communities, on the path to realize their immanent concept of freedom. As a whole, freedom in the state is the direct result of a "rational system of spirit," and this system is the method and content of the logic.

In the political world, the logic's task is the equalization of the individual with the state as its other. This is the undoing of the liberal dichotomy of the political subjectivity of the citizen on the one hand, the objective authority and mechanism of the state on the other. As in the logic, this unity is found in a concept of personhood and will which unites the two in a spiritual whole. This whole is sustained in the idea of the free will, the basis of the doctrine of right where "Right therefore is by definition freedom as Idea." Though all stages move toward freedom in their momentary expression of right, the prioritization of either the state or the individual personality represents political arrangements which equate right with a limited and one-sided element of the absolute Idea.[38] Hegel rejected either alternative and neither achieve the demands of modern politics. The dilemma arises in the pre-modern stage of abstract or formal right in its totalization of the abstract universal as the basis of right. The contrary moment in morality realizes its opposition and sets up the particular against the prior universality. These two moments abide as the contest of the one and the many, universal and particular and remain to find a final form of unity which realizes their inner unity as individual singularity. In absolute freedom, a condition mirroring the integral unity of the absolute Idea, there are no conflicts where harmonization of these moments has been achieved. This was Hegel's intent and one which he held to be a thoroughly descriptive position. That is, he claimed to render forth the fully formed synthesis of the political universal (the state) and particular (the individual of civil society) in his conception of freedom. This is an achievement of harmonization which each age, in its turn, is capable of in its thought and application of reason.

Hegel elaborated the ideas of political right and will in reflection of the concepts which underlie political consciousness itself. Such a political task for Hegel could only be imagined in terms of speculative logic: "The method whereby ... the concept develops itself out of itself is expounded in logic and is here likewise presupposed."[39] In the *Philosophy of Right* as in the logic, then, the proper task of thought is to read from the outer layers of particularity the coherence of the outer with an inner and regulative universal concept. The *Philosophy of Right* reads the ideal out of the actual and sees the inherent concept as reason in things as they are so as to offer, to articulate, the ideal that is already actual. This for Hegel is the witnessing capacity of philosophy which brings to consciousness "the matter's *very soul* putting forth its branches and fruit organically."[40]

It is under this conception that he conceived of the now famous *Doppelsatz*, his "double dictum," of the actual as the rational and vice versa, and the full development of the inner possibilities of an age for itself in thought. Far from intending a doctrine of passivity and inert reflection, the actualization of the ideal potentials of an age or nation—which might otherwise remain obscured by the tendencies of either abstract or traditionalistic thought—are brought to light through reason. On his account, politics is a moving shape of the Idea in its striving to become aware of itself and render its inner potentials concrete and necessary. The Idea, though, must not be understood as a mere object of thought; it is always a will, moving forward to greater self-realization through syllogistic reconciliation. This remains true in the politics as much as it does in the logic.

As brought out above in Chapter 3 and as well documented by Walter Kaufman, in the 1830 version of his *Logic* Hegel informed and reminded us that he was well aware that "These simple sentences have seemed striking to some and have been received with hostility" and that "when I spoke of actuality ... [I] distinguished it not only from what is contingent ... but also. .. from existence [*Dasein*]."[41] The fixation of conservative enthusiasm or liberal criticism upon the latter half of Hegel's doubled equation—that the actual is rational—mistakes empirical reality for the actual when in fact it cannot be so. This conforms with Hegel's own idealism which distinguished the full realization of the rational ideal from that which simply exists.[42]

Beyond the double dictum, the overt relations of the method of the *Logic* and the structure and intent of the *Philosophy of Right* go yet further. The development of the *Philosophy of Right* itself maps the concepts of the *Logic* onto the synthetic architecture leading up to ethical life (*Sittlichkeit*). The preliminary immediacy of the universal is contained in the concept of abstract right. The subsequent moment of mediation and negation, the dialectical moment, is found in the realm of subjective morality and its contestation of abstract right. Here the particular opposed to the universal arises to present the dilemma of the part and the whole, particular and universal to be dialectically resolved in the realization of the singular individual. Finally, the synthetic turn of speculative thought arrives in the concept of *Sittlichkeit* which unites the first two moments epitomized by the family and the civil individual held within the completed whole that is the individual state. That is, the outer layer of the *Sittlichkeit* is the state holding within itself these two substrata as its grounding moments in sublation (*Aufheben*) so as to realize their inner unity in its own identity. Freedom emerges in this third and last moment alone, and the state in its outer objectivity is the organic nation as a spiritual and political unity.

The metaphysics of the Preface and Introduction then have rendered Hegel's key concepts of political life—right, will and freedom—in terms which are a direct translation of dialectical relations articulated in the logic. As Hegel clearly indicated, these introductory sections integrate his political conclusions with the syllogistic plan of the *Logic* in a very direct way. Dismissing this dimension of his plan is thus to misunderstand the primary significance of the outer shell of the state and ethical life as the outward display of a deep and foundational commitment to their universal concept. It is, by extension, certainly to miss the classical legacy at work under the surface of Hegel's thought as it sought to reinstate the unity of the universal and particular where it has been sundered in the oppositions of ancient and modern thought, logical and political.

## The philosophical context of Hegel's modern political project

In the brief metaphysical work of the Preface and Introduction, Hegel put forward an abridged sketch of his *Encyclopedia* Logic's rigorous philosophical system with a view to theorizing the relations of the social and political part and whole. His dialectical conception of these relations are a reflection of the process of historical change itself, insofar as change represents the mediated expression of ideas over time.[43] As he first laid out in his *Phenomenology* and elaborated in his theory of right, they are understood through their decisive historical manifestations so that any philosophy of the state could no more find a once and for all time model than one could "overleap his own age, jump over Rhodes."[44] Dialectic is historical and not merely cognitive or conceptual. In this way Hegel understood the ideality and abstractness of the concept of the "whole" and "part" as embedded (i.e., immanent) aspects of the historical process through which societies and individuals develop. Thus there is no wholly intellectual level of universalist abstraction upon which to ground universal and final legitimacy for political authority. In this way political "reason" itself, "right," is understood as going through the process of historical transformation to the point where individual human beings—who become full members of this process only with the onset of the modern era—come to equally possess the capacity for rational political agency as part of a developmental process.[45] It is through this deduction, and as a child of his time, that Hegel recognized the radical need to provide for the equilibrium of the social "whole" and "part" through political participation.

The "substance" or ground which legitimates authority in the modern era, one which brings about popular sovereignty through the pluralization of reason, is its peculiar ethical life. Here the state as the embodiment of the concept of freedom holds within itself both the social basis of the family and the individual–particular levels, and represents the unifying level of the "ethical order" that establishes sovereignty. It is the institutional life of the state itself, as opposed to the subordination of either the principle of the whole or the part to the other in the abstract, where "the prodigious unification of self-subsistent individuality with universal substantiality has been achieved."[46] For Hegel the ideal–conceptual opposition of the whole and the part is resolved in the political fusion of the singular state that takes freedom to its core as the moment which overcomes the opposition: the collective individuality of the state as "freedom in its most concrete shape."[47] The universal and its political relationship to the particular is mediated and synchronized through this historical framework in Hegel's logic of the dialectic and its realization of concrete freedom. Hegel's political thought here conceives of freedom as the very universalist idea of history realized over time, understood in the terms of dialectical progression and speculative consummation. Where the institutional expression of this realization is possible only through the state, the *Philosophy of Right* translates the syllogistic resolution of the metaphysical problem of universals into a method for the resolution of the political problem of the universal. In attending to the question as to how the state can be both one in itself and in its many members at the very same time, the problem of universals acts as a paradigmatic concern in both metaphysical as well as political ways. While Hegel has not yet articulated his particular social and political arrangements, his introductory statements made his programmatic intentions clear. From this starting point, Hegel's explicitly political project is given a metaphysical christening as it makes way toward the fulfillment of freedom in the forms of modern society—*Sittlichkeit*—and politics.

Prior to delivering his theory of modern politics and the state in the context of the "ethical life" (*Sittlichkeit*), Hegel first moved through two prior stages of the will. These are abstract right and morality and they represent the movements of being and essence, universal and particular, which emerge prior to the consummation of thought in the Idea through the concept.[48]

## Foundations of the modern state

### *The family*

The first emergent consummation of the ethical ideal of right, family, is united to the spirit of the nation through the intermediation of the ethical order. "*Sitte*" or "custom" as ethically regulated behavior, forms the positive bond which unites individual consciousness with the family, and in this way conditions and unites the family with the larger ethical body. This is the syllogism of the intermediation of universal and individual through the particularity of the family, underpinning Hegel's understanding of freedom where individuality is formed through its dependence upon the community. In both the *Encyclopedia* Logic and the *Philosophy of Right*, it is this being "situated" which characterizes the basic substance of the ethical community, the actuality of the idea which unites individual, family and nation.

Within the family, the relations of self-conscious love accord with the rule of freedom, and the family is the most basic element within the larger complex of the ethical life. Here, in contradistinction to the liberal contract theorists, marriage is made as an "anti-contractual" contract. That is, within the contract of marriage, partners forego and transcend their individuality, and as such, contractual relations. A merely consensual form of love, Hegel argues, is reduced to ritual and formality. Here, the independence of the married members "brings disunion into the loving disposition and, as an alien factor, ... [runs] counter to the inwardness of their union."[49] That is, the inner unity of the family is disturbed by the presence of the contractual relations which ought to be restricted to the sphere of civil relations. Sexual differences themselves present no threat to domestic unity, where the ordering of men and women's physical differences find a common basis in reason. In this way gender precedes the subject; men are "powerful and active," and women "passive and subjective" in Hegel's view.[50] Marriage transforms the two previously independent selves and capacities into a unified and greater individual and herein asserts the first moment of the unifying capacity of the ethical order itself. As the most basic element of the ethical life, the family represents the first sublation, or synthetic-integration, of the individual particular into the objective universality of the communal whole.

The objective, and outward expression of familial unity is expressed in the holding of property. The foundation of the family in right transforms the caprice and selfishness of private property into the ethical form of estate capital

(*Vermögen*). In the domestic sphere the conjugal relationship takes priority over its prior and consanguine relations. In this way, the newly formed union is understood as consummate in its differentiation out of its prior familial ties, and establishes it as a universal and "enduring person." From this basis in the family, Hegel's transition to civil society represents the developmental maturation of the ethical concept into a fuller, self-subsistent and objective form, i.e., a concrete society of familial "persons." This evolution is both historical on the objective level, and abstract on the ideal. It is a process which witnesses the dialectical movement within the familial sphere from marriage through property with the final dissolution of the family realized in the maturation and individuation of children through education. Civil society thus represents a further development in the evolution of the concept of freedom, and the potentiation of the subjective particularity which remained latent and sealed off in the undifferentiated universality at the heart of the family.

## Civil society and the mediation of propertied individuals

In the development of freedom towards its consummation in the state, Hegel conceives of civil society as a mid-ground. Here, the basic tenets of liberal consent and freedom are developed. Though this is the sphere of the individual conceived of in the terms of classical liberalism, it does not present us with Hegel's conception of the true individual. That is, it is here where self-centered, egoistic interests of particular individuals find their fullest expression, though it is only the state which is able to forge familial universality with particular identity into individuality.[51]

The complex web of interdependence that is civil society weaves the fabric out of which this sphere develops into a "system of needs." Yet this interconnectedness is external and contractual, and ridden with the disintegrating forces of particularist interest. Despite this external form of the relations of civil society, one of dislocation and fragmentation, it nonetheless abides in the immanent universal: "inner necessity behind the outward appearance." In accord with civil society's uninhibited expression of particularity and personal individuality, a concomitant physical and ethical degeneracy arises. In emphasizing external appearances here, Hegel's vision recalls the *Republic's* city of pigs, where the self-subsistence of egoistic interests find their legitimacy in the realization of their aims.

The appetitive and desirous momentum of the civil sphere poses an immediate threat to the rational equilibrium and immanent balance of the universal and the particular, familial society and the individual particular. A higher form, then, must politically mediate between the self-interestedness of civil society and the ethical interests of the whole through the objective authority of superior right, i.e., the state. The integration of the subjective and self-seeking particularity of the individuals within civil society into the larger ethical order thus is crucial to Hegel's plan for overall political stability and order as well as the preservation of personal freedom. For Hegel, the grave failing of Plato's polis was its resistance to this subjective element and the inevitable consequences to the flourishing of the overall order which such stultification implies either destroying the whole or stultifying its development.[52]

The three key moments of civil society—the system of needs, of justice and the corporation—form Hegel's fully developed sphere of subjectivity and personal freedom. Unimpeded by the ethical and religious concerns of the state, the aims of civil society find expression and grounding in law and institution. The core character of this sphere, as a matrix of interdependent needs, is the freely contractual expression of self-interest. Corporations and the judiciary serve as collective institutions which integrate interests and secure the essential foundations of the system of needs within the larger ethical order. Hegel clarifies that, unlike the social contract theorists, it is civil society alone, and not the state, which constitutes the collective of particular interests in contract with one another.

The state, above and beyond civil society, is itself composed of all substrata as the integrated moments of the total ethical order. It is the objective expression of a whole and unified ethical body in its expression of law and institution as the highest realization of the ethical universal, i.e., the idea of right itself. Thus, where Locke and Rousseau subsume the state within civil society, Hegel intentionally nests it within the state in order to give the latter its ethical and political primacy. For Hegel, civil society thus forms a lower level of consciousness than does the state. The immanent awareness of the necessity and universality of the state is not yet attained, and this sphere is incapable of developing true freedom: "There [in civil society], then, spirit's freedom has existence and spirit comes to be *for itself* in this element which *in itself* is alien to spirit's appointed end, freedom."[53] The purposive self-realization of freedom is herein only wholly actual in the state. In this way, supreme authority rests in it as the only unity capable of containing, and sustaining, the autonomy and specificity of the lesser spheres. Derived from its speculative power of integration, it is the consciousness of the organic unity of the universal and the particular in its objective and individual form.

The level of freedom actually attained in civil society is one of asserting the subjectivity of need over and against the objectivity of nature. Needs are satisfied by consuming the products of others' labor, and it is this interdependence which emancipates humanity from nature's scarcity. Unlike animals, who express only physical needs for Hegel, men and women are rationally informed through the abstraction of the idea of freedom. In this self-creative process, consciousness multiplies both the degree and kind of need through its involvement in developing means of satisfying these very needs. This capacity for abstraction, through the ideal of freedom, reifies social relations as they differentiate, and in this ongoing manner presents a highly specialized mechanism to respond to the diversity of developing interests.

Essentially, members of civil society reformulate their needs by way of an implicit aesthetic and utilitarian awareness of the logical concept: "Understanding, with its grasp of distinctions, multiplies these human needs, and since taste and utility become criteria of judgment, even the needs themselves are affected thereby."[54] That is, needs participate in an ongoing and reflective process of self-transformation, moving towards embracing the latent concept which is projected into the objects of their own subjective strivings. This is the rationality behind the outward appearance of this sphere's selfishness and avarice. Reinforcing the syllogism of the particular's concept (freedom), the system of needs is driven teleologically by its many wills towards the actualization of the idea of freedom, and in this way anticipates—and mandates—the universal state. This is the foundation of Hegel's optimism in the reconciliation of civil society with the demands of the ethical order writ large and of the part with the whole. Civil society herein forms a completely integrated moment of subjective universality within the larger ethical order, existing in continuity with the interests of objective universality. Thus conceived, civil society and state are held to be in no inherent opposition with each other, and the liberal conception of the "negative state" is side-stepped and denounced as inherently false.

The system of needs brings about both the division of labor and the universal dependence of all upon all. Hegel speculates that the abstract and technological process of rationalized instrumentality, the result of the developing needs and wants of society, finds its utmost expression in the complete dehumanization of labor, i.e., the universal implementation of automated machinery. What one can see in this is the incessant drive towards the manufacture and satisfaction of needs, in essence the rudiments of commodification: "What the English call 'comfortable' is something inexhaustible ... a need is produced not so much by those who immediately experience it, but by those who hope to make a profit from its creation."[55] In this arrangement Hegel witnesses the inevitable rise of an accompanying underclass of paupers and their potential to develop into a "pauperized rabble." He confronts this problem by handing over certain limited powers of economic intervention to the state, e.g., price fixing, taxation and public works. However, in the end, civil society must be left essentially untouched; Hegel assumed "the market" has its own universal laws which must freely and uninhibitedly express themselves to engender the greatest economic prosperity and free personal expression.[56]

The key to Hegel's stabilization—political and logical—of the ethical world may be seen to lie specifically in civil society. Where particular members are reconciled to the whole through the institutions of rights and law, individual freedom comes about as the consciousness of subjective immediacy with the objective order established in the state and by the family. The realization of freedom in coherence with the overall order is thus the stabilizing crux of his modern political project of freedom and the resolution of the modern political problem of the whole and the part.[57] The subjective particular is the intermediating moment between the universal family and the individuality of the state. In this regard it plays a central role in legitimizing the state in modern terms, making possible the equalization of the political subject and object in conformity with the underlying logic of the ethical order.

Against those who would conflate it with society, the universal state retains its ideal autonomy in relation to its particular instantiations. While the state may be said to stand in a holistic and interdependent relation with its citizens, it nonetheless retains independence in its capacity to sustain the relation of its concrete members with the inner concept of right which freedom realizes in the modern world. Thus the state "individual" as institution carries out the speculative syllogism of the political world ("ethical life") which elevates the alienated and atomic particular to its inner potential and universal concept. This restates the private, particular person's universality, one seeded by the absolute Idea's historical development, nesting the apparent transience of civil relations within the ethical firmament of a purposeful historical development. Even in the depths of civil subjective particularity the pronounced syllogistic unity of the overall ethical order (*Sittlichkeit*) witnesses Hegel's logical program.

## *Civil society's classes and the problem of capitalism*

Hegel points to civil society and characterizes its individual members as "burghers," or the bourgeoisie. Civil society is, in fact, nothing but the realization of the bourgeois spirit: *bürgerliche Gesellschaft* (burgher or bourgeois society). In construing the economic relations of need and satisfaction as he does, Hegel infused the theoretical rudiments of liberal capitalist society into the ethical order. When looked at in retrospect, he underestimated its potential transformative and disfiguring impact upon the whole of the ethical order. Hegel somewhat anticipated this contention and responded to it by maintaining that self-interest is realized solely through its recognition of the universal ethical substance within itself. That is, underlying all subjective pursuits within the matrix of diverse interests and the division of labor, a rational equilibrium inherent to the differentiating ethical order presides so as to reconcile self-interested individuals to the universal interests of the body-politic: a "hidden-hand" so to speak. Thus, the "political" and the "economic" are inalienably and rationally fused to each other, despite their dichotomous expressions in the state and civil society. Differentiating the two into autonomous spheres in this way creates no immediate problem for Hegel. A dualism in "actuality" does not necessitate an accompanying dualism of its essential substance rooted in the eternal Idea.

Where Hegel's conceptualization of free-willing subjectivity rests upon the economistic grounds of civil society, he emphasizes the way needs and labor reflect each other's development and revise class consciousness in the process. However, in making the individual free only out of the rising complexity of the system of needs, and so grounding free subjectivity upon the reflection of differentiating self-interests, Hegel seems to leave the individual particular stranded in a culture of fetishism where individuality is rooted in commodified social and material experience. Hegel characterizes the movement from community (*Gemeinschaft*) to society (*Gesellschaft*) as a historical differentiation of the system of needs. However, this development is not merely historical, not merely empirical. Rather, it conforms to, and actualizes the ideal which the transition expresses historically. In this way, his conception of free-subjectivity within civil society promotes a self-interested freedom highly problematic from an ethical standpoint. That is, by founding individual autonomy and interest on the consumptive and avaricious grounds of free-market activity, Hegel's conception of free subjectivity seems at odds with the normative integration of the dialectic of state and civil society as he conceives of it. Despite Hegel's explicit critique of classical liberalism's political and metaphysical presuppositions, he has nonetheless employed some of its central tenets which seem to hinder the core project of his express program as an all-encompassing and ethically integrative social-being realized in, through and for the historical state. His means of addressing these problems comes in the form of the classes and corporations which serve to unite the persons of civil society into collectives and to resist the proliferation of class divisions into pervasive forms of material inequality.

Furthermore, and following a brief sketch of the class system, I outline a conflict which arises between class and subjective autonomy. In both its productive and its consumptive character, civil society is characterized by the prevalence of three distinct classes. Hegel described the relationship between class and consciousness to be one rooted in the concrete experience of daily life. In this way, the nature of one's labor decisively influences one's general world-view expressed through class consciousness. The division of labor and the technical classifications of production and exchange distinguish the class types. These classes are hierarchically ordered in relation to their realization of the political universal, of freedom.

The first class type, the agricultural class, is the most context-specific and nature-bound in character; i.e., it is the least reflexive and self-willing of the classes. It finds its development restricted by its reliance upon nature as a completely self-contained "stranger." The primacy of family relations is secured in lineage and trust, and forms the patriarchy which is most compatible with this class's sense of dependency and arrested consciousness. The second class type, one of a higher-order self-awareness, is the business class. Its core function is the manipulation of raw materials characteristic of its labor, reflection and intelligence. This class is most representative of civil society insofar as it drives the progressive division of labor through the conscious mediation of the diverse interests within it. Craftsmanship, trade and manufacture characterize this class's economic activities and fix within it a spirit of self-interest and universalized subjectivity. This class mediates between the excesses of the poverty and wealth of the other two classes, and in so doing stabilizes the ethical order and forms the bourgeois "heart" of the civil order in its epitomization of *Bürgerlichkeit*. The third and final class type, the genuine universal estate for Hegel, is composed of civil servants; the bureaucrats of the state. This sphere functions to represent and mediate between the interests of all social strata and the state itself. In brief, the bureaucratic class serves to ensure that the oppositions and contradictions between the integrated elements of the ethical order do not overwhelm the ethical body as a whole. The practical issues which arise with the actual ability of such a bureaucratic class to successfully mediate these interests will be dealt with in greater depth below.

Hegel emphasizes the free expression of subjective opinion and "arbitrary will" within civil society as the decisive factor in determining the individual's station and class. However, at the very same time, he argues for the necessity of class distinctions as the only means by which individuals attain self-realization. That is, prior to the individual particular's potential for self-realization, the person already belongs to and shares in a class based world-view or ideology. This Hegel made quite clear in his description of the "character" indicative of each class. However, he subsequently argues that the individual only becomes a genuine individual through self-restriction to an exclusive sphere of class. In maintaining these two positions, Hegel sets up an opposition of class and freedom. That is, first, individuals are predisposed to class as the formative source of their essential consciousness. Individuals are here "born" into a class which conditions the trajectory of their "natural" capacities and willing intentions. Second, and in opposition to the first point, the individual's "will" is held to ultimately mediate its own class personification, its class identity. To describe this problem logically: if the individual is made free through a self-determining "restriction" to a specific class and so is made free only after this choice has been made autonomously, there was in fact no freedom prior to this choice which was made as yet within the bounds of class consciousness (i.e., prior to this belonging to a class). Thus, since the individual always already belongs to a class by virtue of birth, the legitimacy of the individual autonomy with which this self-restriction to class is performed is undermined. Hegel attempts to resolve this dilemma of agency by attributing class divisions to an external and objective source, i.e., nature:

> People are made unequal by nature, where inequality is in its element, and in civil society the right of particularity is so far from cancelling this natural inequality that it produces it out of spirit and raises it to an inequality of skill and resources, and even to one of moral and intellectual education. To oppose to this right a demand for equality is a folly of the empty understanding which takes as real and rational its abstract equality and its "ought-to-be."[58]

Nature is made responsible for social and economic inequalities. Civil society, alternatively, is the mediating force which seeks to equalize disparity. Class divisions thus represent the immutable "unfairness" of nature forcibly superimposed on human communities, which themselves play little role in either forming, or sustaining these inequalities. To this extent, Hegel seems to here offer us a restatement of Plato's "myth of the metals."

However, and in an implicit sense, Hegel's unresolved tension between civil society and nature, individual and class, seems to lead toward the ethical logic of a "social-contract." That is, if, as argued above, one is always necessarily "bound" to class, then the individual can never have had the free will to have chosen class membership free of the reign of class influence in the first place. Thus, the act of rationally contracting into a class is always hypothetical and never actual. Yet, and in contrast with this logic, Hegel wants us to accept that the individual can at once be born into a class, in the full sense of its material

*Political dialectic* 189

and ideal self-awareness, and at the same time express a genuinely free subjectivity in rationally defining its own "class destiny," i.e., its socio-economic and ideological future. Thus, if we dismiss this "social-contract" analysis as being in basic conflict with civil society's dialectical sublation of class stratification, then we would only be left with the alternative of the one-class society. That is, only in a single-class society could the individual be both the member-inheritor of class values, expectations and potentials, and at the same time be truly capable of socio-economic self-determination.

In this context, we are faced with a question: if the individual will is ultimately decisive, and birth, natural capacity and contingency merely have their influences secondarily, what is the purpose of class divisions to begin with? Speculatively, in incorporating the three spheres of the family, civil society and the state into the overall operative consciousness of the ethical order, Hegel intends a grand, "modern" synthesis of the previous feudal estates in a way which reconciles the alienation of these elements in resolution of the modern political problematic of the universal. In this way, the distinctions amongst the levels of class within civil society, in terms of the conceptual evolution of freedom and consciousness, are directly reflected in their economic stratification. What each class represents in terms of the syllogistic potentialities of the universal concept thus has its reciprocal expression in the actual world of material want and need. As has been pointed out, economy is for Hegel one instantiation of the progressive expression of the universal ideal's drive towards ever greater forms of self-realization. However, despite what this understanding offers in terms of a descriptive tool for explaining objective historical developments, it nevertheless lacks in terms of sustaining an ethical ground for critique.

These issues have long been a source of debate amongst Hegel commentators, some of whom have lamented that where the actual is made the rational and vice versa, we have but to reconcile and adjust ourselves to the world as it necessarily, and already ideally, is. In anticipating this, Hegel countered that these are essentially abstract and "youthful" arguments which refuse to "move beyond the universal and so never reaches the actual." What Hegel is stressing is that only through the realization of right, manifested in the social hierarchy of class, can the individual ever truly realize subjectivity and make it valuable. Herein, Hegel understated the ethically invidious aspects of class divisions by interpreting them away as "moments" in the evolution of the absolute Idea historically expressed in civil society. Class divisions thus seem to present a problematic, and inconclusive, aspect of Hegel's thought. As Karl Marx would later assert in his *Critique of Hegel's "Philosophy of Right,"* Hegel often moves from a descriptive "is" to a prescriptive "hence" with little concern for the logic of his ethical and political entailments.[59]

### *The state: a "system of three syllogisms"*

Where the state is itself the "ethical whole," it is to the ethical life what the concept is to the absolute Idea: the initial emergence of its actual existence. It is in the state that the universal concept of right achieves its foremost historical expression. As the concrete unification of all the sub-spheres of the ethical life, the state stands as the very embodiment of ethical objectivity and the summing up of the total spiritual life or organism of the parts: "The state is the actuality of the ethical Idea. It is the ethical mind or spirit qua the substantial will manifest and revealed to itself."[60] That is, the state physically embodies the substance of the ethical order; it is the Idea's consummating expression of reason in the historical world. The dialectic of right defines the state itself: it exists in the universal state as custom, the particular as the individual of civil society, and the individual as the state. The state, however, only becomes fully rational with the realization of its inner universality and the closing of the dialectical circle between itself and its others in the family and civil society. The state thus represents the conformity of right and institution in its most complete expression; the ideal dialectic balance is struck between the "concept of right together with the actualization of that concept."[61] In this way the state anchors right in the world, and establishes the fundamental stability of the overall ethical order in a balance of freedom and belonging, right and duty. For these reasons, the state reigns over the individual particular, where the latter realizes its highest freedom through its paragon commitment to the former.

The spiritual individuality of the state, the third moment of the political syllogism of the ethical order, is thus the moment which reproduces Hegel's speculative logic of resolution and follows closely its method in seeking a reconciliation of whole to part which secures legitimate authority for the political sphere. The political sphere is the completion of the ethical world but, at the same time, is but a prelude to the larger life and destiny of the nation. In the consummation of the three moments of state—universal, particular and individual—Hegel intended to catalyze the political whole into a unity which witnessed the underlying idea of spiritual unity as a basis of rationality. This is as much as to say that the political logic of the state surpasses the mechanical, and out of its teleological moments creates a new unity which focuses and unites the national will on the basis of syllogistic reconciliation. It is from this inner unity of logical thought and historical substance drawn from the *Logic* with which Hegel's state projects itself outward as a world historical entity. As discussed above, Hegel clearly wished to distinguish his idea of political life from those founded upon classical liberal ideals, and his notion of the state as a precursor to the ethical life aspires to restore the integrated communality of polis life in accord with the demands of modern freedom.

In accord with the triadic relationships of the *Logic* in mind, Hegel asserted a strict distinction between civil society and the state. While Hegel argued that civil society should not be understood to exhaust or subsume the ethical and political auspices of the state, he upheld the inverse. To extend the fractious and avaricious logic of civil society into the state itself would be to make inclusion and allegiance to it optional. Since the state is both the essential universal substance and end-state of freedom, both its content and its form, meaning and objective identity ultimately come to the citizen particular through it alone. To undermine this relationship is to undermine the structure of the whole order resulting in the loss of freedom for all. In this way, the state's organic unity grounds "objective freedom"; it is a conscious and "self-determining" agent which "thinks" and so creates its laws in conformity with the universal Idea. It is the absolute and final individual, encompassing all constituent subjects as its elements. In its highest conceptual form, it remains the idea of its "actual," constituent parts understood in terms of the fullest realization of freedom.

The three forms of the abstract idea of the state, its physical forms, are thus the differentiated moments of the idea of political totality and this is the outward show of the syllogism itself. The constitution (i.e., a system of law and order) forms the rational foundation from which these three objective forms, or "powers," spring, and so reflects the objective inclusion of the three essential moments of dialectic. Each of these moments finds its objective form in the powers of the state, in respective order, as crown or monarch, the executive and the legislative. By extension, the powers of state reflect the interests and substance of the classes themselves. The executive, agent of applied right, carries out the subordination of the particular case to the rule of the universal in law. The legislative writes the actual law in accordance with the principles of freedom and ethical universality founded in the constitution itself. This component of the state represents the middling moment of particularity for Hegel where the crown, the executive and the representatives of the three estates are conjoined to the rational development of law in the parliamentary forum of the Estates Assembly. It is this aspect of Hegelian governance which sustains the unity of the functional arms of state, and herein rejects Montesquieu's ideal of the separation of powers.[62] The presence of the representatives of all three estates is a bulwark against social atomism and marginalization and an intentional mediation of the mass of private particulars and unified public consciousness "preventing both the extreme isolation of the power of the crown ... and also the isolation of the particular interests of communities, corporations and individuals."[63] The crown then represents the individual autonomy and unity of the two other branches of state.

Though Hegel discussed the monarchy first, it is in actuality the third and singular moment in the internal dialectic of the state.[64] Where the monarch is the individual symbolically elevated to the whole, it equalizes the individual with the state which reciprocally reaches down to embrace all individual citizens. The monarch in its relation to the state thus portrays, yet again, the ethical dialectic itself; the universal and the particular projected one into the other, each finding as its own idea the substance of the other immanent within itself by virtue of the speculative unity of the whole at the level of the state's individuality. The interplay of the three powers thus directly reflects the triad of syllogisms, the logic's categories "shining" into the elements of the ethical life as its ideal ground.[65]

In keeping with the organic interdependence of the three dialectical moments as the objective parts of the state, Hegel stressed the essential coalescence, and internally related unity, of the three state powers to be found in the idea of the state. Thus, each part carries out its specialized function to the same end as the other powers of state. Though their instrumental and functional activities diverge, their ethical aims lie in the same goal—the preservation and development of the social and political organism along the lines of freedom:

> The powers of the state, then, must certainly be distinguished, but each of them must form a whole in itself and contain within itself the other moments. When we speak of the distinct activities of these powers, we must not slip into the monstrous error of so interpreting their distinction as to suppose that each power should subsist independently [*für sich*] in abstraction from the others. The truth is that the powers are to be distinguished only as moments of the concept.[66]

This dialectical unity in the consciousness of the state's concept—its self-awareness per se—is the foundation of its sovereignty and it underlines the logical presence of the concept (*Begriff*) as the basis of the political rationality, and therein legitimacy, of the state. This is not to be conceived in terms of capricious license or monarchic hegemony. Rather, it is the direct expression of the rational ideal ensconced in law, embodied by the constitution and the objectivation of the state in coherence with its logical concept. For Hegel, the legal and constitutional structures are independent so that the monarch has but to "say 'yes' and dot the 'i'." This amounts to a ritual and symbolic expression of the nation's unified willing endorsement of codified law: the ethical order's willing consciousness objectified and the equalization of the one and the many in the monarch as the "spiritual individual" of the ethical order. Sovereignty, as the consummate de jure legitimacy of right, lies in this legal formulation and establishes the form of rational necessity (i.e., *Sitte*) unique to the ethical order of a nation where its laws and constitution are characteristic of this uniqueness. Laws are in this sense the ideal thoughts of national custom put into rule, the logic of its objective mind in principle and in conformity with the universal dictates of reason at a particular moment of its historical development.

Where the monarch exists as the equalization of the whole ethical order with the individual, Hegel intended to embody the freedom of the absolute individuality of the state. The state is herein made the supreme element and achievement in the life of a nation's development towards freedom. It represents the innermost purpose of a modern people's historical development. Without this form of political community, there can be no individuality and it is through the evolution of the state alone that freedom comes to be possible for individuals. The dialectic of duties and rights which the constitution promulgates is herein central to the political and spiritual coordination of the individual state and the citizen particular. Duties sustain the presence of the universal throughout the ethical life and so ground the substance of right by extension. Far from the universal being a negative and constraining burden opposed to liberty, it is rather its precursor and the "the interpenetration of the substantial and the particular."[67] This duality of duty and rights serves to display their unity in the ultimate ethical basis of right as an expression of the absolute Idea itself.

The political problem of the particular, from the point of view of the state, is thus sidestepped in its immanent belonging to the larger unity of the state as itself in its other. The syllogistic reconciliation of family and civil society in and through the state bonds the universal to its particular citizen and unifies the ethical order as a spiritual organism. While civil society is the classically liberal component in his overall system of society and allows for untrammeled individual agency, the state is custodian of a yet higher and deeper form of individuality which only emerges from the individual particular's membership in the state; one which bonds individuals to the whole in a way which neither private property nor self-interest are able to do.[68] For this reason, Hegel was unwilling to pose the question of the legitimacy of the state's existence in empirical terms, or to see the state as a "merely" political form of administration.[69] Instead, he understood the legitimacy of the state in terms of its fulfillment of the universalist project of freedom and the most basic interest and birthright of human communities and their individual constituents.

The idea of the state which unites right, freedom and will in the spheres of the ethical life presents us with the basis of its legitimacy in reason that freedom expresses politically. This idea forms the basis for political theorization and apprehends the reciprocal relation of reason and the historical ideal for Hegel so that "*What is rational is actual; and what is actual is rational.*"[70] As discussed above, this dynamic permits for more than the philosophical quietism and the relegation of reflective thought to the merely descriptive with which Hegel has historically been charged.[71] His idealist grounding of the state mirrors Plato's understanding of the ideal-political content which simultaneously lies at the heart of both the political community and the citizen (as apprehended through dialectic and logic).[72] Hegel envisioned a constitution as the script and text of this rational basis of right for the founding and preservation of the modern political community in a way which serves to unite the three spheres of the ethical order and the interests of the estates. The constitution serves as the direct and rational expression of the *Logic* applied to the task of the unity and integration of the political whole and part within the ethical order as a mirror of the dynamic and syllogistic integration that is the absolute Idea.[73] The logical development of the Idea is here everywhere behind the analogical development of the state through its constitutional form. The actual constitution of the state is not a form of law which perfectly embodies reason, but rather the dialectical movement and life of its concept in the rational projection of its subjective will into history. Hegel's state is unified and omnipresent through its replete reciprocity with all its citizens where the universal is found "articulated in the particulars."[74] This reciprocity is material as well as spiritual for Hegel and serves to thwart the totalitarian or, more reservedly, authoritarian implications of his "double dictum" or *Doppelsatz*.

To ensure this unity and stability of the state, the particularity of interests which run free in civil society are transformed and translated over to the will of the "universal": the ethical self-consciousness of a people or society itself.[75] This collective will represents the realization of the modern nation's freedom and remains in harmony with the extreme form of self-interest and particularity in civil society.[76] It is the national will as a whole which has been realized through the collaboration of the part. Hegel here brings the state to its completion in recognition of the complex subjective potentialities within the whole of society which coincide, compliment and conflict with the political. Hegel informs us that the "essence of the modern state is that the universal be bound up with the complete freedom of particularity and with the well-being of individuals."[77]

Historicity aside, Hegel's understanding of the state as contextually integrated with the other spheres of social existence thus markedly differs from Plato's conceptions of the unchallenged role of the political office of the state. By extension, he directly opposes Hobbes' realism in charging that it is the bond of duty which holds the state together, opposing a shared sense of civic duty and belonging to the politics of security and power.[78] Hegel unabashedly conceived of the constitution as the "organism of the state," holding that it is in the constitutionally regulated balance of its offices that the state, as a whole, is brought to completion and related back to the overall social order of the *Sittlichkeit*. It is thus *Sittlichkeit* (ethical life) which stands as Hegel's unique and logical paradigmatic resolution to the problem of universals in political terms, and his understanding of the organistic relation of whole and part.

The political form which sustains the equilibrium of *Sittlichkeit*, Hegel found in a mixed republican constitution. The branches of the legislature, the executive and the crown are seen as syllogistic reflections of the three prime spheres of society: family, civil society and state; universal, particular and individual. These political branches reflect the socio-economic levels of class (estates, *Stände*) with an emphasis on the level of the executive which is dominated by the bureaucratic class—an emphasis on the 'middling' class. Hegel aspired to make political place for all classes and engrained a pluralist character in his organization of the three levels of government. Yet Hegel shared an agoraphobia with Plato, though to a lesser degree. He held public opinion in generally low esteem as a philosopher, and referred to it as a "standing self-contradiction" in its expression of both popular want and unreflective opinion:

> The *many*, as individuals—a favourite interpretation of "the people"—are of course something connected, but they are connected only as an *aggregate*, a formless mass whose commotion and activity can therefore only be elementary, irrational, wild, and frightful.[79]

"The Many" of the masses are thus not to participate directly in the course of the activities of state. Rather, they are held to be best represented by plenipotentiaries who carry over their interests, understood as an agglomerate mass held together in the estates, while sustaining the rationality of the state which is necessary to the preservation of organistic unity. Though democracy is a possible form of organization for rational states, a strong degree of representative mediation is held as necessary to overcome its atomistic and irrational vicissitudes. For these reasons Hegel concluded that, if all haphazard forms of state are sidestepped, that "sovereignty is there as the personality of the whole ... in the reality adequate to its concept, as the *person of the monarch*."[80] Representation thus takes on two maximal forms for Hegel: those of the corporations and *Stände* of civil society translated over to the *Stände* of the state, and, second, the people as infinite particulars given voice in the perfunctory sweep of the monarch's quill in approving legislation.

Though the *Philosophy of History* witnesses a progression of one to the few to the many in the transition from the Oriental to Greek and Germanic Christian worlds, Hegel was there far from asserting that the state take up a democratic shape for "the fancies which the individual in his isolation indulges, cannot be the model for universal reality."[81] The spheres of society and state do not revolve around the individual as their star, much as the syllogistic analogy of the solar system presented in the logic.[82] Rather it is the primacy and latency of the state which mediates the universality of the natural person in the family with the particular of civil society as their center of gravity so that "the Universal is to be found in the State, in its laws, its universal and rational arrangements."[83] Though "the many" realize the universal of history through the self-knowing freedom of modernity, the state entwines this freedom in mediated reciprocity with the three moments of the dialectic within itself as the consummate and universal whole; the fulfilled actuality of the state as individual reinstates and overcomes the universal's earlier negation by civil society. It is through the state that all are able to fulfill their excellence and it is thus given priority in his formulation of the resolution to the political problem of the universal.

Yet, and despite his agoraphobia and the highly mediated forms of representation which it entails for the relations of state and civil society, Hegel sought an integration of the extremes of "the many" of civil society and "the one" of monarchy through a middling bureaucratic "political class" where "The monarch is *one* person; the *few* come on the scene with the executive power, and the *many* in general with the legislative power."[84] This ordering represents his installment of the bourgeoisie (*bürgerliche Gesellschaft*) as ruling class. Albeit representative and class structured, his theory brings the state to the fore as a preserve for the expression of free political "will" by the citizen. This freedom is never severed from social and class belonging, and is understood as developing alongside of it.

As the moment of the Idea in historical time which overcomes the opposition of the ideal universal and its concrete particulars, the state represents the core of his political response to the philosophical challenge posed by the problem of universals. The question of the legitimacy it offers in these terms stands or falls with the unifying logic of speculation its realizes in *Sittlichkeit*. That is, where the dialectical equalization of the universal and particular is taken as fulfilled in the dialectic of the Idea there are grounds for accepting Hegel's juxtaposition of state and citizen. Hegel's conception of the state is intimately bound up with his understanding of the historical development of the relation of the political part and whole. The progression from the abstract universality of right, through morality and into the ethical life intentionally elaborates this in conformity with the syllogistic form of dialectical progression. In this way his conception of freedom stands as an alternative to Plato's extreme form of collective political harmony (Justice), and as one which avoided the extremes of atomistic accumulation (Property)[85] or social conflict (War),[86] as the justification of the state's existence as well.

In appealing to the development of universal ideas through the dialectical processes of history in order to resolve the philosophical problem of universals in terms of the oppositions of the "in-itself" with the "for-itself," Hegel's conception of the state was led towards resolving the tension between it and its particular citizens by analogy with the logic of syllogism embodied in the state. This is a relation which witnesses the intimate and extensive coordination of his logic's philosophical method, both as form and content, with political theory as a "soul putting forth its branches and fruit organically."[87] The ideal order of the state finds its justification beyond empirical grounds in the logic of thought itself. He here seems to stand side by side with Plato where Hegel held that the actual history of states are ultimately "no concern of the Idea of the state" where "these things are mere appearance and therefore matters for history."[88] Thus the ideal state emerges from the life cycle of the thought where its existence is the eternal and necessary being of spirit. This mental life is at once the substance of the logical dialectic and the integrative fabric which overcomes and outflanks the classical antithesis of the universal and particular, one and the many in modern political life:

> The principle of modern states has prodigious strength and depth because it allows the principle of subjectivity to progress to its culmination in the self-sufficient extreme of personal particularity, and yet at the same time brings it back to the substantial unity and so maintains this unity in the principle of subjectivity itself.[89]

The foundational presence of the life and power of speculative logic of the Idea, as presuppositional for the attainment of a well ordered and free society, presents the aspect under which the total organization of the ethical life serves to respond to the political problem of the universal. The archetypal forms of universal being, particular essence and the singular Idea give form to the three powers of the state as the first reflections of the newly differentiated ethical order and the "*appearing in them* as the power of reason in necessity." Where "the ground and ultimate truth of these institutions is mind," Hegel's philosophical genealogy of the modern state presents us with the life of the absolute Idea which "knows what it wills and knows it in its universality, i.e., as something thought."[90] This state is the historical thought of the absolute Idea in the form of willing itself as an ethical order. The inner truth of the state as political will, of the *Philosophy of Right*, is none other than this procession of the logical and spiritual categories of dialectic given physical and historical form in the political sphere. A "bad state is one which merely exists" and is no state at all where it has not brought about the living unity of the universal and part in dialectical reflection of the speculative unity of the Idea. The project of reconciliation, and the core of the stability of the ethical order, witnesses the coalescence of freedom and reason so that the state is made transparent with the interests of its particular members. Though he restricts his task to his own age, this holds for all stages of history; the reality of a state can only be measured against its relative development of the idea of right.

## Coordinating categories

### Logical problems and political propositions

As the previous chapter on logic laid out, the problem of universals invites relation and comparison with Hegel's categories of opposition. The problem itself asks whether ideas exist independently of the things they predicate and is thus reducible to the question of whether such universals exist either in a permanent and unalterable unity, or whether they exist not at all as mere constructions of language and thought. This division of the question into the possibility of unity and plurality is the legacy of Parmenides' Eleatic thought, and is recapitulated in Plato's dialog of the same name. The basic problem of universals is convertible to the question of the whole and the part in asking whether ideas exist as undivided unities which collect their instances within themselves, or whether there are no ideal wholes and only parts which constitute a unity understood as a convention of language and thought.

Hegel addressed this dynamic issue and treated it in terms of a logical opposition between an intelligible realm of the Idea accessible to reason and a sensible realm accessible to experience. While he took the opposition as concrete and fixed, he did not "mythologize" the relation into a fundamental opposition as Plato had. Rather, the opposition of ideas and things is a process which constantly recurs, and is without beginning or end. The parts themselves are generated out of the very nature of the whole; universal "being" severs its relation with itself in negation and gives birth to the many particular essences of the world and experience.

The universal ideal is ever present in experience and reason seeks to discover the essences residing behind the accidents registered by the senses. Once the particular has manifest itself alongside and in opposition to the universal, the essential problem of universals is disclosed. The opposition is one of unity and plurality and it demarcates the limits of the family and the origins of civil society, community and modern society. Though the opposition is antagonistic, the recycling of the universal and its form-giving to the particular offers the opportunity for reconciliation. They share a singular basis in the teleological drive towards individuation, a process which fulfills their inherent concept, their nature: "Actuality is always the unity of universal and particular."[91] This unity is the singular or true individual which takes shape in the form of the political organism of the state harmonizing the diverse entities of the political, economic and social world. The ethical life's syllogism of state individuality overcomes the fundamental oppositions of freedom and authority, state and citizen, and formulates a spiritual organism that suspends their fundamental, logical opposition.

Hegel considered this dialectical drive to the reconciliation of the universal and particular in individuality to abide in the highest form of thought: speculation. Speculation takes up the problem of universals as the basic condition of thought and historical transformation, all change restating the three basic moments of the dialectic in an ever recurring cycle. The development of understanding, dialectic and speculation emerge in reflection of the ongoing relations of the universal, particular and individual. Each form of thought is translated into a form of political life in reflection of a particular social sphere and class, and in pursuit of the historical reconciliation which the individual state makes possible in the closure of the political problem of universals through the power of speculation. The equilibrium of universal and particular that is found in modern *Sittlichkeit* is thus an accomplishment of logic and is precisely dependent upon the development of thought that moves from Eleatic being (family), through essence (civil individuality and subjectivity) and into ideal unity—individuality—in the state. This equilibrium, and the specific relations of immanence contained within it, is an achievement which cannot be taken for granted prior to the third and synthetic phase of the *Logic* which makes possible the emergence of the "singular" in sublation.

Though Hegel did not accept the existence of uninstantiated universals, the prior forms of thought of the first two phases of the logic, understanding and dialectic, do not yet permit such a conclusion; speculation is his specialized response to the specialized problem which the opposition of universality and particularity present for thought and actuality. The transcendence of the universal remained a suspended possibility in the perseverance of the ancient and medieval metaphysical worlds, one which the modern world recovers from heaven in order to "ground" the earthly and empirical. *The very pendulum of negation which Enlightenment understanding swung against the logic of medieval monism and feudal collectivity is overturned in speculation, herein recovering the problem of universals as a means of reinstating contradiction as the continuity of thought's dynamic momentum and the organism of political life.*

From the ancient world and the Eleatic and Platonic monisms of being, through the dispersion of essence in medieval revelation and emanation to its final material sublimation and concealment within the causal matrix of empiricism, Hegel had witnessed the incessant and temporal rending of the universal through its syllogistic forms. Each moment declared its finality and conclusiveness in and against its predecessors. In denying the truth of the others each drew its own negation closer. Each outburst of totalization—metaphysical and political—amounted to an abstract denial of the form giving conditions of its predecessors and its own existence. Aware of these crises, the Hegelian state seeks to circumscribe and contain the familial collective and civil individualistic forms that provide the basis for the emergence of modern social and political life.

## *Freedom and the creative resolution of the aporetic universal*

A conception of organic unity runs through the structure of Hegel's *Sittlichkeit*, each of the elements of his social institutions and classes reflecting a larger dynamic. The concept of the organic is one of internal differentiation and plurality which maps the tripartite dynamic of speculative logic onto the arrangements of the parts so that each—citizens, classes and ethical spheres—are themselves imbued with the faculties and potentials of the whole.

Hegel's approach to the organic conception of the social and political was rooted in a concern for the preservation of what he saw as the great flood tide of subjective freedom which confronted Plato's time, and which had remained the challenge of politics and thought ever since. The spheres or moments of a modern society—family, civil society and state—must necessarily be internally differentiated so as to accommodate the absolute demands of subjective particularity in freedom. Yet and at the same time, in order to inaugurate order and unity of purpose in the modern social arrangement, these spheres must be integrated and the subject particular must not be alienated in this overall organization; the viability of the modern political organism is held up by Hegel against this very standard. In order to accomplish this, Hegel fashioned his *Sittlichkeit* as a system which imbues all particulars with rational capacity and expression so as to participate in the public dialog of the universal. As earlier considered, this is not to say that Hegel's political arrangement seems robustly democratic. This rationality is often ascriptive and present in the form of representative structures, institutions and relations reflecting what Hegel considered to be the objective potentialities of all citizens in relation to the higher rationality and ethical universality of the whole. The condition of the partial rationality of the agents of civil society, unknowingly participating and conjoined to the larger ethical life of the state, is exemplary of this subordinated aspect of the rationality of the individual particular.

Yet, and in line with the logic, no single syllogism defines the whole. In making access to the synthetic power of speculation, the singular "one" of the rational state and the natural many of the family are syllogistically conjoined to one another through the intermediating sphere of civil society's subjective particular. This intermediation, key to the modern social and political arrangement, plays a central role in holding together the legitimacy and sovereignty of state with the natural persons of the family and their consanguine interests. As his earlier *Logic* had made clear, the synthetic aspect of the dialectic ensures that, despite the specificity and particularity of the three spheres, they each participate in a mediated process which unites in an equally persistent whole. Hegel described this organic development of the elements of ethical life out of the immanent Idea of the state as its telos:

> the state as such is rather what is first. It is within the state that the family is first developed into civil society, and it is the Idea of the state itself which divides itself into these two moments. Through the development of civil

society, the substance of ethical life acquires its infinite form ... the form of thought whereby spirit is objective and actual to itself as an organic totality in laws and institutions which are its will as *thought*.[92]

Hegel articulated the conception of the dialectic of the organic ethical world as one which takes up the central project of creating the conditions of totality and unity, while at the same time promoting the interests and development of particular will. This condition then encapsulates his response to the political problem of the universal, and it organizes his total formulation where the *Sittlichkeit* is "the *Idea of freedom* ... the concept of freedom *developed into the existing world and the nature of self-consciousness*."[93] The crowning moment of the ethical life, the state, realizes actual freedom for the individual and thus legitimates its authority and the individual's allegiance:

> The state is the actuality of concrete freedom. But *concrete freedom* consists in this, that personal individuality and its particular interests ... pass over of their own accord into the interest of the universal, and ... they even recognize it as their own substantial spirit; they take it as their end and aim and are active in its pursuit.[94]

The syllogism of the three spheres of the ethical life and the classes are in constant inter-mediation and intra-mediation so that the parts of organism "are not parts but members."[95] The family, civil society and the state each contain within themselves the three moments of speculative logic, and each participates both as whole in relation to the other, and as part in relation to the whole. Thus, the human being is no mere microcosm of the state for Hegel. The emergent totality of the state is a formal condition for the freedom of the subject or citizen particular, but is never exhaustive as the determinant of its content. Justice passes over to modern freedom where the organic interaction of the universal and particular is reciprocal and leads to reconciliation in the creation of the individuality and sovereignty of the state.[96]

## The sovereignty of the metaphysical in Hegel's political thought

In his 1964 introduction to *Hegel's Political Writings*, Zbigniew Pełczyński initiated an influential line of argument for a split between the metaphysical and political components of the *Philosophy of Right* which seems inimical to the self-declared vocation of Hegel's political treatise: once the metaphysical element becomes dominant, as it does in some sections of the *Philosophy of Right*, the character of political theory changes. The teaching, or the insight, it provides ceases to have any practical significance.[97]

As I have argued, the metaphysical work of the *Logic* and its emergence in historical reason through political participation brings about a fusion of Hegel's metaphysical perspective and the demands of political practice. Hegel seated his politics precisely upon the metaphysical groundwork of the *Logic* to order the political realm on the firmament of the concept and in a way which is not merely political but conceptually presuppositional to other spheres of life as well. Pełczyński justified his theory and practice division upon a construal of Hegel's *Logic* as a search for truth:

> Hegel thought that only by transposing politics to the metaphysical plane and giving his concepts a speculative underpinning could he establish their validity. It is this quest for absolute proof, this passion for certain knowledge in politics, which constitutes one of the distinctive features of Hegel's political thought.[98]

Yet Hegel's "philosophical science" as a metaphysical approach to politics sought less for "absolute proof" than it did philosophical justification and "reconciliation of the reason that is conscious of itself with the reason that *exists*" in the world.[99] That is, he did seek an iron science of politics but rather applied his speculative method in order to ensure that the contents of political theory do not fall prey to false antinomies between wholes and parts, states and citizens. It is in this sense that Steinberger has called Hegel's political theory a "perfectionist" project, one which insists upon a prevailing harmony between states and citizens as much as it does between subjective and empirical phenomena.[100] Hegel's search for political unity in the world thus only followed his search for unity in the life of the Idea. As K.H. Ilting has cogently asserted, the unity of philosophical form and political content must remain intact if we are to understand Hegel's project on his own terms. He further held, in light of Hegel's claims for this unity, that "Only an exposition of the dialectical structure of his *Philosophy of Right* will make clear whether or not this is the case."[101] It is precisely this task that I have attempted to carry out.

In concluding that "[although] some intellectual curiosity may be unsatisfied when metaphysics is left out; a solid volume of political theory and political thinking will still remain"[102] Pełczyński may, strictly speaking and in a limited sense, have been correct. By accepting such a view, however, we would no longer be entertaining Hegel's overt intentions or organizational structure in the *Philosophy of Right*. Having removed the soul from the body and the animus from the apparatus, such a reduction would leave us with a Hegelian politics that is a "bland 'rational reconstruction' of it, which fits more or less loosely on his text,"[103] alienated from the very energetic conceptual dynamic its author envisioned for modern politics.

Short of eviscerating Hegel's authorship and appropriating his thought to our own ends, then, I hold that his total organization of the political world of citizens and monarchs, as well as their intermediating institutional forms, remains inextricable from his philosophical commitments. It is this marriage which has turned much pragmatic theoretical interest in Hegel's political thought away from its logical moorings, and which has resulted in misunderstanding of its metaphysical creed. A more thorough reconsideration of this dimension may yet lead to renewed appreciation and interest in Hegel as the philosopher who conceives of the modern state as a response concerned as much with the recurrent political challenges implicit in the abstractions of Eleatic "being" as with the convulsions and convolutions of the pre-modern orthodoxies of his day. It may also serve to diminish the degree of embarrassment which Hegel felt had befallen philosophical inquiry where it might otherwise have advanced the interests of worldly political thought.

## Dialectic paralyzed: the distortions of the non-metaphysical reading

My presentation of the strong bonds and development between Hegel's logic and politics has made a positive case for the import of the relation of these portions of his thought. Yet I have left the non-metaphysical approach to the politics intact; for while I have made the case for the importance to Hegel, his corpus and his historical legacy, I have as yet left open the possibility that the non-metaphysical approach is able to offer a perfectly adequate account of the contents of Hegel's *Philosophy of Right*. That is, while I have argued that the metaphysical reading is correct, I have not made the inverse case that the non-metaphysical reading is wrong.[104] As Robert Stern has pointed out, exponents of the non-metaphysical view will eagerly respond to my reading with a retort. They can concede that Hegel has a metaphysics and that he intended it to relate to his politics, but this in and of itself does not render the non-metaphysical reading of the *Philosophy of Right* beyond the *Logic* incorrect. This camp claims that they not only get him right without the metaphysics, moreover they claim that shedding the *Logic* is the only way to truly arrive at the pragmatic import of his politics uncorrupted by his abstruse and nonsensical metaphysical program. While the case delivered in this and the preceding chapters certainly overrides the assertion that we ought to bypass the *Logic* in order to avoid having to substitute a study of Hegel's *Logic* for that of his politics, the prior challenge yet stands. Against this position I hold that not only does the non-metaphysical reading problematically dismiss Hegel's overt metaphysical intentions, but it also mistakenly asserts the independence of Hegel's political from his logical thought and deforms its subject in the process.

Given this chink in my argument's armor, I respond to this charge against Allen Wood's highly respected *Hegel's Ethical Thought*[105] as the leading representative of the non-metaphysical reading below. I do so, first, by taking up Stephen Houlgate's brief but insightful exposé of the shortcomings of the non-metaphysical approach, and Wood's reply, insofar as the latter is led to draw flawed conclusions regarding Hegel's positive political arrangements by ignoring their speculative conceptual framework. Second, I proceed to critically apply my own reading of Hegel's project of metaphysical resolution in the *Philosophy of Right* to Wood's reading. While Houlgate's comments unsettle a variety of Wood's claims about Hegel's political project, my interrogation of Wood's anti-metaphysical reading goes further in undermining his representation of Hegel's concrete social and political cosmos.[106] This seems especially true on the matter of Wood's reading of *Sittlichkeit* and the overall ordering of the relations of citizen and state within the context of Hegel's universalist scheme.

## Houlgate's challenge

Stephen Houlgate recognizes the inherent pitfall that sidestepping the *Logic* entails on the path to an understanding of Hegel's political thought. On Houlgate's account, the actualization of spirit in political life can only work in reflection of an "intrinsic *Bestimmung* [determination] when it achieves a clear understanding of the self-developing concept of spirit in philosophy."[107] Without recognizing the metaphysical seed, in other words, Wood's representation of the concept of freedom and its historical actualization in the state can in no way reflect Hegel's understanding of what human development or potential entails. This "dimension of logical necessity" underlines the self-realizing character of spirit for Houlgate and represents a central component of the development and internal structure of freedom in the political realm. For Houlgate, the logical background of the *Philosophy of Right* is addressable to Hegel's comment in the 1830 *Logic* that "the whole development of the spirit is nothing other than the [process of] raising itself to its truth."[108] Freedom then is in a constant and teleological striving to fully realize its inner concept historically and necessarily coheres with the speculative method of the logic.

Houlgate concedes that Wood's reading of spiritual self-realization in Hegel recognizes and accepts this teleology. Yet, he claims, at the very same time it problematically redefines such a telos in terms of a "model of human agency" where "the agent creates or 'posits' an external object."[109] This sets up the dialectic of self-development through the new form of mediation that this relation to the object has now created or "posited." In other words, Wood's willing agent stands as the ground of self-realization, manifesting itself in its self-projection and transformation of the natural world into objects of the will. This externalized self found in the objects of the external world, in turn, must now be understood and brought back into relation with the inner self. The myth of the given at work here can't be missed; the self is a given starting point in Wood's reading, taking the place of the *logical* universal of spirit, and stands in as the purposive origin of the dialectical development of the self. Yet, as with Feuerbach's critique of Hegel's taking being for granted as the starting point of the logic,[110] so too does Wood problematically take the self as a given basis for its own development and completion. Moreover, he does so in a way which is completely at odds with Hegel's own understanding.

For Hegel, this self and its form of freedom are not rooted in the development of subjective agency per se, but are given to a form of freedom which already takes the individual particular as wedded to the larger ethical world. To sow the seeds of the ethical life upon the individual and its destiny of freedom in this way is to interrupt and impede the strong form of intersubjectivity necessary to the realization of the state and the overall ethical order. As I have explained previously, clear and plural warnings against such a totalization of the agentive subject are asserted in the *Philosophy of Right*. The problem of the political universal is evaded in such a strategy where the development of the part is realized in and through the part itself, lending itself to an atomism that upsets the overall integration of the body politic.

Houlgate's analysis leads him to assert that Wood takes Hegel's dialectic for granted in a significant sense. For Wood, according to Houlgate, Hegel is "already standing on historical ground in the *Philosophy of Right* and to view Hegel in that text as analyzing specific historical and social self-images of human individuality."[111] This descriptivist strategy on Wood's part reduces Hegel's portrayal of the development of human freedom to that of a positivist observer of his era. At the same time, it is to undermine Hegel's normative and logical narrative in the most fundamental of ways. Where Houlgate claims that Wood's rendering of the *Philosophy of Right* is primarily "analyzing specific historical and social self-images of human individuality and human agency in the world" in the *Philosophy of Right*, Wood recasts Hegel as a psycho-social phenomenologist divested of his primary metaphysical claims. This historicist rendering diffuses Hegel's influence and trans-historical claims, and replants him firmly in the soil of his age beyond reach of the historical landscape he explicitly described and engaged. A kind of anthropological historicism, then, is the result of Wood's strategy. This lack of attention to Hegel's historically developmental essentialism is for Houlgate the lens which "distorts" Wood's "understanding of Hegel's text at several points."[112]

Houlgate traces the consequences of Wood's positivist reading into the issue of interpreting punishment in the *Philosophy of Right*. Where Wood abandon's the speculative logic of right informing Hegel's development of institutions, Houlgate reads Wood's interpretation of social institutions on the basis of "the self-image and consequent practices of concrete social, historical human beings."[113] In other words, in sidelining Hegel's conceptual groundwork, Wood inherently subverts and ascribes exogenous reasoning to the rationale structuring his institutions. For Houlgate, and myself, such a reading is "unwarranted and misleading."[114]

In correcting Wood's reductionist reading of Hegel's concept of punishment to "a social mechanism for protecting individuals' property,"[115] Houlgate argues for the form and content of the concept of right itself. On his revised reading, punishment not only addresses the actor and action of the crime, but also restores the actuality of "violated right itself."[116] In so doing, Houlgate asserts the need to take seriously the working of the conceptual matrix of logical dialectic within which Hegel is operating in order to understand and make bare sense of what Hegel's political thought amounts to where punishment "can be seen to follow necessarily from the very concept of right."[117] Though Thom Brooks differs with Houlgate regarding the ultimate basis of justification for punishment in the *Philosophy of Right*, arguing that "Hegel's theory is only minimally Retributive,"[118] he nevertheless recognizes speculative logic as a key for making sense of Hegel's theory of punishment in the first place. With Houlgate, Brooks argues that Hegel's treatment of punishment "can make sense only if we take seriously the relationship between the *Philosophy of Right* and Hegel's larger system."[119] It is therefore one thing for us to be wrong about Hegel's arguments, it is another for us to embrace an alternate foundationalist ground of interpretation which leads to appropriative and ascriptive readings. Such a conclusion wholly conforms with the conclusions drawn out in chapter three above. Revisionist readings responding to the plethora of contemporary ideological and epistemological demands do not merely bring Hegel up-to-date and allow him to respond to our "ethical concerns and cultural identity crises."[120]

In the case of private property, the very same set of grounding assumptions driving Wood's reading of Hegel leads Houlgate to conclude, very similarly, that "the *Philosophy of Right* quite clearly presents private property as the logically *necessary* concretization of right, rather than as a historical product".[121] Houlgate's conclusion overall is unequivocal. Despite real appreciation for Wood's explication of Sittlichkeit, he holds that "Wood's preference for regarding Hegel as above all a social and historical thinker, rather than a speculative logician who is concerned in the *Philosophy of Right* to develop the implications of the concept of freedom in a systematic way, leads him to misunderstand Hegel at certain crucial points."[122]

## Wood's reply

While Allen Wood recognizes that Hegel's political thought has witnessed a grand revival in the last decades, he says that this is specifically despite "the narrowminded sectarian arrogance often found among his admirers."[123] Against this claim, I argue that behind this so-called arrogance is a loyalty to Hegel's program as sustaining some kernel of independence from our needs and interests such that we must at the very minimum attempt to traverse the gap. Wood's program, unfortunately, sees this as an unworthy journey and I think that this lack of adventure on his part leads not merely to a metaphysically neutralized version of Hegel's ethical thought, but to a misleading one in significant ways.

Wood's reply to Houlgate's assertion of the importance of the logical development of right as a central plank of Hegel's political thought underestimates Houlgate's rather overt intent. In repeatedly denouncing Hegel's speculative logic as dead and decrepit,[124] Wood does himself the favor of liberating his arguments from all traditional Hegelian critique. Yet, and in light of my reading of the *Philosophy of Right*, it is clear that Hegel is not merely waxing metaphysical, but is rather participating in a perennial line of political philosophizing. That is, Hegel's systematic response to the problem of universals reflects both his positive metaphysical intent behind the *Philosophy of Right*, as well as his response to the classical metaphysical problem of universals in political terms. Clearly, sidestepping the logical dialectic as an end in itself and its historical outcomes obscures this latter dimension of the *Philosophy of Right* altogether. This obfuscation then permits Wood to proceed with Hegel's "historical concerns" first, where "logic and metaphysics" become derivative, rather than the other way round, in his primary approach to Hegel's political project.[125]

Wood's response to Houlgate on the issue of punishment is even more difficult to accept in light of the Aristotelian grounds of Hegel's developmental logic. For Wood, "the conceptual argument is just no good," so "we do Hegel no favor by ascribing the conceptual argument to him."[126] That is, in rejecting the *Logic's* categories and their development as a basis for understanding Hegel's political arguments, we liberate the latter from the fundamentally flawed dynamics and influences of the former. As Frederick Beiser has brought out, "Hegel's theory about the sources of normativity is based on his social and historical conception of reason, which ultimately derives from his Aristotelian view that universals exist only *in re* or in particular things."[127] Wood's approach accomplishes much of what is implicitly demanded by this in recognizing the anthropological specificity of reason belonging to a particular people at a particular time. Yet he wholly misses out on the teleological aspect of this process that Beiser's reading makes a crucial component: "reason also consists in the telos of a nation, the fundamental values or goals that it strives to realize in all its activities."[128] This teleology only operates in reflection of an essential concept which itself is generated by the larger sweep of the history of the universal and its pluralization of being. This development, of course, is captured by the logical cycle of universal, particular and singular through which the concept is wedded to and developmentally reflective of its content. With Beiser, it seems plausible to argue that "Whatever the success of Hegel's arguments, it should be clear that his entire account is intelligible and defensible only as a metaphysics. So if we insist on a non-metaphysical reading of Hegel's social and political theory, we cannot appreciate its foundation."[129] Not only do we underestimate foundations, we also inevitably get Hegel's political conclusions wrong in missing out on his program of logico-political synergy.

Wood retires the "conceptual argument," that the essential key to understanding Hegel's politics is to be found in speculative logic, on the basis of its inherent contradiction with the Hegelian imperative of rationally justifying a given political community as a "form of life."[130] He refers his argument to Hegel's Preface which seeks to "demonstrate the rationality of what is commonly accepted as right and ethical."[131] Yet where Wood emphasizes the positivity of the rationality of the actual, he underestimates the equally crucial aspect of the actuality of the rational which discloses the logical impulse of the development of the concept beyond its positive grounding. This critique stands behind Houlgate's remonstrations against historicizing Hegel's thought against Hegel's own intentions. The sweep of Wood's logic certainly provides a rationale for doing so, for on his account "the conceptual argument is so bad, and so remote from anything that is explicitly present in Hegel's texts, that we can do right both by Hegel's texts and his ethical theory only if we do not saddle him with it."[132] Yet this apologetic revisionism is so distorting, and as I have and will continue to argue, grounded in a specific set of contemporary liberal-positivist axioms of an epistemological and ontological nature, that Wood participates in the unfortunate project of eviscerating core elements of Hegel's thought in order to save it. I argue that such a cure for Hegel's metaphysical incorrigibility seems far more harmful than the disease. As Brooks has argued we "are simply mistaken to suppose we need to perform philosophical surgery on Hegel's views in order to retain our interest in them."[133]

My involvement in this debate, between metaphysical and non-metaphysical approaches to Hegel's political thought, takes off precisely on the basis of Wood's own invitation: "It would be a reasonable kind of criticism if someone said that my refusal to treat speculative logic as the basis of Hegelian ethics prevented me from appreciating certain of Hegel's insights or correctly interpreting certain of his arguments."[134] While I have already shown that the *Logic* plays a crucial and instructive role in both the development and the content of the *Philosophy of Right*, a sort of "logical animus" inspiring the micro and macro formulations of the political world, this section has moved further. Following Houlgate, it took up the argument that not only does the non-metaphysical approach miss out on a critical layer of Hegel's political thought, but that it goes astray in crucial ways as well.

## *Citizen, state and* Sittlichkeit*: beyond liberal rights and negative liberty*

Though Wood rejects the metaphysical approach—or "conceptual argument"—as an end in itself, he does seek to find some justification within Hegel's writings themselves for the non-metaphysical view. In stating that Hegel occasionally takes his politics as a "'practical philosophy' (PR §4A)"[135] Wood seeks a Hegelian basis for asserting that "the *Philosophy of Right* must be looked at simultaneously in two ways":[136] as both philosophical science as well as a practical theory of ethics and politics. As we have seen above,[137] Wood's wholesale rejection of the speculative, conceptual approach seeks no license or justification from Hegel's intentions. Yet here we see Wood seeking just that sort of textual and authorial support. The question thus arises as to whether we ought to reference Hegel's views when it comes to theory and not merely practice, and what this would mean for Wood's, and others', non-metaphysical readings. With Stern, Ware, Brooks, Plant, Beiser and others, the answer is clear. We ought not to systematically invoke Hegel on our terms short of reducing his work and thought to an instrumentalist *Doppelgänger*.

Wood takes this theory and practice split further to Hegel's *Doppelsatz*.[138] In describing the practical aspect of the maxim as grounded in empirical concerns that proceed "from a rational comprehension of what is"[139] he underestimates the speculative side of the double maxim. In taking speculation as a "philosophical wisdom" which "consists in contemplating the inner rational essence"[140] in and against appearances, it seems hard to avoid a Platonic association. Yet for Hegel the outer appearances of things were certainly not bereft of intelligibility and this speculative/practical binary is hardly meaningful in Hegel's thought. The speculative take on the double maxim on Hegel's account would demand no less than the mediation of outer and necessary appearances with their inner conceptual ideal as part and parcel of their rational development. Reducing the speculative to this platonic monism seems to be part and parcel of a basis for its dismissal, finding, instead, in the practical aspect of the maxim a preferable basis for reading Hegel's political thought in its entirety. Where Wood accepts the double maxim "in its practical meaning while repudiating it in its speculative meaning" by giving "a conception of human self-actualization some other basis,"[141] he eliminates that which is actually thought as a process of thinking development from Hegel's politics and infuses his preferred version: "an empirical, historical analysis of the nature of human beings in modern Western culture."[142] This reductionism is not only to read Hegel against his own intent as Wood admits, but is also to eliminate and revise the inner logic and metaphysical concerns animating Hegel's political thought as a whole. As Houlgate, Brooks and others have pointed out, this reductionist and revisionist strategy has direct and substantial implications for how we ultimately understand and render the concrete institutions and political forms Hegel deployed in his *Philosophy of Right*. Understanding the practical precisely requires that we take the speculative seriously.

In taking the citizen as a political end in itself, Wood's portrait endorses a liberal interpretation of Hegel's state. Wood claims that "because the state is an organic unity in which no member is end and none is means" he is able to compare Hegel's state–citizen relation to that of John Stuart Mill where "the well-being of individuals who comprise the collective"[143] is the only possible end of the collective. Yet, as earlier argued above, where the state is both the essential universal substance and end-state of freedom, both its content and its form, meaning and objective identity ultimately come to the individual particular through it alone. To undermine this relationship is to undermine the structure of the whole order resulting in the loss of freedom for all.

Where the happiness of citizens is made possible is in the realm of civil society, happiness understood as the fulfillment of subjective desire. Yet at the level of the ethical universal realized through the state, the happiness of the citizen is transformed in reflection of the universal as Hegel tells us that "substantive unity" "maintains this unity in the principle of subjectivity itself"[144] precisely through the modern state. This universality, too, is reflected surreptitiously in civil society which, inadvertently, reflects the larger ethical order even as a spiritual animal kingdom. Where individuality is transformed in citizenship as a member of the organism of the state, individuality is displaced and a higher rationality is realized. This is the basis of Hegel's critique of Rousseau's general will as too contractualist in its conflation of the state with civil society. Hegel tells us that "it is one of the commonest blunders of abstract thinking to make private rights and private welfare count as absolute in opposition to the universality of the state."[145] Yet where Wood argues that Hegel is unable to "conceive of anything except the well-being of individuals who comprise the collective"[146] as the aggregate end of collective life, he seems to do precisely this.

On these grounds Wood underestimates Hegel's devotion to a positive version of liberty through which individuals are transformed and bonded in political belonging, realizing themselves as more than mere "aggregate" individuals of the whole. Hegel makes this clear where he insists that the essence of the state is more than the mere collective well-being of individual members: "happiness lies in everyone's subjectivity and feeling, this universal end is for its part particular, and consequently there is still not present in it any genuine unity of form and content."[147] In other words, the political problem of the universal remains unresolved at the level of civil welfare, leaving the state to bring about a higher form of unity as a means of overcoming the rampant particularism which the civil sphere generates.

Wood's liberal and historicist bent in reading Hegel stretches further. In taking Hegel's thought as a sort of cultural relativism, "historicized universalism" in Wood's terms, where each cultural tradition aspires from its own foundations towards a version of the universal which reflects its experience and resources, Wood is able to conclude that Hegel's approach "looks like the best way to achieve rational tolerance."[148] Yet, in drawing this picture, Wood makes the concomitant claim that the most developed or "rational and progressive" cultures will be the ones which are most humble and the most open to difference. Herein Wood reads the script of Hegel's development of reason through freedom in terms of the ideals of tolerance, pluralism and mutual respect. Yet there is no inherent inclination built into Hegel's evolution of freedom that would necessarily or inherently valorize these liberal ideals over others. Against these very value judgments Wood had earlier claimed that "there is no universal standard" by which any society can "be criticized or regarded as superior one to another."[149] In doing so he leaves behind Hegel's own evolution of reason, freedom and right which clearly do entail benchmarks of development. Both at the level of intra- and international relations, Wood's Hegel is a liberal who appreciates happiness, tolerance and pluralism above all. Thus in his implicit depiction of Hegel's response to the political problem of the universal, he consistently yields a Hegel who privileges the individual in relation to its others in a form of pluralistic harmony. Yet, at the very same time, his articulation of Hegel's strong notion of organic unity, the core concern at the heart of the problem of universals both conceptually and political understood, goes largely underdeveloped in conformity with this rendering of Hegel's political thought as compatible with liberal ideals.

In taking freedom to consist in Hegel's "complete development of personal individuality and the recognition of its right for itself" ... so that individuals "recognize it as their substantial spirit and are active for it as their final end"[150] and where a people "choose to devote themselves to a universal or collective end which they acknowledge,"[151] Wood again emphasizes Hegel's individualized agency and the right of an aggregate whole as the basis of the state in a way which borders on social contractualism. Yet Hegel would have none of this selective reading: our belonging to the state and society are not mediated through private right and choice. While the modern state for Hegel permits subjective freedom "to progress to its culmination" he nonetheless insists that it "at the same time brings it [subjectivity] back to the substantive unity and so maintains this unity in the principle of subjectivity itself."[152] In other words, a synergy of state and citizen is pre-established in accord with the perfectionist paradigm Peter J. Steinberger has outlined.[153] This undermines Wood's liberal reading of the state–citizen relation and exposes the conceptual groundwork underwriting Hegel's political thought. To imagine our having agency outside of the state and our belonging to it would be to imagine a historical and social transcendence that Hegel's organicist thought simply does not offer. Moreover, such a proposition runs against the grain of Wood's own assertion that "fallible, culturally conditioned, and historically limited reason is the only reason we have."[154] To reframe individual choice in this manner, even where it is seen as belonging to an aggregate social and ethical collective, is to undermine what choice means on Hegel's account of politics. Certainly, there is some form of choice but it is pre-dated and presupposed by the presence and development of the universal itself. That is, the state in more ways than one teleologically precedes the individual, and this foundation means that Wood's liberal evocation of Hegel's work amounts to one-sided and systematic misrepresentation. This also exposes and restates the ways in which the presence of the universal as a conceptual problem haunts Hegel's work and frustrates those who seek to sidestep or write it off. To overemphasize the autonomy of the individual and its "right for itself" as unassailable as Woods seems to do is to posit a liberal-positivist metaphysics at the heart of Hegel's thought, ignoring as it does the dynamic and unceasing dichotomy of social part and universal. It is also to conceal a set of metaphysical presuppositions in a supposedly non-metaphysical reading.

As is evident then, Wood is at pains to elaborate Hegel's freedom as belonging to citizen individuals rather than the state collectivity. He claims that it is "a serious distortion of Hegel's view to say that he regards true freedom as the freedom of a collective rather than the freedom of individuals"[155] and thus emphasizes the individual as the beneficiary of right and freedom in the *Philosophy of Right* itself. Yet, and again, this is a distorted and one-sided view of the ongoing dialectic of universality in the *Philosophy of Right* conceptually and politically understood. The state, too, is an "individual" where "freedom comes into its supreme right"[156] such that its more complete form of universality demands "supreme right against the individual."[157] To take the end of the actualization of freedom through the state as "the freedom of the individuals" in civil society is to trespass against the spiritual unity and personhood, "individuality" the state embodies for Hegel, above and beyond the sphere of individual well-being. With Hegel, where "the state is confused with civil society," I argue that for Wood "the interest of the individuals as such becomes the ultimate end of their association, and it follows that membership of the state is something optional."[158] This would clearly amount to a serious violation of Hegel's state–civil society dialectic where

> the state's relation to the individual is quite different from this. Since the state is objective spirit, it is only as one of its members that the individual himself has objectivity, truth, and ethical life. Unification as such is itself the true content and aim, and the individual's destiny is to live a universal

life. His further particular satisfaction, activity, and mode of conduct have this substantial and universally valid life as their starting point and their result.[159]

As I pointed out above in my reading of the *Logic* and *Philosophy of Right*, there is clearly ambiguity in the dialectic of the universal and particular, civil society and state, that can make it difficult to distinguish between synergy and subsumption, harmonization and hegemony, in Hegel's logical and political thought. Yet for Wood to consistently come down on the side of Hegel's championing the autonomy of the particular seems conspicuously ideological. How else can he sweepingly conclude that "Hegel's political ideas leave the liberals' state pretty much intact"?[160] As Michael J. Sandel has brought out,

> [the Liberal] vision ... gives pride of place to justice, fairness, and individual rights. Its core thesis is this: a just society seeks not to promote any particular ends, but enables its citizens to pursue their own ends, consistent with a similar liberty for all; it therefore must govern by principles that do not presuppose any particular conception of the good.[161]

Yet Hegel's teleological vision of the good as freedom realized through the historical state is not amenable to the Rawlsian, consensus-based politics that Wood's reading calls for. The consummation of the syllogism in and through the ethical life is the emergence of the good as freedom that binds the individual and state. As brought out above, this unity stands as Hegel's resolution of the political problem of the universal. Hegel writes of the opposition of the political universal and particular that

> the unity and truth of both these abstract moments [family and civil society]—the Idea of the good not only apprehended in thought but so realized both in the will reflected into itself and in the external world that freedom exists as substance, as actuality and necessity, no less than as subjective will; this is the Idea in its absolutely universal *existence—Ethical Life.*[162]

Wood does concede that any justification for the liberal state in Hegel is delivered on a non-liberal platform and that his ethical theory proposes an "antiliberal vision of what modern society is."[163] Despite this, his primary claim for the culmination of the liberal state in the *Philosophy of Right* simply flies in the face of Hegel's strong formulation of positive liberty achieving the universal "destiny"[164] (*Bestimmung*) of the individual in and through the state to begin with.

Allen Wood's *Hegel's Ethical Theory* is one of a variety of versions of the non-metaphysical reading of Hegel's *Philosophy of Right*. As examined in Chapter 3, it is part of a well-established tradition in Anglo-American discourse that has been dominant for nearly a century. While Wood's reading in no way exhausts the strategies employed by this trend, his work nevertheless has and continues to play an important role sustaining it. As such, undermining it does not fully defeat the non-metaphysical tradition, but is rather intended to be demonstrative about its rather substantial and conspicuous shortcomings. The dynamic of speculative resolution of categorical antinomies has been shown to be crucial for the way Hegel's thought animates the social and political landscape. Behind this dynamic stands the metaphysical problem of universals and the triad of syllogisms which fix Hegel's logical and political thought to a set of conceptual problems. In the light of these findings and those of Chapter 3, it is all too easy to lose sight of these imperatives and to imbue Hegel's political thought with our own when we consider it in their absence. The overall organic achievement of *Sittlichkeit* relies and thrives on the problem of universals as an integration of opposites that is irreducibly conceptual and in a way which creatively draws upon metaphysical resources. Where the *Philosophy of Right* and its concrete political formulations carries on with the form and content of thinking initiated in the *Logic*, then, there is no excluding an appreciation of speculation from their consideration. Coming to terms with the modes of collectivity and integration that Hegel there lays out requires nothing less.

With the primary justifications for the descriptive program which has dominated Hegel scholarship for nearly a century overturned, the concluding chapter is set up to challenge the equally dominant and chronologically prior prescriptive challenge: that political theorization *ought* to be kept separate from metaphysical concerns.[165]

## Notes

1 Portions of this chapter were previously published as Eric Goodfield, "The Sovereignty of the Metaphysical in Hegel's Philosophy of Right," The Review of Metaphysics 62, no. 4 (2009), 849–73.
2 Georg Wilhelm Friedrich Hegel and Henry Stewart Macran, Hegel's Doctrine of Formal Logic (Oxford: Clarendon Press, 1912), 100.
3 As Mathew J. Smetona has brought out, Hegel's overall system is not foundationalist in the sense of a clear starting point of being or knowledge. The idea, instead, is that logic, spirit and nature all presuppose each other in a circle that is without foundations, which is thought itself.
4 Matthew J. Smetona, Hegel's Logical Comprehension of the Modern State (Lanham: Lexington Books, 2013), 56.
5 A clear statement of this discursive context, Karl Popper included, is elaborated in Zbigniew A. Pełczyński's "Hegel Again" and Sidney Hook's "Hegel Rehabilitated," both in Walter Arnold Kaufmann, Debating the Political Philosophy Hegel (New Jersey: Transaction, 2010), 80–86 and 55–70 respectively.
6 Georg Wilhelm Friedrich Hegel and Z.A. Pełczyński, Hegel's Political Writings (Oxford: Clarendon Press, 1964); Dante Germino, "Hegel as a Political Theorist," Journal of Politics 31, no. 4 (1969), 885–912; Mark Tunick, Hegel's Political Philosophy: Interpreting the Practice of Legal Punishment (Princeton, NJ: Princeton University Press, 1992); Allen W. Wood, Hegel's Ethical Thought (Cambridge, UK; New York: Cambridge University Press, 1990).
7 Hegel and Pełczyński, Hegel's Political Writings, 136.

8 Dante Germino, "Hegel as a Political Theorist," 885–6.
9 Frederick Beiser "Dark Days: Anglophone Scholarship since the 1960s," in Espen Hammer, German Idealism: Contemporary Perspectives (London: Routledge, 2007) 79–90: 82.
10 Raymond Plant, *Hegel* (Bloomington: Indiana University Press, 1973); Henry S. Richardson, "The Logical Structure of Sittlichkeit," *Idealistic Studies* 19, no. 1 (1989), 62–78; Smetona, *Hegel's Logical Comprehension of the Modern State*; Peter J. Steinberger, *Logic and Politics: Hegel's Philosophy of Right* (New Haven: Yale University Press, 1988); Robert Stern, *Hegel, Kant and the Structure of the Object* (London; New York: Routledge, 1990); Robert Stern, *Routledge Philosophy Guidebook to Hegel and the Phenomenology of Spirit*, Routledge Philosophy Guidebooks (London; New York: Routledge, 2002); Robert Stern, *Hegelian Metaphysics* (Oxford; New York: Oxford University Press, 2009); Robert Bruce Ware, *Hegel: The Logic of Self-Consciousness and the Legacy of Subjective Freedom* (Edinburgh: Edinburgh University Press, 1999); Stephen Houlgate, *An Introduction to Hegel: Freedom, Truth, and History*, 2nd edn (Malden, MA: Blackwell, 2005); Stephen Houlgate, "Hegel's Ethical Thought," *Bulletin of the Hegel Society of Great Britain*, 25 (1992), 1–17; Thom Brooks, *Hegel's Political Philosophy: A Systematic Reading of the Philosophy of Right* (Edinburgh: Edinburgh University Press, 2007); Goodfield, "The Sovereignty of the Metaphysical in Hegel's *Philosophy of Right*."
11 Hereafter also referred to as the *Logic* or simply *Logic*.
12 Hegel, *Logic*, §86 and §86, no. 2.
13 In short, the task of Hegelian dialectic itself.
14 Shlomo Avineri, *Hegel's Theory of the Modern State*, Cambridge Studies in the History and Theory of Politics (London: Cambridge University Press, 1972); Michael Beresford Foster, *The Political Philosophies of Plato and Hegel* (Oxford: Clarendon Press, 1935); Z.A. Pełczyński, *The State and Civil Society: Studies in Hegel's Political Philosophy* (Cambridge, UK; New York: Cambridge University Press, 1984) and Wood, *Hegel's Ethical Thought*, among others, many of whom are examined in Chapter 3.
15 Such as H.S. Macran's position referenced above.
16 As Lawrence Dickey and H.B. Nisbet bring out in their introduction, Knox and Pełczyński's work is an attempt to bring Hegel back into the fold of liberal, mainstream, political thought. This coheres with a larger Anglo-American program to make Hegel amenable to the norms of analytic and empirical "sobriety" that carries on to the present day. Georg Wilhelm Friedrich Hegel, Laurence Winant Dickey and Hugh Barr Nisbet, *G.W.F. Hegel: Political Writings*, Cambridge Texts in the History of Political Thought (New York: Cambridge University Press, 1999). These and other themes are comprehensively addressed in Chapter 3.
17 Georg Wilhelm Friedrich Hegel, Klaus Brinkmann and Daniel O. Dahlstrom, *Encyclopedia of the Philosophical Sciences in Basic Outline. Part 1, Science of Logic* (Cambridge, UK; New York: Cambridge University Press, 2010), §24
18 Benjamin Jowett, *The Dialogues of Plato*, Vol. IV, (London: Oxford University Press, 1892), Steph. 15.
19 Steinberger, *Logic and Politics*, 207.
20 Ibid., 115–16.
21 Jean-Jacques Rousseau, *The Social Contract*, Penguin Classics (Harmondsworth: Penguin, 1968), 6.
22 The *Philosophy of Right* was last revised in 1827 and so was written prior to the *Encyclopedia* Logic of 1830. Hegel's most advanced statement of logic at the time was thus his 1816 *Science of Logic*. Despite this, his later work on logic remains a useful and perhaps more accessible, if somewhat condensed, entry to his logical system, and it largely retained a fidelity to the earlier edition.

23 The term "basis" and its association with "foundation" here is intended to indicate the interdependence of metaphysics and politics, and not to suggest that the latter has its "absolute start" in the former.
24 The prescriptive challenge is outlined in the Introduction.
25 Georg Wilhelm Friedrich Hegel and Stephen Houlgate, *Outlines of the Philosophy of Right*, Oxford World's Classics (Translated from the German) (Oxford; New York: Oxford University Press, 2008), 4.
26 Ibid., 14.
27 Ibid., §21.
28 Ibid., 1.
29 *The Science of Logic* and *The Encyclopedia* Logic,
30 Ibid., 26.
31 Ibid., 28.
32 Ibid., §7.
33 Ibid.
34 Ibid.
35 Hegel and Houlgate, *Outlines of the Philosophy of Right*, 7.
36 Ibid., §24.
37 Ibid.
38 As it is acquired and apprehended in the context of its development and its modern form.
39 Ibid., §31.
40 Ibid., §31.
41 Hegel et al., *Encyclopedia of the Philosophical Sciences in Basic Outline. Part 1, Science of Logic*, §6.
42 The source of much of this confusion likely originates with an oration which Friedrich Engels made that translated Hegel's *wirklich* as "real" rather than "actual."
43 Hegel and Houlgate, *Outlines of the Philosophy of Right*, Preface.
44 Ibid., §15.
45 Ibid., §10. Hegel's understanding of this process is teleological.
46 Ibid., §33.
47 Ibid.
48 As these are not essential to his equalization of universal and singular in the speculative move of the state, I leave them out of my consideration of Hegel's specifically modern political response to the problem of the universal.
49 Ibid., §164.
50 There seems no "logical" necessity behind Hegel's gender ascriptions here.
51 The speculative move overcomes the mere appearance of the part in recognition of its inner-concept, one which binds it to further development and the overturn of the negation of the prior universal it initiated.
52 Ibid., §206
53 Ibid., §187.
54 Ibid., §190.
55 Ibid., §191.
56 Hegel was influenced by Sir James Steuart's *Principles of Political Economy* as well as others on these matters.
57 Ibid., §206.
58 Ibid., §200.
59 Karl Marx and Joseph J. O'Malley, *Critique of Hegel's "Philosophy of Right"*, Cambridge Studies in the History and Theory of Politics (Cambridge, UK: University Press, 1970), 12–13.
60 Hegel and Houlgate, *Outlines of the Philosophy of Right*, 257.
61 Ibid., §1.
62 Ibid., §300.

63 Ibid., §302.
64 Steinberger provides a good overview of opinion on the forces and reasoning behind Hegel's seemingly contradictory statements and intents vis-à-vis the role of the monarch. Steinberger, *Logic and Politics*, 211–28.
65 This triad of syllogisms in the logic is discussed in detail above in the section "Teleology and Syllogistic Revolution," Chapter 4.
66 Ibid., §272.
67 Ibid., §261.
68 Ibid., §258.
69
> The spiritual individual, the nation—in so far as it is internally differentiated so as to form an organic whole—is what we call the state. This term is ambiguous, however, for the state and the laws of the state, as distinct from religion, science, and art, usual have purely political associations. But in this context, the word "state" is used in a more comprehensive sense, just as we use the word "realm" to describe spiritual phenomena. A nation should therefore be regarded as a spiritual individual, and it is not primarily its external side that will be emphasized here, but rather what we have previously called the spirit of the nation.
>
> Georg Wilhelm Friedrich Hegel and Johannes Hoffmeister, *Lectures on the Philosophy of World History: Introduction, Reason in History*, Cambridge Studies in the History and Theory of Politics (Cambridge, UK; New York: Cambridge University Press, 1975), 96

70 Ibid., 14. This of course is Hegel's *Doppelsatz* and its intention is to unite reason as a specific historical practice to the ideal or concept to which it inherently strives at a given time or place. Against conservative interpretations which suggest that he here associates the actual with the status quo, Hegel made clear that the full realization of this concept in actuality is a process never fully complete: "God ... alone is what is truly actual." Hegel *et al.*, *Encyclopedia of the Philosophical Sciences in Basic Outline. Part 1, Science of Logic*, §6.
71 Chapter 3 addresses this issue and its debates.
72 In contrast to Plato, this logic was not entrusted to an exclusive autocratic and oligarchic group of elite who administer justice for the sake and benefit of the rest of the community.
73 Ibid., §259.
74 Ibid., §270A.
75 Hegel goes to great lengths to distance his notion of universalist will from Rousseau's, holding that the latter was far too contractualist in his conception of the foundations of political community.
76 Ibid., §260.
77 Ibid., §260A.
78 Ibid., §268.
79 Ibid., §303.
80 Ibid., §279.
81 Georg Wilhelm Friedrich Hegel and J. Sibree, *The Philosophy of History* (New York: Dover Publications, 1956), §21, 28.
82 Hegel *et al.*, *Encyclopedia of the Philosophical Sciences in Basic Outline. Part 1, Science of Logic*, 198.
83 Hegel and Sibree, *The Philosophy of History*, §41
84 Hegel and Houlgate, *Outlines of the Philosophy of Right*, §273.
85 John Locke.
86 Thomas Hobbes.
87 Ibid., §31.
88 Ibid., §258.

89 Ibid., §260.
90 Ibid., §270.
91 Ibid., §270A.
92 Hegel and Houlgate, *Outlines of the Philosophy of Right*, §256
93 Ibid., §142.
94 Ibid., §260.
95 Ibid., §278.
96 In recognition of Plato's substantial legacy of the organic conception of the state, Hegel expressed gratitude in recognition of his discovery of the "the organism of the moral commonwealth." G.W.F. Hegel, *Lectures on the History of Philosophy*, trans. E. Haldane (New York: Humanities Press, 1974), 2, 99–100.
97 Hegel and Pełczyński, *Hegel's Political Writings*, 136.
98 Ibid.
99 Hegel et al., *Encyclopedia of the Philosophical Sciences in Basic Outline. Part 1, Science of Logic*, 14.
100 Steinberger, *Logic and Politics*.
101 K.H. Ilting, "The Dialectic of Civil Society," in Z.A. Pełczyński, *The State and Civil Society: Studies in Hegel's Political Philosophy*, (Cambridge, UK; New York: Cambridge University Press, 1984), 211–226: 212.
102 Hegel and Pełczyński, *Hegel's Political Writings*, 137.
103 M.J. Inwood, *Hegel*, Arguments of the Philosophers (London; Boston: Routledge & Kegan Paul, 1983), 5. Though not addressing the relations of philosophy and politics directly, Inwood here stresses the ambiguity inherent to Hegel's writing so as to preserve its richness and depth. In doing so, he opens up an encounter with Hegel's wider systematic purposes.
104 Many thanks to Robert Stern for making this deficiency abundantly clear.
105 Wood, *Hegel's Ethical Thought*.
106 Of course, Houlgate restricts himself to the writing of a short critical review.
107 Stephen Houlgate, "Hegel's Ethical Thought," *Bulletin of the Hegel Society of Great Britain*, 25 (1992), 10.
108 Ibid., 9.
109 Ibid.
110 See above, Chapter 1, on Feuerbach and "The doctrine of being and the illusion of origination."
111 Ibid.
112 Ibid.
113 Ibid., 10.
114 Ibid.
115 Ibid.
116 Ibid.
117 Ibid., 11.
118 Brooks, *Hegel's Political Philosophy*, 51.
119 Ibid.
120 Wood, *Hegel's Ethical Thought*, 5–6.
121 Stephen Houlgate "Hegel's Ethical Thought," 12.
122 Ibid., 14.
123 Ibid., 34.
124 In both his book as well as his reply to Houlgate where he assures his reader that "on no interpretation does Hegelian speculative logic have any credibility at all for philosophers today." Allen Wood, "Reply," *Bulletin of the Hegel Society of Great Britain*, 25 (1992), 34–50: 34.
125 While these are Houlgate's descriptions of Wood's approach to Hegel, Wood admits that he is correct. Allen Wood, "Reply," 42.
126 Ibid., 44.

127 Frederick C. Beiser, *Hegel*, 1st edn (New York: Routledge, 2005), 210.
128 Ibid., 213–14.
129 Ibid.
130 Allen Wood, "Reply," 45.
131 Ibid.
132 Ibid., 46.
133 Brooks, *Hegel's Political Philosophy*, 131.
134 Allen Wood, "Reply," 35.
135 Wood, *Hegel's Ethical Thought*, 11.
136 Ibid.
137 Both in this section as well as Chapter 3.
138 Hegel's "double dictum" or maxim that "what is rational is actual; and what is actual is rational."
139 Ibid., 14.
140 Ibid.
141 Ibid.
142 Ibid.
143 Ibid., 29.
144 Hegel and Houlgate, *Outlines of the Philosophy of Right*, §260.
145 Ibid., §126.
146 Wood, *Hegel's Ethical Thought*, 29.
147 Hegel and Houlgate, *Outlines of the Philosophy of Right*, §20A.
148 Wood, *Hegel's Ethical Thought*, 204.
149 Ibid., 202.
150 G.W.F. Hegel, quoted in ibid., 237.
151 Ibid.
152 Hegel and Houlgate, *Outlines of the Philosophy of Right*, §260.
153 Steinberger, *Logic and Politics*.
154 Wood, *Hegel's Ethical Thought*, 205.
155 Ibid., 238.
156 Hegel and Houlgate, *Outlines of the Philosophy of Right*, §258.
157 Ibid.
158 Ibid
159 Ibid.
160 Wood, *Hegel's Ethical Thought*, 258.
161 Stephen Eric Bronner, *Twentieth Century Political Theory: A Reader* (New York: Routledge, 1997), 73.
162 Hegel and Houlgate, *Outlines of the Philosophy of Right*, 33.
163 Wood, *Hegel's Ethical Thought*, 259.
164 Determination as destiny or vocation as Michael Inwood has clarified. M.J. Inwood, *A Hegel Dictionary*, Blackwell Philosopher Dictionaries (Oxford; Cambridge, MA: Blackwell, 1992), 77.
165 An overview of the prescriptive challenge is outlined in the Introduction.

# Part III
# Political theory, thought and metaphysics

# 6 Political theory and the metaphysical presuppositions of thought

> Find a scientific man who proposes to get along without any metaphysics—not by any means every man who holds the ordinary reasonings of metaphysicians to scorn—and you have found one whose doctrines are thoroughly vitiated by the crude and uncriticized metaphysics with which they are packed.... A man may say 'I will content myself with common sense.' I, for one, am with him there, in the main.... But the difficulty is to determine what really is and what is not the authoritative decision of common sense and what is merely *obiter dictum*. In short, there is no escape from the need of a critical examination of "first principles."[1]
>
> C.S. Peirce

Having squarely confronted the descriptive program undermining the integrity of Hegel's body of metaphysical and political thought in the previous two chapters, what remains is to meet the chronologically and theoretically prior challenge issuing from the prescriptive program. The prescriptive challenge, as should be recalled from Chapters 1 and 2, took root in the overt nineteenth-century drive to found positivist inquiry beyond the reach of the hubris and theology of metaphysics traditionally understood. As developed in Chapter 3, this diagnosis became part and parcel of the majority Anglo-American representation of Hegel's political thought as an axiomatic set of ideological and methodological norms and starting points. Though a historical derivative of the prior prescriptive challenge examined in Chapters 1 and 2, I first presented a critique of the descriptive program holding that Hegel's political thought bears no necessary relation to his metaphysics in Chapter 3. This critique was subsequently extended in Chapters 4 and 5 in the form of a defense of the counterposition which affirmed their meaningful interconnectedness. The goal there was, once and for all, to overturn the remainder of the descriptive program that intends to drive pragmatic, methodological and theoretical wedges between them.

As a background to the current task of confronting the prescriptive challenge which follows, Chapters 4 and 5 excavated the deep metaphysical concern for the universal which drove Hegel's logical and political thought in train. Having anchored the political in the logical, and in finding the ground of the metaphysics of the *Logic* in its response to the underlying problem of universals, the idea of meaningfully or intelligibly reading the politics beyond Hegel's speculative framework is dissipated insofar as we intend to represent Hegel, and not merely our contemporary surrogate. Moreover, not only were the two concerns inseparable for Hegel, but the central finding of this study and of my criticisms of Hegel's critics goes beyond this to the prescriptive issue of practicality and usefulness.[2] Where Pełczyński, Wood and others have argued for the necessity or utility of setting aside Hegel's metaphysics in our readings of his political thought, they have underestimated the pragmatism of Hegel's actual political theory as well as their own metaphysical commitments.

As I have argued above, and as I will defend in detail below, there is no getting beyond such commitments. The capacity to be useful, to involve ourselves in practical and prudential politics inherently implies theoretical starting points which sustain metaphysical commitments. Thus, with the descriptive program put behind us, I will here make a concluding case against the prescriptive challenge in favor of the utility and value of metaphysical problems and questions for political thought, both for Hegel and for ourselves.

## Metaphysical foundations and the theorizing subject of political thought

I understand thinking as inherently involved in advancing a conception of universality from its foundations in the unquestioned and un-thought. Ontological claims that seek to sidestep the metaphysical thus, nonetheless, sustain deep-seated metaphysical structures which inform and precede thinking as a form of grounding. Within such a framework, the ground of thought is not open, not transparent to the thinking subject. Rather it forms a conceptual context for thinking. Hegel specifically addressed this unseen metaphysical net which suspends our thinking:

> [E]veryone possesses and uses the wholly abstract category of *being*. The sun *is* in the sky; these grapes *are* ripe, and so on *ad infinitum*.... All our knowledge and ideas are entwined with metaphysics like this and governed by it; it is the net which holds together all the concrete material which occupies us in our action and endeavour. But this net and its knots are sunk in our ordinary consciousness beneath numerous layers of stuff. This stuff comprises our known interests and the objects that are before our minds, while the universal threads of the net remain out of sight and are not explicitly made the subject of our reflection.[3]

Behind particular thinking universalist presuppositions invest thought and play a structural role. In Hegelian terms, the presence of the logical universal in thought, nominally or realistically understood, mediates the particular. As such, universalist presuppositions necessarily participate in empirical and positivist claims. The case of Moore and the myth of the given examined in Chapter 2 presents a case in point. There we found that perceptual reflection of the phenomenal thing is not divested of thinking mediation. Rather the particular thought was found to be fixed and suspended by the interaction of a set of prevailing epistemological prejudices with the object of thought itself. I there found that, in Moore's thinking on the object, the thinking of the thought of the object was found to be obscured and concealed. In this light, both thought and object are inextricable elements of our theoretical claims. To further illustrate, and as argued in Chapter 3, just as the positivist tradition is rooted in a groundwork of metaphysical axioms which defy empirical validation, so too does all thinking emerge from antecedent grounding within which particular thoughts are embedded, and, ultimately, embodied.

Does this basis of thought reflect "experience" as an epistemic posit, or does it reflect an actual reality that is mind independent? An inescapable question of philosophy, Moore's and ours, the epistemological question of the relation of the idea and the thing, mind and world, is thus itself a primary metaphysical question which no subsequent thought escapes. The rationale for either the rejection or the affirmation of nominalist and realist epistemologies takes metaphysical claims as starting points; i.e., this is what is or is not a mind, this is or is not what satisfies the criteria of mind-external reality and relation. All responses to this epistemological question sustain metaphysical commitments, and all systematic responses imply metaphysical systems. As a result, insulating our political arguments in positivist or scientific language will not lead us to the promised land of metaphysical neutrality. P.F. Strawson enlarges on this view: "the general theory of being (ontology), the general theory of knowledge (epistemology), and the general theory of the proposition, of what is true or false (logic) are but three aspects of one unified enquiry."[4] Thus epistemological claims, even from a realist perspective, have metaphysical resonance. The ways in which the nature of thinking conditions our ontological pursuits here becomes a significant concern.

In making epistemological claims about the nature of thought interdependent with claims about what actuality exists, some would argue that the realist position is foreclosed; where a clear division between thought and being is dismissed, our ability to make strong claims about actual existence seems beyond reach.[5] To the contrary, my position does not deny such claims or consign us to an idealist perspective which makes metaphysics reducible to an investigation of our conceptual schemes (such that all being is either thought, or merely the thought of being) because there is no denial of a world beyond thought. As Steinberger puts it, the substantial interrelatedness of the two spheres of epistemology and metaphysics "does not in any way compromise the sense in which objectivity can really be objective."[6] Metaphysical suppositions affect our epistemological theories, and our theories about epistemology bear implications for our metaphysical claims.

As argued above, in the self-reflexiveness of thought as a form of awareness, the grounds from which thought itself emerges are beyond full cognizance. Thought emerges without self-transcendence, and, as such, claims for strong forms of rational self-transparency and autonomy are precluded. In this context,

## 224  Political theory, thought and metaphysics

A.W. Moore takes this logic further to a limit condition, identifying the aporias that the rejection of metaphysics as an inherency of thought implies:

> there may be no way of registering the thought that our sense-making is limited to what is immanent except by distinguishing what is immanent from what is transcendent, and thus either doing the very thing that is reckoned to be impossible, that is making sense of what is transcendent, or failing to make sense at all.[7]

The rejection of the possibility of metaphysics or its acceptance both generate metaphysical dilemmas and embroil us in metaphysical questions.

In attending to these questions, our thinking makes reference to a basic set of conditions, whether ultimately mind independent or dependent, transcendent or immanent is beside the point and, possibly, beyond reckoning. While the epistemic limits of thought are herein suggested, the possibility of drawing a conclusion on their ultimate status is prohibited by virtue of a metaphysical impasse.[8] As Hegel's invocation of metaphysics asserts, the necessity of reconciling substance and subject is foreclosed at the level of "understanding." Unable to move beyond positivist categories of sense perception, understanding is succeeded by a metaphysical procedure—speculation—in rereading the text of the world beyond the binary of spirit and nature, animate and inanimate categories. Whether we embrace Hegel's speculative checkmate or not, his point is clear. Our attempts at understanding the world are unable to recede to metaphysically neutral ground. Rather, our epistemic juxtapositions of knower and known mirror and reify our most basic notions of reality and—by extension—involve us in metaphysical claims that resound with the ontological presuppositions of the world and community we know and are.[9]

Against this background, the claims which our systems of thought and theory issue or renounce must be reconciled with our foundationalist schemes in order to come to terms with metaphysical implications, limits and possibilities.[10] In the exchange between thinker and thought, our thinking is accountable to a prehistory within which *this thought* and *this thinking* are made possible. In rejecting the paradoxical contingency of this framing, we divest our thinking of origins and assert the final universality of the foundation, even where and when universality itself is formally rejected as a metaphysical strategy. Theoretical reification and tautology seem to be the result where we take thought as an object of self-creation without attempting to come to terms with the condition of thinking within which it is enmeshed. The latter demarcates the formal and logical boundary of the thought as object, as well as informs the theorizing subject from the outset. To the degree that other versions of the universal conflict with our own, we resolve and adjudicate these in correspondence with our own implicit foundations. That is, where other responses to the problem of universals, freedom or the relation of thinking and thing (etc.) conflict with my own, I tautologically resolve the difference in relation to my axiomatic and foundational paradigm. Steinberger comments:

despite recurrent and insistent protests to the contrary, the simple fact is that traditional practices of theoretical speculation, ontological as well as prudential, continue to hold sway over us today. Such practices are deeply inscribed in each and every one of our beliefs about how things really are; and those beliefs cannot but reflect an elaborate conceptual and theoretical apparatus, a complex structure of thought on the basis of which we seek to make sense of the world.[11]

Groff further reinforces and specifies this thought with the

thesis that social and political theories have metaphysical commitments built into them.... These assumptions shape and constrain the express content of a theory, making it more or less natural, or possible, for its proponents to articulate or defend given concepts or lines of argument.[12]

Our responses to metaphysical problems are inescapably metaphysical. In this light, the rejection of the metaphysical dimension of thought by way of methodological neutralization or ideological reduction becomes a metaphysical act. The liberal-positivist paradigm that has been elaborated and traced through Anglophone appropriations of Hegel has shown us just that. What was at first a wholly overt project to eliminate the metaphysical in the name of the positive, in the end resulted in the occlusion of that project. In its place emerged a program that silenced the very set of fundamental metaphysical questions which first animated it. Steinberger again:

It is true that making sense of the world now involves us, more than ever, in the protocols of the natural sciences. But even these reflect, however unselfconsciously, an underlying structure of truth—a set of metaphysical presuppositions about the nature of things.[13]

As I have brought out, the eclipsing of these questions under the shadow of liberal ideology and the natural sciences, and the foundational metaphysical presumptions in which the sciences partake, has had a seriously deforming effect on contemporary Anglo-American representations of Hegel's political thought. The extremity of the deformity is made evident and given its central meaning in the elimination of the very questions which Hegel himself sought to answer in terms so unfamiliar to the Enlightenment tradition. What was, and is, left is a mutilated, "non-metaphysical" version of Hegel that has been reinstated on the grounds of an alternative and privileged framework of metaphysics.

The implications of my claim for the inherent metaphysicality of thought presents a direct challenge for the theorizing subject traditionally understood and contemporaneously deployed in the wake of liberal-positivist theoretical orthodoxy; a subject who holds a transparent and detached capacity in thought and who remains autonomous in the act of reasoning beyond antecedent influence. In short, the rudiments of subjective freedom in autonomous rationality forms the basis of the conventional currency of Anglo-American theoretical agency, one which privileges the theorizing subject as transcending the very conditions of subjectivity, their own thinking. As Michael Sandel extrapolates from Kant's construction:

> Who or what exactly is this subject? It is, in a certain sense, us ... but "we" qua participants in what Kant calls "pure practical reason," "we" qua participants in a transcendental subject.... The unencumbered self and the ethic it inspires, taken together, hold out a liberating vision. Freed from the dictates of nature and the sanction of social roles, the human subject is installed as sovereign, cast as the author of the only moral meanings there are.[14]

Against the modern and contemporary paradigms of political theorizing, our thinking is inherently grounded in foundational metaphysical claims in ways which tether the theorizing subject to a wider and deeper horizon of thought than can be assigned to autonomous subjectivity per se. This dimension forms the contingent underpinning of our thinking. Without such origins and the holography of a claim about the nature of reality that is posited in the particular thought, the discrete act of thinking itself would be challenged. In recognizing the way heteronomous foundations inevitably situate thinking, Steinberger witnesses this metaphysical horizon as forming

> the conditions of our unfreedom; it determines what it is possible for us to think. But it explains, as well, the precise sense in which we are in fact quite free, for it defines not only the horizons but also, at the same time, the as-yet-unimagined possibilities of our intellectual life. It is, in effect, a prison-house of ideas without which, however, we could not even begin to think for ourselves.[15]

The variety of skepticisms which reject or assert epistemological access to the totalities of absolute claims are themselves embroiled in metaphysical culpabilities. This understanding of thinking subjectivity and its conditions challenges the theoretical monopolies of Enlightenment humanism and the contemporary liberal-positivist version of freewheeling, autonomous rationality it has propagated. Rather than seeking to supplant this program with another, this critique and its recognition calls for the pluralization and revivification of metaphysical debate, reflection and exchange.

As I have argued, the problem of universals, for both Hegel and for us, has a direct political resonance. In Hegel's thought it represents the possibility for the reconciliation of the state and citizen by reference to a conception of the whole, rather than the exclusivity of the pair. The political problem of the universal makes explicit the dilemma of whole and part in a way inaccessible to the contemporary liberal-positivist frame of reference. The metaphysical commitments belonging to these perspectives dismiss a version of universality claimed for the state or simply for strong versions of political collectivity. This was brought out explicitly at the end of Chapter 5, in my critique of Allen Wood's liberal rendering of Hegel's political thought as mired in aggregate individualism. Recognizing the incommensurability running between contemporary positivist metaphysics and that of the philosophers of the past for whom metaphysical reflection was a necessary prelude to political theorization, Steinberger gravely asserts of the latter that

> We have, of late, lost touch with this commitment.... It reflects, in part, a failure to see that the interdependence of part and whole is, as both Hobbes and Kant recognized, characteristic of artificial as well as natural organisms. And when political society is misconceived in this way, it becomes difficult or impossible to reconcile notions of civic virtue, patriotism, loyalty and community, on the one hand, with conceptions of individuality, rights, tolerance and negative freedom, on the other. Such a reconciliation is arguably the most serious problem of contemporary political thought.[16]

In addition to recognizing the need for political theorizing to come to terms with the way it participates in the groundedness of its claims, Steinberger gives voice to the centrality of the problem of universals in alluding to its intersecting and double meaning for political thought. The problem of "the part and whole" is at once paradigmatic for thought itself and it intersects, at the very same moment, with the way we continue to conceive of political unity and multiplicity in practical terms.

Ruth Groff's recent work strengthens these insights. Groff makes clear,

> social and political philosophy is not metaphysically neutral at all. Received beliefs of the day notwithstanding, even the most deontological of theories connects up, in the end, with an attendant set of basic commitments regarding what kinds of things exist, what they are like and how they are or are not put together.[17]

Though Groff does not herself make the claim, I add that behind the assumptions of the foundationlessness of empirically oriented political theory lies a set of commitments which are themselves beyond empirical verification. As such they remain metaphysical. Groff writes:

> the very idea of metaphysical neutrality turns out to be an unselfconscious affirmation of what is called Humeanism (or, less technically, mechanism): the presumptive, anti-essentialist ontology of the contemporary period.... In this respect, the notion that social and political theory is metaphysically neutral ... is the meta-theory generated by the dominant philosophical position.[18]

In Aristotle's shadow, Groff asserts that political theorists need not do metaphysics, but that they must come to terms with the political implications that their implicit metaphysics generate. Groff again:

Aristotle himself, of course, was both a social-political theorist and a metaphysician, as were many other canonical philosophers. Most contemporary thinkers are not. But the point is not that one may not specialize. Rather, it is that *the compatibility in question is not guaranteed*. Social-political theories cannot be mixed and matched with any and all ontological commitments.[19]

In this context, all political theorists work within a set of metaphysical commitments. Where these are taken for granted, practical political theorizations run the risk of running aground on the shores of incommensurable political claims which they otherwise intend to uphold. This is very much the insight that is illuminated in Groff's exposé of Humean event causation. Humean metaphysics are demonstrated to categorically undermine any notion of agency, human or otherwise. Yet, as Groff points out, this did not spare Hume or latter day Humeans from the necessity of deploying such forms of agency in their political theorizations.

Insofar as political theory is understood as always already deep in metaphysical waters where its conclusions are ultimately sustained on such grounds, Groff charges that "It is a mistake ... for social and political theorists to believe themselves to be disinterested parties vis-à-vis debates in metaphysics."[20] I wholly concur; the inexorable entwinement of political theory within metaphysical frameworks demands metaphysical accountability. In making normative or ontological claims, political theorists ought to come to terms with their metaphysical presuppositions for at least two substantial reasons. First, as a means of avoiding ideological and ontological reification in their normative and critical enterprises—much as was seen to be the case in Anglo-American appropriations of Hegel's political thought. Second, and as Groff's study of Humean mechanism entails, such accountability is necessary to sustain coherence between a set of metaphysical commitments and the political theorizations they make possible in the first place lest the former "undercut its [their] content."[21]

## Political theory and the metaphysical frontiers of the liberal-positivist paradigm

As I have brought out in the case of Hegel, the metaphysical bypass that is advanced by liberal-positivist strategies generally take either the form of explicit condemnation (the prescriptive strategy) or simply a passing over of the issue altogether (the descriptive). In both cases, the question of the value of metaphysics for political thinking is taken as over and done with. These strategies take their origin in a cocktail of ideological and methodological convictions, as well as a common sense epistemology that coheres with the dominant priorities of liberal-democracy. This was illustrated in Chapter 1 through the interrogation of Moore's and others' writings, in Chapter 2 through an exposé of the development of twentieth-century political science and in Chapter 3 through a consideration of the revisionism that has beset Hegel's political thought in the context of his wider body of philosophical writing.

As examined in Chapter 2, the serendipitous union of scientific realism and liberal institutionalism revealed the theoretical and practical alliance at the core of the displacement of the very discussion of political metaphysics. Such deep intellectual and institutional commitments have repelled and eclipsed a variety of philosophical questions which, nevertheless, reside at the historical and theoretical roots of the modern program of political science. With its ideological and metaphysical opponents sidelined and largely marginalized in the contemporary Anglo-American academic worlds, those roots have been canonized and generally put beyond the threshold of critical awareness and reflection. They have played the role of a new "world intuition"—*Weltanschauung*—and epistemological dogma in a host of theoretical territories. All in all, the normative force of this program has carried political thinking towards an ever greater intellectual narrowing. Caught up in a landscape of competing ideological priorities, mainstream Anglo-American political theory has been progressively alienated from direct and reflective engagement with the presuppositions sustaining its ideological imperatives. Witness both David Easton's and John Gray's contemporary admonitions for political science where it reifies and valorizes the ideological regimes which nourish it.[22]

In extension of my arguments above, the reification of a many-over-one strategy, as I term it, reflects the privileged status of the liberal-positivist response to the political problem of the universal and hinders interest in political metaphysics as a productive theoretical concern.[23] That is, since at least the early analytic triumph over the idealist project of organic relations consummated in Moore's seminal work,[24] there has been a further conflation. In line with Hobbes, Locke and Hume, the particular is granted autonomy and equated with the thing that is seen, the ideal thing in mind (a "one") is made equivalent with the plural phenomenon of experience. As I take Steinberger's work to further suggest, such a positivism does away with the possibility and potency of the universal altogether where consciousness of the thing is taken as the singular datum of experience and rarely as a question rooted in substantial mediation with thought. While we always think with universals, as Josiah Royce has argued, "the facts of the world always appear to our senses to be individual. Man, as a mere abstraction, doesn't exist; individual men do."[25]

In this way the liberal-positivist many-over-one strategy does not merely eclipse the alternative or an equilibrium. More than that, it equates the one with the many such that, in this ontological arrangement, all possible ones as universals are always already many. This is the ultimate blind spot of this perspective; the only universal that is possible is already posited in the form of the particular, such that the particular is universal. In political terms these metaphysics endorse an atomistic social and political ontology. In epistemological terms, they reinforce Moore's realism in fixing the object in a perspectivist matrix of the empirical experiences of discrete, individual subjects. The trajectory of this logic is clear; atomism is the central and underlying trend in this strategy, subsuming and arrogating to itself all logical and practical alternatives. Groff takes up the atomist gambit:

> Atomists have no place for genuine wholes in their ontology. At the level of social and political theory, this means that the atomist is not entitled to talk of the polis, as Aristotle does—or of societies, or families, or corporations, etc. They are entitled to talk only of pluralities of individuals, of "aggregates...."[26]

As a politico-metaphysical program, liberal-positivist prejudices founded upon pluralist forms of atomism have remained largely beyond question as supporting columns of the established Anglo-American architecture of political thought. Elements of this program varyingly include, amongst others: the ethical primacy of individual right and interest, private property, contractualism, negative liberty, methodological individualism, ontological atomism, democratic legitimation, ethical pluralism, empirical common sense, moral relativism, etc.[27] In short, many of the central ideological and epistemological pillars of the historical Anglo-American world connect up with this broad program in meaningful ways.

A challenge to this state of affairs on the basis of renewed philosophical debate carries strong ideological implications. Liberal-positivism as a dominant paradigm must manage, sort and accommodate many perspectives, political and theoretical, according to its epistemological and political priorities. However, as has been brought out by countless social critics of various stripes,[28] its political logic marginalizes universalist and holistic versions of the good and opts instead for normative pluralization, inherently denying the possibility of "the one" of the ethical community or political state. The most fundamental challenge to the liberal-positivist paradigm would therefore seem to be found in a version of organic unity. As Groff has brought out, alternatives to Humean metaphysics could sustain commitments to a unified subject endowed with real agency. Implicitly running against the grain of the liberal-positivist paradigm from an Aristotelian critical realism, Groff

> does not imagine agents to be purely material entities bearing purely mental properties. [but rather] as unified, intentional beings ... bodies are enformed through and through by the "rational principle".... This is a way of thinking about mind and body, subject and object, that is deeply unfamiliar to post-Cartesian moderns. The idea is that our powers are the powers of an integrated whole.[29]

What does this exposure imply for liberal-positivist political commitments? As well, where does this leave contemporary Anglo-American political theory in relation to its illiberal opponents whose universalist claims it commonly decrypts as oppressive metaphysical interventions against difference and autonomy? The implication is apparent: confronting the subordination of theory to ideologically dominant ends raises the possibility of a widened political theoretic horizon. I do not mean to suggest that metaphysical transparency is just around the corner subsequent to removal of the liberal-positivist veil. Rather, I do mean to say that a return to theoretical inquiry and questioning, vibrancy of debate and the reinterpretation of hardened norms and presuppositions would be made possible in a way that is currently beyond reach. Such theoretical reflection would have profound implications for the way we understand the thinkers, such as Hegel, as well as texts that have become part and parcel of the subfield. With Gregory Kasza, the implications for the discipline and its empirical concerns would be substantial:

> Political philosophy, understood as inquiry into the big ontological, epistemological, and normative questions, has lost its place in political science ... the biggest losers are not those in the subfield of political philosophy but the rest of us in the discipline, who are rendered incapable of thinking in a sophisticated way about the most basic aspects of our research.[30]

The idea then is to return to the big questions, but not necessarily to grand system building. What diverse thinkers would see and do with a renewed attention to philosophical interrogation and practice is an open question. With A.W. Moore, and Peirce before him,

> metaphysics can fulfil the function of rectifying bad metaphysics ... there is a real need for something to counteract the debilitating and damaging effects of our relatively instinctive, relatively primitive efforts. There is a real need, that is, for good metaphysics.[31]

Steinberger witnesses the direct value these insights imply for political theory:

> To understand truly our own theory of the state ... of policy and government, thus requires that we attend precisely to that foundation. We need to examine our own presuppositions with care, and attempt to determine exactly what kind of political theory they entail, if we are to make sense of the social and political problems that confront us.[32]

There is no necessity that the particular metaphysical avenues I have explored should provide the sole paths to greater perspective. Indeed, metaphysical concerns—agency, causation, being amongst them—are many, and the demands of the day will always press and repress those challenges and issues into its own molds.[33] While I have issued admonitions that put brakes on the wholesale cooptation and reification of the philosophical potentials of theory aligned to present day ideological demands, the inverse problematic represents an equal danger. Should theory be pursued as a singular dedication to the demands of metaphysical inquiry in a way which turns political thought away from lived experience, an equally deadened and otherworldly dialectic looms. Such an admonition yet remains largely unnecessary in today's atmosphere of academic and empirically oriented "post-foundationalism."[34] Where metaphysics is understood as grounded in and emergent of lived experience, as well, no such concern or proscription should be necessary.

In this vein, where the metaphysical dimension of theoretical questions themselves, and not their solutions made instrumentally servile, become the primary point of departure for inquiry of the political, the ideologization of theory seems a less likely outcome. Ongoing liberal, post-structuralist and post-modern denials of the value of the metaphysical dimension of political theory seem only to serve to limit their own theoretical potentials. Moreover, the dangers of metanarrative totalization, paternalism and power which they witness there are not part and parcel or the inevitable issue of metaphysical questions themselves. Rather, it is service to historical expediencies—theocratic, nationalist, classist, economic, racial, sexist—that has foreclosed on the relative autonomies of the great metaphysical programs: Christ become Constantine.

As Jean Hampton has brought out, it is not the pursuit of philosophical truth and its enterprises that reduces metaphysics to a tool of power. Rather, such instrumentalist faithful "are not committed to the truth; instead, they are true believers committed to their cause" and "It is their blind faith, not their metaphysics, which results in discord and even war."[35] In my view, Hampton takes Steinberger's and A.W. Moore's thoughts forward to a normative extent in claiming that the crux of her "argument for metaphysical political philosophizing"[36] boils down to a fundamental respect for the other that metaphysics specifically attains to. On this account, only with a conception of true and false, right and wrong, and the "substantive metaphysical beliefs" which presuppose such philosophical agency, can "disrespectful ideas and practices" be rejected for the false entities they are.[37] From this point of view, proscriptions of metaphysics as ascriptive and reifying political agendas imposed upon real consensus and political dialogue seem tantamount to cancellations of truth as a possibility—a position which itself entails a strong metaphysical claim and closure. Closing off philosophical inquiry and exchange on these accounts doesn't merely serve the ends of peace and justice as is often claimed. Rather, it seems to essentialize difference and to freeze the conflict grounded in it as well; prejudice unexpressed is prejudice beyond revision. Where such admonitions against the closure of the metaphysical dimension of political theoretic practice are ignored, the latter loses access to the foundational questions which animate its thought in the first place. The agapeic dimension which William Desmond has witnessed in the metaphysical tradition is cynically rejected in exchange for a thorough politicization of the field of thought.[38] The will to power herein becomes synonymous with the efforts of theory, balkanizing thought through and through in the process.

What then lies beyond the threshold of the atomistic ontology and frontier? The liberal universalization of the one as many seems to have shut off several obvious alternatives: the many equalized to the one, the one over the many or the radicalization of the many as one.[39] Why and how should their value be assigned and to what extent has discursive and ideological tradition already foreclosed such options in the Anglo-American academic worlds?

Hegel tells us that the historical "diremption" or rupture of modernity was such that its political and scientific revolt sought the elimination of all that was pre-modern. In this transformation liberal scientific modernity stands in diametrical opposition to that which had been part and parcel of the feudal world: the many of the senses supplanted the one of mind, the earth, the heavens.[40] Enlightenment liberals, then and now, see the liberty of the ancients across this divide as undesirable in its privileging of positive liberty and the unity of political organism. In its stead they raise detachment, privacy and property to the fore. The notions of subordination and subsumption of the citizen in political collectivity, and the option to annihilate the part altogether by totalizing the whole, seem untenable in the context of so-called contemporary politics. The sole remaining option, that which has been heralded by the communitarian likes of Taylor and Sandel, following in the footsteps of Hegel and Rousseau, is the equalization of the one and the many. Despite these alternatives, forms of strong unity inspired by communitarian visions of positive liberty have made limited headway within contemporary Anglo-American political theory. The case of Hegel's reception and representation explored throughout this study makes just this case; the ideological persistence and ubiquity of liberal individualism and positivist atomism have proven powerful bulwarks to their revision. The social and material forces of history, and not metaphysical poker chips taken as playing in their stead, form the ultimate context within which a theoretical "time and place" emerges. Yet the resources for moving beyond the current impasse are seemingly not on offer given the obstacles to renewed metaphysical reflection which liberal-positivist matrices have implied for social and political inquiry.

Those who read my appeal to metaphysical thinking and questioning as inevitably invoking this matrix of practical political permutations will immediately dispatch with the larger questions and emphasize the results: what good does the meditation on the universal and particular, or the one and the many present where history, in large part, has already pronounced harsh and negative judgment? The response to these challenges is clear: political thought is stultified where it seals itself off from internal development and external dialogue. More than this, Hegel persuasively asserts that such self-absorption and reification ought to be its own undoing; the triumph of the many is the herald of the one. Many so-called critics of Hegel's thought and those who would see themselves as disciplined liberals lose sight of this point in standing too closely with Isaiah Berlin in seeing the political universal as all fascism, charisma and paternalism.[41] What seems more true, and under the current conditions of the crisis of political thought, is that the atomized many in absence of a one has ceased to play the creative theoretical role it once did. This is not a resentful denial of liberal democracy in favor of an aggrandized resurrection of past or future forms of romantic community. Those who claim the terms of the debate are settled—as most Anglo-American Hegel commentators over the last century seem to do—stand on a hubris vulnerable to the very forms of undesirable reaction that historically justified and underwrote their liberal commitments in the first place.[42]

Where metaphysical questions are taken as an inevitable correlate to political thinking, as has been argued here throughout, denying this theoretical other becomes an act of self-defeating censorship. The recognition of metaphysical discourse, then, does not merely and only open up the route to a fearful politics of coercive unity in the one. Rather, the dialectical reflectivity it engenders implies a diversifying and deepening of what pluralism, particularism and identity can mean as well. The liberal project is only diminished by lack of contact or the theoretical eclipse of its conceptual and ideological opponents. William Desmond's position seems an invaluable pearl in the wake of the post-Hegelian break with philosophy and its theoretically narrowed horizons: "The claim that Hegel represents the culmination of metaphysics has had disastrous consequences ... because the reiteration of this claim has stood in the way of rethinking metaphysics."[43]

The question of Hegel's place in the history of political thought in the context of the writing and rewriting of Hegel scholarship in the last 150 years explored above sheds light on the question at hand. Indeed, the rejection and revision of Hegel's thought has simultaneously been a rejection of history as an open arena—agora—of conceptual, political and normative change. While Berlin saw the most ominous rejection of the market place of ideas in Hegel and his ilk, the liberal-positivist fixation upon atomized plurality and its normative prerogative of negative liberty have been far more constricting. The triumphalism of the liberal-positivist theoretical program has led to a compulsion to contain Hegel precisely because his project works to reunite lost dimensions of political thought and practice from the past. His legacy has proven a double-edged sword. On the one hand Hegel is omnipresent and his mark upon diverse threads of theory and practice is beyond question or erasure. Yet, on the other, "we" cannot tolerate Hegel's methodological indulgence of universalist propositions which not only challenge our own dogmas and norms, but also seem bent on reintegrating the pre-modern past with the modern world into some form of Greek *Gemeinschaft*. The dialectic does not merely seek to conjoin whole and part, it also intends to reconnect past and future and against this the liberal-positivist paradigm is inherently and existentially opposed. In this context, where liberal-positivism was once revolutionary it has now become reification.

Hegel's great power and lasting appeal is not merely witnessed in his attendance to a dynamic methodology and politics that seeks system in contradiction alone. Perhaps the most powerful element in Hegel's thought is his attempt to restore historical memory and with it a deepened understanding of the past and its implications for the present and future. Through Hegel's system historical modes of thought and action speak to us and infuse our ideas with historical experience. This invasive dimension posed a serious danger for William James and continues to do so for his contemporary descendants. The material and spiritual implications are clear; the particular is born out of and inextricably betrothed to a whole not of its own making or knowing. This social and spiritual "oceanic feeling"[44] is taken as the repugnant sovereignty of the collective and a threat to the epistemic pillars of modernity and their ideological self-production and reproduction within the social and political sciences. This dimension presents a boundary condition of contemporary liberal thinking and its exposure calls into question this program's core raison d'être: resistance to the absolutization of any one good or group in favor of the sustenance of the many on the one hand, and suspension of the tyranny of the past over the present on the other. What is left then is to imagine a mode of political theorizing in which we recognize and advance both its historical and metaphysical dimensions.

## Political and metaphysical: analytic and continental

These boundary issues which confound static knowing and present its conditions, arise in the use of conceptual language and immediately juxtapose political theorization with the inexhaustible questions which metaphysical inquiry takes as origin. William Desmond greets this point, where "There is no being beyond metaphysics ... for the very effort to be beyond inevitably invokes its own dilemmas of the one and the many, unity and difference, community and pluralism, and hence is not beyond."[45] The question of practicality is not sidelined by such questions, indeed the paradoxes which such problems give rise to are inherent in the way we localize and interpret the very positive political phenomena and pragmatic concerns which theorists intend to address. Whether these questions haunt the mind independent world in the same way they do the world of conception, whether they attain to realist and not merely idealist criteria, makes little difference in the wake of the rejection of the "myth of the given" as a starting point for self-conscious theorization.

These concerns will undoubtedly be met with skepticism; does not the recollection of or immersion in the relentless metaphysical issues which intersect with politics imply immobilization and "omphaloskeptic" paralysis? How can such *Sehnsucht* and "poetry of the soul" lend any utility to our theorization of politics? The response is positive. Practical thinking and solutions are shot through and through with the destabilizing questions and conceptual aporia that metaphysical reflection reveals in even our most mundane acts of thinking. Metaphysical questions, not their grand solutions, are what makes the metaphysical an inexorable component of our understanding and theorizations of the world in the first place. Desmond writes:

> Despite our protections and resistances, agapeic astonishment will still strike home. It may come from anywhere and from nowhere, from any direction or no particular direction, to anyone, for any or no reason, at any time, or it may come and seem to suspend time. It does not have to arrange an appointment before it arrives disturbingly at our door. It gives its gift, and no preconditions are extracted for its offer. In fact, its gift is what makes each of us to be primally metaphysical.[46]

The agapeic dimension returns a philosophy of politics to the origins of what political consciousness implies and aspires to. It builds into our thinking a transformed awareness of what ethical and political problems conceptually demand. While these concerns destabilize boundaries and bring indeterminacy to our discursive paradigms, they do not eliminate attendance to the practical, discrete and determinate findings of empirical research which science pursues. Nor do they impose rationalism as a surrogate for the engagement of the lived politics of everyday life and its world of political practices and common sense. Thought or unthought, they form the basis of understanding upon which such a world is built and stands.

Whether taken in an "analytic" and nominalist vein as with Steinberger's embedment of the metaphysical in a socio-cultural world of intelligibility, or in Desmond's classical "continentalist" realism of sensuous immersion in being, the questions persist.[47] Whether they riddle thought as wholly conceptual or mind independent, objective concerns, there is no getting beyond them in political theorizing. In falling into the dogmas of "analytic" or "continental," empirical or rationalist camps, forgetfulness or denial of fundamental questions which animate our theoretical and practical worldviews only invites the latter's transformation or regression.[48] The tides of change ebb and flow with little concern for our humanist pretensions or methodological hubris.

## Notes

1 C.S. Peirce in Robert Stern, *Hegelian Metaphysics* (Oxford; New York: Oxford University Press, 2009), 37.
2 Usefulness in the sense that action too participates and presupposes judgment and the mediation of thought. Thanks to Matteo Morganti for pointing out the possible ambiguous association of the notion of usefulness I propose with that of action.
3 Georg Wilhelm Friedrich Hegel, T.M. Knox and Arnold V. Miller, *Introduction to the Lectures on the History of Philosophy* (Oxford; New York: Clarendon Press; Oxford University Press, 1985), 27–8.
4 P.F. Strawson, *Analysis and Metaphysics: An Introduction to Philosophy* (Oxford: Oxford University Press, 1992), 35.
5 Thanks to Ruth Groff for pointing this out.
6 Peter J. Steinberger, *The Idea of the State* (Cambridge, UK; New York: Cambridge University Press, 2004), 133.
7 A.W. Moore, *The Evolution of Modern Metaphysics: Making Sense of Things*, The Evolution of Modern Philosophy (Cambridge, UK; New York: Cambridge University Press, 2012), 10.
8 Both nominalist and realist epistemological claims rely upon metaphysical representations of the nature and relation of mind and world, idea and thing.
9 This embedment in foundations does not require that we fatally resign from metaphysics altogether simply because we can never fully liberate ourselves from the conceptual structures of our metaphysical presuppositions to begin with. The implication, instead, is that all thinking proceeds from a set of commitments and that, in order to come to greater grips with these, we must engage their counterparts. The dialectical circle allows that we move critically between one set of foundations and its others all the while gaining perspective on our origins. In agreement with Steinberger "the critical engagement with our structure of metaphysical supposition must itself emerge from our structure of metaphysical presupposition" (Peter J. Steinberger, "Re: Conclusion for feedback," email to Eric Goodfield, August 2, 2013.). Yet to be clear, this contextualization does not lock us into the conceptual analysis of a metaphysics of experience either. The argument that our presuppositions are themselves only subjectively or conceptually real or knowable is itself undermined by the aporia that it

generates. As Robert Stern has raised the problem, "How can our knowledge of the necessary structure of our cognitive structures *itself* be explained in a Kantian manner, by *further* appeal to such structures, where at this level it is hard to see how the explanation could work?" (Stern, *Hegelian Metaphysics*, 24). In giving up being and instead restricting ourselves and retreating to mind and concept, we nonetheless seem to be restrained and frustrated by irremovable and irresolvable problems and questions. For Hegel, the breakout is achieved in speculatively tracing the "universal" threads of the net of our metaphysics back to the absolute out of which it is woven.

10 I use the term "foundationalism" here in the sense that I am making a claim for the metaphysical inherency of thinking in general, not because I am making a claim about ontological monism or pluralism, mereological or otherwise.
11 Peter J. Steinberger, *The Idea of the State*, 32–3.
12 Ruth Groff, *Ontology Revisited: Metaphysics in Social and Political Philosophy*, Ontological Explorations (New York: Routledge, 2013), 106.
13 Steinberger, *The Idea of the State*, 33. David Lay Williams makes a similar claim:

> There is little doubt that the move to exclude metaphysics from discussions of ethics and politics in this century has been inspired by the success of the natural sciences.... From Logical Positivism to Legal Realism, it has been our Zeitgeist to remove metaphysics from legitimate normative discussion. What has replaced metaphysics, however, is either veiled metaphysics, which is a form of intellectual dishonesty, or what is perhaps worse, a contest of purely bald assertions, which is the worst form of dogmatism.
> 
> David L. Williams, "Dialogical Theories of Justice,"
> *Telos*, no. 114 (1999), 109–31

14 Michael J. Sandel, *Public Philosophy: Essays on Morality in Politics* (Cambridge, MA: Harvard University Press, 2005), 84, 87.
15 Steinberger, *The Idea of the State*, 34.
16 Ibid., 288.
17 Groff, *Ontology Revisited*, 1.
18 Ibid.
19 Ibid., 116.
20 Ibid.
21 Ibid.
22 David Easton, *The Political System: An Inquiry into the State of Political Science*, 1st edn (New York: Knopf, 1953), 51; John Gray, *Enlightenment's Wake: Politics and Culture at the Close of the Modern Age*, Routledge Classics (Abingdon, UK; New York: Routledge, 2007), 215–76. The latter writes of political thought: "The tacit or declared objective of philosophical inquiry has been the delivery of a rational justification of liberal political morality—a transcendental deduction, that is to say, of *ourselves*" (p. 215).
23 For Steinberger "the problem of the state" and for me the political problem of the universal. Steinberger, *The Idea of the State*, 32.
24 G.E. Moore, "The Refutation of Idealism," *Mind* 12, no. 48 (1903), 433–53.
25 Josiah Royce, *The Spirit of Modern Philosophy: An Essay in the Form of Lectures* (Boston and New York: Houghton, 1892), 218.
26 Groff, *Ontology Revisited*, 90–1. Groff is not addressing the specific context I here cite her in, but the ramifications of her analysis reinforce and align with the conclusions I draw.
27 In her discussion of rational choice thinkers, Sonja Amadae identifies a very similar set of concerns:

> Their understanding is that science, democratic liberalism, and capitalism are based on toleration; free trade and free association; personal autonomy permitting

subjective moral standards; an experimental epistemology based on universal laws subject to empirical test; and legitimate rule as a reflection of individuals' interests.

S.M. Amadae, *Rationalizing Capitalist Democracy: The Cold War Origins of Rational Choice Liberalism* (Chicago: University of Chicago Press, 2003), 256 As my discussion of rational choice theory argued in Chapter 3, it is an extension of the liberal-positivist program.

28 Theological, communitarian, socialist, Aristotelian, Platonist amongst them.
29 Groff, *Ontology Revisited*, 85.
30 Gregory J. Kasza, "The Marginalization of Political Philosophy and Its Effects on the Rest of the Discipline," *Political Research Quarterly* 63, no. 3 (2010): 697–701, 700.
31 Moore, *The Evolution of Modern Metaphysics*, 17.
32 Steinberger, *The Idea of the State*, 93.
33 Ruth Groff's examination of the metaphysical dimensions of Humeanism and its take on causal powers provides one recent example. Groff, *Ontology Revisited: Metaphysics in Social and Political Philosophy*.
34 Keeping in mind the foundationalism/s which positivism and neo-positivism themselves represent.
35 Jean Hampton, "Should Political Philosophy Be Done without Metaphysics?" *Ethics* 99, no. 4 (1989) 791–814: 812.
36 Ibid., 813.
37 Ibid., 814.
38 William Desmond, *The Intimate Strangeness of Being: Metaphysics after Dialectic*, Studies in Philosophy and the History of Philosophy (Washington, D.C.: Catholic University of America Press, 2012); William Desmond, "Being, Determination, and Dialectic: On the Sources of Metaphysical Thinking," *The Review of Metaphysics* 48, no. 4 (1995), 731–69. This dimension of his thought and its relevance for political thinking is considered below in the section "Political and metaphysical: analytic and continental" of this chapter.
39 The complete subsumption and diffusion of the parts in the whole.
40 Georg Wilhelm Friedrich Hegel and J.B. Baillie, *The Phenomenology of Mind*, 2nd edn, Library of Philosophy, edited by J.H. Muirhead (London; New York: G. Allen & Unwin; Macmillan, 1931), §8.
41 Berlin presents a liberal critique of Hegel's "vices" and "erroneous views" in his *Freedom and Its Betrayal: Six Enemies of Human Liberty*.
42 With Adriaan Peperzak, the political battle over metaphysics is not over. Adriaan Theodoor Peperzak, *Modern Freedom: Hegel's Legal, Moral, and Political Philosophy* (Dordrecht; London: Kluwer Academic, 2001).
43 Desmond, "Being, Determination, and Dialectic," 733.
44 To borrow a phrase from Sigmund Freud.
45 Desmond, *The Intimate Strangeness of Being*, 35.
46 Ibid., 42.
47 Peter Steinberger's political thought invokes the philosophy of thinkers such as Robert Brandom and P.F. Strawson, and William Desmond's takes up strong ties to Plato, G.W.F. Hegel and Friedrich Nietzsche.
48 Without wishing to suggest that these—*our*—camps exhaust the range or depths of metaphysical thinking whatsoever.

# Select bibliography

Adcock, Robert, Mark Bevir and Shannon C. Stimson, *Modern Political Science: Anglo-American Exchanges since 1880* (Princeton, NJ: Princeton University Press, 2007).
Allen, Gay Wilson, *William James*, University of Minnesota Pamphlets on American Writers (Minneapolis: University of Minnesota Press, 1970).
Amadae, S.M., *Rationalizing Capitalist Democracy: The Cold War Origins of Rational Choice Liberalism* (Chicago: University of Chicago Press, 2003).
Aristotle, *De Interpretatione 7*, in Porphyry and Paul Vincent Spade, *Five Texts on the Mediaeval Problem of Universals: Porphyry, Boethius, Abelard, Duns Scotus, Ockham* (Indianapolis: Hackett, 1994).
Avineri, Shlomo, *Hegel's Theory of the Modern State*, Cambridge Studies in the History and Theory of Politics (London: Cambridge University Press, 1972).
Bachmann, Carl Friedrich, *Über Hegels System und die Notwendigkeit einer nochmaligen Umgestaltung der Philosophie* (Aalen: Scientia-Verlag, 1968).
Baldwin, Thomas, *G.E. Moore*, The Arguments of the Philosophers (London; New York: Routledge, 1999).
Beiser, Frederick C., *The Cambridge Companion to Hegel* (Cambridge England; New York: Cambridge University Press, 1993).
Beiser, Frederick C., *Hegel*, 1st edn (New York: Routledge, 2005).
Beiser, Frederick, "Dark Days: Anglophone Scholarship since the 1960s," in Espen Hammer, *German Idealism: Contemporary Perspectives* (London: Routledge, 2007), 79–90.
Bell, David, "The Revolution of Moore and Russell: A Very British Coup?" in Anthony O'Hear, *German Philosophy since Kant*, Royal Institute of Philosophy Supplement, (Cambridge, UK; New York: Cambridge University Press, 1999), 193–208.
Bellamy, Richard and Terence Ball, *The Cambridge History of Twentieth-Century Political Thought* (Cambridge: Cambridge University Press, 2008).
Berlin, Isaiah, *Freedom and its Betrayal: Six Enemies of Human Liberty* (Princeton, NJ: Princeton University Press, 2002).
Bernstein, Richard J., *The Restructuring of Social and Political Theory*, 1st edn (New York: Harcourt Brace Jovanovich, 1976).
Bernstein, Richard J., "Why Hegel Now?" *The Review of Metaphysics* 31, no. 1 (1977), 29–60.
Brooks, Thom, *Hegel's Political Philosophy: A Systematic Reading of the Philosophy of Right* (Edinburgh: Edinburgh University Press, 2007).
Burbidge, John W., *The Logic of Hegel's Logic: An Introduction* (Peterborough, Ont.: Broadview Press, 2006).

Burbidge, John W., *Hegel's Systematic Contingency* (Basingstoke, UK; New York: Palgrave Macmillan, 2007).
Candlish, Stewart, *The Russell/Bradley Dispute and Its Significance for Twentieth-Century Philosophy*, Pbk edn, History of Analytic Philosophy (Basingstoke, UK; New York: Palgrave Macmillan, 2009).
Carritt, E.F., "Hegel and Prussianism," *Philosophy* 15, no. 58 (1940).
Catlin, George Edward Gordon, *The Science and Method of Politics* (Hamden, CT: Archon Books, 1964).
Collier, Andrew, "Critical Realism," in George Steinmetz, *The Politics of Method in the Human Sciences: Positivism and Its Epistemological Others*, Politics, History, and Culture (Durham: Duke University Press, 2005), 327–45.
Crick, Bernard R., *The American Science of Politics: Its Origins and Conditions* (Berkeley: University of California Press, 1959).
Desmond, William, "Being, Determination, and Dialectic: On the Sources of Metaphysical Thinking," *The Review of Metaphysics* 48, no. 4 (1995), 731–69.
Desmond, William, *The Intimate Strangeness of Being: Metaphysics after Dialectic*, Studies in Philosophy and the History of Philosophy (Washington, D.C.: Catholic University of America Press, 2012).
Ducasse, C.J., "Introspection, Mental Acts, and Sensa," *Mind* 45, no. 178 (1936), 181–92.
Easton, David, "The Decline of Modern Political Theory," *Journal of Politics* 13, no. 1 (1951), 36–58.
Easton, David, *The Political System: An Inquiry into the State of Political Science*, 2nd edn (New York: Knopf, 1971).
Engeman, Thomas S., "Behavioralism, Postbehavioralism, and the Reemergence of Political Philosophy," *Perspectives on Political Science* 24, no. 4 (1995), 214–17.
Farr, James, "The New Science of Politics," in Richard Bellamy and Terence Ball, *The Cambridge History of Twentieth-Century Political Thought* (Cambridge: Cambridge University Press, 2008), 431–45.
Feuerbach, Ludwig, *Kritik der Anti-Hegels: Zur Einleitung in das Studium der Philosophie*, 2nd edn (Leipzig: Wigand, 1844).
Feuerbach, Ludwig, *The Fiery Brook: Selected Writings of Ludwig Feuerbach* (Garden City, NY: Anchor Books, 1972).
Feuerbach, Ludwig, *Principles of the Philosophy of the Future* (Hackett, 1986).
Findlay, John Niemeyer, *Hegel, A Re-Examination*, Muirhead Library of Philosophy (London; New York: Allen & Unwin; Macmillan, 1958).
Foster, Michael Beresford, *The Political Philosophies of Plato and Hegel* (Oxford: Clarendon Press, 1935).
Franco, Paul, *Hegel's Philosophy of Freedom* (New Haven, CT: Yale University Press, 1999).
Germino, Dante, "Hegel as a Political Theorist," *Journal of Politics* 31, no. 4 (1969), 885–912.
Goodfield, Eric, "The Sovereignty of the Metaphysical in Hegel's *Philosophy of Right*," *The Review of Metaphysics* 62, no. 4 (2009), 849–73.
Grattan-Guinness, I., "Russell and Karl Popper: Their Personal Contacts," (DigitalCommons@McMaster, 1992), 10.
Gray, John, *Enlightenment's Wake: Politics and Culture at the Close of the Modern Age*, Routledge Classics (Abingdon, UK; New York: Routledge, 2007).
Groff, Ruth, *Ontology Revisited: Metaphysics in Social and Political Philosophy*, Ontological Explorations (New York, NY: Routledge, 2013).

Gunnell, John G., *Between Philosophy and Politics: The Alienation of Political Theory* (Amherst: University of Massachusetts Press, 1986).
Gunnel, John G., "History of Political Science," in George Thomas Kurian, *The Encyclopedia of Political Science* (Washington, D.C.: CQ Press, 2011), 1278–85.
Hammer, Espen, *German Idealism: Contemporary Perspectives* (London: Routledge, 2007).
Hampton, Jean, "Should Political Philosophy be Done without Metaphysics?" *Ethics* 99, no. 4 (1989), 791–814.
Hanna, Robert, "From an Ontological Point of View: Hegel's Critique of the Common Logic," in John Stewart, *The Hegel Myths and Legends*, Northwestern University Studies in Phenomenology and Existential Philosophy (Evanston: Northwestern University Press, 1996), 253–81.
Hardimon, Michael O., *Hegel's Social Philosophy: The Project of Reconciliation*, Modern European Philosophy (Cambridge, UK; New York: Cambridge University Press, 1994).
Hartmann, Klaus, "Hegel: A Non-Metaphysical View," in Alasdair C. MacIntyre, *Hegel: A Collection of Critical Essays*, 1st edn, Modern Studies in Philosophy (Garden City, NY: Anchor Books, 1972), 101–24.
Hauptmann, Emily, "Defining 'Theory' in Postwar Political Science," in George Steinmetz, *The Politics of Method in the Human Sciences: Positivism and Its Epistemological Others*, Politics, History, and Culture (Durham: Duke University Press, 2005), 207–32.
Haym, Rudolf, *Hegel und seine Zeit: Vorlesungen über Entstehung und Entwickelung, Wesen und Werth der Hegel'schen Philosophie* (Berlin: Gaertner, 1857).
Hegel, Georg Wilhelm Friedrich, *The Philosophy of Right*, trans. T.M. Knox (London: Oxford University Press, 1952).
Hegel, Georg Wilhelm Friedrich, *Hegel's Briefe*, Hamburg: Felix Meiner Verlag, 1952, vol. ii.
Hegel, Georg Wilhelm Friedrich, *Lectures on the History of Philosophy*, trans. E. Haldane (New York: Humanities Press, 1974).
Hegel, Georg Wilhelm Friedrich and J.B. Baillie, *The Phenomenology of Mind*, 2nd edn, Library of Philosophy, edited by J.H. Muirhead (London; New York: G. Allen & Unwin; Macmillan, 1931).
Hegel, Georg Wilhelm Friedrich and Carl J. Friedrich, *The Philosophy of Hegel* (New York: Modern Library, 1954).
Hegel, Georg Wilhelm Friedrich and Johannes Hoffmeister, *Lectures on the Philosophy of World History: Introduction, Reason in History*, Cambridge Studies in the History and Theory of Politics (Cambridge, UK; New York: Cambridge University Press, 1975).
Hegel, Georg Wilhelm Friedrich and Stephen Houlgate, *Outlines of the Philosophy of Right*, Oxford World's Classics (Translated from the German) (Oxford; New York: Oxford University Press, 2008).
Hegel, Georg Wilhelm Friedrich and Henry Stewart Macran, *Hegel's Doctrine of Formal Logic* (Oxford: Clarendon Press, 1912).
Hegel, Georg Wilhelm Friedrich and Z.A. Pełczyński, *Hegel's Political Writings* (Oxford: Clarendon Press, 1964).
Hegel, Georg Wilhelm Friedrich and J. Sibree, *The Philosophy of History* (New York: Dover Publications, 1956).
Hegel, Georg Wilhelm Friedrich and William Wallace, *Hegel's Logic: Being Part One of the Encyclopaedia of the Philosophical Sciences (1830)* (Oxford: Clarendon Press, 1975).

242  Select bibliography

Hegel, Georg Wilhelm Friedrich, Klaus Brinkmann and Daniel O. Dahlstrom, *Encyclopedia of the Philosophical Sciences in Basic Outline. Part 1, Science of Logic* (Cambridge, UK; New York: Cambridge University Press, 2010).

Hegel, Georg Wilhelm Friedrich, Laurence Winant Dickey and Hugh Barr Nisbet, *G.W.F. Hegel: Political Writings*, Cambridge Texts in the History of Political Thought (New York: Cambridge University Press, 1999).

Hegel, Georg Wilhelm Friedrich, John Niemeyer Findlay and Arnold V. Miller, *Phenomenology of Spirit* (Oxford: Clarendon Press, 1977).

Hegel, Georg Wilhelm Friedrich, Michael George and Andrew Vincent, *The Philosophical Propaedeutic* (Oxford; New York: Blackwell, 1986).

Hegel, Georg Wilhelm Friedrich, T.M. Knox and Arnold V. Miller, *Introduction to the Lectures on the History of Philosophy* (Oxford; New York: Clarendon Press; Oxford University Press, 1985).

Hempel, Carl G., *Aspects of Scientific Explanation, and Other Essays in the Philosophy of Science* (New York: Free Press, 1965).

Hobhouse, L.T., *The Metaphysical Theory of the State* (London: G. Allen & Unwin, 1918).

Hook, Sidney, "From Plato to Hegel to Marx," *New York Times*, July 22, 1951.

Hook, Sidney, "Hegel Rehabilitated," in Walter Arnold Kaufmann, *Debating the Political Philosophy Hegel* (New Jersey: Transaction, 2010), 55–70.

Hook, Sidney, *From Hegel to Marx: Studies in the Intellectual Development of Karl Marx*, Ann Arbor Paperbacks for the Study of Communism and Marxism, (Ann Arbor: University of Michigan Press, 1962).

Houlgate, Stephen, "Hegel's Ethical Thought," *Bulletin of the Hegel Society of Great Britain*, 25 (1992), 1–17.

Houlgate, Stephen, *An Introduction to Hegel: Freedom, Truth, and History*, 2nd edn (Malden, MA: Blackwell, 2005).

Inwood, M.J., *Hegel*, Arguments of the Philosophers (London; Boston: Routledge & Kegan Paul, 1983).

Inwood, M.J., *A Hegel Dictionary*, Blackwell Philosopher Dictionaries (Oxford; Cambridge, MA: Blackwell, 1992).

Ishiyama, John T. and Marijke Breuning, *21st Century Political Science: A Reference Handbook*, 21st Century Reference Series, 2 vols (Thousand Oaks: SAGE Publications, 2011).

Jackson, M.W., "Hegel: The Real and the Rational," in Jon Stewart, *The Hegel Myths and Legends*, Northwestern University Studies in Phenomenology and Existential Philosophy (Evanston, IL: Northwestern University Press, 1996), 19–25.

James, William, "On Some Hegelisms," *Mind* 7, no. 26 (1882), 186–208.

James, William, *A Pluralistic Universe: Hibbert Lectures to Manchester College on the Present Situation in Philosophy* (New York: Longmans, Green, and Co., 1909).

Kant, Immanuel, Paul Guyer and Allen W. Wood, *Critique of Pure Reason* (Cambridge, UK; New York: Cambridge University Press, 1998).

Kasza, Gregory J., "The Marginalization of Political Philosophy and Its Effects on the Rest of the Discipline," *Political Research Quarterly* 63, no. 3 (September 1, 2010), 697–701.

Kaufmann, Walter Arnold, *Debating the Political Philosophy of Hegel*, (New Jersey: Transaction, 2010).

Kaufmann, Walter Arnold, "The Hegel Myth and Its Method," *Philosophical Review* 60, no. 4 (1951), 459–86.

Kaufmann, Walter Arnold, *The Owl and the Nightingale: From Shakespeare to Existentialism* (London: Faber and Faber, 1959).
Kaufmann, Walter Arnold, *Hegel's Political Philosophy*, 1st edn (New York: Atherton Press, 1970).
Kaufmann, Walter Arnold, *From Shakespeare to Existentialism: An Original Study. Essays on Shakespeare and Goethe, Hegel and Kierkegaard, Nietzsche, Rilke, and Freud, Jaspers, Heidegger, and Toynbee* (Princeton, NJ: Princeton University Press, 1980).
Kaufman-Osborn, Timothy V., "Political Theory as Profession and as Subfield?" *Political Research Quarterly* 63, no. 3 (2010), 655–73.
Knox, T.M., "Hegel and Prussianism," *Philosophy* 15, no. 57 (1940), 51–63.
Kreines, James, "Hegel's Metaphysics: Changing the Debate," *Philosophy Compass* 1, no. 5 (2006), 466–80.
Kurian, George Thomas, *The Encyclopedia of Political Science*, 5 vols (Washington, D.C.: CQ Press, 2011).
Lamb, David, *Hegel: From Foundation to System*, Martinus Nijhoff Philosophy Library (The Hague; Boston Hingham, MA: M. Nijhoff, 1980).
Lamberth, David C., *William James and the Metaphysics of Experience*, Cambridge Studies in Religion and Critical Thought (Cambridge, UK; New York: Cambridge University Press, 1999).
Lane, Melissa, "Positivism: Reactions and Developments," in Richard Bellamy and Terence Ball, *The Cambridge History of Twentieth-Century Political Thought* (Cambridge: Cambridge University Press, 2008), 321–42.
Laslett, Peter, *Philosophy, Politics and Society: A Collection* (Oxford: Blackwell, 1956).
Löwith, Karl, *From Hegel to Nietzsche: The Revolution in Nineteenth Century Thought* (New York: Columbia University Press, 1991).
MacIntyre, Alasdair C., *Hegel: A Collection of Critical Essays*, Modern Studies in Philosophy, 1st edn (Garden City, NY: Anchor Books, 1972).
Marcuse, Herbert, *Reason and Revolution: Hegel and the Rise of Social Theory*, 2nd. edn (London: Routledge & Kegan Paul, 1955).
Marx, Karl and Joseph J. O'Malley, *Critique of Hegel's "Philosophy of Right"*, Cambridge Studies in the History and Theory of Politics (Cambridge, UK: University Press, 1970).
Marx, Karl, *Early Writings*, Penguin Classics (Harmondsworth; New York: Penguin in association with New Left Review, 1992).
Merriam, Charles E., "The Present State of the Study of Politics," *American Political Science Review* 15, no. 2 (1921), 173–85.
Merriam, Charles Edward, *New Aspects of Politics*, 2nd edn (Chicago, IL: University of Chicago Press, 1931).
Moore, A.W., *The Evolution of Modern Metaphysics: Making Sense of Things*, The Evolution of Modern Philosophy (Cambridge, UK; New York: Cambridge University Press, 2012).
Moore, G.E., "The Refutation of Idealism," *Mind* 12, no. 48 (1903), 433–53.
Moore, G.E., *Some Main Problems of Philosophy*, Muirhead Library of Philosophy (London, New York: Allen & Unwin; Humanities Press, 1953).
Moore, G. E., *Principia Ethica*, (Cambridge, UK: Cambridge University Press, 1959).
Moreland, James Porter, *Universals*, Central Problems of Philosophy (Montreal; Ithaca: McGill-Queen's University Press, 2001).
Neuhouser, Frederick, *Foundations of Hegel's Social Theory: Actualizing Freedom* (Cambridge, MA: Harvard University Press, 2000).

Patten, Alan, *Hegel's Idea of Freedom*, Oxford Philosophical Monographs (Oxford; New York: Oxford University Press, 1999).
Pełczyński, Zbigniew A., *The State and Civil Society: Studies in Hegel's Political Philosophy* (Cambridge, UK; New York: Cambridge University Press, 1984).
Peperzak, Adriaan Theodoor, *Modern Freedom: Hegel's Legal, Moral, and Political Philosophy* (Dordrecht; London: Kluwer Academic, 2001).
Pippin, Robert B., *Hegel's Idealism: The Satisfactions of Self-Consciousness* (Cambridge, UK; New York: Cambridge University Press, 1989).
Plant, Raymond, *Hegel* (Bloomington: Indiana University Press, 1973).
Popper, Karl R., *The Open Society and Its Enemies*, 2 vols (London: Routledge, 1945).
Porphyry and Paul Vincent Spade, *Five Texts on the Mediaeval Problem of Universals: Porphyry, Boethius, Abelard, Duns Scotus, Ockham* (Indianapolis: Hackett, 1994).
Quine, W.V., *The Ways of Paradox, and Other Essays*, Rev. and enl. edn (Cambridge, MA: Harvard University Press, 1976); reprinted in Rockmore, *Hegel, Idealism, and Analytic Philosophy*, (New Haven: Yale University Press, 2005).
Ricci, David M., *The Tragedy of Political Science: Politics, Scholarship, and Democracy* (New Haven, CT: Yale University Press, 1984).
Richardson, Henry S., "The Logical Structure of Sittlichkeit," *Idealistic Studies* 19, no. 1 (1989), 62–78.
Ritter, Joachim, *Hegel and the French Revolution: Essays on the Philosophy of Right* (Cambridge, MA; London, England: MIT Press, 1982).
Rockmore, Tom, "Analytic Philosophy and the Hegelian Turn," *The Review of Metaphysics* 55, no. 2 (2001), 339–70.
Rockmore, Tom, *Hegel, Idealism, and Analytic Philosophy* (New Haven: Yale University Press, 2005).
Rousseau, Jean-Jacques, *The Social Contract*, Penguin Classics (Harmondsworth: Penguin, 1968).
Royce, Josiah, *The Spirit of Modern Philosophy: An Essay in the Form of Lectures* (Boston and New York: Houghton, 1892).
Russell, Bertrand, *A History of Western Philosophy* (New York: Simon and Schuster, 1945).
Russell, Bertrand, *My Philosophical Development* (London: Allen and Unwin, 1959).
Sabine, George H., "Hegel's Political Philosophy," *Philosophical Review* 41, no. 3 (1932), 261–82.
Schelling, Friedrich Wilhelm Joseph, von and Bruce Matthews, *The Grounding of Positive Philosophy: The Berlin Lectures*, Suny Series in Contemporary Continental Philosophy (Albany: State University of New York Press, 2007).
Schmitt, Frederick F., *Socializing Metaphysics: The Nature of Social Reality* (Lanham, MD: Rowman & Littlefield, 2003).
Schoedinger, Andrew B., *Introduction to Metaphysics: The Fundamental Questions* (Buffalo, NY: Prometheus Books, 1991).
Schoedinger, Andrew B., *The Problem of Universals* (Atlantic Highlands, NJ: Humanities Press, 1992).
Sellars, Wilfrid S., "Empiricism and the Philosophy of Mind," *Minnesota Studies in the Philosophy of Science* 1 (1956), 253–329.
Sellars, Wilfrid, Richard Rorty and Robert Brandom, *Empiricism and the Philosophy of Mind* (Cambridge, MA: Harvard University Press, 1997).
Sheldon, S. Wolin, "Political Theory as a Vocation," *American Political Science Review* 63, no. 4 (1969), 1062–82.

Sirkel, Riin, *The Problem of Katholou (Universals) in Aristotle* (London, Ont.: School of Graduate and Postdoctoral Studies, University of Western Ontario, 2010), http://ir.lib.uwo.ca/etd/62.

Smetona, Matthew J., *Hegel's Logical Comprehension of the Modern State* (Lanham: Lexington Books, 2013).

Smith, Steven B., *Hegel's Critique of Liberalism: Rights in Context* (Chicago: University of Chicago Press, 1989).

Steinberger, Peter J., *Logic and Politics: Hegel's Philosophy of Right* (New Haven: Yale University Press, 1988).

Steinberger, Peter J., *The Idea of the State*, Contemporary Political Theory (Cambridge, UK; New York: Cambridge University Press, 2004).

Steinmetz, George, "The Genealogy of a Positivist Haunting: Comparing Prewar and Postwar U.S. Sociology," *boundary 2* 32, no. 2 (2005), 109–35.

Steinmetz, George, *The Politics of Method in the Human Sciences: Positivism and Its Epistemological Others*, Politics, History, and Culture (Durham: Duke University Press, 2005).

Stephen Eric Bronner, *Twentieth Century Political Theory: A Reader* (New York: Routledge, 1997).

Stern, Robert, *Hegel, Kant and the Structure of the Object* (London; New York: Routledge, 1990).

Stern, Robert, *Routledge Philosophy Guidebook to Hegel and the Phenomenology of Spirit*. Routledge Philosophy Guidebooks (London; New York: Routledge, 2002).

Stern, Robert, *Hegelian Metaphysics* (Oxford; New York: Oxford University Press, 2009).

Stewart, Jon, *The Hegel Myths and Legends*, Northwestern University Studies in Phenomenology and Existential Philosophy (Evanston, IL: Northwestern University Press, 1996).

Stirling, James Hutchison, *The Secret of Hegel: Being the Hegelian System in Origin, Principle, Form, and Matter*, 2 vols (London: Longman, Green, Longman, Roberts, & Green, 1865).

Taylor, Charles, *Hegel* (Cambridge, UK; New York: Cambridge University Press, 1975).

Taylor, Charles, *Hegel and Modern Society*, Modern European Philosophy (Cambridge, UK; New York: Cambridge University Press, 1979).

Toews, John Edward, *Hegelianism: The Path toward Dialectical Humanism, 1805–1841* (Cambridge, UK; New York: Cambridge University Press, 1980).

Travis, Don Carlos and Texas University, Dept. of Germanic Languages, *A Hegel Symposium; Essays by Carl J. Friedrich [and Others]* (Austin: Dept. of Germanic Languages, University of Texas, 1962).

Tunick, Mark, *Hegel's Political Philosophy: Interpreting the Practice of Legal Punishment* (Princeton, NJ: Princeton University Press, 1992).

Wallas, Graham, *Human Nature in Politics*, 3rd edn (New York: F.S. Crofts, 1921).

Ware, Robert Bruce, *Hegel: The Logic of Self-Consciousness and the Legacy of Subjective Freedom* (Edinburgh: Edinburgh University Press, 1999).

White, Alan, *Absolute Knowledge: Hegel and the Problem of Metaphysics*, Series in Continental Thought (Athens, Ohio: Ohio University Press, 1983).

Williams, David L., "Dialogical Theories of Justice," *Telos* 1999, no. 114 (1999), 109–31.

Wood, Allen W., *Hegel's Ethical Thought* (Cambridge, UK; New York: Cambridge University Press, 1990).

Wood, Allen W., "Reply," Bulletin of the Hegel Society of Great Britain, 25 (1992), 34–50.

# Index

absolute being, Eleatic monism of 132, 140, 160
absolute Idea 24, 29, 128, 145; British form of 31; concept fulfilled and 155–60; in constant self-realization 175; development of 19, 132–4; dialectical dynamics of 144; in Hegel's version of reality 26; integral unity of 179; mediation of the purpose of 163; notion of 13; progressive objectivation of 131; self-conception of 163; self-consistency of 161; self-differentiating of 138; teleological vocation of 25; universality of 175
agoraphobia 194–5
agricultural class 187
Amadae, Sonja 66–7
American institutional values and norms 60
American Political Science Association (APSA) 49, 60, 62–3
ancient abstractionism, limitations of 120
Anglo–American: break with metaphysics, origins of 30–42; empiricism 25; Hegel's place in theoretical imagination of 75–80; political science's project of scientization 50; political theory 1, 230; reception and transmission of Hegel 47; representations of Hegel's political thought 225; scholarship 74–5, 87, 170; social sciences 48; struggle against idealism 61
Anglo–Saxon philosophy 56
"anti-contractual" contract 182
antiquity and modernity, problem of universals between 104–10
aporetic universal, creative resolution of 199–200
appearance, idea of 139–40
Arendt, Hannah 105

Aristotle 160, 227–8; *Categories, The* 106; *De Interpretatione* 106; rationality, concept of 152; subdivisions of logical classification 106
*Aufhebung* (sublation, dialectical "synthesis"), theoretical role of 11
Avineri, Shlomo 86–8, 104
Ayer, A. J. 62

Bachman, Karl Friedrich 20
behavioral revolution 49–50, 62–3
behavioralism, legacy of 60, 62, 65–8
being, doctrine of 13; dialectic, Parmenidean origins of 132–6; particularization of 135; problem of universals and 132–3; quality, quantity, and measure 136–7; self-completing 136
Beiser, Frederick 3, 111, 171, 206, 207
Bernstein, Richard 29, 31, 48, 56, 61, 81
Bhaskar, Roy 60–1
Boethius, Anicius Manlius Severinus 7n1, 107; translation of Isagoge 106
Bradley, F. H. 29–31, 47, 76, 95
Brooks, Thom 88, 94, 204, 207
*bürgerliche Gesellschaft* 186, 195

Catlin, George 48, 53–5, 59–61
chemism, framework of 151, 152, 154
Christian doctrine 78
Christianity, negation of 18
citadel of idealist dialectic, withdrawal from 11–12
civil liberty 173
civil society 153, 179; classes and the problem of capitalism 186–9; distinction with state 190; Hegel's transition to 183; and mediation of propertied individuals 183–6; reconciliation of 185; *Stände* of 195; syllogistic reconciliation of 193

class: consciousness 186–8; destiny 189; metaphysical justification of 22
class divisions 188–9; proliferation of 187
classical liberalism 67, 183, 187
concept, doctrine of 123; individual and syllogistic resolution 145–7; judgment of 147–9; self-identity 158; subjectivization of substance and 143–5; syllogism and the object 149–60
conceptual liberation, project of 158
conjugal relationship 183
consciousness, idealist confusion of 37–41
Contra Feuerbach (raw data of the senses) 22–5
coordinating categories, of opposition: freedom and creative resolution of aporetic universal 199–200; logical problems and political propositions 197–8
Crick, Bernard 49–50, 66, 93
*Criticism of the Anti-Hegelians* (1835) 20
cultural relativism 209

democratic realism: enlightened elitism of 62; science of politics and 60
Descartes' wax 137
Desmond, William 232, 234–6
determinate being 13, 134, 136–7; categories of 135
dialectic: of correlation 142; dualism in 138; of integrity and revulsion of form and content 141; Parmenidean origins of 132–6; philosophical limits of 129; self-generating 135
division of labor 185–7
Ducasse, C. J. 38, 40

Easton, David 49–50, 54, 55–60, 80, 229; American political theory 58; approach to transformation of political theory 56; assault on political theory 55; interaction of political theory 60; post-behavioral revolution 63; scientific study of politics 56
economic determinism 50
Eleatic logic, limitations of 136
emancipation, doctrine of 25, 61, 112
empiricism, principle of 11, 25–7, 30, 51, 53, 58, 65, 114–20, 124, 126, 129–31, 140, 159, 163
*Encyclopedia* Logic 150, 177–8, 182; dialectics of 171; first philosophy and foundational system of universals 113–15; Hegel's metaphysical corpus and 111–15; overcoming positivism 120–7; sense, concept and thought 124–7; speculative philosophy of 127–31; transition to 115–20; understanding, limits of 127–31
*Encyclopedia of the Philosophical Sciences in Outline* (1817) 113, 163, 173
Enlightenment 54–5, 61, 67, 77, 87, 137, 150, 175, 226, 233
*esse est percipi:* Berkeley's 40; interrogation of 35–6; reduction of idealism to 34–5; truth or falsehood of 34
essence, doctrine of: appearance 139–40; existence 138–9; of man 22; one and the many as content and form 140–3
estate capital (*Vermögen*) 182–3
ethical community 182, 230
ethical Idea 182, 190
ethical life, elements of 199
evolution of truth 122
existence, idea of 138–9
experience, denial of 25–30

family, concept of 182–3; syllogistic reconciliation and 193
Feuerbach, Ludwig: challenge to Hegel's monistic thought 19; conception of human nature 22–3; and curse of metaphysical ascription 12; dialectical idealism, criticism of 14; doctrine of being and illusion of origination 13; on Hegel's universalism 12; intolerance of Hegel's metaphysics 11; materialistic intuitionism 25; metaphysics and incomplete evacuation of theology 16–20; negative mediation with Hegel 23; *Principles of the Philosophy of the Future* (1843) 16; problem of universals, critical approaches on 13–15; sensuous consciousness and common sense, primacy of 15–16; "third man" argument 14; young Hegelians and the ambiguities of legacies of 20–2
Findlay, J. N. 82, 112
finitude 28, 129, 135–7, 156
Franco, Paul 90
fraud and force, use of 78
freedom, principle of 144, 179, 182, 184; and creative resolution of aporetic universal 199–200
French revolution 18
Friedrich, Carl Joachim 20, 80, 82–3
"fullness of divine thoughts" 147
*Gemeinschaft* 186, 234

*German Ideology, The* (Marx) 21
Germany: idealism in the English-speaking world 26; metaphysical revolution 21; nationalism 171
goodness, religious notion of 127–8
Goodnow, Frank J. 62
Gray, John 229
Groff, Ruth 7, 225, 227–30

Hampton, Jean 232
Hardimon, Michael 90
Hauptmann, Emily 66
Haym, Rudolph 20, 30, 74, 76, 78–9, 83; notion of the Spirit 23; rejection of Hegel's metaphysics 21
Hegel, Georg Wilhelm Friedrich: "the actual is the rational" dictum 84; anglophone appropriations of 225; apotheosis of the mind 17; appropriation of reason 16; *Begriffe* (concept) 15, 144, 192; books on 79; collective vision of positive liberty 78; comprehensive system of logical resolution and integration 131; critique and reaction to Kant 111; cultural hermeneutics 88; declaration on "the One" 136; dedication to romantic expressivism and moral freedom 87; defense and deformation of legacy of 81–92; defense of Prussian nationalism 20; doctrine of logic 113; "double dictum" 17, 86, 179–80, 193, 207; *Encyclopedia of the Philosophical Sciences* 113; as father of idealism 76; Feuerbach's negative mediation with 23; first philosophy and foundational system of universals 113–15; free subjectivity, concept of 187; freedom, principle of 144; idea of the absolute in spirit 26; immediacy, concept of 133; intellectual solipsism 12; internal relations, doctrine of 28; interpenetration of opposites 131; James's misperception of 29; logical and historical dialectics 11; logical and political thought 75, 89, 94; logical system of metaphysics 18; Lutheran Christian principle 176; metaphysical and political thought 74, 77–8, 86–7, 110–11, 221; metaphysical conception of human subjectivity 22; metaphysical corpus and *Encyclopedia* Logic *see Encyclopedia* Logic; modern political project, philosophical context of 180–1; notion of being 14; organic concept of the whole 36; "perfectionist" project 201; *Phenomenology, The* 111–13, 119; *Philosophy of Right* 21, 82–7, 90–1, 94–5, 103, 109, 116, 151, 170, 172, 174–80, 182, 196, 200, 202, 205–10; philosophy of the State 77; place in Anglo–American theoretical imagination 75–80; place in the history of political thought 234; plan of philosophy 123; political life and action, vision of 87; political theory 3, 5; politics of its metaphysical presuppositions 83; portrayal of development of human freedom 204; project of political reconciliation 162; project of the absolute 112; response to the dilemma of the understanding 111; scholarship 1–2, 4, 31; *Science of Logic* 113, 116, 170; science of reason 14; sovereignty of metaphysical political thought of 200–2; spiritual and natural realms for thought 110; state-citizen relation 208, 210; theory of right 3; total and complete self-subsistence, concept of 153; transition to civil society 183; universals, theory of 104–10, 118; vicious intellectualism 25–30
*Hegel und Seine Zeit* (1857) 20
*Hegel's Ethical Thought* (1990) 88, 174, 202, 211
*Hegel's Theory of the Modern State* (1972) 86
Hegel-Schelling project 110
Hobhouse, Leonard Trelawney 78–80; anti-authoritarian interpretation 77; Hegel's political thought, views on 76–7; *Metaphysical Theory of the State* (1918) 76
Houlgate, Stephen 73, 171, 203–5, 207–8
human energies, conservation and canalization of 52
human essence, spiritualization of 16, 19, 23–4
*Human Nature in Politics* (1908) 62
human self-actualization, concept of 208
human technological organization 52
human-sensuous activity 23

idealism, refutation of 30–42, 61, 64; to *esse est percipi* 34–5; notion of 35; and origins of positivism 41–2
idealistic association, guilt by 75–80
Ilting, K. H. 5, 201
immediacy, concept of 32, 39, 119, 126, 132–3, 138, 140, 142, 146, 157, 163, 176, 180, 185

Index 249

immutable absolute, theological principle of 17–18
individuation, "Western" principle of 28, 136, 143, 156, 173, 183, 197
infinity, notion of 107, 135–6
internal motivation 54
internal relations, doctrine of 28, 30, 124
interpenetration, notion of 29, 131, 148, 155, 158, 192
*Isagoge* (Porphyry) 106

*Jahrbücher* (Arnold Ruge) 12
James, William: *ad hominem* attacks on Hegel's work 47; anti-Hegel program 26; misperception of Hegel 29; radical empiricism 30; rejection of monism 28; vicious intellectualism, analysis of 25–30
judgment of the concept 147–9

Kant, Immanuel 33, 226; cognitive conditions of knowledge, analysis of 37; Copernican revolution 31; *Critique of Pure Reason* 110, 113; dualism of understanding and sensibility 110; Hegel's critique and reaction to 111; metaphysics, definition of 110; sensuous experience, analogy of 41; transcendental logic 157
Kasza, Gregory 66, 231
Kaufman, Walter 81–2, 84–5, 180
Kaufman-Osborn, Timothy 66
Knox, Malcolm 77, 83, 85–7

Lane, Melissa 62–3
law of contradiction 26, 35; Hegel's rejection of static notion of 36; and logical crisis of organicism 36–7; violation of 36, 41
LeConte, Joseph 51
Leibniz's monads, philosophy of 150
liberal-positivist program, for political thought 7n10, 73–5, 93
logico-metaphysical project 143

Marx, Karl 4, 6, 11–12, 16–18, 20–6, 30, 32, 47, 73, 78–9, 81, 189; "Eleven Theses on Feuerbach" 22; on human historical development 25; and materialist termination of Hegelian 22–5
material humanism 22
materialism, concept of 23–4, 120
mediation of thought 120, 138
mental spirituality 33

Merriam, Charles 49–53, 55, 59, 61–3, 73, 93; apologetics for social science 51
*Metaphysical Theory of the State* (1918) 76
Metaphysics 1–7, 25, 62, 64, 77, 86, 92, 103, 106, 110–11, 116, 127, 180, 221–2; analytic and continental issues 235–6; *ancien régime* of 18; Anglo–American break with 30–42; in context of *Encyclopedia* Logic 111–13; curse of 12, 18; deduction 77; empirical resolution of 56; Feuerbach's intolerance of Hegel's 11; foundations of 222–8; German revolution in 21; of Hegel's historicism 84; Hegel's logical system of 18; Hegel's metaphysical and political thought 74, 76, 85, 87, 89, 94–5; imposition of 23; and incomplete evacuation of theology 16–20; liberal-positivist paradigm in 228–35; Platonism and 77; problem of universals 104, 181; rejection of the possibility of 224; sovereignty of 200–2; of the Spirit 16; supra-personal rationality 89; and theorizing subject of political thought 222–8; vocation of political philosophy 170–4
methodological positivism 5, 48, 63, 65, 93
modern science and politics, development of 137
modern state, foundations of: civil society and mediation of propertied individuals 183–6; civil society's classes and the problem of capitalism 186–9; family 182–3; state as "system of three syllogisms" 189–97
monarchic hegemony 192
Moore, A. W. 224, 231–2
Moore, G. E.: idealist confusion of consciousness 37–41; reframing of sensation 39–40; "Refutation of Idealism" essay 30–42, 61, 64
myth of the given 27, 45n97, 64, 109, 203, 222, 235

Nazism 53, 60, 79–80
negation and concrete inception, cycle of 136
*New Aspects of Politics* (1925) 51
non-metaphysical reading, distortions of 202–3; citizen, state and *Sittlichkeit* 207–12; Houlgate's challenge 203–5; Wood's reply 205–7
*Nous* (spirit), Greek idea of 118

"the One," notion of 137, 172; Hegel's declaration on 136; internal negation of 136
*Open Society and Its Enemies, The* (1945) 78
organic unity, concept of 29, 36, 162, 184, 191, 199, 208–9, 230
organicism, logical crisis of 28, 36–7, 77, 172
origination, illusion of 13, 28, 114, 147, 157

Parmenides 107, 129, 132–4, 150, 160–3, 197; abstractionism of 119–20; Eleaticism 13
Pełczyński, Zbigniew 83–5, 87–8, 91, 171, 200–1, 222
Peperzak, Adriaan 3
perception, identity of 36
personhood, concept of 179
*Philosophy of Right* (Hegel) 21, 82–7, 90–1, 94–5, 103, 109, 116, 151, 170, 172, 174–80, 182, 196, 200, 202, 205–10
Plato 110, 117, 141, 157, 193; becoming, concept of 128; ethic of freedom 77; good-in-itself concept 147; myth of the metals 188; *Philebus* 107, 135–7; polis, concept of 128, 183; *Sophist* 160
*Pluralistic Universe, A* (1909) 25, 29, 41
political Catholicism 21
political control 51, 67; scientific governance of 53
political ideals, logical pursuit and realization of 176
political logic, *Philosophy of Right* and 174–80
*Political Philosophies of Plato and Hegel, The* (1935) 77
political philosophy 20, 48, 62–3, 66, 68, 77, 90, 227, 231; metaphysical vocation of 170–4; pre-positivist tradition of 65
political right, Hegel's idea of 179
*Political System: An Enquiry into the State of Political Science, The* (1953) 57
political theory 3, 5–7, 31, 49, 55–60, 62, 64, 66, 68, 84, 86–9, 104, 171, 174, 196, 200–1, 227–8; Anglo–American 1; decline of 53; humanist paradigms of 226; ideological prerogatives of 2; and metaphysical frontiers 228–35; need for 227; orientation of 48; practice of 4; regulation of 175; social science and 65, 225; Western European 83

politics movement, science of 49, 59, 60, 63
Popper, Karl 2, 64, 74, 78–84
Porphyry 107; Aristotelian provocation 106; *Isagoge* on medieval philosophy 106
positivism: influences of, in the social sciences 65–8; legacy and persistence of 60–5; origins of 41–2; scientific and theoretical 60–5; vulgar positivism 63
post-behavioral revolution 63
practical philosophy (PR) 21, 207
*Principles of the Philosophy of the Future* (1843) 16
problem of universals *see* universals, problem of

rational choice theory 48, 65–8
rationality for choice and agency, idea of 89
reason, concept of 158, 176
reflection, as form of thought 125–6
Refutation of Idealism (Moore) 11, 30–42, 61, 64
right, concept of 190
Ritter, Joachim 20
Rockmore, Tom 29, 31, 37, 44n79
Rousseau, Jean-Jacques 6, 91, 184, 208, 233; project of modern political thought 173; theory of legitimacy 178
Royce, Josiah 29, 108–9, 229

Sabine, Henry H. 77–9
Sandel, Michael J. 211, 226, 233
Schoedinger, Andrew 105
scholastic metaphysics 143
science of democracy 62
*Science of Logic* (1812) 113, 116
*Science of Logic* (1830) 111–12
scientific society 53
self creation of the self 125
self-consciousness 18, 111, 120, 124, 176, 178; ethical 193
self-generating system 123
self-knowing, project of 121, 144, 164, 195
self-ordering system 123
self-preservation, act of 152
self-realization 112, 175, 178, 180, 184, 188–9, 203
self-relation, condition of 142, 148, 161, 178
self-standing thought, transformation of 25
self-transformation, process of 152, 185
Sellars, Wilfrid 27

sensory experience, 73, 124, 131, 159
sensuous experience 33, 35, 112; Kant's analogy of 41; presentation of awareness in 40; theory of 15–16, 23, 38
separation of powers, Montesquieu's ideal of 191
sexual differences 182
*Sittlichkeit* (ethical life) 25, 182, 194–5, 198–9, 207–12, 227; concept of 180; social and political arrangement of 150
Smetona, Mathew J. 73, 170–1
Smith, Steven B. 87–9
social atomism 76, 191
social equalization 23
social hierarchy, of class 189
social sciences 50, 52, 56, 61–3, 93; Anglo–American 48; Merriam's apologetics for 51; rational choice theory 65–8
social scientific timidity 64
social-contract, ethical logic of 188–9
socio-economic stratification 22
Soviet Union 67
speculation (*spekulation*), notion of 129–30, 198
speculative rationality 130
spirit, concept of 2, 12, 18, 23, 26, 84, 118, 120, 159, 164, 184, 203
spiritual individual 163, 190, 192
spiritual unity, idea of 190, 210
standing self-contradiction 194
state: abstract idea of 191; concept of 189–97; distinction with civil society 190; political form of administration 193; self-awareness 192; *Stände* of 195; three moments of 190
Steinberger, Peter J. 6–7, 90, 92, 172, 201, 210, 223–7, 229, 231–2, 236
Steinmetz, George 48, 63
Stern, Robert 73, 171, 202, 207, 237n9
Strawson, P. F. 93, 223
subjectivity, principle of 209
substance, concept of 143–5
syllogism, doctrine of: and absolute Idea 155–60; chemism, framework of 151; dialectic force of 160; dialectical progression 196; ethical life 200; of family and civil society 193; individual and 145–7; and judgment of the concept 147–9; mechanism 149–51; metaphysical method 175, 181; and the object 149–60; and the problem of universals 160–4; "system of three syllogisms" 189–97; teleological thought 152–3; teleology and syllogistic revolution 153–5
"system of needs" 183–6

*tabula rasa* 25
Taylor, Charles 2, 74, 79, 87–91, 233
technocracy of governance 52
teleology: concept of 152–3; and syllogistic revolution 153–5
thought 198; concept of 153; mediation of 120, 138; nature of 223; as object of self-creation 224; self-reflexiveness of 223; stages of 130
totality, principle of 153, 160
truth, principle of 16
Tunick, Mark 89–90, 171

understanding, limits of 127–31
universal idea/s, 111, 123, 132–3, 139, 156, 171, 175, 178, 189, 191, 197; alienation of 141; articulation of 118; development of 135, 138–9, 196–7; of thought 112; *see also* absolute Idea
universal: development of 130; particularization of 138
universalist logic: elements of 127–31; role of 171
universality of diversity, phenomenon of 137
universals, problem of 104–10, 117, 141, 144, 157; critical approaches on 13–15; definition of 149; dialectical resolution of 127; and dialectical reunion with particularism 120–3; and Hegel's categories of opposition 197; Hegel's philosophy and foundational system of 113–15; Hegel's resolution of 163; at physical and logical level 159–60; speculation and 198; at the stage of being 133–4; syllogism and 160–4
unmediated and pure being, notion of 13

*Verstand* 127
vicious intellectualism, analysis of 25–30
vulgar materialism 137
vulgar positivism 63

*Weltanschauung* (world intuition) 229
Western Christianity 2
Wolin, Sheldon 65
Wood, Allen 2, 6, 75, 88, 171, 174, 202–11, 222, 227

# Routledge innovations in political theory

1. **A Radical Green Political Theory**
   *Alan Carter*

2. **Rational Woman**
   A feminist critique of dualism
   *Raia Prokhovnik*

3. **Rethinking State Theory**
   *Mark J. Smith*

4. **Gramsci and Contemporary Politics**
   Beyond pessimism of the intellect
   *Anne Showstack Sassoon*

5. **Post-Ecologist Politics**
   Social theory and the abdication of the ecologist paradigm
   *Ingolfur Blühdorn*

6. **Ecological Relations**
   *Susan Board*

7. **The Political Theory of Global Citizenship**
   *April Carter*

8. **Democracy and National Pluralism**
   *Edited by Ferran Requejo*

9. **Civil Society and Democratic Theory**
   Alternative voices
   *Gideon Baker*

10. **Ethics and Politics in Contemporary Theory**
    Between critical theory and post-Marxism
    *Mark Devenney*

11. **Citizenship and Identity**
    Towards a new republic
    *John Schwarzmantel*

12. **Multiculturalism, Identity and Rights**
    *Edited by Bruce Haddock and Peter Sutch*

13. **Political Theory of Global Justice**
    A cosmopolitan case for the World State
    *Luis Cabrera*

14. **Democracy, Nationalism and Multiculturalism**
    *Edited by Ramón Maiz and Ferrán Requejo*

15. **Political Reconciliation**
    *Andrew Schaap*

16. **National Cultural Autonomy and Its Contemporary Critics**
    *Edited by Ephraim Nimni*

17 **Power and Politics in Poststructuralist Thought**
New theories of the political
*Saul Newman*

18 **Capabilities Equality**
Basic issues and problems
*Edited by Alexander Kaufman*

19 **Morality and Nationalism**
*Catherine Frost*

20 **Principles and Political Order**
The challenge of diversity
*Edited by Bruce Haddock, Peri Roberts and Peter Sutch*

21 **European Integration and the Nationalities Question**
*Edited by John McGarry and Michael Keating*

22 **Deliberation, Social Choice and Absolutist Democracy**
*David van Mill*

23 **Sexual Justice/Cultural Justice**
Critical perspectives in political theory and practice
*Edited by Barbara Arneil, Monique Deveaux, Rita Dhamoon and Avigail Eisenberg*

24 **The International Political Thought of Carl Schmitt**
Terror, liberal war and the crisis of global order
*Edited by Louiza Odysseos and Fabio Petito*

25 **In Defense of Human Rights**
A non-religious grounding in a pluralistic world
*Ari Kohen*

26 **Logics of Critical Explanation in Social and Political Theory**
*Jason Glynos and David Howarth*

27 **Political Constructivism**
*Peri Roberts*

28 **The New Politics of Masculinity**
Men, power and resistance
*Fidelma Ashe*

29 **Citizens and the State**
Attitudes in Western Europe and East and Southeast Asia
*Takashi Inoguchi and Jean Blondel*

30 **Political Language and Metaphor**
Interpreting *and* changing the world
*Edited by Terrell Carver and Jernej Pikalo*

31 **Political Pluralism and the State**
Beyond sovereignty
*Marcel Wissenburg*

32 **Political Evil in a Global Age**
Hannah Arendt and international theory
*Patrick Hayden*

33 **Gramsci and Global Politics**
Hegemony and resistance
*Mark McNally and John Schwarzmantel*

34 **Democracy and Pluralism**
The political thought of William E. Connolly
*Edited by Alan Finlayson*

35 **Multiculturalism and Moral Conflict**
*Edited by Maria Dimova-Cookson and Peter Stirk*

36 **John Stuart Mill – Thought and Influence**
The saint of rationalism
*Edited by Georgios Varouxakis and Paul Kelly*

37 **Rethinking Gramsci**
*Edited by Marcus E. Green*

38 **Autonomy and Identity**
The politics of who we are
*Ros Hague*

39 **Dialectics and Contemporary Politics**
Critique and transformation from Hegel through post-Marxism
*John Grant*

40 **Liberal Democracy as the End of History**
Fukuyama and postmodern challenges
*Chris Hughes*

41 **Deleuze and World Politics**
Alter-globalizations and nomad science
*Peter Lenco*

42 **Utopian Politics**
Citizenship and practice
*Rhiannon Firth*

43 **Kant and International Relations Theory**
Cosmopolitan community building
*Dora Ion*

44 **Ethnic Diversity and the Nation State**
National cultural autonomy revisited
*David J. Smith and John Hiden*

45 **Tensions of Modernity**
Las Casas and his legacy in the French Enlightenment
*Daniel R. Brunstetter*

46 **Honor**
A phenomenology
*Robert L. Oprisko*

47 **Critical Theory and Democracy**
Essays in honour of Andrew Arato
*Edited by Enrique Peruzzotti and Martin Plot*

48 **Sophocles and the Politics of Tragedy**
Cities and transcendence
*Jonathan N. Badger*

49 **Isaiah Berlin and the Politics of Freedom**
"Two Concepts of Liberty" 50 years later
*Edited by Bruce Baum and Robert Nichols*

50 **Popular Sovereignty in the West**
Polities, contention, and ideas
*Geneviève Nootens*

51 **Pliny's Defense of Empire**
*Thomas R. Laehn*

52 **Class, States and International Relations**
A critical appraisal of Robert Cox and neo-Gramscian theory
*Adrian Budd*

53 **Civil Disobedience and Deliberative Democracy**
*William Smith*

54 **Untangling Heroism**
Classical philosophy and the concept of the hero
*Ari Kohen*

55 **Rethinking the Politics of Absurdity**
Albert Camus, postmodernity, and the survival of innocence
*Matthew H. Bowker*

56 **Kantian Theory and Human Rights**
*Edited by Reidar Maliks and Andreas Follesdal*

57 **The Political Philosophy of Judith Butler**
*Birgit Schippers*

58 **Hegel and the Metaphysical Frontiers of Political Theory**
*Eric Lee Goodfield*

# eBooks
## from Taylor & Francis
Helping you to choose the right eBooks for your Library

Add to your library's digital collection today with Taylor & Francis eBooks. We have over 45,000 eBooks in the Humanities, Social Sciences, Behavioural Sciences, Built Environment and Law, from leading imprints, including Routledge, Focal Press and Psychology Press.

**Choose from a range of subject packages or create your own!**

Benefits for you
- Free MARC records
- COUNTER-compliant usage statistics
- Flexible purchase and pricing options
- 70% approx of our eBooks are now DRM-free.

Benefits for your user
- Off-site, anytime access via Athens or referring URL
- Print or copy pages or chapters
- Full content search
- Bookmark, highlight and annotate text
- Access to thousands of pages of quality research at the click of a button.

**Free Trials Available**

We offer free trials to qualifying academic, corporate and government customers.

## eCollections
Choose from 20 different subject eCollections, including:

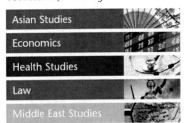

- Asian Studies
- Economics
- Health Studies
- Law
- Middle East Studies

## eFocus
We have 16 cutting-edge interdisciplinary collections, including:

- Development Studies
- The Environment
- Islam
- Korea
- Urban Studies

For more information, pricing enquiries or to order a free trial, please contact your local sales team:

UK/Rest of World: **online.sales@tandf.co.uk**
USA/Canada/Latin America: **e-reference@taylorandfrancis.com**
East/Southeast Asia: **martin.jack@tandf.com.sg**
India: **journalsales@tandfindia.com**

**www.tandfebooks.com**